To Cricket —

Best Regards,

12/3/2000

FAMILY CENTENNIAL

Johnny Moore

Johnny Moore

Published by Sugarpine Aviators

© 1999 by Johnny Moore
Author of I MUST FLY!

Published by Sugarpine Aviators
P.O. Box 1450 • Quincy, CA 95971
email: sugarpine@thegrid.net
http://www.thegrid.net/sugarpine

Library of Congress Catalog Number 98-96576
Photographs from the author's collection.
Photo Art and Cover Design by Lori Reynolds
Manufactured in the United States of America

Quality Books, Inc., has catalogued this edition as follows:

Moore, Johnny, 1940 —
        Family centennial / by Johnny Moore. — 1st ed.
        p. cm.
        "A prequel to the author's I must fly"— Back cover.
        Includes bibliographical references.
        Preassigned LCCN: 98-96576
        ISBN: 0-9658720-6-8

        1. Moore family. 2. Pioneers—Maine—Biography.
3.   Maine—Biography. 4. Aeronautics—History.
5.   Aeronautics—Biography. 6. World War, 1939-1945—
Aerial operations. I. Title.

CS7I.M662 1999   929'.2'0973
                                       QBI9S-1446

FAMILY
CENTENNIAL

JOHNNY MOORE

This book is dedicated to my
mother and father
whose lives
were full of promise.

TABLE OF CONTENTS

Acknowledgments i

Foreword ii

Part I – **PIONEER LEGACY**

Chapter 1 – Deep Woods of the East 11

Chapter 2 – Wide Open West 27

Chapter 3 – Civil War 33

Chapter 4 – Children of the East 94

Chapter 5 – Children of the West 103

Part II – **AVIATION LOVE STORY: A World War II drama**

Chapter 6 – Before 149

Chapter 7 – 1943 153

Chapter 8 – 1944 304

Chapter 9 – After 367

Epilogue 372

References Cited 374

Appendix 375
        Family Centennial Geneolgy

About the Author 379

ACKNOWLEDGMENTS

My cousin from Maine—Elliott Hersey, a genealogist—got me more interested in my families and opened up wondrous new connections for me with the past, which, after some research, inspired me to put this book together.

My wife, Judy, must be commended for dragging around the country stacks of old, yellowed documents and manuscripts authored by my ancestors (but unread by me until recently). When I finally did get to them one stormy day, I was catapulted into tumultuous times past kept alive with amazing clarity due to the skill of the mostly unpublished writers.

Thanks to Lori Reynolds with her patience and skill with graphic arts and editing in the production of this book.

FOREWORD

My first involvement with *Family Centennial* was when Johnny Moore came into my studio and approached me about designing the cover. A few days later, he brought me the first draft of his manuscript and wondered if I would be interested in editing along with providing graphics throughout the book. I agreed but at first wasn't sure what I was getting myself into. Did I really want to undertake such a monumental task from a local author I knew virtually nothing about?

However, It didn't take long for me to become totally immersed in the project; in fact, I was hooked from the first page. As with other great novels I have read, the only thing wrong with this one is that it was too short—I didn't want it to end. Now that I have read his other book, *I Must Fly!* I see that it doesn't. *I Must Fly!* picks up at the end of World War II where *Family Centennial* leaves off.

I believe Johnny Moore has created a masterpiece with *Family Centennial*. He has taken the writings of his ancestors from the mid-1800s up through World War II in a book that rivals epic novels by more established authors. It's a page-turner that's sometimes hilarious, sometimes gut wrenching, but always fascinating. It was the most engrossing book I have ever had the pleasure to edit, and it serves as an intriguing prequel to Moore's other book, *I Must Fly!*

L. C. Reynolds
October 28, 1998

Cyrus Barker   Mary Jane Berry Barker

Addison Barker

Part I

PIONEER LEGACY

Mary Elizabeth Barker

Chapter 1
Deep Woods of the East

I am Mary Elizabeth Barker. During the period between the years of 1820 and 1860, there was quite an extensive migration from the older portion of New England to the fertile lands along the eastern border of Maine. The term "going Down East" became a slogan, which I often heard. My people were of that group of pioneers who opened up the Northern Maine Wilderness.

My earliest recollections have remained with me in the form of a series of pictures. The first is a half-day spent in a country school, of which my father was the teacher. The desks and benches were hand made, without paint. The one vivid object was a huge fireplace in which a pile of sizable logs was sending up the chimney leaping, roaring flames. Father brought a low stool and seated me in a corner of this fireplace where I was most warm and comfortable during the morning session. Indistinctly, my mother was somehow vaguely connected with this picture.

The next is a bright morning in early spring. A group of people is moving in a forest that is just beginning to show a mist of green. By a rude trail, the first promise of a highway through swamp and over hill, they followed the leader, which was a horse hitched to a sled commonly called a jumper. My grandfather Cyrus *[Cyrus Barker (I)]* drove this horse. The jumper was loaded with trunks, bags and various household utensils. After the load, my father walked with some small bundles. There was also Rod, a lad of sixteen who was my uncle, and an older boy, a neighbor who bore me, a child of three, perched on his shoulder. We were having a jolly time together. He gently soothed my fright when we walked on a log over the black water of the stream. He pointed out the flying birds and chattering squirrels, the first yellow dogtooth violets, and the crimson trillium, and he was very patient with my endless questions.

We were a small band of pioneers going into a temporary home while a permanent one was being builded. Grandfather and two sons came first and selected five lots of one hundred and sixtyacres each. This was uncleared land situated on a beautiful ridge. He then transported his family and all his belongings by a team a distance of several hundred miles. The little log camp to which we were bound on the morning was builded by some men who, for a time, lived there while they cut cedar and shaved shingles. It was very comfortable with a stone fireplace in the middle of one side wall at the back. The furniture was all made on the spot, for the nearest place to purchase anything was Patten, twelve miles away, and the only vehicle fit to go over the trail was a hand-made jumper. A bed stood in one corner with a trundle bed for the children, which shoved under the larger one in the daytime. There was no stove. All the cooking was done at the fireplace and served on a rough table in the end of the room near the door. A small shed, attached, covered the woodpile, and a log hovel housed the horse and the cow.

My father *[Addison Perley Barker (I)]* was educated in city schools followed by a course in a military institution. He brought very little into this new country except good physical and mental equipment and the habits of industry. His farm was covered by the primeval forest and must be cleared and cultivated before he could hope to obtain much return; but with a vision of a comfortable home before him, he could attack and surmount all difficulties.

To provide a comfortable place for the family was his first task. The log house stood in a small opening from which the trees had been cut to build it. The surroundings were rough with the stumps still standing, and rocks and roots and brush covered the ground. He dug the ground among the stumps and planted a vegetable garden. He put the camp in order and filled the shed with wood. He also brought supplies from his father's store, enough to last a year.

There were only two families living at the Falls until Grandfather occupied the abandoned house that was builded by a man who went with the Forty-niners for gold. He brought with him—besides his food supplies—a herd of cows, horses, sheep, farm equipment, and one thousand dollars toward the new buildings.

Though so young, I was most intensely interested in all this activity, and my awakening mind was absorbing all the wonders of this new world. The forest rapidly taking on its green garments was a perpetual mystery and source of delight. The gay little birds, the spring flowers, the small animals of which there were plenty, and a dear little brook near, so jolly to play in, all added to the charm and joy of life.

We lived at the foot of the ridge on which the farms lay. The trail led up the hill joining Grandfather's on the south side. All the men began felling trees and clearing a portion of land for next year's crop. At the same time, logs were transported to the nearest mill, and men were found to begin preparing the frame for Grandfather's barn.

Each morning Father went away with his dinner pail on the jumper drawn by the horse and did not come back until sunset. Mother *[Susan A. Brown]* and we children stayed in the cabin, tended the cow and hens and watched over the garden. There were wild animals (especially bears) in the woods, but we did not fear them. They were considered harmless if left to themselves.

During the summer, Father built a root cellar to house the garden vegetables for winter. I watched each step of the process. First, the excavation, then the stoning of the walls, the frame and roof, and finally the covering with earth. It made quite a mound. There were bins for potatoes and larger vegetables. He cut little shelves and cupboards for food that needed protection from frost in winter and heat in summer.

Settlers paid the State of Maine for their farms by a certain amount of roadwork each year. Our men had already made considerable improvement on the trail from the Falls by working odd days.

One little incident made such an impression on me that I never will forget it. The sun was already down behind the trees one evening in midsummer. The nighthawks were booming and robins and thrushes were making the air musical. Father and Mother were looking over the garden, exulting in its thrifty appearance and speculating as to whether the melons would have time to get ripe, when they suddenly became rigid, listening intently. A faint halloo came from somewhere on the hill.

"Someone calling for help?" asked Mother under her breath.

"No," said Father. "It's Rod *[Rodney Clinton Barker]*; probably exercising his lungs. Doctor's orders, you know."

Nothing more was said at the time; but the following night, as Father was preparing for supper, he said: "It was not Rod who was calling last night. It was Steve *[Steven Cutler Barker.]* He was treed by a bear."

Mother looked startled. Her mind flashed back two nights when she had been searching in the woods for the cow. She had sprung up on a big fallen log and then stepped down on a sleeping bear who slipped from under her foot and bounded off with aloud woof.

"I didn't suppose they would attack a man," she said.

"He probably would not have done so, but Steve had a shotgun and didn't know any better than to fire in his face. Of courses it did not hurt him much, but it made him mad. He charged, and Steve went up a tree. The bear sat down to wait for him to come down."

"Well, what did he do?" asked Mother as Father paused to take a drink of water.

"Spot was along and barked and nipped the bear's behind until he drove him off."

As I listened, I added one more item to my knowledge of bears: It is not safe to fool with them.

As summer faded into autumn, Mother spent her evenings reading or knitting by the light of the log fire. One night she glanced up at the low window through which the firelight shone. Her heart gave a leap, for a bear was looking in at her. He disappeared as she rose to her feet. In after years she would say that she often heard them walking about the camp sniffing at every box or barrel. She had little fear because there was no way they could get inside. A heavy wooden bar held the solid well-built door.

There was no lack of meat. Deer, moose, caribou and partridges could be obtained with little effort. There was no law on game, and there was an abundance stored for winter use. There was a good crop of vegetables from the garden. Through the summer, raspberries and fine blueberries were to be had, but no other fresh fruit at any price. We could buy dried apples at the stores. Grandfather was skilled in fruit raising and he began at once to plant an orchard with apples, plums, pears, cherries, grapes and smaller fruits. Space about the buildings was set apart for a garden and orchard.

When the snow covered the ground, Father hired with a lumber operation not far away. He came home on Saturday night and sometimes for a night during the week. Grandfather spent the winter cutting and hauling lumber to a mill in an adjoining town for the house he hoped to erect next summer. New energy came with the budding trees and flowers of spring. Everybody worked with a will from daylight until dark. The cleared fields were sowed to wheat and oats, and while that grew, more trees were felled. Carpenters were hired to build the house and sheds, and by autumn, all were up and covered in.

As the grain headed, a new difficulty appeared: The bears began to destroy it. One Sunday morning, we walked up to the new fields to look at the grain. I was delighted.

To climb that path was like *Pilgrim's Progress* to one beset with the difficulties for small feet, but with promising stations along the way and a radiant goal at one end. Halfway up the hill, a mother partridge was clucking to her half-grown brood who were busy filling their crops with wild seeds and berries. Later, beechnuts would be plenty on the ground. When we were near the field, Father said, "Let us keep very quiet. We may see a bear."

I tiptoed along, eagerly, for I had not yet seen one of those black beasts of which I had heard so much. There he was, to be sure, not many rods away. His back towards us, sitting on his haunches, he was absorbed in gathering as many stalks of grain within his long forelegs as they would hold and stripping the heads off with his powerful jaws.

Father motioned us to step back out of sight and turned back to get Grandfather's gun. We waited in silence while he was gone, but the bear had become alarmed and was gone.

The destruction of the crops was so great; it was decided to take some measures to scare the beast, if nothing more was accomplished. The deer were troublesome but more easily managed. They came at daylight or late in the day and could be easily hunted, but bears were worse offenders. They came silently in the night and were very wary and suspicious. They also destroyed more. To watch for them at night seemed the most feasible procedure.

"It's a slim chance," said Steve. "But we may scare them some."

"It's not easy to tell bears from stumps," said Rod, "and it isn't easy to hit them by moonlight, either, if they are at any distance."

Grandfather said, "if you go early and get a good position overlooking the field, with the moon at your back and the wind toward you, possibly you may hit something if it gets near enough."

The boys laughed and replied, "We will make sure of using all those suggestions." The moon was nearly full and the sky cloudless. Not even a light breeze rippled the grain.

Father and Steve selected a good position overlooking a section of the field and hidden by the bushes behind them. Rodney went farther down the opening and settled himself near the woods with a pile of brush at his back.

"Was there a black stump just south of that stub over to the right?" asked Steve in a whisper.   "I don't remember," said Father.

"Well, I believe there was one there," insisted Steve.

"There's something black there now," from Father.

"Yes, but it hasn't moved. You had better watch it. If it's a bear, he is listening and sniffing for scent to find if the coast is clear."

Five minutes later came Steve's excited whisper, "It's moved!"

"All right," said Father, "we'll both fire."

Two shots rang out on the still night. The black thing suddenly disappeared, and near where Rod was hiding, a large animal bounded off into the forest.

"Another bear gone, by gosh!" lamented Rod. They went over to the stub, and truly there was no stump but a trodden path to the woods and a trail of blood. Nor did they ever find the bear, though in daylight they followed the trail until satisfied they could not overtake him. They kept up their vigilance on clear nights, often getting shots at some animal until they ceased to be much troubled by them, and a very good crop was finally harvested.

One morning I was told I could go to the Falls with Father and spend the day with Grandma. Such days were always glorified holidays to me. I did not mind walking the distance now, and choked down my fright at walking the log over the deep black brook. I did not return until the following morning, when I found Mother in bed and a neighbor from two miles away was holding a new baby in her lap, my little brother *[Addison Perley Barker (II)]*.

The crops were harvested, the shed filled with wood and everything again made ready for winter. Once more Father went to work for the lumber company. The snow covered the ground, and the cold lonely winter days were here.

A month passed by; then, one day, Grandfather drove into the yard with the horses and sled. When he opened the door, Mother said sharply, "What is it, is Addison hurt?"

"Yes," said Grandfather. "A log fell on him."

"Oh Father!" And she fell on his shoulder and shook with sobs.

"Perhaps it is not so bad. They are bringing him to our house. He was trying to get out of the way of a tree that was lodged. A stick caught in a hole in the bottom of his moccasin and threw him."

"Oh yes," said Mother. "He tried to get time to patch that hole Sunday. He said he would come home some night this week and mend it."

Meantime, she was getting herself and the children ready to go with him.

My recollection of what happened in the following days were just certain pictures retained in my memory. The first is of several men in a room where Father lay in bed helpless.

"There is no feeling in the legs, hips or arms."

There was a short, stout man with gray hair and a young face who said but little, but that little was apparently of importance. When I entered the room, he sat with his chair tipped against the wall, the right leg thrown over the other. It was a characteristic attitude, especially if he was seriously considering some matter. He was Dr. Luther Rogers of Patten, and the family physician of most of the families in several townships.

As I went in to say goodnight to Father, they had tied scarves to his hands to lift them towards the ceiling. Though there was no feeling in them, they felt tired to him.

"To rest my arms," he told me with his quiet smile.

The third day, I was conscious that something had happened. I did not know what it was, but everyone was much distressed; early in the day, I was sent across the river to stay with the Sewells. No bridges had been built in town. In the winter, people crossed on the ice; in summer by boat or raft. Mrs. Sewell was a bright, vivacious little person who beamed on everyone with the most hospitable smiles. The other members of the family ranged from a boy of sixteen to men and women. Among them I found the young man who carried me on his shoulder to my new home. There was one more picture—a room full of men and women, my own people whom I knew, and others who were strangers. In the midst, my father, so white and silent in his strange new bed.

There was a break now in my life. Mother's people, the Browns, wanted her to go back to her own family, and this she did. For three years, we lived under the shadow of the White Mountains. The love of all wild things begun in the wilderness so early in life was still fostered and strengthened in my new home on my grandfather's farm. The buildings were small and very old fashioned. One side of the land was bordered by a small river, while on the other side a still smaller stream flowed the length of the farm and emptied into it. Over this brook the road crossed by a bridge and led to the ridge where was the main road to the Franconia Mountain, towering high. Across the river was a steep forest-covered mountain.

Grandmother [Achsah Hart] had a garden of old-fashioned flowers, and there were shade trees and an orchard. The chief charm of the place to me was a pasture lying back of the buildings. It was very like many other New England pastures, more or less rocky, with scattering young pine and fir growing on it to provide shady spots. There were also grassy hollows and daisy-covered knolls. There were damp spots in the shade of great boulders where the greenest mosses grew. It was an enchanted country. One could pretend anything there.

Three years passed, and I was eight years old when my little brother and I jour-neyed back "Down East," as everybody called the new country. In that time, much had been done to develop it. My aunt *[Mary Ellen Barker]*, whom I had never seen, met us at Patten Village, which was the terminus of a hundred-mile stage route. Mother, weary with the long journey and the care of the children, was glad to see her. It was too late in the day to go the ten miles to Grandfather's, but friends living about half the dis-tance made us welcome for the night. There was no longer the need for people to travel with a jumper. The road was good, at least in winter, and the comfortable sleigh and fur robes drawn by a spirited horse had replaced the old makeshift. It was equip-ment Grandfather had brought with him from his former home.

The improvement was no less marked in the Barker homestead. The buildings were finished, except the upstairs rooms, which were partitioned with carpets, cur-tains and blankets. It was a pleasant, comfortable home, and Grandma *[Mary Jane Berry]* was its presiding genius.

To the west and south stretched wide fields, but to the north and east the forest of lofty beeches and sugar maples was left untouched. Back of the buildings, a thrifty young orchard of carefully selected trees was growing. Small fruits were already bear-ing, and in summer the vegetable garden was a delight to behold.

Grandfather was a strong advocate of clean, careful tillage. He fed many roots to his young stock, and he was very particular about their cultivation. Grandma loved flowers and raised all the old-fashioned varieties. Her flowers gave an artistic touch to the air of comfort and plenty, which prevailed. It was into this busy, loving atmo-sphere that we two fatherless and practically motherless children came.

A few nights later, Mother kissed her children goodnight; and, when we awoke in the morning, she was gone—back to a life of toil for her daily bread. It was three years before we saw each other again.

I had no difficulty fitting into the family at Grandpa's. I was quick physically and mentally; eager to be of service, and interested in all the simple industries that made up the daily life. Steve and Rod were still members of the family, though both worked in the lumber woods in the winter.

Father's farm had been sold to his brother-in-law *[Winchell Woodard]* whose family was living there in a roomy log house. There were three boys and one girl, Jane, who was one year my senior. The next lot on the road, which had belonged to Steve, had been sold, and that family contained several boys and girls. Two more families belonged in the Barker Ridge colony, but in these there were no children.

The deep snow covered the ground. It was before the days of skis, and children did not travel on snowshoes as men did. Addison and I had to keep to the yard on the road when we went out to play. There were rides on the sled behind the gray horses, and a particularly interesting tramp. That was behind the herd of cattle when they were driven each morning down the long path to the spring in the woods for their drink of water.

We were never tired of tending sheep. They were so gentle and tame, and when the young lambs began to appear, my enthusiasm soared. Often Grandfather brought one wrapped in a blanket into the kitchen to be warmed and fed until it could stand firmly on its legs. There were always a few whose mothers refused to own them, and they became my special care and pets. They had to be fed milk from a bottle several times each day.

The pleasantest part of the day was in the evening when, the work all done, Grandpa sat by the fire with his pipe and Grandmother with her knitting, and I read aloud to them from some book brought from the Sunday School library at the Falls or borrowed from the neighbors. Grandpa and Grandmother were great readers and kept themselves well informed about the affairs of the day, but books were not common. Not much money was spent for them by ordinary people. There were very few books in the house suitable for a child. A few on agriculture and orcharding, a church history, several books of travel and biography, and one prize, *Robinson Crusoe*, which I read over and over.

Occasionally, Grandpa and Grandma told stories of things, which took place in the first years of living in the wilderness. Stories of battles with moose in the hunt, or of wolves and bears.One bear story especially intrigued me, perhaps because the sequel happened after I came back there to live. I have said that Grandpa had a flock of sheep, seventy-five in fact. He was very careful and gentle with them. They all knew and trusted him. They had a section of the barn and a yard opening into the cattle yard and their own pasture, the only field of grassland, it having been made before he began to clear the land. In the meadow, surrounded by woods, was a spring from which flowed a tiny brook. A path led into the main road a hundred rods below the buildings.

Both cattle and sheep were brought to the yards at night and securely fastened in. The fence was of cedar, five rails high. The gate was made like a hay rack with wooden standards set into the top and bottom pole, the upper one being long, and heavy with a weight to balance the gate.

One hot summer night, when everyone was supposed to be sleeping and it was very still, Grandma heard the cowbells tinkle as if the cows were moving slowly about the yard. She called Grandpa's attention to it, and after listening a few moments he said, "I think it's because it's so hot. I left the sheep gate open so they can get out into the yard."

Nothing more was said. Next morning Rodney had a hurry call to get up, and when he appeared, Grandpa said, "Something got among the sheep last night. They are gone. They broke the standards out of the gate pushing each other out. Pieces of wool are left on the broken standards."

"They must have been mighty scared," said Rod. They went to the yard to look for tracks. The road was full of sheep tracks, nothing else. Rod continued the search while Grandpa followed the sheep. He found them on the far side of the pasture huddled together, too frightened to feed. They saw him when he came out of the woods and rushed towards him, every one voicing a loud complaint as though trying to tell him all the trouble.

They did tell him some of it, for he counted them as they went through the bars and found one missing. When they reached Rod, he had found bear tracks. A pile of boards had been laid on the outside of the fence, and on these boards were muddy bear tracks while marks of claws were deeply embedded in the top rail. Careful scrutiny revealed a trail, not in the road, but on the harder ground beside it.

"There is no sign of the sheep being dragged either over the fence or on this trail. Do you suppose he carried it?"

"It looks that way."

"Well, he must be some size. It was one of the biggest sheep in the flock."

They followed the track past the cleared land, alongside the woods, until they came to a pile of brush left when the road was made. Here, for awhile, they were baffled, until going around the brush they found the bear had jumped over it, laid the sheep down and dragged it two or more rods, and then eaten of it until his hunger was satisfied. The remainder lay there before them.

That day, Rod built a trap known as a deadfall around the remains of the sheep. Bears will go back to their kill even though there is the human scent about it. They love mutton and will dare much to get it. He did come back that night, and left the hide of his back on the big log, which ought to have crushed an ordinary bear.

One thing was lacking at the buildings of the Barker farm. That was good drinking water. Halfway down the hill near the road was a fine spring, and to this spring every night, when his day's work was done, went Grandpa to get a turn of water. For that purpose, he had made a wooden yoke that fitted his shoulders. Pieces of rope were tied to the ends of the yoke. Each rope had a wooden hook to hang the pail of water on, and his hands steadied both pail and hook.

The following night, he went as usual for the water. Not far from the buildings, he saw coming towards him, his nose on the sheep tracks, a bear. He stopped, and at the same moment the bear stopped also, threw up his head, and they took a good look at each other; then Grandpa yelled. The bear jumped sideways from the road and for several minutes could be heard bounding off through the forest.

"No wonder he got out of that trap," Grandpa said to Rod, "I knew he must be a big bear to carry off a sheep in his mouth, but I never saw one as big as that bear. He stood four feet high. His legs were long but his body was large. He had a white face. That is very unusual."

He gave them no more trouble, nor was he seen again in the vicinity. In the spring, a hunter living in Sherman told my Grandfather that, while looking for game, he fired at a very large bear; feeling sure he had hit him in the shoulder, he followed him for several hours in the direction of Barker Ridge. Finding he was not gaining on him, he abandoned the chase.

Two years later came the sequel. A group of five men, all of one family, settled on land east of our farm, and one, who was the owner of a sheep and lamb, moved into the log cabin once occupied by my father.

One morning in early spring, the sheep was gone; search revealed the half-eaten body in the swamp back of the hovel. Each man owned an old-fashioned muzzle-loading gun. These they set around the sheep, attaching cords to the trigger, the other ends being tied to the carcass. That night they all slept in the old camp. At daylight, they were awakened by a regular fusillade of shots and were soon on the spot expecting to find a dead bear. Not so. Bruin was gallantly facing the crowd, growling and snapping his teeth, the blood flowing from five bullet holes.

There were still patches of snow, and all the hollows were full of water. The bear slowly retreated, drinking at each puddle as he went, while the men reloaded their guns and fired repeatedly at him. At last, his strength failed him. He stooped to take a swallow of water and fell head-first into the pool and drowned. I remember that I was glad the plucky old fellow died by drowning rather than by bullets.

In size and markings, he answered perfectly to the bear that two years before had taken one of Grandpa's biggest sheep. Moreover, there was a bare spot on his back where some time the hide had been scraped off, probably by a deadfall. When they cut up the meat, they found a bullet, embedded in the flesh of the shoulder, having completely healed over.

The evenings were not always quiet and uneventful. Neighbors frequently dropped in for an hour's chat. They even came occasionally from the Falls to bring some piece of news or on some other errand.

Times were stirring out in the world, and excitement even penetrated the far frontier, where we lived. It was the winter of 1860 to '61. The papers were full of discussion for and against the policy of the administration. The slavery question was the central thought of it. There was not much chance for argument or division in the little groups gathered around our winter fireside.

Both Grandpa and Grandma had long been enthusiastic abolitionists, and Abe Lincoln was their chosen leader. The others were equally loyal to the issues for which the North was contending.

"There will be war," said Grandpa. "The South has gone too far to back down now."

"In my opinion," said Woodard, a near neighbor, "they have been planning just that for several years."

"What I can't swallow," said one young man, "is their calling the people of the North mudsils, just because we work for our living."

"I don't see what the government is thinking of, letting them get hold of the arsenals and so many arms. They have most of the trained men, too, trained at West Point at the government's expense. Our folks must be drunk or asleep."

"There's a book printed about slavery. It's written by a woman and shows what a terrible thing it is. I saw it at the village the other day. The South and a lot of Northern people are furious about it." This bit of information came from William Craig. It was some time before I, who was eagerly but silently absorbing all the talk, read *Uncle Tom's Cabin*. Then I remembered this bit of publicity.

Very little else but the increasing evidences of the coming struggle was talked about for the next two months. Then came the shock of the attack on Sumter. The news ran like fire throughout all the frontier towns.

Uncle Rodney came home from his work. "Mother, I'm going to enlist."

Grandma, pale but game said, "I expected it."

If the air had been filled with excitement, it was tense now. The young, over-eighteen, gathered in groups and made plans.

"It won't take long to quell this disturbance," was the prevailing opinion.

Grandpa, however, said gravely, "Don't be so sure."

It was midsummer before they got off to the capitol for mobilization, a goodly company of young, stalwart men from the towns around the village. Nine men enlisted from Island Falls, only recently organized into a town.

Before mobilization was complete, two—George Sewell and William Craig—were brought back dead of measles.

Steve came home from bidding Rodney good-bye, and as he ate his late meal, he said, "I've had a letter from Steve's brother *[Silas Barker]*. He has enlisted and is at the capitol. He says they are forming a regiment of sharpshooters. He has qualified and is sure I can. He wants me to go with him. I've got to go, Mother. I can't let the other boys go and I stay here."

Grandma was distressed. "If my country needs all my boys, I have nothing to say, but I don't believe it does. We can't spare you, Steve. What will we do without you?"

"I'll stay until the crop is harvested, Mother. I can get a man to do the plowing. We will all be back in the spring."

So he went, and with him, or soon after, were ten others.

On one of his trips to Patten, Grandpa brought back very disquieting news. A disease had broken out about which little seemed to be known other than that it was reported by the newspapers as an epidemic prevailing in cities, and many deaths were occurring as a result. The doctors called it diphtheria.

"It's the same sickness that spread over the country many years ago," said Grandma. "They called it Putrid Sore-throat then."

It certainly became an epidemic in all the towns about us. Hardly a family escaped, and many households lost all the children. There were funerals every day, and nobody seemed to guess its contagious nature. Professional nurses were unknown in our new country. The neighbors helped each other, and the funerals were all public. Fred Sewell and two Craig girls besides several younger children died in our town.

It finally ran its course and died out, leaving many wrecks as well as much sorrow in its train. When spring came and restored health to the land, there were many sore hearts and empty homes. Nor was the news from the front reassuring. It was being borne in on the consciousness of everyone that this was no unimportant episode in our history. Help was getting scarce on the farms. Men were hired to plant the spring crop, but they enlisted before it was half finished.

I did much light work out of doors to keep the routine going: planting potatoes in the burnt land, corn, beans and pumpkins in the orchard, and helping with the cattle and sheep. Both Addison and I learned to ride horses that summer. The task I enjoyed most was hunting the cows. They had very little pasturage, picking their living wherever they could find it, in the woods, on little meadows and swales, often getting miles from home. They generally wandered back as the sun began to drop in the west, and we nearly always found them within a mile of home.

Addison and I were started off at four o'clock and wandered leisurely along, stopping here and there to look at many fascinating things on the way, keeping an ear open the while for the sound of a bell of which there were several in the herd. There was one dignified old cow who seemed to be the acknowledged leader of the herd, and no one of them ever sought to supersede her. She always headed the procession. Her name was Kentucky; why, I never knew.

The "Down East" boom reached its heights. People from all over New England traveled "Down" to the Aroostook, where rich lands were to be had for a song. They appeared at all times of day and night.

There were no hotels or boarding houses in our town. The three or four families with the best accommodations had to feed and house these pioneers. Our house was often full, as were also those belonging to the Sewell's and Craig's. These newcomers were mostly a good class, and many of them became permanent residents. They came to Grandpa for all sorts of supplies, having brought none with them and often having no team to transport stuff far.

Crops were good in our new country and brought excellent prices during the war. It became necessary to have more barn room, and that winter Grandpa cut and hauled the logs for lumber for another barn. A sawmill had been built at the Falls which supplied the settlers with lumber for building purposes.

A log schoolhouse had been built at the Falls three years previously and a school established, two terms each year of twelve weeks each. On every Sunday there was a Sunday school, and twice a month a minister came from Patten to preach in this primitive house. We children on the Ridge used to walk to the Sunday School, the distance being two miles and a half, and the road rough and muddy in places, but we did not mind either the distance or the road.

The town had what it called a grand celebration of the Fourth of July the following summer. There was a beautiful poplar grove on the edge of the settlement, which was an ideal place for a picnic, and here were built tables and a stand for speakers, and flags were hung to decorate the place. A parade of "horribles" was planned, and singing, and musical events of various kinds, and there were swings and so forth.

All the people were invited, and the women cooked the spread. The day was ideal, and I remember with what a thrill Addison and I set out from home quite early in the morning. There was plenty of noise, helped out with a fife and a drum or two. The "horribles" were sufficiently horrible, and the guns were a delight. There was not much going on that we did not see. But the best of all were the pails of lemonade and the board shanties where we could buy for a cent a thick stick of striped candy.

A large crowd had gathered from our own and other towns. The tables were loaded with bread, butter, cakes, pies and doughnuts. It only remained to dish up the hot baked beans and vegetables when the cry went around, "There's a shower coming up! Get the dinner ready quick!"

Everyone in charge of the food worked like mad and nearly finished setting the tables. But alas! The rain came down in torrents. Instead of sitting down to the tables, the people crawled under them, into the booths, the barns, houses, anywhere for shelter. The rain ceased shortly, but everything was wet and the food was a mess. Nevertheless, they straightened things out the best possible and sat down and ate what was not utterly spoiled. Afterwards, there were speeches and patriotic songs, which everyone sang.

The sun came out from behind the clouds and soon dried the grass and trees, and the fun went merrily on until the West began to glow with the afternoon sun. We were a tired but happy pair of children when we crawled into our beds that night, very enthusiastic about our nation's birthday.

Late in autumn, Grandma remarked one day, "It's time we dipped the candles."

The butchering was all done, and there was a large supply of beef and mutton tallow. This had all been tried out in the big farmer's boiler set in an outhouse. Next day began the task of making the year's supply of candles. Balls of wicking were cut and twisted into the proper lengths. These were strung on small wooden rods long enough to reach across a wash tub. Enough of these rods were used to cover a tub, carefully keeping the wicks apart lest they interfere with each other. Another tub was then filled with hot tallow, and each rod full of wicks was dipped in it and returned to the empty tub to cool.

When sufficiently cool, the tub was replenished with hot tallow and the process repeated until the candles were the right size, when they got their final cooling. They were then slipped from the rods and new wicks substituted. That job lasted two or three days, for it took a lot of candles to light our house through the long winter.

"The corn meal is getting low," said Grandma one morning as Grandpa brought in the foamy pails of milk.

"All right, "was his reply.

There was one room with which I had become very familiar since coming to the farm. It was the grainary, a long room over the wood shed and wagon house where carpentry work and other repairs were done. It was also more or less a storeroom for supplies for the kitchen and other useful articles. The larger part was used to store the products of the farm. Bins of oats, wheat, rye, barley, buckwheat, and barrels of beans. But I admired most the bins of shining ears of yellow corn. It was husked on the barn floor, and the ears were put in this airy room to dry.

That night, while we were washing the dishes, Grandpa brought into the kitchen a basket of corn, an empty tub and a board. I, at my work, listened while Addison asked questions.

My curiosity was as great as his, however. "What are we going to do with the corn?"

"Shell it," answered Grandpa.

Addison fingered an iron strap nailed along the edge of the board and a hole six inches long just back of the strap.

"Watch and you will see," was the reply to his questioning look.

Grandpa placed the board across the tub, sat on it, and thrusting the fingers of his left hand into the hole, which was shaped to fit his hand, took an ear in the right hand. He held it against the corn partially supported by the left fingers and quickly scraped the kernels off the cob.

Little brother Addison gave a shout, "Oh, Grandpa, let me help!"

And he began to pass the ears, which he inveigled himself into believing greatly expedited the process. Other baskets followed on successive evenings, and soon a load of corn and rye was ready to be carried to Houlton to be ground into meal for the johnnycake and "injun" loaves.

The mill was thirty miles away, but the bulk of the crops were marketed there. Grandfather had other work with which he busied himself in the long winter evenings. He repaired all rips and breaks in the harness. He made moccasins for himself and mended his shoes, which were made by a shoemaker in the town. All our everyday shoes were made there.

"See the hole coming in my shoe, Grandpa," said Addison.

Grandpa looked the small shoe over very carefully. "I guess I'll have to tackle that shoe tonight. They both need taps too."

In the evening, he brought in his mending bench, and we drew up our chairs to watch him. That mending bench was a fascinating object. It was finished in little compartments containing different articles. There was one for the ball of shoe thread after doubling and twisting it, another for hog's bristles, which he fastened by some mysterious process to the waxed thread and used like needles. There were the awls to make the holes in the leather to be sewed and little pieces of leather to make patches or taps. One corner was full of tiny wooden pegs to fasten the tap to the sole of the shoe, and a cute little hammer to drive them in. How I admired the straight rows of holes made with the awl and into which the pegs were so easily driven.

Our hands were small, so it was our task to find if any point were sticking up inside the shoe. These he would wear down to smoothness with an iron rasp. All our shoes for common wear were made in like manner. In summer I wore, as did most women, cloth shoes with leather soles and elastic at the sides.

When the housework was done in the morning, Grandma would spin. I, on my favorite seat, a low stool, kept busy with my "stint," knitting a certain number of rounds on a stocking or doing "over and over" on a sheet. I often paused to watch her swift, graceful movements. A bunch of wool rolls lay on the bench of the wheel. From it she picked a single roll and twisted the end onto the end of the thread always left on the spindle by slowly turning the wheel round. Slipping her hand down the roll about eight inches, she then grasped it tightly and again, slowly turning the wheel with a small tool called a pin, she retreated, stretching and twisting the piece into a strong, even thread about five feet long. Then, giving the wheel a quick whirl to complete the twisting, she swung the left hand across the right shoulder and, still turning the wheel, wound the yarn on the spindle. This process was repeated until the spindle was full, then was wound onto a reel. This was a stick eighteen inches long with a twelve-inch stick dovetailed in to each end at right angles to it. She first doubled a short length of the yarn to make a string, tying it to the long stick which shegrasped firmly and began winding the yarn on both end sticks, counting as she wound. When there were forty rounds, she tied it with the string and called it a knot. Seven knots made a skein.

It was not yet yarn, however. Two of these skeins were stretched on the winder, which whirled on its own standard. Here I came into a job. I soon learned to double or wind the two threads together into balls. Grandma twisted them on the wheel; they were again wound on the hand reel into skeins, secured, and were ready for use unless dyed.

There were coarse yarn for mittens, medium for stockings and a fine quality for cloth and blankets. Grandma made her dyes. Indigo for blue, copperas and alum for yellow, cedar boughs for brown, sumac for red, and green was made by combining other colors. She combined a black wool with white for gray. She produced clouded effects by braiding the yarn or tying strips of new cotton cloth tightly about the skeins.

Grandpa's ordinary working clothes were always of homespun cloth which Grandma cut and made, and when he donned a new suit, I thought he was a grand man. He had a fine, tall, well-proportioned figure. He was clean—except for a beard under his jaws and chin. His black hair, with some gray mixed, was combed straight up from his forehead like a pompadour, and at the center back again, straightforward over his ears.

Grandma's hair was very white, and she always wore what she called a front of brown hair. The back of her head was covered with a black lace cap with narrow black ribbons and made curls covering her ears. Some of the discarded curls furnished the hair for a rag doll she made for me soon after I came to live with her. It was one of the treasures of my little playhouse in a corner of the "open chamber" as long as I cared to play with dolls.

The supplies for the household were bought at Patten. A ride to town meant a day off from work, and a list of things needed to last for perhaps three weeks. Addison and I always remained at home to keep the fires. A man attended to the stock.

It was on one of these journeys that they brought home the first kerosene oil and a glass lamp. This was a great boon to me, who loved all things to read after the supper was over until my early bedtime. There were in the house whale oil lamps with tubes for wicks. But for some reason, probably scarcity of oil, they were never used. This new light was very superior to candles, which Grandma said looked more than ever "like white beans."

My spare time was made happy by bundles of illustrated periodicals sent to us by the boys at the front: *Harper's Weekly*, Frank Leslie's *Illustrated Weekly* and others. They were full of war, but the pictures were very good, and I was introduced by them into a world outside my ken. We also had Peterson's and Godney's Fashion Magazines. I greatly admired the charming ladies. The living room needed redecorating, and we papered it with the accumulated heaps of picture papers. I have in my mind a picture of myself on my way from the dining table to the pantry, with a pile of plates in my hands, pausing to read something pasted on the wall. Grandma's stern "Mary" quickly brought me back to ordinary life.

When we were not too busy out of doors, I always had to do a "stint" in sewing or knitting before I could go and play. They were not hard, just enough for practice. My grandmother conscientiously taught me to do all the kinds of work needed in a household. She was an expert with the needle, and I learned to sew quite well. I was very proud and happy when, under her direction, I cut and made myself a gingham dress. Grandma, on one of her shopping expeditions, bought me a hoop skirt made for a girl of my age. "That's because you are a good girl and do your stints every day," she said. I was very proud of that hoop skirt. I practiced until I could make the proper spread and curve under my skirts while sitting.

Jane Carr, Addison and I walked to Sunday school one fine morning in summer. From the foot of the Ridge, the road stretched through woods all the way to the Falls. We were going along a turnpike which had a deep ditch on either side, busily talking, when a bear stalked across the road in front us a short distance. We stopped, quite astonished, saying nothing. At once our attention was called to two cubs on the outside of the ditch, whimpering and whining because they thought they could never get over the ditch alone. There was water in it, too.

It was too much for us; we all shouted. Instantly, they disappeared in the bushes behind them. We walked along to where we had seen them and stopped. There they were, about ten feet up a large tree, hanging by their claws to the bark, watching us with their black, twinkling little eyes. They were such fat, cute little fellows, like little puppies, with pointed ears and white noses. We talked at them and laughed at them, but they wrinkled their noses and watched us silently.

Suddenly it came over us with a shock that we were between the cubs and their mother, and I whirled about fully expecting to see her charging at us with snapping teeth and growls, but she was not in sight, and we went on in a hurry. We stopped at a safe distance, hoping she would go back to the cubs, but she did not.

Winter again shut down with its cold and its blocking storms. There were still activities. The hauling of the farm produce to market, getting the grain and corn to mill to make flour and meal for our use and for the barn creatures, and the cutting and preparing the year's supply of wood. The first threshing machine run by horse power in that section went the rounds that autumn. There were two terms of school during the year in our district, though we had no schoolhouse yet.

A tragic event happened on our Ridge about the middle of the winter. The Darlings, who came early into the settlement of the neighborhood, were having company. The usual family consisted of the two old people and an unmarried son, George. This winter, a married son and family were living with them. The eldest daughter was married and lived east of the Ridge, two miles off the main road. The company was a daughter, who worked in a factory in Massachusetts, home for a few days' visit.

Thursday morning George harnessed his horses into the sled to carry her to her sister's for the weekend. She called to see Grandma on her way. The road to her sister's turned east just beyond our place. She was tall and muscular, with vivacious face and red cheeks, the embodiment of abounding life and health, certainly a woman able to care for herself in an emergency.

Sunday morning was cloudy, and by nine o'clock was spilling snow. She said to her sister, "I think I had better go home. I'm afraid we shall have a heavy storm, and I want to get back to Mother before that happens."

Her brother-in-law had no horse but offered to go with her as far as the main road. "The path is good yet; it won't take us long."

The temperature was dropping fast, and the storm increasing in intensity. Halfway lived the Johnson's in the log cabin where my father first lived. Being somewhat cold, she stopped in for a short time to get warm. She told them she was taking the snowshoe trail a few rods up the Ridge. This was a beaten path used by her brother-in-law and others and led to her brother George's shingle camp in the woods near her father's house.

It was a wild storm. A fierce wind blew from the northeast, and the air was thick with the falling snow. Grandpa said, as he came from the barn, "I don't know as I ever saw the snow so thick in the air. One can't see across the road."

Night closed down early, and sometime before daylight it ceased to snow; but the wind, now in the north, and cold still, blew a gale. The large body of snow was piled in drifts everywhere. Now and then the sun shone out for a few minutes through the driving clouds, but no one was seen on the roads. The wind did not let up until Tuesday, when the sky became clear in the afternoon. Wednesday, all the men were out with teams and shovels breaking the roads.

A number of teams with their crews came from the Falls. While they were breaking by the house, George Darling came in to ask Grandmother if she had seen Lucy or her brother-in-law since the storm began. When he heard that she had not seen them, he said that early that morning he had found Lucy's handbag and a pair of frozen stockings hanging in his camp. His story suggested only one thing to the men gathered around him.

"I am going to break through to Jeff's," he said.

Two men offered to go with him to help him, and others promised to remain at our farm if needed when he got back.

They did not have to go far. They met Johnson on snowshoes who told them of her call and her plan to take the trail. The storm was getting so bad, he went to the path after she had gone to make sure she went that way. It was evident that she made the camp without much difficulty. It was through the woods, therefore sheltered, and it saved her a mile of travel.

The majority of men working on the road made up the search party. They were equipped with shovels, axes, restoratives, some food, blankets and a long hand-sled.

We, at home, and the anxious family, were left in suspense during the long hours of that day. At first, they thought perhaps she was lost between the camp and the house, being unable to make her way in the black storm, but the wind had swept the ground clean of the new snow. They turned to the woods. They reasoned that her long heavy skirts spread by the crinoline she wore would make a trail in the old snow already quite deep before the new snow fell. Acting on this idea, they circled the camp and soon found her track. It led straight off into the swamp *[Thousand Acre Bog]*, which was nowhere less than two miles broad. And they followed it in single file, a group of silent men.

She had sunk in the snow to her knees at each step, but on she went over fallen logs, around the tops of fallen trees, brush and thicket. They found where she had stopped to rest. After that it was plainer. There was less snow on the track and finally none.

They began to find clothing hung up on limbs. First the heavy shawl, then two or three frozen skirts. All these garments were telling the story of exhaustion and a desperate fight for life.

Suddenly they were at the end of the trail. Then they saw what they had not noticed before—she had doubled on her tracks. Somewhere they had passed her.

They turned and went slowly back. The man at the end of the line saw a step off the trail beside a small tree. He stepped around the tree and found himself within an open space made by the tops of several down spruces. One glance was enough. He motioned to the man in front to ask her brother to leave the sled, which he did, going on without question. She had trodden down the snow, sat down against the boughs and fallen asleep.

There was one queer incident that might be added to this story. A year later Rodney was asked by the family to remove the remains from their temporary resting place to the new cemetery. When the casket was lifted out, he yielded to a sudden impulse and opened it. She lay as if asleep, as freshand fair as when her friends last saw her. For three minutes they gazed at her, then before their eyes, she crumbled to a mere handful of dust.

Our household was awakened one cold morning about four by a loud knock on the door. It aroused me, and directly I heard the excited tones of both Grandpa and Grandmother mingled with a deeper yet familiar note. I woke Addison, and we hurried into our clothes and ran downstairs.

Stephen was there, and we were so glad to see him. Even old Tom, the cat, sprang straight into his arms at sight of him.

Grandma proceeded to get breakfast, but the rest gathered about the stove to listen while he talked. He had walked all night, thirty-five miles, because he was too impatient to wait for the next day's stage. There had been some changes in the company officers, and he had been promoted to Captain, with a few days' furlough.

How hard it was to have him go back. Indeed, it was the last time Addison and I ever saw him.

While we waited for breakfast, someone opened the door and called us to listen. Wolves, evidently a small pack, were chasing some animal, probably a deer, on the brook. Because it was open to the sky, the sound came to us very distinctly, though they were perhaps two miles away. The mingled yells, barks, howls and growls were cruel and bloodcurdling. I could not forget the poor deer, which stood little chance of escape with the snow so deep.

There were but few wolves in that region. Now and then some incident made us aware of their presence. Before he became a soldier, Rod had a line of traps covering several miles. He had to re-cross his track several times, and he discovered that one lone wolf followed him all day. Rod did not see him then or afterwards.

We were reminded of them by something which occurred the previous autumn. A man died on a lonely road east of us. The other two men who lived near him went to Patten with our team for a coffin, returning as it began to be dusk. For some reason, they decided to carry the coffin on their shoulders the remainder of the way.

It was two or more miles over a rough and muddy road, the last half being after it had become dark. They had to sit down frequently to rest. Very soon, they became conscious that animals were keeping abreast of them on each side of the road. They could hear their stealthy movements.

After reaching their house, they heard now and then the yelp of a wolf. Hunters and trappers say they are attracted a long distance by the smell of a dead creature.

It was almost impossible to get help for the work on the farm. Grandpa succeeded in obtaining labor for the more strenuous work from some of the new settlers who worked by the day. Generally they were paid by supplies from the farm. Addison and I were his steady helpers and could accomplish many of the lighter tasks.

CHAPTER 2

WIDE OPEN WEST

Carr family ancestors came to Rhode Island from London in 1635. Reverend Carr delivered the first Protestant sermon in Buffalo, New York and settled on a farm near there. When Byron Oscar Carr and his brothers moved with his prosperous parents *[Clark Merwin Carr and Delia Ann Torry]* to Illinois, he had already taught school. He then served as a surveyor's assistant on the new Chicago, Burlington and Quincy line.

When the Civil War broke, B. O. and two brothers became officers in the same Illinois regiment. With his sociable good humor, competence born of a photographic memory and plenty of experience with railroading, he wound up as Quartermaster to the Army of the Southwest. His brothers did well, too, with Clark *[Clark E. Carr]* in business and Horace *[Horace M. Carr]* the Ambassador to Denmark.

Yet another, General Eugene A. Carr, served in Texas in 1854 and Kansas in 1857. During the Civil War, he was west of the Mississippi winning the Medal of Honor at Pea Ridge. Later, it was in his service that Buffalo Bill Cody achieved fame as a scout. *[Marian Carr, some years later, remembers Buffalo Bill riding up to shake hands with all the family during one of his shows. – JM]*

While the Carrs were fighting the Civil War and subduing the Western Indians, the Pratts were settling California and helping connect it to the rest of the Union by building the transcontinental railroad.

The first Pratt had arrived at Weymouth, Massachusetts, in 1623. Simeon Pratt was born in Maine in 1797. At various times he was a storekeeper, bookkeeper, fisherman, teacher, town selectman, town clerk, justice of the peace and a Colonel in the state militia. He was also the teacher of singing schools for the whole countryside. All was quiet when he sat by the hearthstone and poured out a stream of song.

Simeon's eldest son *[Robert Henry Pratt]* was a seaman and navigator. He was among the early settlers in California. When he married Louisa Merrill in Freeport, Maine in 1849, he and about a hundred New England men left by ship to California. After a mutiny by his fellow gold seekers, he was left as the ship's first officer. Under his leadership, the trip around Cape Horn was uneventful.

In a year of mining along the Trinity River of northern California, Robert and his brothers did well enough to purchase a ranch in Colusa County. There, along the Sacramento River, they built a hotel, operated a ferry, and helped organize the county, with Robert becoming the first county auditor.

Louisa and Baby Sarah *[Sarah Amelia Pratt]* could now afford to ship to Panama. They crossed the isthmus on muleback, and sailed north, arriving in 1851. Louisa became a pioneer, living ten miles from the nearest other white woman and forty miles from a doctor. The Pratts dipped their own candles and rarely obtained fresh fruit.

Livestock was destroyed by disease, and bandits were laying wait for couriers. Once, to deliver gold to Sacramento, Robert put the precious metal in a gunnysack, dressed in shabby clothes, and took passage on the lower deck of a riverboat.

Robert sold out to his brothers and about 1863 became involved in the trans-Sierran railroad project when there was still doubt of its feasibility. His family stayed with him as the railroad construction crept up the ridges toward the crest of the Sierra Nevada. Sometimes they lived in a boxcar.

Louisa, a former schoolteacher, wrote poetry and painted watercolors in her spare time and took great pains with Sarah's education. As Sarah, the eldest child, grew up, her parents saw to it that she graduated from high school. Although yearning for a higher education, Sarah found herself teaching school on the frontier.

Robert Pratt became well acquainted with Colonel B. O. Carr, who was Superintendent of Construction of the Central Pacific, and was working day and night to meet the schedule. Sarah was a buxom, rosy-cheeked girl, very assured, and very spoiled being one of just a few unmarried girls among the vast army of railroad builders. B. O. was very courtly, awfully good looking and accustomed to leadership.

After inviting Sarah to several dances and "socials" and getting nowhere, he finally asked her to a dance which, unbelievably, she hadn't been bidden! *After* getting her promise, he arranged with their "set" to give the dance. Of course, Sarah's "regulars" found her already engaged. Sarah Pratt and Colonel Carr were married in the remote railroad community of Carlin, Nevada, in 1872. The nearest preacher was the agent at the Pyramid Lake Indian Reservation hundreds of miles away.

Sarah's active imagination was eventually displayed in her published books such as *The Iron Way,* where she writes about romance and guile:

"Mr. Cadwallader, I cannot accept nor parry your extravagant compliments as a city girl would. Surely you can't be interested in the simple things I can say. Please let me go." Once again she moved as if to pass him.

"A beautiful woman doesn't need to say things to be interesting. You haven't asked what it is I wished to say."

"Did you expect me to ask?"

"Most girls would. That's where you are the more attractive. Sit down here, and we'll talk it over. I'll make you comfortable." He reached for some of the overhanging boughs, intending to place them on the rock seat. The movement took him a pace from the opening.

"Really, Mr. Cadwallader, I'm sure you could tell me as well at the hotel. Good afternoon." She started toward the low, thorny opening.

He was after her with the spring of a cat. "No you don't, my beauty! If you won't stay and talk, you shall give me a proper farewell."

The inequality of the ground availed him; and before she could divine his intentions, he threw his arm around her, gave her an audible kiss, and stepped back out of her reach.

"There, my wood-nymph, don't break your heart; and don't think I was intending to ask you to marry me. I only wanted to tell that inflated skipjack, Vincent, that his modest dove wasn't above a sweet little flirtation with your humble servant. I have your handkerchief, and—"

His sneering words ceased suddenly, not for the menace in Stella's pale face, but for hasty, approaching strides. He sprang forward past Stella to meet Gideon's crashing blow.

Sarah ends her colorful book with the dramatic scene when the East and West segments of the transcontinental railroad are finally connected:

"Under the desert sky, the spreading multitude was called to order. There followed a solemn prayer of thanksgiving. The laurel tie was placed, amidst ringing cheers. The Golden spike was set. The Trans-American telegraph wire was adjusted. Amid breathless silence the silver hammer was lifted, poised, dropped, giving the gentle tap that ticked the news to all the world! Then, blow on blow, Governor Stanford sent the spike to place!"

"A storm of wild huzzas burst forth; desert rock and sand, plain and mountain, echoed the conquest of their terrors. The two engines moved up, 'touched noses,' and each in turn crossed the magic tie. America was belted! The great Iron Way was finished."

[Another relative, Temtyan Dunn, writes of a different branch of the new railroad and of a much different lifestyle. Temtyan never went to school in her life, but she taught herself to read and write. — JM]

I came to Abilene Kansas in the year of 1866 with my father and mother and three brothers. We drove through from Illinoise in a covered wagon called a schooner wagon. It was a long and tedious trip, and when we arrived at Abilene it was a desolate looking place, not more than a dozen houses, all little log huts scattered all a round. Not a street in either direction.

Thare wasent a house in Abilene for us to live in so we went down near the river along Mud Creek. Thare was a little log house some one built and we moved in it. We stayed thare one year. That was one of the drye years. The wells and creeks went drye. We would take our cloths and tubs and go to the river and do our wash. Thare was just a little stream of water running through the center of the stream bed not more then 3 or 4 feet wide.

The country was a vast prairie as far as a person could see; not a house in site and not any way for a man to make a living. We planted garden and potatoes, but it all burned aup. This was just after the war and every thing was so high priced. I have seen my mother take wheat ban and mix a little syrup in it and brown it over the fire and put in some coffee essence and make a drink. The old people thought they could not live if they dident have coffee every day.

When we moved into town thare wasent any railroad. All the provisions had to be hauled from Junction City to Abilene and on out west to Fort Haze. The government hired it done. They halled in covered wagons, 15 or 20 wagons in a drove. They had to go a lot of them to geather on account of the Indians. Once in a while they could see one loan Indian a way off on the highest hill watching for the train of loaded wagons—then he would give the signal to the other Indians and they would make a raid on the company and take all the provisions they could get and some times take the best horses.

They built the Union Pacific Rail Road through—then the town began to boom. They graded the road through, then they came along laying ties and rails and the train followed aup as fast as the track was laid. We could see the train 2 or 3 days before they got into town. My brother and I was anxious to get close to the train. When the train pulled up close to us the ingeneer and fire man was watching us and they blew the whistle and turned off steam. We were two scared kids. We tried to run but I would fall down every 2 or 3 steps.

Thare was only one store in Abilene, a grocery and drye goods and the post office all in one room. Then they built the first big hotell and the town built aup fast. The saloons opened aup and the Texas trade came to Abilene. Thare was "cattle men," as we called them, every where, drinking, fighting, swaring and gambling day and night. As it was we had the only good well water in town and every body stopped thare for water. The yard would be full of men all the time. We got so tired of it my father went out on Holland Creek and took a homestead.

My father built us a dugout house. The house was dug down about 5 feet in the ground and had 3 rounds of logs on top of the ground with a board roof with dirt on top of the board. It was a one room house with a board floor on one half and the other half was dirt. The dirt part was our kitchen. We lived in that dugout about 6 years. We could see the buffalows travling over the hills and deer and antelope and prairie chickens.

It was a clear day and all at once it seem to get a little dark as if a thin cloud had come over the sun. I went to the door and look aup in the sky and I could see something flying in every direction and in a few minuts they began to com down. They com so fast and so thick it just sounded like hail as they hit the roof and sides of the house. We had a nice garden, but by evening thare was nothing left. The grasshoppers eat every thing that was green and then they disappeared.

The Indians would com through every fall going out in the western part of the state hunting buffalow and other wild game. They are a snoopy kind of people. They would stop at every house on the road and at the school house, and they always go all around the house before they com in. Then some of them will com in the front door and others will com in the back way at the same time and others will be looking in at the windows.

They go all through the house looking into every thing and they beg or trade for almost any thing to eat. Once my father was feeding a bunch of cattle and one stear got mired in the creek and they pulled it out, but it died that night. The next day a tribe of Indians came along and they see that anamel. One big Indian came in and he wanted to cut some meat from that stear and father couldent understand him. The Indians always cary a big knife in their belt, so he pulled out his knife and reached over and took hold of my little brother and commence to mark a crost his back with the knife. It scared the boy nearly to death. The Indian laughed and said, "Me no hurt little papoose."

My Husband *[Perley Brown Ross]* drove cattle from Texas to Abilene. He looked just like all the rest of the cattle drivers—his hair was long, down over his shoulders and he wore a wide brimmed hat just like Wild Bill did. He and Wild Bill were great friends. *[Wild Bill Hickock gave Perley his gun after accidentally shooting his best friend. — JM]*

Back to the Carr family in the Far West. In an amazing show of generosity, Sarah named her firstborn after the Colonel's first wife, Mary Buck, who died in childbirth. Daughter Mary Louise shows much imagination as she writes of her parents [Byron Oscar Carr and Sara Amelia Pratt]:

I once horrified Mother and some of her callers by insisting that I was at the wedding of my father and mother! These good ladies were already inclined to be somewhat askance because in conservative New Albany my mother was from the "Far West." Pinning me down, Mother learned that I was a little pink angel in the corner of the ceiling and saw the minister raise his arms so high that Papa almost laughed at the display of shirt front. But Mamma, being really praying, had her eyes shut and could say "I do," at the right moment. Many hearings of this incident had convinced me that I had been present on that momentous occasion.

Mother was an expert horsewoman, and Father was always proud to take her for a canter. One afternoon my father and a fellow officer rode up in front of our house. A colored boy brought up a prancing beauty for Mother who appeared in her voluminous broadcloth habit of olive green. I recall it had acorns and oak leaves embroidered on collar and cuffs and an ostrich plume trailing from her mannish hat. The children next door, watching with me the mettlesome mount, said; "Oh Mamie! Aren't you afraid your mamma'll be killed?"

"Oh, no!" I replied, very high-hat, "My mamma used to be a circus rider!" It seems that it was months before the story got back to Mother. She realized my impressions of the "circuses" she and the neighbor children used to get up (neighbors in those days being five to ten miles distant) and was able to understand the pointed coolness of the next-door neighbors.

My dear father was the second of five sons, all of whom distinguished themselves in the Civil War. About the outbreak of the war, my father was a young civil engineer who was later admitted to the Bar in the State of Illinois and was acquainted with many of those whose names are history.

He suddenly found himself, instead of the devoted husband of "the prettiest girl in Knox County" and father of a fine boy, unbelievably a widower with two little sons.

His mother, coming to the rescue, took the two babies, and Father threw himself into that bitter campaign, trying to stifle his grief and making himself very useful to his country.

After the war, Father went into the West, and there into railroading—becoming, of course, well acquainted with Mother's father [*Robert Henry Pratt*], who was then Superintendent of Construction of the old Central Pacific and was working day and night to meet the schedule. Grandmother, who had been a New England school mistress and a beauty, always made Father welcome at the little home on wheels which moved forward every day to the end of the track. Mother was a buxom, rosy-cheeked girl, very assured; and as Grandmother had a new baby (her seventh), Mother was in charge of the household, although Grandmother planned to resume her school teaching when term began.

After a few more months of railroading, Father was given a fine presidential appointment, which took him for a time to Memphis, Tennessee. His two boys, then fifteen and thirteen years old, came to make their home with him. Mother promptly found herself a full-fledged mother of almost grown boys, in a strange Southern town, with a Northern husband! But fortunately, she had a Southern sister-in-law whose position and influence and prompt sponsorship of the little Western bride did much! It was a summer climate where vegetables and fruit bought in the morning was crawling away by night! Mother learned, later on, the knack of handling her colored help. Poor little thing—far away from everyone she knew, and homesick. Ill, but ever valiant!

Luther Bailey Rogers

CHAPTER 3
CIVIL WAR

The Rogers family was descended from Robert Rogers, who emigrated from England in the 1630's and settled in Newbury, Massachusetts. A descendent, Dr. Luther Rogers, migrated north to Harrison, Maine, and finally to Patten in the early 1840's.

In the spring of 1861, I, Luther Bailey Rogers, *[eldest son of Dr. Rogers]* was twenty-one years old, and I began life for myself by going on the drive. I started the 14th day of April, the day the South fired on Fort Sumter. I drove into the boom at Old Town, arriving home the 4th of July. The war was on. I had a chance to enlist in Bangor, but I thought if the war continued there would be a company raised in Patten, and I preferred to go in that one.

I helped Father hay and was mowing with a hand scythe in front of the house on the Rogers farm when Mr. Ichabod Morrill came along. In great glee, he told me of the battle of Bull Run. It pleased him that, as he said, "Our men ran like sheep."

To say that I was mad and aroused to a fighting pitch seems tame. I dropped the scythe, went to the village, hunted up James B. Hill, the Captain of the Rifle Company, and urged him to raise a Company for the war. This he did at once, and I was the second one to sign the roll. We were some time getting together. Most of the boys boarded at the village hotel where they had a lively time getting their meals. I boarded at home. Through the influence of Alfred Cushman, and because of my experience in the Rifle Co., I was made Second Lieutenant.

About the first of August, we started for the seat of the war. We loaded into wagons, and all the country was out to see us off. It was a great occasion for the countryside. At Sherman, Mr. Ambrose made a very patriotic speech. We reached Mattawamkeag the first night; the second, we were in Bangor, where we got our first taste of camp life. From here we took the train and arrived in Augusta the next day.

We considered ourselves a fine lot of men, all dressed in red flannel shirts, the lumbermen of Penobscot. Our regiment, known as the 8th mobilized, was camped in front of the state house. The 7th of September, we were mustered into the U. S. service. I was lieutenant in Company B.

A short time after, we went by rail and boat to New York and camped on Hampstead Plains. We camped in a field east of the Capitol, I think near where the Congressional Library is now. There were no buildings between our camp and the Capitol. It was just one big field.

From there we were sent to Annapolis where an expedition was mobilizing, as we found out later, to capture Hilton Head, South Carolina. We went by steamers to Fortress Monroe where the expedition rendezvoused. It was of some size, 10,000 soldiers, a big fleet of war vessels, and any amount of supply vessels. There were so many that when we started off, the ocean was covered with ships of all descriptions for miles.

While we lay at Fortress Monroe, there were stories going about of a big iron clad that the Rebels had, or were building, at Norfolk. It was supposed to becoming down to sink our whole fleet. They didn't get it ready until long afterwards, however, when the little "Cheese box on a raft" stopped their fun.

At last we sailed away into the broad Atlantic. A big gale struck up off Cape Hatteras, which scattered our fleet. I shall always remember those big waves: our steamer pointing straight up to heaven, then straight to the bottom of the ocean. I was so sea sick, I did not care if we did go to the bottom.

Eventually, we reached our destination, Hilton Head, South Carolina. Our fleet of transports lay outside of the men-of-war for a few days waiting, I suppose, for our storm-scattered fleet to gather.

One fine morning, the flagship Wabash of fifty guns steamed up the harbor followed by the other war vessels, mounting in all four hundred guns. When the flagship was between the forts, she opened both broadsides. The air over the forts was full of exploding shells. For hours the fleet circled the harbor pouring in their fire; how the Johnnies stood it was more than I could see. Just as we soldiers were getting ready to land and storm the forts, the Johnnies took to their heels and the fort was ours.

It was the ninth of November when we landed and pitched our tents in a sweet-potato field. While at Hilton Head, we assisted in the capture of Fort Pulasky. Five companies were sent to Lybee Island. They manned the guns that sometime later reduced the fort and caused it's surrender. The five companies, which included Company B, were stationed on Daubuskey Island. Our job was to cut off communication between Savannah and Pulasky.

From Daubusky Island to the Savannah River stretched a wide marsh at high tide covered with water. We got the cannons across the marsh and built platforms to prevent their sinking in the mud, then carried bags of sand on our backs to build a magazine and breast works. After this was done, we were moved across the river to Bird Island where we helped to establish batteries, which completely closed the river to communication.

The living conditions here were bad. They were more or less so on all the islands. There was a little dike built around it to keep out the ocean, but at high tide it generally broke through somewhere and covered the island with water. We had to get the water we used at low tide, and it was muddy and brackish. I felt that we were too much exposed here; and, if the Rebels had attempted to raid upon us, we should have all been killed or taken prisoners.

After the surrender of Fort Pulasky, we were moved to Lybee Island and loaded vessels with the powder. The greatest enemy we had was the sand flea. Our blankets were so full of them, and at every seam in our clothes was a windrow of them. Our tents being pitched on the sand, there was no escape. Our only relief was the salt water bathing which was very fine.

After we were moved to Hilton Head again, we were sent on an expedition to reduce Morris Island. I was given command of a company of sharpshooters. For some reason, no attack was made and we returned to Hilton Head. Our Colonel did us one good turn for which we were thankful. He kept us out of three fights that amounted to very little except that in each instance many men were killed.

After a short time, our regiment, with several others, was sent to Jacksonville, Florida. While there, we were sent out on a scouting hike on the plank road. On a railroad running parallel with the plank road, the Johnnies had a cannon mounted on a car. They shelled us, and one shell passed over our company and struck a company in front of us killing two men and wounding several. We all landed in a ditch in a heap. They shelled us through the night but did little damage.

We were taken back to Hilton Head again; but, just as we were leaving the city of Jacksonville a fire broke out doing much damage. Its origin was charged to our regiment, which I am sure was a mistake. We returned to Hilton Head. While doing picket duty on Pinkney Island, we had one man killed and one taken prisoner. The company who relieved us was all killed or taken prisoners.

Our next move was to Beaufort, South Carolina. As we marched ashore, we passed a New Hampshire regiment tenting under some live oaks, very nice and shady. The boys said probably they will put us right out in the sun, which they did. We began to get strong and well while the New Hampshire regiment had two or three funerals a day and were finally obliged to move out in the sun also.

In the spring of 1864, all the white troops were transferred to the front in Virginia. The army of the James under General Ben Butler mobilized at Glosister Point of Revolutionary fame. From there we took steamers up the James, landing at Bermuda Front, so called after we fortified it. Afterwards, it became a part of General Grant's line around Richmond and Petersburg.

We went out on the pike between Richmond and Petersburg, south towards Petersburg where we had a brush with the Johnnies and then turned back up the pike towards Richmond. I remember as we marched toward the city there was quite a heavy cannonade going on in our front. There came up in my throat a hard bunch, which I could not swallow; I felt sick to my stomach, but nothing came of it. We camped quietly down in the mud and rain for the night. Toward morning, a rebel prisoner tried to make his escape. He got possession of a mule and charged through the camp. There was a cry of "The Rebel Cavalry"; guns were fired; we all turned out and fixed bayonets to resist cavalry. The camp quieted down again but not for long. We were turned again out and marched towards Petersburg. This gave us another scare, but we were returned to camp.

In the morning, we were marched towards Richmond arriving in front of Fort Darling drawn up in line of battle. We tore down a board fence in our front, which we used to build camps to shelter us for the night, for it was cold. We had hardly gotten them finished when we were ordered up the line, to our disgust. It was a fortunate thing for us, for it was there that the battle of Drury's Bluff began.

The Johnnies swept the camps of the New Jersey regiment that took our place with grape and canister, almost annihilating them. Our regiment was in thick woods behind log breastworks. My Company B and Company F were sent out in front under the Rebel fort as pickets. It seemed a long way out there. The bullets were ticking through the limbs of the felled trees over which we had to climb.

At last we got into our positions and things became quiet. In the night, the Johnnies opened fire without hitting us. This lasted but a short time. In the morning, which was foggy, there was a terrible cannonading on our right and I heard in front, from someone unseen, the command, "Forward, forward."

I discovered that the pickets on our right were gone. I ordered my Company to fall back and notify Company F on our left that we were going. We went over the felled trees without noticing them, into the woods toward our main line. We found the Rebels in the woods ahead of us. They ordered us to surrender. Lorenzo Hackett of the color guard said "Not by a d___ sight," and, snatching the fellow's gun, he gave him a kick and sent him with several others back to the main line, prisoners.

At this point the Rebel charging line burst through the fog so near we could almost touch their guns. I said to the boys "Fire, why don't you fire?"

Someone said, "They are our men."

"No, no," I said and they fired and sent them running back into the fog.

We got into company formation and marched back to our regiment and took our place in line. Meantime, there was a great roar of cannon and musketry on our right, and it sounded as if the lines were being driven back, which was true. The Johnnies, however, gave us enough to do. They charged our line several times but failed to start us.

We stayed until the bullets began to come from the rear, when we had our orders to face back. I remember the crazy action of a dog that belonged to Company D. He ran back and forth howling. He evidently realized that the sound of bullets falling around him meant danger.

The night before, three days' rations had been distributed in piles along our line for our use, but they were not issued to the men, so we had to leave them for the Rebels. No more were issued until three days. The men got whatever they could at the supplier, when they could get where he was.

As we were marching through the thick woods, we met a general on horseback who inquired what troops we were. He ordered us to face about and go back to our old line. Some of our regiment did get back to the old works but had to fight beyond the logs. I remember of seeing one man I knew scouting not far from us. I heard a voice say, "What troops are these?" The man said, "Union, of course." A whole brigade of Rebels was there in line of battle. At the word Union, they fired. We dropped on our faces as it came like a clap of thunder, but their aim was too high. We were covered with leaves, but only one man was hit. A bullet struck his cap and made him so crazy that I had a hard time keeping him anywhere. We lay on our faces and gave those fellows as good as they sent. They said later that if they had known there was but one regiment they would have charged and captured the whole of us.

We got orders after burning a lot of gun powder to march back to the rear as our line on the right and left had been driven back. The Captain of Company A had the shell fever badly. His company was scattered and kept trying to form in my company.

I said, "Why don't you go to your own company?"

They said, "There's our company," and pointed to their Captain on his hands and knees behind a tree.

He sang out, "Company A this way," and they all gathered around him and his tree. A shell came whizzing along and landed near the tree. He came creeping back in front of Company B, but they kicked and whacked him to keep him out from under their feet. It was a capital crime to strike an officer, but nothing was ever done about that performance.

At last we came out of the woods and formed a line at its edge. Colonel Boynton wanted me to take Company B and deploy as skirmishers in front of the line of battle in the woods. I did not like the job, as I knew our line would open fire as soon as it found the enemy in the woods. I told him my company had been on picket all night and were the first to take fire in the morning, so he sent some other company out. It was as I expected.

When the Rebels opened fire, Colonel Boynton gave the order to fire, which placed the skirmishers between two fires. I ordered Company B to hold its fire which gave them a chance to come out on our front, at least all those alive and able to move.

Many skirmishers were undoubtedly wounded by the Union fire. I was pleased to see one man from some company fire straight up in the air. A bullet struck Sergeant Swett and bowled him over. We thought he was dead. Sergeant Ingalls said, "Let's get his cartridges." While we were rolling him over, he came to and got to his feet. Throwing us his cartridge box, he headed for the rear. The bullet had stopped in his watch. He had a serious time with the bruise later.

We kept on shooting until we were ordered back after the rest of the line had gone. Colonel Boynton got a piece of shell in his back and that was the last of his service with us and the end of the Battle of Drury's Bluff. I was in command of Company B in all the fighting we did though I was not the captain. Our captain was not a fighting man.

We marched back to camp at Bermuda Front where the Johnnies followed us and established their line near our works. Our pickets and theirs exchanged shots as they closed in on us. We had several skirmishes, and they continually shelled our camp.

On the 18th of May, two hundred of our regiment were ordered out to support that picket line. As we came out of our entrenchments in the open field, a battery shelled us. Their range was wild, though some of the shells came very close. We went into a sunken road behind the picket line where we were well protected. The shells went over us and exploded beyond.

I felt so safe I borrowed a piece of paper of one Private Troop who was, in a few minutes, killed. I was busy reading the news when the Johnnies suddenly, with their peculiar yell, charged our picket line. We instantly sprang to meet them. Their picket charged our pickets and drove them out of their entrenchments, following them until they met our fire. Then they were driven back over the entrenchments they had captured.

Meanwhile, a Rebel line of battle followed their pickets into the entrenchments. We were facing, with two hundred men, a line of battle half a mile long. Their fire was concentrated on those two hundred men. A part of our troop found another sunken road, which saved them. But my company was in plain sight of the enemy with nothing to protect them, so we got the heaviest of the fire. Of forty men, twenty-five were killed or wounded in the time it takes to tell of it.

I had just turned to give an order, when a bullet took effect in my overcoat, rolled in a bundle on my back. It had nine bullet holes in it, but I was pleased that it had not made one in me. Those of us still in fighting condition protected ourselves as well as we could giving shot for shot all day. In the afternoon, the 47th Pennsylvania Regiment came out and formed a line of battle. I knew the major and asked him what they were going to do.

"Charge the enemy," he replied.

I said, "They will kill you all."

"Well we can only obey orders," was the answer.

They started with a yell but were met with such a rain of bullets, grapeshot, and shell it seemed to wipe them off the face of the earth. I was left behind a fence and the stuff going through the rails left me covered with splinters. A rifle I was holding was hit and knocked out of my hand. A few of the Pennsylvania Regiment came back wounded, among them the major, blood streaming from his sleeve.

Sergeant Ingalls was all of my company left with me, and we started for the entrenchments. As I remember it, we didn't hurry, but walked leisurely along. The bullets were going past us, and we could see the brush of the felled trees being trimmed as with a wind.

Ingalls asked, "What is the reason we don't get hit?"

We had reached the point where we didn't seem to care whether we were hit. That was a day to be remembered. I could not help crying, as I thought of the many men I had known so well, now dead or wounded.

Grant needed men, so the 18th Corps to which we had been transferred from the 10th boarded transports at City Point and sailed down the James River and up to the Pamunkey. At West Point, a part of us landed and marched along the railroad to White House Landing, of Washington fame, where we camped for the night.

The next day, we were on the march to join the Potomac Army then fighting Lee near Richmond. That night, we struck the Rebels who let us know they are there by sending over a few shells. For two days we were shifted from place to place but did not get into much trouble.

The night of the 2nd of June, our brigade was formed in a wood and a ration of whiskey was issued to each man. We were expecting to charge, but a big thundershower came up so we slept on our arms till daylight. We were formed as columns closed en masse at half distance, five regiments, five hundred men in a regiment, a solid body of men. That was part of the great charging column at Cold Harbor. This charge cost the Union Army ten thousand men in a few minutes.

The order came, "Remove priming. Fix bayonets. Charge." Then all hell broke loose. Shell and rifle bullets met us as we went through the woods. Great pine trees came crashing down. Our regiment just got through the woods when we were met by two regiments in front running back in a regular mob. They left the ground in front of the entrenchment covered with dead. They carried us back with them. They were mixed together. When they were passed, all we had left in the formation was the color guard.

I was in command of the color division consisting of two companies, which gave me the command of the color guard. We lay down behind the entrenchment and let the mob run over us. When they were by, we stood up, and in a few minutes our regiment had extricated themselves from the crowd and were back in their places, column closed in mass ready to march towards the Rebels again. We soon got the order. We were marching over the same ground we had been over twice before, the enemy all the time busy with their cannon and rifles. I noticed a steel scabbard on the ground, and, as mine was leather, I picked it up and threw mine away and hitched the steel to my belt.

In the edge of the wood close to the Rebel works, and deployed into the line, we were in full sight, and their fire was something fierce. While deploying, as we presented our side to them, a bullet went through to the rubber blanket I had folded to my chest. An inch or two farther along and I would not be writing this. I said to myself, "They are coming pretty thick here."

After deploying, we closed up the line to the left. The men were lying down, but the officers had to stand until the maneuver was executed, which I thought was a long time. They then built breastworks, the rear rank digging the dirt with their bayonets, the front rank piling it up with their dippers and plates. As there was a lull in business, I squatted behind a tree and practiced shooting at the rebels whenever I could get a glimpse of one.

While busy at this, there came a shell from the flanks that caught me in the stern tearing off the seat of my pants and the heel of my shoe. The shell was two feet long and had struck a tree, which set it to whirling end for end. The edge struck me. If it had come straight, it would have cut me in two pieces. I sprang to my feet; whirling around in a daze, then realizing I was exposed to fire, I dropped again behind the tree. Everybody laughed except the Colonel. He surely looked ugly. There was a continual rebel fire all day long.

A day or two later, I wanted to see my brother, Edwin, who was about a mile to the right on the firing line. It was a side hill back of our entrenchments, and my way lay along this side of the hill. Of course, as soon as I got to my feet, I was a target for what seemed to be the whole rebel army. A regiment in nice new uniforms, evidently new to the service, lay at our right. They had thrown up low entrenchments, and they shouted, "Come down here." I was glad to go. I crawled along over them until I came to some woods where I was protected.

I found Edwin, and while we stood talking, a shell exploded near us. If I had been alone, I would have dodged behind something and probably he would have done so also. We didn't want to be seen dodging by our family relations, so we stood by our guns. Two days later, he came to see me. I can recall him now as we said good-bye and see the look on his face. It was the last time I ever saw him.

We remained at Cold Harbor doing siege work. They would put us outside our works at night, and we would have to have new entrenchments dug by morning. You know that shovels and picks were busy. From there, we went by the way of transports from White House Landing down the Paumukey and up the James River to City Point again. Grant had moved the Potomac Army across from Cold Harbor to Harrison Landing and from there to Petersburg. We were in advance of the main army. A division of colored troops was in advance of us. When we took the road from City Point, we could hear their cannon as they attacked the enemy. As we went on, we met and saw the dead lying about and the wounded limping back to the rear. When we reached the firing line, the battle was over. The enemy had been driven back to their entrenchments near the city.

At night (a beautiful moonlit night), we formed in line expecting to attack, but I remember lying down to take a nap and slept undisturbed until morning. There had been no attack. We marched a short distance into the edge of the wood where we lay all day. Toward night, we marched out on a good wide road where the Johnnies got sight of us and opened fire on us with a battery. The shells kept coming closer until we could see one coming straight at us down the road. We all instantly piled into a deep ditch beside the road. There were several men on top of me, which showed that I was one of the first to dodge.

We maneuvered for some time across fields and through woods, the rebels following us with their fire. At last, we were halted on the ridge in full view of the enemy, and they practiced on us with their guns while we had no orders to fire back. We had several men killed and wounded. To hear bullets striking our men without having any chance to reply was about the hardest stunt we had to endure.

We went back to our camp for the night. The next morning, Grant's Army of the Potomac, having all arrived in front of Petersburg, there was to be a grand assault on the city. Lee's army had also reinforced the rebels in the night, so we had our task cut out for us.

We marched over the same ground we had gone over the night before, but this time not under fire. We were formed in line of battle, and when I stepped out in the front of the line, I saw that every man's face down the line was white and set. I suppose mine was too. The order came: "8th, we, as skirmishers, take intervals." The other companies on our right deployed.

After we had deployed, we faced the west and charged through an orchard. We captured 150 men. I formed the company, which had been scattered in the charge. We filed by some houses down into a field to some trees where we faced and charged the enemy. It was there that Asbury Caldwell of Sherman was killed and I was wounded in the leg.

We were about half way down the hill when I discovered all the men had laid down. When I ordered them up, Sergeant Ingalls suggested that we wait and charge with a regiment that was coming. It was the 1st Maine Heavy Artillery. They were formed in column, and their loss of killed and wounded was very heavy. We charged with them, but I soon got a bullet through the shoulder, and I went to the rear as soon as I was able. I began by crawling on my hands and knees but found that too slow, so I stood up and went back over the hill on the run. I thought the whole rebel army was shooting at me. The bullets were striking each side of me, kicking up the dust. There seemed to be just a path for me to go in. I was much relieved when I reached the other side of the hill.

An ambulance picked me up. In it were several officers of our regiment, among them our Colonel McArthur. I stopped at a Negro field hospital for first aid and got my first glass of whiskey. It had no more effect on me than so much water.

We went by steamer to Fortress Monroe. I had a furlough home and did not get back to the regiment until fall. The three years for which I enlisted were expired, and my brother was dead. Father and mother were very anxious that I should come home and not re-enlist, so I did this, ending my fighting days. I was wounded three times and three bullets took effect in my clothes but did not wound my body. Our regiment came up from the South 800 strong. In two months, they were reduced to 150 by death, wounds or sickness.

L. B. Rogers continues with his brother's obituary: Edwin Searles Rogers, Junior in class of 1865 at Bowdoin, was mustered March 12, 1st Lieutenant into the 31st Regiment Infantry 1864. The regiment was sent immediately to the front, was in the Battle of the Wilderness and in all the following engagements of the Army of the Potomac including Cold Harbor. Although commissioned as lieutenant, he had command of his company during all that time. We exchanged visits while the battle was in progress.

After it was over, he and his company were doing picket duty. A troop of rebels dressed in Union Coats came up in the rear. They had come through a gulch, which was held by a Pennsylvania Dutch regiment. The pickets supposed they were the relief and only found their mistake when the rebels opened fire. Lieutenant Rogers was mortally wounded and taken with the other men prisoners to Richmond; he, being unable to ride, was left at a rebel field hospital the same day, June 7. Thus, much was learned from a wounded man in an Annapolis hospital and from the exchange of prisoners.

It was nine years before we knew anything more about him; then our father, Dr. Rogers, received a letter from a man whose son had been a surgeon in the Confederate Army. He said his son would write and send a pin that Edwin had given him. The son wrote the particulars of his death. He discovered this soldier among the wounded and knew at once that he had but a few hours to live. He also discovered by a pin he was wearing that they belonged to the same college fraternity.

He did everything he could to make him comfortable and finally buried him, placing at the head of his grave a board inscribed with his name, rank and regiment. He said he published the account in such newspapers as he thought would be most likely to reach Edwin's friends.

Mary Elizabeth Barker: In the casualty lists from the battlefields, there were frequently names known to us, either our own townsmen or others of neighboring towns. Our own loved ones were still untouched, though Uncle Steve wrote of very narrow escapes. There was continuous fighting. It was a time when each man searched his neighbor's soul to know if it harbored disloyalty. The people all voted the Republican ticket in our town, which meant that they backed the party and administration supporting the war.

In some of our neighboring towns, there were those who were with the South. It was well known that they not only talked treason, but also helped deserters, bounty jumpers and men who were liable to be drafted to get across the lines into Canada. These people were called Copperheads. At Lincoln's re-election, feeling was very tense in both parties.

A rumor was going about the town that one man, suspected of copperhead sympathies, who lived on a road used only by himself, was flying a rebel flag which his wife had made. The men appointed a committee to investigate the story, and they did. If he was flying a rebel flag, he did not have Barbara Fritchie's courage to keep it flying, for they found none.

This was the year Grandfather built the new barn. He hired two men to prepare the frame. How eagerly we children watched the process, as we did any unusual activity. They hewed the big timbers until they were squared to the proper dimensions for the foundations, uprights and great beams to hold the roof. Then they were mortised at the ends and the proper places to insert the crosspieces and braces. The usual arrangements were made for bays and doors according to the owner's plans. Lastly, the rafters and ridgepole were cut and piled in a heap ready to be quickly used without confusion, and wooden pins were made to fasten the frame together.

The day was set for the raising, and the men of the town invited to come in the morning and help. Meantime, Grandma, with my help, was preparing the dinner.

The men baked the beans, which was the important dish of the meal. They borrowed two iron pots from a lumber-camp cook that would hold enough to feed fifty men. The night before the raising, they dug holes in the ground somewhat larger than the kettles. In the holes, they built fires of hard wood, dropping in a half a dozen small rocks to heat.

When the wood was burned to coals, they shoveled them out along with the rocks and set the pots previously filled with parboiled beans and a sufficient quantity of fat salt pork, seasoning, a cup of molasses and water to fill each kettle. The covers were carefully put on, the bails lifted upright and the hot coals and rocks put back around and over them. The hole was then covered with earth. The men then left them to be shoveled out at noon next day, piping hot and done to perfection.

We had no granulated sugar, but a rather expensive variety called loaf, or crust sugar, a refined article in irregular lumps. It was used only when we had company. We bought brown sugar of a coarse quality, and molasses. Most people made maple sugar or syrup and used it for many things. So there were no elaborate frosted cakes. There were cookies, gingerbread and doughnuts; pies of custard, mince, pumpkin and squash. There were loaves of homegrown wheat and steaming plates of Indian cornbread, pickles and cucumbers from the garden, and there was tea. Some of the neighborhood women came to help, and on the whole it was quite a gala day. To all the children, it was as exciting as a circus.

I was a young pagan in my worship of all nature. It gave me a joy next to ecstasy to stand under the windows next to the garden on a sunny summer morning and look into the green maze of fruit trees, shrubs and flowers, where birds of many kinds builded their nests, gathered their food and sang the warm summer day. I loved the glint of sunshine through the leaves and on the rustling corn that always grew in the orchard, the flash of a scarlet tanager, or yellow birds dashing out of the asparagus. I loved the impudent robins and cedarbirds swinging on the topmost limbs, their bills and throats stained with the juice of cherries, raspberries or thimbleberries. I reveled in all this close, intimate contact with the natural world about me. I imagine I was somewhat lonely for fellowship with someone of my own age. Perhaps Grandma understood that; she was very kind and sympathetic.

Grandma was very superstitious. Charged with it, she would be very indignant; nevertheless, she had a large stock of signs, warnings and even ghostly appearances stored up in her memory. She was not slow to tell me if I inadvertently placed the backs of two chairs together that it was a sign we were about to have visitors; or, if the last Friday in the month was stormy, there never failed to be much foul weather the next month. If I dreamed of deep black water, I was in for trouble of some kind. Even Grandpa killed his hog and planted his beans on a given phase of the moon.

We did have a little ghost story on one beautiful moonlit night in early summer. I was in a room above the kitchen sitting by the open window. It was perfectly still, except for the low tones of those sitting in the dark kitchen below. Suddenly, there came a succession of sharp raps beginning in a low tone and increasing in volume and rapidity. It lasted for a half-minute and ceased. There was dead silence until a visiting cousin ran into the next room and picked up her sleeping baby.

Uncle Rodney called up the stairs, "Do you know what caused that noise?"

"No," I said. "I thought it was in the kitchen."

"You people all keep still. I'm going to find out what it was if I can."

He stole noiselessly out through the woodshed and the wagon house, stopping near the hog house. Three hogs were quietly sleeping, scattered about in their straw. While he stood there listening, it came again, sharp and distinct. He came back with a grin. It was just a hog who lay quite near the side of the bin. Everyone who has seen a hog scratch himself knows that he makes a succession of quick dives at his side with his hard little hoofs. In this case, with each move of this foot, he struck the side of the pen. We called it Grandma's Ghost.˜

The news from the front was discouraging. There was much fighting in Virginia, which kept everyone's nerves taut, but the rebels seemed to gain all the victories, and word was frequently coming of young men we knew who were killed or wounded.

"Magnificent Retreat," cried Grandma, quoting from newspaper headlines. "It makes me furious to see how the newspapers gloss over the failure of our armies to accomplish anything."

There was much criticism and grumbling "back home" on the way the war was being managed. Meantime on the farm, help was scarce and prices soared. The last of the young men enlisted, and the news came slowly.

We got only three mails each week, brought from Bangor to Patten by a stage. Our office was Sherman, ten miles away. Whoever went to the office brought the mail for those living on his road. It was understood that those living within four miles of us on the main road would bring our mail to his home.

That summer, I began horseback rides after the mail occasionally. Grandpa would stop work early, and I would saddle "Old Charley" and ride until I found it. Sometimes it was more than four miles, and I would be correspondingly late home, but Charley knew every foot of the way.

I was known in the neighborhood as being afraid of nothing, a reputation of which I was very proud. I had no adventure during the summer, but later I fell into difficulty. It was Thanksgiving time. The ground was frozen some, and the mud holes were covered with thin sheets of ice. There was one especially bad place in the woods at the foot of a long hill. Charley was a shrewd old beast. He reasoned that if he refused to break the ice and wade in the mud, I would not make him go. He was right, of course.

There was a log about twenty inches through that had been rolled to one side of the road when it was repaired. Behind it were several smaller logs; and on top, a heap of brush. I dismounted and walked the log, leading him alongside where there was no mud worth mentioning. When we had nearly reached solid ground, he plunged over the big log behind me. His two feet went down among the small logs, and he was fast. The brush held him up else both legs would have been broken. I held up his head and spoke to him. He struggled a little, then lay back on the brush as if he knew it was useless.

I dropped off my wraps and ran up the hill as fast as I could, fearing he would plunge and break his legs. My worry was needless. Apparently he never moved while I was gone.

Over the hill, down at its foot, there was a farmhouse and a shingle camp where the owner was working. With him was a man who lived farther along the road. They took axes and went back with me and had to chop through the big log twice before they could roll it off the horse. He stood up and shook himself, as good as ever. There was one peculiarity about Charley—I could handle him without fear when he was out of his stall, but when I had finished tying him to his halter ring, I had to get out immediately. He would never tolerate a woman within reach while in the stall. When he stood beside me on solid ground and I reached for the bridle, he laid back his ears, thrust out his head and snapped his teeth at me. When I commanded him to behave, he threw up his head and turned indifferently away, as if he said, "The matter is closed." Faithful old horse!

There was little social life in the town during this season. Depression like a black cloud hung over the whole country. Anxiety for the fate of those at the front and for the outcome of the war, also sorrow for those taken by sickness at home, were like a weight inescapable. The three years for which the first men enlisted was expired. Many, most of them, re-enlisted, but a few, for various reasons, came home. Among those who returned were my Uncle Rodney and his friend Luther Rogers, whose brother had been killed. Both returned because of the entreaties of their parents.

Uncle Rodney made the acquaintance of young people in Patten where there were already some returned soldiers who were welcomed to the social life of the village. People did much visiting and we came to know many who lived in other towns and who some-times rode long distances to spend the day.

I remember we had several parties of young folks from Patten who came for overnight. I was not much in evidence at such times. I was well developed for my age, but to these young people I was a child, my Grandmother's helper.

Early in the summer, she had a fall and badly sprained her wrist, which she carried in a sling for several weeks. For a while the cooking and general housework became my task under her direction. It was a good experience for me, though hard. When school opened, a girl was hired for the summer.

Uncle Rodney announced to the young people of the Ridge that he would give them a straw ride to their socials. They accepted, of course, and we were a merry party packed into the two-horse farm wagon, or later the sled, spinning over the road to the accompaniment of songs or bells, singing—mostly war songs. The houses were always filled with people happy to have an evening together. In all the town, there were only two musical instruments: a violin, which George Darling played principally for kitchen dances, and a piano, which the Pratt's—quite newcomers—brought with them. I dated my connection with a dozen boys and girls of my own age who lived at the Falls from these events. Most of our social plans included each other until we were finally scattered.

The armies, comparatively quiet in winter quarters, were now fighting with great intensity. Battle followed battle, and both Uncle Silas and Uncle Steve were in the thickest of the struggle. Grandma's face grew worn and lined with dread and anxiety. As for me, it seemed as if there had always been a war, and it would never cease.

People scanned the lists of wounded, missing and dead, and waited in suspense for more certain news.

Uncle Rodney often saddled the horse and rode to the village on mail night. There came a night when he did not return, but sent a neighbor who happened to be in town to tell us that he had a letter from Steve, who was wounded, and he was going to him.

"Didn't he give you the letter?" asked Grandma.

"No," was the reply.

That appeared to be all the man knew about the matter. Later we knew that he had been instructed not to tell any more. The letter had marks of blood on it; it was only a pencil scrawl. It was written on the battlefield where he fell, and where he lay for three days before he could be moved to a hospital.

The case was pronounced hopeless, and both nurses and surgeons were so driven there was little prospect of any attention being paid to hopeless cases. It was not until Uncle Rodney got there that anything was done for him outside of temporary relief.

In spite of the surgeon's decision, under Rod's watchful care, he slowly recovered until two months later he could sit in a wheel chair; then Rod left him to the care of the doctors and nurses and came home. Not for very long, however. A crutch slipped and a bad fall sent him back to bed again, and a large part of the work of recovery had to be done over again. Rod went back to him, returning in midwinter.

In March, we had a visit from my beloved teacher *[Mary Matilda Hersey]* and her newly acquired husband *[Luther Bailey Rogers.]* He was the son of Dr. Rogers and an officer in the same company as Uncle Rodney. He had only lately returned from the war. His brother had been wounded, and died a prisoner.

He was tall, with a very military bearing and rather a stern face. I was afraid of him and kept out of his way. However, the men went off for a deer, and we three womenfolk had a pleasant time visiting together. When they left us, I decided that, when I married, I would have a husband very like the man Matilda had married.

In April, the assassination of Lincoln shocked the country. I felt a heavy sense of calamity and loss aside from the horror of the deed, which entirely swallowed up the exhilaration of victory and relief at the close of the war.

In June, Uncle Rodney went away to the western part of the state and married [Mary Gove]. He drove the horses and the big farm wagon, and they came riding home in it one sunny afternoon. The bride looked very sweet and happy in spite of the rough equipage piled high with her trunks and boxes.

Gradually, Grandma resigned her duties as head of the house, and the relief from care and hard work came none too soon.

Uncle Steve gained slowly and in August, after eighteen months in the hospital, he began the journey home—a cripple, but living. He traveled as far as his Uncle's near Monmouth and Lewiston, when his wounds broke out afresh. Grandfather and Grandmother went to him. He died in a short time.

The following two years were filled with schoolwork for me; at home, when our own school was in session, and in other towns where I worked for my board. I did good work and took some studies out of hours not in the common school curriculum. I also did a great deal of reading in my spare time. During the last two years of the war, there was in circulation in the army a paper-covered book called the dime novel. There were very cheap, sensational stories of adventure. Knowing my propensity for reading, they sent home many of these books. Grandma looked very grave and gave me much good advice, but I read them all, and with that I tired of them. They were not what I wanted. They were not satisfying.

The citizens of our town established the beginnings of a town library. It was a small, though-well-selected collection, and contained some books of poetry. After such an orgy of sensational literature, I thought it time to improve my mind, so I brought home *Paradise Lost* and read it all aloud to the teacher, who was boarding at our house. Quite stiff reading for a beginning, and it was my private opinion that it was dry. But certainly I was cured of reading trash. The contrast was too great. I became familiar with Burns, Tennyson and Longfellow, and could recite whole pages of the *Lady of the Lake*. It paved the way to a keen appreciation of Scott's prose works.

We had another Fourth of July celebration, which I remember very well because I had a part in what was supposed to be an important feature of the coming program. Some new neighbors, who were college graduates and professional teachers, were the Committee of Arrangements for this program. One of the numbers was a pantomime illustrating two songs popular at the time. Mr. L. asked me to take the part of little Mary, singing the first song in the barroom scene. He sang the second song, which was addressed to little Mary in the living room of their home. Mrs. L. had the mother's part, two or more verses composed and set to music by Mr. L. I was much excited, and not a little anxious, since it was my first attempt at theatricals.

The entertainment was staged in a new building destined for a barn. It was quite roomy and clean. A rough stage was builded and seats arranged. A small gallery was also made to accommodate a portion of the audience. I peeped through the stage curtains at the people coming in to their seats.

In the gallery was quite a party from Patten, among them several ex-soldiers, comrades of Uncle Rodney, with their newly wedded wives. Lieutenant Rogers was there, but Matilda, his wife and my teacher, had died several months before, leaving a babe *[Matilda Hersey Rogers]* which was being cared for by her grandmother. I thought the Lieutenant looked very personable in his black civilian suit.

For two years, Grandpa had been slowly failing in health. One morning he quietly and silently passed into the unknown. After that, Grandma spent much of her time with her daughter, Mary Ellen, who had moved to a farm near Patten village.

I began to think of earning some money for myself. Therefore, one summer day found me in a small room in a log dwelling house, the mistress of a dozen scholars. Though barely large enough to seat the children, it was light and sunny and overlooked the beautiful Mattawamkeag Lake. We all did our best together and wound up the term with a little entertainment to which all the people came.

The lake, which fills the valley between the hills and stretches away fifteen or more miles, has for many years been the favorite spot for campers.

One sultry night at the close of the afternoon session I had a thrilling encounter on it which illustrates the spirit of adventure, the daring and utter lack of caution, which characterized me.

Near the shore where I was teaching grew many water lilies, and I conceived the idea of going after some of them. I took a rough road across a field through a narrow belt of woods and a much overgrown path leading along a point of land stretching into the lake. The distance was a mile, probably.

The water formed a cove behind the point of land, and on a beach there was a boat which anyone was welcome to use provided it was returned. I had to paddle down the lake some distance to avoid sunken rocks at the point, but when I had paddled back to the beds of lilies I forgot all else as I gathered the fragrant white cups.

When I had a fine bunch, I became engrossed with ascertaining how near I could float the boat toward that exceedingly wary creature, a loon, who was eyeing me with more curiosity than fear. I was suddenly aware that a great black cloud was boiling swiftly over the top of the mountain. The drops of rain were already falling. A flash of lightning and a crash of thunder warned me that speed was necessary and I bent to the paddle with all my might.

Luckily the storm was at my back, for the wind was heavy, a gale, with the rain soon coming down in torrents. It was such a downpour, it flattened what would otherwise have been dangerous waves. I was soon past the point and still driven on by the wind.

The problem now was to turn the boat and head into the wind without shipping water enough to sink it or being blown onto the rocks of the shore. I did ship a quantity of water, and I did get near enough to the shore to give me a few black moments, but at last I was headed toward the beach and in comparatively calm waters. I was certainly a thankful child when I stood on solid ground and pulled the boat after me.

It was now dark. The thunder and lightning were still as bad as ever, but the rain was not as heavy. I found the path. The difficulty was to keep it, so thick were the bushes, which reached above my head. I had frequently to get down on my knees and search for it with my hands.

At last, I reached the old lumber road which, though very rough and muddy, I could not lose. The flashes lit up the woods often and aided me.

Finally, I was out in the field and could see the lights of the house. I was so weary I could hardly climb the hill, and so wet the water dripped even from my hair. I found the men with lanterns lighted preparing to go in search of me, and it was nearly midnight. I passed around the lilies which—would you believe me—I had clung to all the way from the boat!

I told the people I had had a difficult time getting along the path, but I told only one or two of my chums that I was on the lake in the storm. The fact was I knew I should not go on the water alone, and I was ashamed I had got into such a dangerous situation. My sleep that night was broken with dreams of falling limbs and swirling water.

My Grandmother was making a long visit among old friends and relatives and was taking me with her for a year at school. Accordingly, I became a student at the Lewiston High School. I threw myself mind and soul into the schoolwork and was a rather silent spectator of the school activities. I made warm friends in my own class, and wanted to remain in the school and graduate. It was a matter of finances. I could have had the money for a time anyway, but I did not choose to accept the conditions. I came back to Patten, finished the year at the Academy, and taught a school in the town during the summer.

When the first snows of winter began to fall in December of 1869, Lieutenant Rogers and I were married. About the first person to welcome me to the town was Squire Fish. It was by that title he was always indicated. He introduced himself and assured me that, since his son *[Charles Fish]* had married my husband's sister *[Sarah Rogers]*, he looked upon me as his daughter. He was, so to speak, the founder of the town, having migrated to the place as early as 1830, when it was a wilderness. He was accompanied by Eli Kellogg; both were young, vigorous men.

They came from Mattawamkeag Point in bateaux, up the Mattawamkeag River, bringing their supplies with them. Their object at that time was to cruise for timber, which they found and later cut, following the lumbering business for many years. Meantime, they made for themselves good homes and fine farms.

Squire Fish grew one of the very fine large orchards to be found in that new country. He was a hale old man, still something of an autocrat from long habit of commanding men. His wife, Sarah, a meek, quiet little woman, ventured to oppose him one day. He lost his patience and shouted, "You know mighty well I don't like to be contradicted."

One thing impressed me, and that was the intense individuality of the people, particularly the men. They differed from one another as only men can who have been largely untrammeled by customs and conventions. They were forceful and intelligent, and they were readers; considering their isolation from any large centers, they kept themselves well abreast of the times. They had ideals and visions concerning their surroundings. I was keenly interested in studying them and what they had already accomplished for their new frontier town.

There was one of the early settlers living in the village tilling a large farm and raising a large family. He was known far and wide as Deacon Wiggin. How he came by the title, I never knew—certainly not from any church.

They told this anecdote about him: There came a man to town whose business was distributing tracts. He inquired for some religious person. A wag—it sounds very like one of the Kellogg pranks—told him Deacon Wiggin lived on the corner. He knocked at the Deacon's door and began at once to talk about his tracts. Mr. Wiggin immediately sensed the joke, and for a space the air was blue. He told him to make tracks himself, and be sure they pointed away from his doorstep. In another instance, the old people told a tale of the bloodless boundary war when the Government stationed troops on the extreme northern point of the state for the purpose of repelling invaders. A body of soldiers marching through the town of Patten camped at night in the Wiggin's field. The commander ordered a pair of the Deacon's oxen killed to feed the men. The people were curious to know what the Deacon would say about it. What he said is not on record, but one fact is vouched for. The commander paid for the oxen, full value, before he left town.

There were three churches in the village. For years the three congregations worshipped in the Baptist church, taking turns holding services, but finally the Congregationalists builded for themselves, and a little later, the Methodists did the same.

In the two latter churches, there were two outstanding characters, each being a pillar in his own congregation. They were Elbridge Stetson in the Methodist and Dr. Rogers in the Congregationalist. Both were men of God who left a lasting impression on the community, and both were as set in their creed and interpretation of the scriptures as the eternal hills. Both had made a life study of the Bible, and both dearly loved an argument. So it was no unusual thing for them to meet at Miles' Shop where half the boots and shoes worn by the people were made, and argue points of their creed about which they differed. There was one thing to be said for them—they could dispute for an hour or two, then part in perfectly good humor, each chuckling to himself over the way he had beaten his opponent.

It will have to be admitted there was not much Christian fellowship between the churches. In fact, to me, who knew nothing about rivalry between congregations, they seemed like three hostile camps, tirelessly watching for opportunities to criticize and condemn each other. I found that one must be very discreet and circumspect indeed not to give cause for offense.

I was told the story of an encounter between William T. Sleeper, the pastor of the Congregational Church, and Samuel Darling, a pillar of the Baptist Church. The parson insisted that his people should have congregational singing only when they worshipped. Mr. Darling had a choir trained, and he insisted that they should do the singing at all services in the Baptist Church. Both parties were naturally aggressive, and there had been friction for some time.

One Sunday morning, the Reverend Sleeper gave out the hymns, and as he was something of a musician himself, he pitched the tune and began to sing. Mr. Darling, from his seat in the singer's gallery, sprang up and began a loud and vigorous protest.

How it would have ended, nobody knows; for just at that moment, the funnel from the stove that heated the church—and which extended the length of the room—fell with a crash, filling the place with smoke and ashes. Needless to say, there was neither congregational nor choir singing that day.

There were only two pianos in the town. The old-fashioned melodeon was used in the church. There was very little opportunity to study music. Therefore, Mr. Darling was a benefactor of a sort; each autumn he taught a singing school which all who could sing or wanted to sing attended. These schools always closed with a grand concert, which generally drew a full house.

He also interested himself in arranging so called conventions, really musical institutes, held each year in the town, obtaining some director of music in Bangor or Portland to conduct them. All this was indirectly much help in the social activities of the village and served to give the young people the rudiments of a musical education.

The largest store in town was operated by Gardner and Coburn. They carried general merchandise and supplied many tons of goods to lumbermen. They also supplied the farmers, taking their produce, shingles, wood or anything else that was marketable.

The firm was early established under the name of Gardner and Stetson when both were young men. The post office was in their store, and they also sold all kinds of liquors to anybody wanting it; and at that, most of the farmers wanted it.

The store had the traditional floor space in the center with its box, stove and chairs for the loafers. It always had its good-sized group in the evening telling stories, gossiping and discussing problems. It was their daily paper and the only one they had.

After a while, it began to be whispered around that there were hilarious times there and that some farmers did not reach home till the wee morning hours.

Then, suddenly, the loafers found themselves high and dry. The firm took the initiative. They maintained that in selling liquor they were being a damage to the community, and they did not desire that. So no more drinks of any kind could be obtained there.

About that time, the temperance movement, which finally resulted in the Prohibition Law of Maine, swept over the state. A chapter of Sons of Temperance was organized in Patten, to which the men of the town largely belonged. They built themselves a two-story hall, afterwards known as Masonic Hall, and since that time the prohibition question has been more or less an issue, sometimes very lively.

The family into which I married came from Newbury, Massachusetts, and they brought with them all the habits and traditions of their Pilgrim Fathers. They were a part of the first settlers, Dr. Rogers being fresh from the medical school, and they were among the civic and social leaders.

The Doctor's practice covered a radius of thirty miles, and he was sometimes called to go even farther. In winter, he made his rounds among his patients in a sleigh drawn by one horse. In summer, he always rode in a high, two-wheeled gig. The seat, just large enough for one person, was perched above the small square platform and attached to it by a stout iron rod at each corner. Under the seat he carried a small, hair-covered leather trunk containing his instruments and bottles of medicine.

His horse, "Old Abe," was as unique as the gig. He was not large or speedy but possessed remarkable staying qualities. He struck a busy jog when he left the stable and patiently kept it up to the end of the rounds. He had a bobtail with which he viciously switched flies, and one or both ears generally lopped. His whole appearance as they bobbed along the country roads was one of apparent indifference to life in general and any possible happening.

But Old Abe was not without his shrewd tricks and devices to soften the dull monotony of his existence. He could untie his halter and steal from the grain box or bag. He was very likely to be found on a summer morning somewhere in the outskirts of the village helping himself to a choice bit of clover.

He would never stand to be harnessed unless tied. It frequently happened that in some midnight call of great emergency, the messenger would offer to harness the Doctor's horse while he made preparations to go. Such messenger, while reaching for the bridal or breast-plate hanging on its peg, would turn to see the last of Abe disappearing through the door.

He did not go far, and came back docilely enough when a hand was laid on his mane. This might happen two or three times if the man, in his hurry and anxiety, neglected to make the old rascal secure. He was never malicious, but patient and faithful, and when the old Doctor had to abandon his gig, Old Abe went on a long, well-earned rest.

The Doctor was a sympathetic friend to all the people he attended and was much beloved. The Rogers family was very devoted to the church and keenly interested in the schools and the town affairs. Both the Doctor and his wife *[Hanna Bailey]* were well educated and had always been great readers. To me they seemed superior people. There was evidence of an unusual degree of both social and intellectual culture. There was also a reasonable self-control and restraint that attracted me. I did not learn until later how much they were bound by tradition and convention, results of early training.

My own life had been very free with no undue restraint or conventions. I had been taught what was proper, kindly and right, but I certainly was not run in a mold. I pondered these things and settled in my mind that I would acquire self-control. I would cultivate all the social graces a lady should have, and I would let nothing prevent the development of what mental ability I possessed. I immediately began to study; and though it was often interrupted—sometimes given up for a time—during the years that followed, I kept some study at hand. I formed the habit of gathering bits of information about things that interested me from every source at my command.

In the town was a remnant of a small but well-selected library. Evidently, whatever books of fiction had been in it were worn out. There was little left except Sir Walter Scott's novels, and the print was so fine it was a crime to read them. But how I enjoyed them! They were as entertaining, nearly, as the novels. I did have a job, however, when I tackled *The History of the Reformation* by a French author whose name I have forgotten. It required determination to wade through six volumes. After that, I remember three or four volumes of Charles Kingsley's stories, which livened up matters. We were by that time getting a greater variety in magazines, which were welcome indeed.

The arrival of the mail only three times each week was bound to become an important event. People from the outer neighborhoods, even from the surrounding towns, lingered about the village on Tuesday, Thursday and Saturday afternoons waiting for the stage which was due at six o'clock but was often later. The times of arrival depended largely on the condition of the roads.

The mail came from Bangor by stage, but when the Civil War began, a railroad known by the sonorous name of European and North American Railway made its beginning at Bangor and crept slowly toward the border. It followed, in a general way, the main highway up the Penobscot River until it reached Mattawamkeag, when it turned east. It did not finally reach its destination until near the close of the war. Our stage line going out on Monday made three round trips each week to Mattawamkeag, forty miles away.

Through all the long, dreadful years of the war, we had only three mails each week, and four towns were served by the Patten office. If one had to travel on the alternate days, or if a telegram must be sent, a private team and a ride to Mattawamkeag was the only procedure.

The roads could be called atrocious. There were long stretches of woods on the main highway, owned by proprietors who paid a small tax. The state could be depended on to furnish some money for so important a road. But altogether the sum was very inadequate for the purpose; consequently, there was little capital with which to improve conditions.

The vehicles were ordinary team sleds, boxed in with seats and plenty of blankets in winter. In summer, they were heavy wagons with stiff springs. Sometimes, not often, they were covered. Paul Peavey, the contractor and driver, was sometimes blamed for the lack of comfort and the slowness and irregularity of the mails. I have often wondered as I have reflected on the long, lonely ride through a country largely uninhabited, over drifted roads where he frequently had to break his own way, was pelted by driving snowstorms and half frozen by the cold of winter or bounced from mud hole to rock across ruts in the rainy springs and autumns, whether he did not after all serve the public as well as the times would permit. He was once heard to say, "I don't amount to much, but the family I came from does."

Nobody seemed to know anything about his antecedents, but a queer little incident happened to me: I was visiting in a small city in the central part of the state. While walking along the street, we met a man who, except that he was better groomed and dressed, more alert in his manner and movements, was the double of Paul Peavey! "How much he looks like Paul Peavey," I exclaimed to my friend. "Doesn't he?"

She answered. "And his name is Paul Peavey!"

"What?" I asked in amazement.

She further related to me that he was the manager of a large clothing store and did a thriving business. Afterwards, I discovered that the store in question was one of a chain with headquarters in Boston, and the senior member of the firm was also called Peavey.

The problem of the transportation of all articles needed by the people was still more serious. The railroad had reached Mattawamkeag. From there, everything sold in the stores; all machinery of any description used by the farmers, and all supplies for the lumber camps not produced in the vicinity had to be hauled on large, heavy wagons, or in winter on long sleds. Four horses were required to haul each load.

When one considers that in winter the snow averaged three feet on the level by the last of February, and in summer rain storms are frequent and mud is consequently a factor always to be reckoned with, it can be readily understood that hardships of many kinds fell to the lot of both men and horses. It took four days for the round trip. The teams went from Patten loaded with hand-made shingles (the only form of lumber hauled) or hay, or some-times meat, or butter and eggs. All the teams went together in order to help each other out of mud holes or drifts, to get each other back on the track when the loaded sleds slued off into the ditch, to assist each other in loading, and last but not least, for company, because many miles of the way lay through forests.

When the snow was deep and the track narrow, this man with one or two horses had to watch out for a "turnout" when he was likely to meet the long line of toters. Sometimes two or three teams would meet them where there was no trodden place to turn out. Then every-body had to stop and wait while some of the men shoveled or trod down a place long enough for the lesser number to get out of the road and let the toters go by. We always got a thrill watching the string of teams come down the Finch Hill south of the town and up the steep Mill Hill into the village. There was often trouble on the latter.

The town was a point of departure for an immense lumber business. Lumber camps were scattered through the forests for fifty miles back of the settlements. Many hundreds of men, also horses and oxen, were employed in these camps, building, making roads and cutting the timber. All the needed supplies not produced in the vicinity had to be hauled to Patten and reshipped to the camps. In the spring and autumn, when the crews were going into the camps or coming out from them, the village was a lively place. The old hotel, a wide, roomy two-story structure, was frequently filled to overflowing, and the large yard was crowded with wagons or sleds. The women of the village were careful to keep within doors after nightfall at such times.

Conditions were worst in the spring. The teams began to appear early in March; a dozen or more double teams, the sleds loaded with camp paraphernalia, and men followed by a long line of loose horses too worn and weary to do anything but plod along to their next stopping place.

The men wore the clothes they had worked in all winter. Most of them were ragged, dirty and unbarbered. Very many of them were crazy with liquor and went whooping and shouting through the street. For the most part, they only stayed overnight. They were from the lumber city, and back to the city they went to spend their wages.

There was another class of men who worked for smaller concerns and lived in this or surrounding towns. Not all of these were sober, but the majority were. These immediately disappeared on getting back to town, scattering to their several homes to reappear, perhaps next day, shaved and dressed in their best, to loaf around the town for a few days of rest before beginning the spring's work.

During the early summer, Mr. Rogers and I went to visit his sister. It was my first experience going on a steamer. We went down the Penobscot River and along the coast, across Frenchman's Bay (Bar Harbor) to East Machias where our friends met us. We spent a very pleasant week in that quaint old town, then we went by stage to Lubec, crossed by ferry to Eastport, and took the Boston boat to St. John. We stayed two days, then took a boat up the St. Johns River. The picturesque scenery of the Penobscot, the coast and the St. John's River, remain beautiful pictures in my memory.

One bright summer day, as I walked along a country road absorbed with my thoughts and only dimly conscious that something was approaching behind me, I heard this question: "Won't you ride, ma'am?"

As I turned, my face must have radiated astonishment, but the man who stood there beside his bony, nondescript horse did not seem to notice. He was a thin, rather small middle-aged individual, dressed in the working clothes farmers usually wore. Sandy whiskers wreathed his innocent, yet kindly face and his head was covered with a battered straw hat. In his hand he held reins made of rope, and I noticed the harness was held together in places with leather or twine strings.

But the vehicle on which he was inviting me to ride was the most unusual. It looked like the toys my young brother makes. The wheels were sections sawed from a log, about eighteen inches in diameter, with holes in the center for the poles that served as axles to go through. The wheels were held in place by wooden pins. On these axles a platform was laid, some blocks fastened to it, and on the blocks boards were nailed to serve as a seat.

"Yes, sir, I will," I promptly replied as I sat down on the board.

"I am just trying out my wagon," he remarked.

"Did you make it?" I asked.

"Yes, I did; and a good job too. It took me all last week. It ain't very springy, but it's good and solid."

He talked fluently about inconsequential matters, during which I gained the impression that his mind was much like his wagon, roughly made and loosely put together. I didn't have to ride into town with him as his way parted from mine before we arrived there. I related this incident at the evening meal.

"Oh, that was Silas Coburn," they said. "He is always appearing out in some strange looking rig."

"What's the matter with him?" I asked.

"I don't know. He belongs to a good family. He is not crazy and not simple. Just queer."

I heard of Silas Coburn and the Cow Team Road, so called because he had the habit of yoking his cows and working them like oxen, and because he lived on that road, the building of which he was enthusiastically promoting. As yet, nothing had been done on it beyond his own small farm. The remainder of the way, ending in a part of the town of Sherman, was still a wilderness. Coming from such an irresponsible source, his arguments were treated rather as a jest, and little attention was paid to them. This did not phase him in the least, or dampen his enthusiasm. He paid no heed to their joshing but talked about it on all occasions to anybody who would listen, and he finally won out. When they began to seriously consider the question thus forced on their notice, it appeared there were excellent arguments to recommend it, and it was finally built. When the Bangor and Aroostook Railroad was built, a station was placed there and a little hamlet gathered about it. Some time later I saw him in the village, bound on a project which had neither rhyme nor reason to recommend it.

"What kind of a rig is that, Silas?" was the question put to him.

"Well, I'm planning to haul goods between Patten and Ashland this winter, so I built a little house on the wagon so I could be comfortable and save expense."

The house, or box, contained a stove and bed. Where the goods were to be stored did not appear. I never saw or heard of it again.

There were two people living in the town of whom I was conscious of a feeling of awe. They were Mr. and Mrs. Benjamin. The lady was, to be sure, very gracious to me, showing plainly that she approved of me. But she was so stately and carried herself with so much dignity. She was also an artist of much ability, and I, in my inexperience, believed that people who could make pictures were in a class by themselves.

Her husband, known always as Squire Benjamin (more affectionately, as I always thought, known to the men as Squire Ben) was a lawyer, the only one in town.

His office was in the upper story of a little old black building in the center of town. Mr. Miles used the first floor as a shoe shop. The law office was a dingy place with only necessary furniture and the bookcases. There he transacted all business pertaining to the law which the community required, and possibly might have had more if he had not persuaded so many of his clients to settle their cases out of court. He undoubtedly had plenty of ability and knowledge and was much trusted and respected. He made a comfortable living and had leisure to read and study. That gave him more satisfaction than fighting his way in the state to a prominent position, and greater competency too. He seldom attended any social function but was very companionable with the men.

Their attendance at church, which was very regular, was like a processional and always interested me. They came down the street arm and arm, he in his Sunday suit and bell-crowned hat. She was always well dressed.

They marched down the aisle to the front pew. She dropped his arm and went in to the far end, and he took his seat at the outer end, carefully laying his hat on the floor at his feet. He always listened attentively to the sermon, be it good, bad or indifferent. There was nothing affected by this procedure. It was simply a formality necessary to Sabbath worship. When he was overtaken by ill health and was obliged to sell his business and leave the town, the community sustained a deep sense of loss.

Across the street from the Doctor's was a little shop kept by Minerva True. She was first of all a milliner, but in addition to furnishing hats and bonnets for most of the females living between Ashland and Mattawamkeag, she kept a great variety of such small articles as women are constantly in need of.

She was known far and wide as Minerva, with a long "a." She had a commanding figure, always well and appropriately dressed, and was of a strong character. She was well educated for the times, read extensively, and inclined to be speculative, mystic and notional.

It was, however, as a businesswoman that she excelled. She had made money in her business, which she loaned to the farmers at a good rate of interest, and she seldom lost on her investments.

No one made any headway trying to circumvent her. She could be very sharp on occasion. I was present when Peter G. Noyes, the stage driver between Patten and Fort Kent, handed her a bandbox containing a bonnet which he had carried on his outward-bound trip saying that the woman was returning it because it didn't suit her. Minerva straightened up and glared at him. "You tell her to go straight to the grass!" She said.

"Yes, yes, I will, I will," said Peter, and without doubt he did.

She had a standing grievance, which she argued without fear to those most concerned, namely, the men. She strongly objected to taxation without representation, and she demanded the right to say how the funds raised by taxing her property should be spent. Of course the men laughed at her, as they did at all revolts of women in those days. She, however, demonstrated the state of her mind by going into the street with a hoe and rake and working out her road tax with the men. Though sharp to condemn faults and dishonesties, she was kind and sympathetic to those in trouble.

I was now quite comfortably settled in a small apartment over Mr. Rogers' store. I was interested in the Sabbath School, Church and many of the social activities of the village. I am sure that though little was said, the young people regretted the unfriendly feeling between the churches, and there was a tacit understanding that they would do all in their power to promote a more cordial and tolerant spirit.

Certainly, as the years passed, the former spitefulness and jealousy almost entirely disappeared. It was here that our first child was born. We named him for his uncle who was killed in the war, Edwin Searls Rogers. A year later, my Grandmother died, and my brother Addison came to live with us for two or three years.

Mr. Rogers and I began to think seriously of giving up his store and moving onto a farm. He disliked the work in the store and felt he was not fitted for such an occupation. His father had bought the business and persuaded him to take it off his hands. His object was really to keep him in the town, for he had a strong desire to go West. He had always been accustomed to active exercise in the open air, and the confinement was irksome and injurious to his health. I was also pining for the fields and woods.

The Doctor owned a farm well situated about a mile from the village. Previous to the war, he had tilled it himself by the aid of his two boys and a hired man or two. It was badly exhausted, still rough and rocky, burdened with too many stone walls and ricks of bushes. Its redeeming features were its beautiful location, a fairly good barn set in the wrong place, and good soil if well tilled.

The house, if it could be called that, was two covered frames joined together. They were formerly used as two houses. One was fifteen by eighteen feet and had windows and a rough floor. The other was fifteen by twenty-two. There was a partition between the two houses.

This domicile sat back several rods from the road and the only landscape decoration was a gnarled and worthless apple tree on the east end. Perhaps I ought to include the barn with its attendant yard, which stood between the house and the main road.

We must have had a vast craving for the wide spaces to exchange a comfortable home for one like that. I think I had also the pioneer spirit of my forbears, who despised hardship and saw only the possibilities of the future.

Anyway, we decided to go out there and do the haying the summer the boy was two years old. I asked the privilege of doing the cooking for the crews. A man was hired to clerk in the store, and we took such kitchen outfit as we needed. When we came back after the haying was done, Luther went to his father with a proposition to live on the farm and work it. The old Doctor was in a panic. He came to me with tears in his eyes to beg me to persuade Luther to drop the idea.

"He never will make a farmer in the world," he declared. "He is too extravagant. He wants to spend too much money. He will run through with everything and then he will be off somewhere."

"I think not," I said. "He has decided not to leave you as long as you live. But he has got to be outdoors. The sooner he goes, the better. He can't stay in the store. He thinks he can get a living farming."

He went away still unconvinced, but the move was made. The home was plastered and put into comfortable shape inside, and we lived there while it was being done. I made it as homelike and cheery as possible. Luther turned his attention to preparing for the spring planting. We were sometimes lonesome but always happy there.

The second year, the next boy, Lore *[Lore A. Rogers]* was born. My mother was with me during that winter. Mr. Rogers had become interested in a small way in the lumber business and was absent from home more than at any time previously.

The following summer we built, over the house, making an extension to the ground floor and good comfortable beds above.

I couldn't resist the desire to grow a flower garden and found the time to set a small collection of shrubs and plants. I began also to transplant some of the wild young saplings; but of all I transplanted first and last, only one lived to grow into a real shade tree.

The farm was beginning to show improvements in more fertility, smoother fields and the gradual disappearance of unsightly ricks and piles of rocks.

With the coming of spring, a sad event cast a shadow in our home. Mother Rogers, after a short, severe illness, died. Sarah, the youngest daughter, stayed at home to care for her father, but it was a sad blow to the good old Doctor; after a few months, he gave up his practice entirely and soon took to his bed. The following year, he too passed away.

The home in the village was soon broken up, and none of my husband's family remained in the town. It was during that anxious summer that our first girl, Mary, was born. Edwin was six years old and Lore three. It was necessary to keep a hired girl during the busy months of the year.

After Dr. Rogers' death, many of the church duties fell upon my husband. He was superintendent of the Sunday school and was later made a deacon. The other two deacons at that time were Mr. Miles and Mr. Scribner, but after several years, Mr. Rowe and Mr. Merrill were added. Mr. Scribner died and his son, Caleb, assumed many of his father's duties. Mr. Rogers and I both taught in the Sunday school, and I was a member of the Ladies' Circle, which worked in various ways for the benefit of the church. We always attended the services, as did our children. Three of them were members of the church. No work in which we engaged together, outside of our own household, was as close to us as the work of the church.

Rogers Farm   Patten, Maine

The Grand Army Post was formed by the Veterans of the Civil War. There were at that time about forty men in the town who had served in the war. Very soon, a Woman's Relief Corps was also formed. Mr. Rogers and I attended the meetings quite regularly, and we sometimes exchanged visits with the Posts and Corps of other towns near us.

There was also a reunion on one day of each year of the company to which Mr. Rogers belonged. This was held in Sherman where many of the company still lived. The meeting was largely for the social intercourse it afforded, the keeping in touch. We seldom failed to attend. Once each year his regiment held a week's reunion in Portland Harbor, in a large cottage, which their former Colonel gave them. Mr. Rogers was a trustee of the building and was present whenever possible. I sometimes went with him when I could leave home.

There was another movement that grew out of the G.A.R. membership, and that was the organization of all the posts of Northern Penobscot and Aroostook companies into a regiment. It began at the town of Sherman where they were all invited to the encampment. The organization was perfected there, and the gathering the following year was at Fort Fairfield in 1884.

There was only one way to go, and that was by team. Edwin and Lore were twelve and nine, and we took them with us. We hitched a span to the Concord two-seated wagon, loaded it with bedding, tent and a box of cooked food and a very few cooking utensils such as tin plates, dippers, etceteras.

We were a little cramped for room but nothing to talk about. The delegation from the towns near us were large. All day, as we rode, teams were being added. At Houlton, a long line joined, and seventy-five went into camp at Littleton. People stared and wanted to know what it was all about.

The next night, we were found in a regular military camp at Fort Fairfield. A headquarters tent faced the end of the streets. The other tents were arranged in streets, each Post by itself. It was some camp; it looked very picturesque with the little fires in front of each tent, the busy groups cooking coffee and other savory dishes. Straw for beds and wood and water were provided by the entertaining post, and milk, bread, and even meat were sold by grocery men on the grounds.

During the evening, there were groups of veterans everywhere relating to each other over their war experiences and discussing the battles in which they fought the Johnnies. At those encampments there was always a band or two, sometimes a drum corps; and music contributed to the festivities. At last, taps were sounded, and the camp became quiet. Reveille called us out at seven a.m., but many were up with fires going before that time.

There were military exercises, guard mounting, some drilling and a day parade. Sometimes, a mock battle was staged in the surrounding fields, and there were addresses on one day out of three. But the dominant feature of the whole thing was the joyous reunion and companionship of the veterans themselves. Of course, as the years went by, their numbers became less and less, and finally the movement had to be abandoned, as did the Posts and Corps.

In our town, as probably in many others, there was one very good result of the organization and that was the establishment of Memorial Day. It became an annual event, which everybody observed. The long procession of school children with their waving flags led by the band and officials, followed by an equally long line of cars and many people in the streets and cemetery, made a thrilling picture. After the exercises and decoration in the cemetery came the address at the town hall by someone of note.

Nor was this all. The day before became one of decoration, not only of the veterans' graves, but of all our dead. Not only individuals, but the town began to take pride in the care of the cemetery. It bloomed like a garden on Decoration Day. Mr. Rogers and I took a great interest and pride in these memorial observances, and when at last he became the only active veteran in town, he rejoiced that the American Legion would assume the work he was obliged to pass along to them.

The condition of the schools of the town was a matter in which we were both deeply interested, and it was one we frequently discussed. The Academy had been founded very early in the history of the town, and it had done good work. It was expedient not only that it should keep on doing good work but that it should grow more efficient and that the rural schools should also be made better. The district system was in vogue, and a vicious system it was. The town was divided into districts. Each district built its own schoolhouse, elected its school agent who hired the teacher of his choice, often one not suitable. The district received for the maintenance of its school a certain amount for each scholar. It was generally inadequate for two terms, and two or more extra weeks were added by each family giving its share towards the extra expense. The election of the agent was often the occasion of hard feeling in the neighborhood. He frequently had an axe to grind. Often some friend wanted the school. The pay was very poor, and only poorly equipped teachers would take a rural school.

The state passed a law abolishing the school districts. All school property should be owned and kept in repair by the town, the teachers to be hired by the school committee and paid from the town treasury. The schoolbooks were to be furnished and owned by the town. Immediately, a storm of protest went up from the rural districts. They were indignant that the schoolhouses they had built—and some very good—should be taken from them and made common property. Farmers who had no children complained because they were taxed for books to be used by children of their neighbors. There was nothing to be done about it, however, and the loud protests died away to a grumble. It only took a matter of two or three years to convince them that they were the gainers.

The state offered to furnish a certain sum for the establishing of free high schools in those towns, which would raise an equal amount for that purpose. The trustees of the Academy saw the opportunity for which they had been looking, namely to improve all the town schools. The matter was brought before the town meeting, and a vote taken to raise the required sum, after a hot discussion and by a small majority.

The plan was to hire the Academy to give the scholars a high school training under the supervision of the state. To do this, it would have to be graded, and more teachers would be needed. It was also voted to authorize the school committee to grade the rural schools. The promoters of this movement were George Burleigh, Calvin Bradford, Leroy Miles and my husband. It was the beginning of a fight, which waged year by year until the younger generation became voters. Another term was added to the two, which were the previous limit in the rural districts, and normal school teachers were hired by the committee.

After a few years, the trustees at last had the satisfaction of knowing that the schools compared favorably with other secondary and rural schools in the state. Formerly, the Academy had been considered by the farmers as a village institution for the use of village boys and girls; it was now their own school, and they took advantage of its help. There was also no difficulty now in getting a vote in town meetings to raise all the money needed.

The old Academy took fire one morning and burned to ashes. It was entirely inadequate for its purpose, and most people were glad it was gone. The only difficulty was how to get another. The question was a troublesome one, and it was two or more years before it was decided where it should be put, how much it should cost, and the appropriation made and the work done.

When the dust from the commotion settled, we found we had two good schoolhouses. One ample for the needs of the high and grammar schools, and not far off another sufficiently roomy to house all the lower grades. It was a happy moment for both Mr. Rogers and myself. We by now had six children to educate in the town, and we were glad to have schools for that purpose.

While all this town history was being made, I was interested in some problems of my own. When I was married, I knew nothing about the care and training of children. I had never had any experience in the care of their bodies or the development of their minds and habits. There seemed to be no way of learning all these things except by actual experience. Young mothers were supposed to know by instinct how to care for their children and to profit from the wise council handed out to them by the older women. I soon found the first a fallacy and the last too contradictory to be dependable. Mother Rogers was of much assistance to me until her death. I pondered on the frequent problems that beset me, the fear lest I make irretrievable mistakes and the young lives committed to my charge to care for, train and develop should finally be a failure.

Mr. Rogers and I differed in regard to punishments. He believed firmly in Solomon's law, that to spare the rod was to spoil the child, while I did not have any faith in Solomon. I maintained that his children's record did not commend his theories. But I was not sure of my ground although I have no recollection of suffering punishment of that kind in my childhood. However, Mother Rogers' council strengthened my convictions, and with the last of the group, a rebuke was all that was necessary. In spite of my ignorance, they grew and developed as sturdy, active and healthy as the average, as many another family has done. They came through all the diseases that were considered inevitable accompaniments of childhood. Why should they not? They had good, bracing, pure air from one year's end to another. They had plenty of nourishing food, plenty of sleep and comfortable clothing, though of the plainest. When Mary was two and a half years old, Annie *[Annie Lucasta Rogers]* was born, and after the same lapse of time, David *[David Nathan Rogers]* joined the circle. He was four years old when Luther *[Luther Barker Rogers]*, named for his father, was born.

We were now as busy as a hive of bees. When Edwin was ten years old, he began to tease for a shotgun. We did not make many prohibitions in regard to their amusements and playthings. They had knives and axes or any other tool—under the watchful eyes of their elders, of course. They went where the men went and learned to handle tools and to be self-reliant under any ordinary circumstances. But a gun is another matter. It is dangerous unless used understandingly. We both thought him too young to be trusted with one alone in the woods. We told him he could have a shotgun when someone would go with him and teach him how to use it. Not long after, he came in one day with a partridge, which had been shot.

"Where did you get that?" I asked.

"I shot it," he replied.

"What with?" I wanted to know.

"With Charley Peavy's gun." The Peavy boys were chums just across the field, and I knew they had a gun. His father had said, "If he can shoot a partridge, I'll get him a gun." The next day, Edwin shouldered his new gun and marched off, the happiest lad in the town. From that time on through the years, his favorite recreation was fishing or hunting, but he never had any accident.

One day, Mr. Rogers returned from a business trip to Bangor very enthusiastic over the working of a road machine then being used over the hills in the Seven Mile Woods. Everyone who ever came to Patten over the old stage road from Mattawamkeag knew about those hills and the hair-raising roads over them. Mr. Rogers was one of the town assessors, and Scott Kellogg was also on the board.

He said to Scott, "They are making a trotting park of that road. Go down and take a look at it."

Scott went. He came back enthusiastic, and they both began a campaign to induce the town to buy a machine. Nobody, except a very few who went over the road, believed what they said. As for buying the machine, it was a folly. Just a scheme to spend the town's money.

At that time, twenty-five hundred dollars for any kind of machine was too much for a town like ours to spend. The old way of building roads was good enough anyway. Give the farmers a chance to work out their taxes with their teams and their spades. That was how they reasoned about it. I was, of course, much interested. All my life I had bumped over rocks and ruts, corduroys and cud. The very thought of a good, smooth, dry road intrigued me. Also, I was ambitious for the town. I knew what every thoughtful person knew, that the road building by the old way was a wasteful process.

As the winter went by, it became evident that a vote could not be carried at the town meeting to buy a machine. The board of assessors quietly bought one out of their pockets, and an article was inserted in the warrant to buy a machine. When that article was read, the fight began. The machine had friends, but not enough.

Then someone who had found out about the purchase rose and said, "It's just as well to know that the board has a machine, which they propose to sell to the town."

It was voted to pass over the article.

When the highway was in condition to work, the machine was put upon our section to try it out. To one used only to the old methods, it was certainly amazing to see not only the wide, smooth, hard track, but also the rapidity with which it could be built. Shortly after, the board announced that on a certain day they would demonstrate the machine over the Finch Hill and invited everybody to come and see it done. The commissioner had his men and teams for hauling off rocks and dumping gravel ready where needed, also men to rake sods and smooth up. Mr. Rogers and I drove over there about ten o'clock. Certainly, most everybody of the voting class was there leaning against the fence or sitting about in groups in earnest discussion. A half-mile at the top of the hill had been worked.

We stopped near a man I knew had opposed the purchase. "Well," I said, "what do you think of it?"

He was much excited. "I never would have believed it could do it if I hadn't seen it. I never would have believed it!" And he passed on shaking his head, looking as if he were still mystified about it.

There was no trouble getting a vote to buy at the next meeting. Only one man put in a protest. He said he went in to his farm by a spotted line, had traveled over the road for fifty years, and he never saw it as bad as it was after that machine worked it. The statement was so manifestly untrue and prejudiced that everybody laughed. During the summer, the road movement began.

The barn, blocking the view, was moved back of the house and set on a basement against a knoll. The basement was to be used for stock and the floor above for hay and grain. This added very much to the room and convenience in management of the dairy herd, now quite large. It so much improved the appearance of the place, it began to seem to me like a real home.

Our farm was situated about halfway between the village and the next neighborhood, which we always spoke of as the Hill. It consisted of a cluster of farms on a ridge. I was well acquainted with the people before my marriage and liked them. The men were often at odds and sometimes did not speak to each other, but the women got along fairly well.

I suggested to someone that we get together occasionally for a pleasant social time, and they all accepted the idea at once. We organized what we called a circle. We agreed to take turns entertaining the gathering twice each month except during the three or four months of summer. The ladies attended in the afternoon, the remainder of the family being on hand for the supper and the evening. Each lady brought a contribution to the supper, the hostess furnishing certain things. Each grown person paid five cents, though we did not decide at the time what should be done with the money.

This circle remained very popular for several years. There developed a movement for a Sunday school, and our money was used for a library for it. The school lasted until the children grew up and dropped out of the neighborhood. We then used the money in a magazine club. The magazines were of the best and were not only a treat, but also a benefit to the families represented.

When those interests began, there were four children in our family and my duties as a mother were not light, either as a housewife or dairywoman. I was making all the cream of the eight or nine cows into butter with what assistance Mr. Rogers could give me. I kept a girl to do the heavy work, attending to the cooking myself. I made all the children's clothes and my own as well.

There was no ready-made clothing of all sizes from the infant to the adult. We had to make everything, even the men's shirts. I also knitted our stockings and mittens. I wonder how I ever accomplished it. The old trick of my childhood of reading while I knit served me well now. I did the knitting evenings after the children were in bed and read at the same time. Knitting a stocking was not as monotonous under those circumstances.

On November 23, 1894, an event occurred which nearly cost me my life. Ruth [*Ruth Rogers*], the youngest—a tiny but beautiful baby—was born, "Someone to be with us in our old age," said Mr. Rogers.

Mr. Rogers was now engrossed with the business of lumbering and was away much of the time, from after the crop was harvested until the spring drive was over. This work took him to the Wisattaquoik County and covered a period of about eight years. Our boy, Ed became associated with him, and many exciting and occasionally tragic things occurred.

The Wisattaquoik is a clear, cold, turbulent stream taking its rise from Katahdin, and fed by deep, quiet pools where the surrounding mountains, the blue sky and drifting clouds are beautifully mirrored. In summer time, the water has dwindled into a shallow stream slipping around the boulders so gay and musically as if it never harbored a harsh intention.

It is a different matter in flood time when its waters dash with tremendous force against the boulders that choke its bed. It is impossible of navigation by bateau or canoe because of those great rocks and a dangerous stream to drive logs on for the same reason and also because of the force of the current. Woe to the unlucky man who slips into the icy depths at that season of the year.

Drowning accidents were so frequent, the stream acquired a bad reputation, and it was difficult to hire men for the log driving. The names of the men who lost their lives were chiseled on boulders at the spot where the accident occurred and, in several instances, helped strengthen its bad reputation. Mr. Rogers had these boulders blown out. The blasting of the rocks to improve the channel and a more careful oversight of the men and work had good results. No man lost his life there for several years.

One spring day, Ed was hiring men for the drive, and had succeeded in gathering quite a crew, when there appeared a man to hire who was a stranger to him. He gave his name as Jack McDonald and said he was an old hand with a peavey.

Later in the day, Ed was talking with an acquaintance and asked him if he knew a man called Jack McDonald.

"Jack McDonald?" repeated the man. "Why, yes. Did you hire him?"

"Yes, I did," said Ed.

"Well! He's a good driver. An inveterate gambler. Gets his living that way mostly. There's no tricks with the cards that he doesn't know. Knows how to drive logs. I'll tell you, though, you'll have to keep him off your jams."

"Why?" asked Ed in surprise.

"Loses his head completely. Doesn't know what he's about."

"I see," said Ed, and the subject was dropped.

The men were finally assembled, and the work was well under way. Loose logs set adrift at the landings were already running into Deasey Dam, and men were stationed at important points along the banks to prevent jams, or if that were impossible, to report at once to the boss of the head crew.

One group was taking in the rear. Another crew was handling the main body of the logs and had reached Roll Dam where the work was being sadly hindered by a bad jam formed below the dam. This was one of the several spots on the stream, which bore a bad reputation. It had cut a channel for itself between rocky walls forming quite a chasm. The water ran through in a series of falls. The rocks had been blown out, widening the chasm sufficiently to run logs through but leaving the walls sharp and ragged.

The immediate cause of the jam was a big boulder, which became dislodged from the bank sometime in the spring and had fallen into the bed of the stream just below the dam. The logs pitching over the wasteway striking end-first behind the rock began the jam. Before the water could be shut off and the logs stopped running, a large mass was piled in there. The key log lay under water, one end braced against a rock, the other end held by a log lying at right angles to it. These two held the mass.

It was an exceedingly dangerous place to work. No man's life was safe an instant after the logjam began to haul, and no man could predict the moment when those two logs would yield to the tremendous pressure. They tried starting it by squirts; that is, the gates in the big mammoth dam above were shut and the pond allowed to fill; then they were hoisted, and the whole body of water turned into the jam. It moved it not a particle.

Then our boy, Luther, saw Fleming bring out a stick of dynamite, tap it with a cap and insert a piece of fuse. As he walked toward the shore, he lighted the fuse, waving the stick to start the blaze. Luther, already having lost a part of a finger and thumb by dynamite, had a wholesome respect for it, so he ran behind a rock.

Fleming threw the dynamite toward the jam but not quite far enough to land it among the logs. The current flung it out into the water, and away it went down stream. Just in front of the shelf on which the three men were perched, it exploded, throwing barrels of water into the air, a large part of which came down on the men.

That was all the damage it did. The situation had now become acute. There was a nervous tension on the part of the men and anxiety in the faces of the bosses. The whole crew sat about on the shore while the boss and more experienced men discussed and studied the conditions.

All agreed that if by any means the end of the log at the angle could be pushed down, the whole mass would go. Then Whitlock offered to attempt it.

He had his plan, and it was that they followed. He went down into the water on the key log with his cant-dog or peavey. Six men lay down on the rocks above him and grasped him by his clothes anywhere they could get a hold. He stretched his long arms, and lifting the peavey high above his head, he drove it with all his strength into the end of the log. Instantly, the peavey and log disappeared, and the jam crumbled away in the boiling water; but the six young giants flung him safe and sound on the bank.

After that, young Luther wandered off to the camp and chummed with the cook, and the rest of the story of that day I got from Ed Fleming

After a second lunch, a part of the crew was set to work on a wing jam above the dam. It was not a particularly dangerous task, but the current from it through the pond out to the sluiceway was very strong. As soon as the jam began to "haul," every man must get ashore at his best pace. All that day, it had been perfectly patent to the bosses that McDonald not only shared the general tenseness that seemed almost to pervade the air, but he was really excited and losing his self-control. So Fleming had orders not to send him into a jam, and he was put to work pushing logs out of the eddies into the current..

In a crew of forty to sixty men, it is not always easy to keep track of one man or even to have him in mind. At a distance, they mostly all look alike. Ed came up from below and stopped to watch the men at work prying out the logs, and directly he spied McDonald working on the jam. He strode across the piled logs and, taking him by the shoulders, marched him ashore.

"There," said he. "If you go out on that jam again, I will discharge you on the spot."

Jack had no mind to quarrel and went sullenly back to his safe job near the shore. The men picked patiently away.

Suddenly, a tremor permeated the mass of logs. Every man knew the sign and raised a shout of warning. With their peavies in their hands, they raced to the shore, the logs rolling and tumbling under their flying feet. Every man reached the shore except one. To Ed's consternation, McDonald, shouting for help, rode a log out of the melee and floated towards the dam. Every man who saw him knew his danger. If he got into the middle where the current was strongest, nothing could save him. Two men near the shore ran out on the rocks, and hitching their cant hooks into a log, pushed it toward him as he came along.

"Jump!" they cried. "We'll hold you."

Completely crazed, he paid no heed but ran the length of his log still shouting for help. This movement only served to force him still further towards the current, and in a moment he was beyond help. He saw a submerged rock and jumped on it but his log brushed him off it. Throwing his arm over the log, he drifted on.

A man standing on the dam, heedless of his own danger, reached his peavey as far as possible toward him. Jack made a grab at it but missed. He then dropped the log, and kicking his feet out ahead, tried to brace them against the dam. At the momentary slackening of his speed, the current behind catapulted his body over, and he went out headfirst into the caldron of boiling water and tumbling logs.

Luther, who was telling stories to the cook in the warm camp, finally crawled up on top of the stove wood neatly tiered between the two solid stakes nailed there to hold it, and stretching himself out, went to sleep.

When he awoke, it was dark. The hanging lamps were lighted the length of the long room. The crew of sixty men were all there. What struck him at once was the stillness of the crowd. Even the Frenchmen, always laughing and chattering, were silent. Only such remarks or words as were necessary were spoken. There was something electric in the very air. The men were coming, one after the other, to the stove with their basins and spoons for their soup, quietly helping themselves to their dippers of tea and whatever else they needed from it, then finding a seat somewhere and eating in silence.

Luther curled down beside his older brother behind the stove. "What's the matter?" he said in a whisper.

"A man was drowned today," replied Ed in a low tone. He was watching the men intently and wondering back in his head if he would have to give half the crew a bill of their time in the morning.

He was not worrying so much about the New Brunswick men, but the Frenchmen. He had known a whole crew to be thrown into a panic by less.

As he watched their faces, he was somewhat reassured. A Frenchman is never quiet when he is panicky, and he is never planning anything rash when he is quiet. As a matter of fact, they all stayed by the drive, though in the following days, when they dragged the pools and hunted the banks, the gloom of tragedy was heavy over them all.

I was afterwards told by Bill Fleming, a seasoned river man who had been through many thrilling experiences, that he turned his back on that tragic scene. He could not endure that one of their number should go to his death before their faces and no man able to lift a hand to help him. "But," he added, "his time had come. It had to be."

Two men, during the previous week, made their headquarters at one of his camps. The older man was from a Western city and was spending the winter in the Maine woods hoping to regain some of the vitality lost in too close confinement in a city office. The man who accompanied him was his guide. To the endurance and sagacity of the guide they no doubt owed their escape from death from freezing.

It is true Katahdin is frequently ascended in summer, in spite of its being remote from traveled ways, and rough trails are its only mode of approach. The ascent is seldom attempted in winter, and then only in perfectly still, clear weather. It is perhaps more liable to sudden squalls, fogs and terrible winds than many other mountains.

That, at least, is its reputation. Rising as it does almost alone from the level plain, it gathers to itself the moisture from the air, forms small clouds drifting in a circle about it, often shutting down upon its peaks in a solid bank of fog.

This fog is frequently accompanied by a deluge of rain, sleet or snow, sometimes followed by winds of irresistible force. The Indians believe that the mountain is a spirit, resentful, bitterly avenging the encroachments of human beings.

Sometimes, when the region was a busy lumbering country, a group of ambitious men would scale the steep walls of the North Mountain by cutting finger and toeholds in the ice above the timberline. The top of the tableland is generally good walking except after a heavy fall of snow. Ordinarily, such snow as is left by the winds is packed hard. The trip from the valley below to Monument Peak can be made in a day with an early start.

The MacLeod Camp was on the south branch of the Wisattaquoik in the little narrow valley between Turner Mountain and the north end of Katahdin. The Katahdin side is a sheer rock wall, ice-covered in winter, but Turner is not nearly so steep and is heavily timbered. From high points, beautiful views are gotten of the main mountain, snow-clad, standing out in sharp relief against the blue sky like a beautiful marble ruin.

The valley hummed with busy men and teams cutting and hauling into the Wisattaquoik below the conjunction of the two branches all the merchantable timber growing in the valley. At this camp appeared the two. They were hiking up the river, packs on shoulders. The guide was large and stalwart, the other less robust.

All such visitors were made welcome at the camps, and accommodations were found for them. They made inquiries during the evening about the possibilities and methods of climbing the mountain, but seemed to have formed as yet no definite plan to do so. The Boss explained that several of the men had made the ascent at different times during the winter. There was a fairly good snowshoe trail to a nearby point through the woods, and the climb was not so very difficult if one possessed a level head and quick wit.

The following morning, he, being on his weekly tour of inspection of the work, went out with MacLeod, and it was around ten o'clock when he again appeared.

"Our visitors gone?" He asked the cook.

"Yes. They went on the mountain," the cook replied.

"On the mountain!" exclaimed the Boss. "When did they start?"

"Soon after you all went out. They took a lunch, and the guide borrowed a small axe."

"Well! They are mighty lucky if they don't get caught in a snowstorm up there. The wind is out of the southeast, and the sky is already mostly overcast. They are liable to be caught in the clouds any minute. I wouldn't have let them go if I had known they had any such intention."

The two men, equipped with lunch, axe and snowshoes, had no difficulty in reaching the timberline. The ascent from this point to the highest elevation of the north end was not too difficult. They cached the snowshoes, lunch and axe at the end of the path through the woods and made good time unencumbered. The walking was hard for a mile and descending after that level.

Overhead, the sun was shining, but banks of clouds lay about the horizon. Great stretches of country spread out before them covered with snow and ice; its dead black and white effects lacked the power to inspire enthusiasm that goes with sparkling blue water, green woods and meadows. Nevertheless, it was absorbing.

As they walked, their attention was concentrated on what was below and distant rather than what was above; consequently, they were unaware that the thin haze covering the sky in the early morning was rapidly thickening and the sunlight as rapidly disappearing.

Before them rose Monument Peak, South Peak, and across the Basin the sharp outline of the Narrows, the Chimney and Pomola, all dazzling white against the dark clouds gathering on the eastern horizon. Down two thousand feet below, dark green stretches of fir, spruce and pine relieved the dead white monotony of the landscape.

Suddenly, out of the southeast rolling over Pomola, came a tempest of wind and snow enveloping them as a cloud, filling their eyes and stinging their faces like needles. They were obliged to turn their backs to breathe, and soon they were unable to stand against it.

They crouched on their feet and were carried across the wide plateau like dried leaves in autumn. Over the edge they were swept, now flat on their backs, and brought to a final stop in the scrubby growth at the timber line. They were down to the soft snow. They were also sheltered from the force of the wind and the usual light of a dull, stormy day replaced the blackness of the blizzard, which still raged above them.

They went off the tableland at a point known to woodsmen as the Northwestern Basin, which lies between the western spur and the north end. From near the top flows a brook, which becomes a sizable stream as it nears the bottom and finally breaks into a charming waterfall.

It was near this brook, which at this season was covered with snow, that they stopped and were able—after much labor—to follow it to reach the base of the mountain. The guide took control of the situation, the lawyer quietly following as best he could.

There is no timber of any size on the lower reaches of the west side. It is mostly scrub which, at this time, was quite well covered with snow, dry and unpacked. They sank to their waists among the hidden branches from which they extricated themselves with difficulty; consequently, their progress was slow and painful.

It was the afternoon of a short winter day, and storming at that. They followed the brook until it flowed into a larger one the guide knew must be the north branch of the Wisattaquoik. As he fought their way through the brush, out into the more open and smoother course of the stream, he turned over in his mind the chances of escaping alive from this frozen wilderness. He knew there was absolutely no hope of help on the west side of the mountain. There were no lumbering camps operating there. All the sportsmen's camps were closed. He was sure they would start a search party from MacLeod Camp in the morning, but how would they keep alive until then? Obviously, only by keeping on the move.

If they followed the North Branch, it would eventually take them into the MacLeod logging roads. The distance would be probably about ten miles. It was thirteen miles to the camp. The snow was three feet deep. He looked speculatively at his companion; the other fellow was out for his health. He might be obliged to carry him after a time. Now he wished for that luncheon. It's hard traveling on an empty stomach, sick or well.

"Well," he said, getting to his feet after their brief rest, "we have to make the most of this daylight."

"What are we going to do?" asked the lawyer.

"There is only one thing to do if we want to get out alive," was the reply. "That is to go north to the MacLeod logging roads."

"Heavens," sighed the man, but he straightened up gamely.

The guide cut two stout sticks, trimmed them smoothly, gave one to the other man and kept one for himself. "Use it as a cane," he said. "It will be lots of support and save you many a fall. Now here's where I break trail. It will help some."

"Some" was right. If the snow had been soft, it would have been much help, but there had been no rains since the first fall in the early winter. In this cold, dark valley, the snow was like sand down to the bottom. At each step, it flowed in from the sides half filling the hole as soon as his foot was removed. Their feet pulled up through it as if they were weighted. They had to stop frequently to rest, but only for very short periods; it was plain the lawyer went on more and more reluctantly.

Daylight faded, and darkness shut down upon them. The snow, however, reflected a dim sort of glow, which helped them. The frozen, snow-covered stream was an unmistakable guide. They could not miss it. To veer right or left carried them into bushes. They plodded slowly on for three hours, making hardly more than a mile each hour. The guide was carefully watching the steps of his companion for signs of exhaustion. He had kept up well so far, but the hard, grueling tramp was beginning to task his not-too-vigorous frame. His step was lagging, and his whole appearance was very weary.

They said but little, all their strength being needed to keep them going. Another hour passed. The lawyer begged to lie down for just a few minutes to sleep.

"No," said the guide. "It would be fatal. You would chill very quickly, and I could not wake you up." He reasoned with him until he was persuaded to go on.

Slowly, they plodded on for another hour, but for half that time the guide expected each step his companion took would be his last.

It was hard, cruel, but it might be effective. "Want to rest a minute?" he asked.

"Yes" said the man; "I'm going to rest from now on. I cannot go another step." He dropped on the snow and leaned his head on his hands.

"Well," said the guide, "you've done mighty well. But you don't want to stop now. It won't be long before we get out."

"I cannot go any further," said the lawyer, "and I'm not going to try. I'm completely exhausted. I would rather die than walk another mile."

"Oh come on" pleaded the guide. "You'll feel better soon. Get your second wind."

"No Sir. I'm done."

The guide stepped back behind him and, without warning, struck him a stinging blow across the shoulders. The lawyer sprang to his feet, instantly galvanized into hot, raging life. All his weariness dropped from him.

He faced the guide, his hands clenched, his eyes glaring. "I'll kill you!" he gasped.

"All right" said the guide, nonchalantly. "Any time. Come on."

He turned to the trail and went on, and behind him tramped the man—angry, but yielding.

For an hour, nothing was said. They sat down to rest frequently in perfect silence. The lawyer's drawn, haggard face, the grim, set mouth, told the story of his sufferings, but the eyes had not lost their angry glare. After awhile, they seemed to be getting into more open country and better light. Then, all at once, they walked down into a hard, well-trodden road.

The guide could not restrain a shout of relief, and even the lawyer straightened up. How good it seemed to be walking without having to lift the sucking weight of the snow clinging to their feet at each step. It was yet three or four miles to camp, and up hill at that, but the certainty of the warm camp food and rest at the end gave them a new hold on life. At ten-thirty, they walked into the cookhouse where the Boss and his assistants were detailing men and tying up lunches for a search party to be sent out at daylight.

The next incident is one of summertime, in the middle of June. I remember how happy I was that the trees were again covered with leaves and the vivid fields spotted with the white and yellow flowers. The most beautiful month of the year! The orchards are shedding their pink and white blooms, and all the birds are singing from daylight to dark. Everything is growing with all its power, and summer is fairly on. My husband, "The Boss," had come home today after two months of driving the river, and according to the story he told me, winter had not yet vanished in some places.

He said: The tenth of June, we finished driving, the night before the last log of the Sourdnehunk Drive ran into the West Branch of the Penobscot. From there into the boom was not our job.

On the morning of the tenth, twenty or more men were gathered about the cook's fire on the shore of the river eating our final meal on what the cook called the leavings. The wagon was to be all packed into the boats and taken down the river that day. The men were scattered about sitting on stumps, rocks or logs, each one with a plate in his lap and a knife, fork and dipper in hand. The plates were filled with the odds and ends of food collected in the last clearing-up process. It was chilly there in the shadows, for though past sunrise, its beams were seen only on the clouds in the west because Katahdin rose steeply, darkly behind them and shut off the sunshine.

When I had finished and shied my plate in the direction of the wooden bucket where the cook was packing the dishes, I said, "All you men had better take a lunch with you. You'll need it before you get where there's a square meal."

The big cook tent and the men's sleeping tent were still standing, and the river, carrying drifts of foam from its boisterous passage through chasms, rapids and over falls, looked black and cold. In the center, the cook's fire burned brightly with the logs, which had fed it since last evening. With singing, shouting and rough horseplay, the men filled the half-hour before leaving camp.

The task, long and arduous, was completed, and they were mainly interested in getting out of the wilderness to their families or to the pleasures of loafing and playing until their money was spent. The boats' crews were to take all the tools and other pieces of the outfit in the boats by way of the river until they reached the highway where the stuff could be sent to its destination by railroad or team. All the other men were to go across country on foot. So it was that they scorned the lunch and looked without concern on the nine miles to the tableland, every foot of which was a climb and the last two miles at an angle of forty-five degrees.

The Boss said: I put a handful of doughnuts in my pocket, all that was left of the breakfast, and after some final directions to the boatmen, followed the men who had already taken the trail. There was no snow on the side of the mountain. The trees along the stream were in blossom, and all the small young plants were growing. Spring was here, though not very far advanced, and the sun was warm.

The men were strong and vigorous and took the climb easily, but consuming more time in doing so than they expected. It was fully ten o'clock when the tableland was reached, which we crossed by old caribou trails through evergreen scrub breast-high. It was two miles across the plateau, with comparatively smooth level footing of moss and cranberry vines. The view of the lofty peaks towering on the right and the surrounding country stretching far away in all directions was exhilarating to one with eyes to see and a mind to appreciate it.

We reached the eastern edge of the tableland at a point between the North and South Basins, and here the men threw themselves down for a brief rest. We had also to consider the next move. It appeared to be a difficult one. We were lying on the edge of a perpendicular wall that rose many hundred feet from the ground below. It would seem that all the snow that had fallen on the mountains during the winter had blown off into that abyss until a drift had formed, beginning at our feet and sloping downward. Its farthest edge was lost in the tall trees that marked the opening into the valley, east of the mountain. A hard crust had formed on the drift, which caved very little under our feet, even in the sun. It was a question of getting safely down into the abyss below.

I was familiar with the trails and doubted if the one into the Basin ordinarily used would be safe. It might be dangerous. There was one leading down the north end of the mountain, but it was long and difficult, and we had no food. It was necessary to get to the East Branch, the first stopping place, as soon as possible. Someone suggested that we slide down on our feet. Another objected that we might not be able to keep our feet. One might slide on his head instead.

At last Johnny Bouleau stood up. 'By Gar! I'm going to dat bottom on my head or my feet, me. Come on boys,' and suiting the action to the word, he crouched on his feet; balancing himself with his hands and arms, he went flying down the slope.

One by one, the others followed, myself last. The top branches of trees stuck up through the snow here and there. Farther down, the trunks began to show. These gradually increased in height as we neared the point where the drift ceased. The most of the men lost their footing very soon and sat down or lay on their backs. They steered themselves somewhat with arms and feet, but their passage was plenty swift enough to satisfy the most hardened speed fiend. When we picked ourselves up at the bottom, it was a relief to know no one was hurt. Johnny straddled a tree but was not badly shaken by the shock.

"Oh, Johnny,' I cried. "How did you like your ride?"

"By gar! I slide down dat mountain again for five dollars."

They were off down the trail. There was much slush and water from the melting drift, also moss-covered rocks slippery and treacherous, but it was descending, which was a pleasant change from the hard climb of the morning.

The men, used to four meals each day, began to wish they had heeded the advice I gave them at breakfast time. One and one-half miles brought us to Dry Pond, by no means dry now, whatever it may be in midsummer, but it could be waded and the trail ran right across it. There was this trouble with Dry Pond. Each bit of shore looked exactly like every other bit; consequently it was very easy to leave it at the wrong point, and not at all easy to find the right one.

When I arrived, the men were grouped in the center, waiting.

"Lost?" I asked.

"Well! We'd like to know where to get off. Jack Gangon and Joe Paradis said it was over there, and that's where they've gone. And Tommy Martin and Mike Comman have gone too."

"That isn't right," I told them, and I pointed out the exact spot where the trail entered the woods. "How long have the men been gone?"

"Jack and Joe have been gone some time, but Tommy and Mike just went into the woods."

"You go on as I told you; I'll go after them."

I had no trouble overtaking Tommy and Mike. A half mile of fast walking and there they were sitting beside the road, exhausted and discouraged. They had given up trying to get anywhere. The men were faint from lack of food, for, like children, they were too excited to eat in the morning, weary with the grueling, nerve-racking strain of these weeks of driving the logs, and last but not least, the climb up the mountain tests the muscles of the strongest man. Then, added to all these things, the uncertainty as to the trail was more than they could endure, they gave it up and preferred to sit down and wait for what came next.

"Have you seen the other two men?"

No, they had not. Now I knew that to go blindly across an unfamiliar country without compass or marked trail is fraught with danger. A man in thick woods, where he has no outlook and no sun, may travel in a circle until he becomes exhausted and so bewildered that he is partially insane and unable to recognize a familiar spot when he sees it.

In this case, there was the far greater danger that these men, who had eaten very little since the previous day, would become so weary that they would lie down to sleep, which might end in death from exposure. Men of that class sometimes succumb easily. On the other hand, Gangon and Paradis were old woodsmen and might keep a general direction toward the Wisattaquoik Valley if they kept in mind one landmark. With Mount Turner always on their left, they would at last get out to the stream above where the others must cross. It would be tough traveling because that section had been swept by fire some years previously and the ground was not only covered with boulders but fallen trees as well. I seriously considered all these things but also remembered I had these two exhausted men on my hands; so I took a chance and said, "They'll probably get to the Wisattaquoik all right."

I had eaten one of the doughnuts. There were just four remaining. These I divided between the men who, after some encouragement and persuasion, concluded to try again. We retraced our steps to the Pond, went off at the proper place, and from that time I kept them in sight. We passed Katahdin Lake and crossed the Wisattaquoik on Robar Dam. Then came miles of tramping over an old tote road, a stiff climb up another mountain. We overtook here and there tired stragglers from the first group of men. At last we stood on the bank at East Branch and saw the welcome light of the long, low building where there were food and beds. The first to reach the shore sent out the usual call for ferry, so there was no waiting when the last tired man stepped out of the woods.

In the morning, they scattered towards the towns, but I staid by. My job was not yet all finished. I still had business right there. I dispatched a man with horse and food back over the road to City Camps. These camps were unoccupied.

The man had instructions to bring back the missing men if they were there; but in case they were not, to come back at once, as it would be necessary to send out a search party. The man found them both at the camp, sick in the berths. They stated how they found a porcupine in the yard and they killed the animal, skinned and roasted it by a fire built in the open. They ate it all, then crawled into the bunks for a good rest and sleep. But alas! All night long, they tossed and writhed in bitter pain, and when the rescuer arrived at noon, their haggard faces and trembling limbs proclaimed it. However, some good, civilized food and hours of sleep refreshed them to such an extent they were able to go on the following morning, and they eventually reached the end of the journey.

These men will tell you such experiences are all in the day's work and sooner or later they all escape by the skin of their teeth. They had a tale of woe to tell. They at first followed what they supposed was an old path, but after a mile or more, it came abruptly to an end and they realized they were wrong. Rather than go back, they decided to keep on, hoping to be able to follow the general direction. The distance from Dry Pond would be seven or eight miles. They skirted the south slopes of Turner without difficulty, but the next two miles was through swampy land covered with evergreen trees and overflowing with water through which they picked their way with great difficulty.

They could get no glimpse of the mountain, and it was not easy to keep the right direction. The sun, nearly overhead, gave very little help in that matter. Both were suffering from hunger and great weariness, but they were too anxious to get out of the woods to stop long enough to rest. At last, the swamp was past, the woods opened out and, to their relief, there was Turner looming up on their left, proving they were keeping the right direction.

But their troubles were not yet over. From the woods they came into the burnt land. A mass of boulders covered the ground. Over these lay a tangle of dead trees killed by the fire, uprooted by the winds, broken by their own decay or still standing, mere stubs awaiting their turn to fall. Up from the scant soil under the rocks was a young growth of all sorts of shrubs and brakes. It was through this hagus of Dry-ky they had to force their way to the Wisattaquoik and at last, when the sun was setting, they stood on its banks, too utterly exhausted to drag one foot after the other. Over the other side was City Camp, but they had to go a long mile upstream and cross on the dam.

One February, there was a catastrophe in one of the camps. I had been very uneasy for about two weeks about matters there. During that time, we had a heavy thaw, warm weather, then much rain. A heavy winter thaw happens only occasionally in this land of deep snows and is always more or less of a disaster. Especially so in the lumber woods where the snow is deep and the roads become so soft no teams can travel them.

Where a cluster of camps are miles from the station or base of supplies, and if the horses number from seventy to a hundred, and the men from a hundred and fifty to two hundred, there must be careful provision for their needs. If, because of heavy storms or for other reasons, the toters have been prevented from getting a sufficient supply ahead to insure plenty for an emergency, then a week's thaw may be a calamity. More than that, the overhead charges of a business of that size are heavy; every day is a distinct loss, not only in cost of maintenance, but in the time needed to get into the stream the logs already cut.

I had heard nothing from camp, meantime, but all at once it turned cold and everything froze solid and very slippery. Two days later, our son, Ed, his wife *[Mattie, daughter of Rodney Barker]* and the eighteen-month-old baby *[Beth]* and also her niece, Thede *[Hersey]*, seven years, arrived by train.

Mr. Rogers, The Boss, had brought them to Stacyville and put them aboard the train and then gone back to camp. Mattie told me the story of their experience. I have already said that the Wisattaquoik is a dangerous stream in springtime. But it does not confine its rampages to the spring freshlet. A winter thaw is fully as bad.

For a week, the thermometer had been slowly rising. The air was heavy and overwarm. The sleek coats of the horses were dripping with perspiration as they "made their turns" from yards in the woods to the landings on the stream.

"The sleds go hard," said Johnny Amboise. "She one mighty steeky day, by Gee Willey."

The men hate a warm, soft day. It is so much easier to work in a cold, crisp atmosphere. Saturday night, it began to rain a steady downpour, and it continued during the hours of Sunday morning until water was freely running in all directions.

Russell Camp was situated on the North Branch of the Wisattaquoik that flows past Russell Mountain which, in turn, butts on the north end of Katahdin. It was built on the edge of a flat bordering the stream and the men's sleeping quarters, the cookhouse, one storehouse and a hovel accommodating twelve horses were on the flat. Next to these structures was the camp yard that was on higher ground extending back to the woods. In this yard, the staved was cut, the teams unharnessed from their sleds, and tote teams unloaded. Back of the yard, and also on the higher level, were another storehouse, a blacksmith shop, the large hovel for horses and the cookee's bean hole, a pit in the earth covered with a roof where the great kettles of beans were baked. A road from this yard led into the main logging and tote road. On the other side next to the stream in a sheltered hollow was a little cabin occupied by Ed and his family. It was a tiny log structure where they lived very comfortably and happily. The Boss was there, and also a visitor, Mr. Thomas. Sunday morning, there was much uneasiness in camp owing to the break in the weather.

Back of the camp was a ridge running from the logging road to the stream. A dam had been built to conserve water for the spring driving between the end of this ridge and the mountain. The flowage covered quite a space making a fair-sized pond. The melting snow of the previous warm days and the heavy rain started innumerable little brooks on the mountains, all flowing into the Wisattaquoik, lifting the ice, breaking it up into cakes large and thick, and forcing it down the stream. These cakes were already beginning to pile up on the dam. The crashing and grinding of the masses of ice filled the air with thunderous connection.

Every man in camp knew the menace of this ice jam. It completely stopped the flow of water through the wasteway of the dam and backed it into the pond. If this body of water, constantly increased by the streams flowing into it, rose beyond a certain point, it would break through to the lowest point, which was at the end of the dam nearest the camp. The little cabin and the camps on the flat would be directly in its path.

The Boss urged them to pack up and move out of the cabin, not run the risk of being caught in a trap, but Ed was reluctant.

"I don't believe it will rise high enough to overflow," he said. "I think the rain is about over. I guess we will wait a while anyway."

They did pack the grips and roll the blankets ready to be thrown into the pung in the yard at a moment's notice. The Boss kept his horse harnessed.

About noon, the rain ceased and the wind breezed up, soon increasing to a gale. The roar of the wind in the trees and mountains added to the crashing of the cakes of ice caught in the rebound of the current. They shot into the air like surf on a reef, and falling with loud report on the already formidable heap at the dam, the sound filled the valley with its tumult.

The clouds began to break up and the sun to shine out. The temperature also began to fall, which was encouraging. By mid-afternoon, the water seemed to be falling a trifle. At four o'clock, the men came in from the pond with the welcome news that the worst was over. The water was steadily falling; so, also, was the temperature. The wind was already sharp. All the camp settled down to its usual routine. The teamsters fed their horses; the cook and cookee hastened to get the supper on the table. Ed put on his camp sweater and slippers. Mattie fed and undressed Beth. Even Thede took off her heavy sport stockings and shoes. Only the Boss kept his outdoor togs on, even his reefer.

The mother was just about to slip the nightie over the baby's head when one of the crew burst open the door and shouted, "The camp floor is all afloat!" And he was gone.

The Boss sprang through the door and Thede, in a panic, rushed after him. Underneath all the noise, he could hear the hiss of the water creeping through the snow. He took two or three steps on the path to the yard and went down in slush to his knees. Thede, behind, was swept off her feet by the stream of water and carried against a post where she hung, screaming. The Boss reached over and, grasping her, floundered back to the door, meeting Ed with the baby wrapped in a fur coat in his arms.

"We can't get across. Get on the roof!" he shouted.

Ed tossed the baby up on the low roof, and wrapping Thede in another coat, threw her up after her. He then tossed up two more fur coats and sprang up himself. The logs of which these cabins are made are put together like cob work. They are notched and fitted into each other near the ends, which project a few inches. These projecting ends form narrow steps to the roof, up which it is not hard to climb. It was such a corner that Ed quickly gained and then lay down, reaching his hands to his wife. When she was safely on top, he turned to help his father who was a heavy man and quite lame from a recent hurt. He was not there. He had gone back into the camp for blankets.

In consternation, Ed shouted, "Father! Father! Come out! You'll be drowned!"

The water was already pouring down the inclined path to the door. In a few minutes, the cabin would be full. After what seemed an age, but was really not over two minutes, he reappeared, struggling with difficulty against the rising current. Swinging himself as far over the edge as he could with safety, Ed grasped him by the shoulders, pulling him out of the water and assisted him to their little refuge. They were safe for the moment, but two of them were wet and the night wind was bitter.

They looked about them considering the next move. There were drifting clouds in the sky that now and then obscured the moon; but, for the most part, it shone brilliantly. The valley between the

cabin and the ridges was full of snow drifted in by the winter winds. It was under this drift the water had come. It was not yet soaked at the top, but it would be very shortly. The snow was far too soft to hold up their weight.

"We have got to have snow shoes," said Ed, and he began shouting, hoping to attract the attention of someone in the camp yard.

From the moment the men discovered the water in their camp, the wildest excitement prevailed. Men seized whatever footgear, mackinaws or caps they could reach and rushed out into the yard. The cooks abandoned the supper steaming on the table; teamsters, snatching their lanterns, ran for the hovels. The one on the flat was the only one in immediate danger, and that had a foot of water inside already. There was no time to untie horse halters. A man with a knife ran along by their heads and cut the ropes while others led them out to higher ground where they huddled, bewildered and uneasy. Mr. Thomas led out Prince and hitched him into the pung, then looked about for the Boss. "Look!" said Tommy Martin. "On the roof. Hark!"

The one word "snowshoes" was heard above all the racket, but it was enough. A man caught up the only two pairs in the yard and, putting on one pair, was soon across the ridge and the drift. Ed put on the extra pair, and each taking a child, they went across the drift as speedily as possible. Ed then took a pair back for his wife to use. They also got across safely, but the slopes filled with water after each step. It now remained to get the Boss over this dangerous crossing. They snowshoed over and took him between them in order to distribute the weights as evenly as possible and to hold him up in the event of his sinking.

A few anxious moments, and they were all safe. Behind them, the water shone in the moonlight. They soon reached the road where the team awaited them. The baby, wrapped in her fur coat, had made no outcry through it all. When her mother took her from the young Frenchman who carried her across, she discovered that, in his excitement he had reversed her, tenderly carrying her feet over his shoulder and her head down. Poor baby, she didn't even have her nightie with her; and then, after a two-mile drive to the other camp, she was much mortified because she had to wear a nice clean print shirt the cookee lent her. A jersey undershirt from the same source made pajamas for Thede, the sleeves serving for pants.

As many of the crew and horses as could be accommodated at this camp were made welcome and fed. The remainder of the horses—twelve in number, with their six teamsters-went over the tote road two miles to a dismantled camp. The roof was partially fallen, but it was some shelter from the cold wind. With an old axe found in a crib, they managed to cut some limbs and kindle a fire in the yard. But the wood was so wet, it gave out neither heat nor much flame, so they went in and stood among the horses to keep warm. The poor animals were hungry, not having had time to eat the last feed. They searched the cribs and nuzzled their drivers, begging for food in their soft, whinnying voices.

Said Joe to Jim, who stood between the next span over, "I wish I had the grain I hung up in a bag behind the horses at supper time. I could get it, too, if I could get to the roof of the hovel."

"The hovel's half full of water by this time, and you couldn't get near it by six feet," replied Jim.

"Yes, but there's a heap of brush and logs behind it. I believe I'll go back. Might as well go back as shiver here."

"All right," said Jim, "I'll go with you." And taking the old axe and a lantern, they went the two miles back to the flooded camp.

Joe got to the roof of the hovel, and prying up the splits with which it was covered, he hauled out his bag of grain, still dry. Jim prowled about, considering the possibility of salvaging something eatable, when he saw Joe jump down from the storehouse to the roof of the cookhouse. A window was set into the roof to aid in lighting the camp, and this window he pried out and thrust his lantern inside to light up the interior.

"What do you see?" shouted Jim.

The camp was two-thirds full of water with numberless tin plates and other cooking utensils floating about. Joe continued to peer about, throwing the beams of light here and there.

At last he called back, "I see a box that looks like the cook's gingerbread box. Bring me a long stick out with a hook on the end."

Jim got there promptly with his stick. Gingerbread sounded good to him. They hooked the stick to the box and gently drew it to him. It certainly was the gingerbread box, but the sodden mass no longer bore any resemblance to gingerbread. Disappointed and hungry, they again turned their faces back to the old camp. Half the distance was traversed when difficulty again confronted them. Since they passed over the road, the flood had covered it for some distance, also flowing back into the woods for several rods. The snow was still too soft to bear their weight, so they crawled around the water on their hands and knees, alternately carrying the bag of grain on their shoulders.

They reached the camp at last, and the horses certainly made them welcome, though one bag of grain is not so much divided among twelve. They had not many hours to stand about waiting for daylight, and they all shouted in unison when at sunrise a team appeared with a sled load of supplies and tools. It was accompanied by cook, cookees and men enough to repair the camps and put them in order for occupation.

They reported that the water of the flooded camp was slowly receding, but everything was embedded in ice. Whatever was salvaged at present would have to be chopped out of it. In a few days, they were settled in their new quarters, and work was proceeding as usual. Nobody but the owners suffered any permanent damage.

Ed and his family were living in their little camp at Pogy where another crew was working. He made the camp rounds each week looking after the work. On this day, they were all at our camp for dinner. Ed was planning to snowshoe from the logging road on the west side of Turner where a crew was at work. They had their headquarters at Robar Camp. When we carried his wife and child back to Pogy after the noon meal, we dropped him at the logging road, which went up the side of the mountain. The sky was dark and lowery, and the clouds thick. Mattie was plainly worried.

"I tried to persuade him to take more time and keep to the tote road," she said. "I think it is unsafe to cross the mountain on a day like this."

"Oh, you can't lose Ed," I said. "He will get there all right."

I really thought so, too. I used to worry about him when he tramped the woods as a boy, but the men assured me there was no danger of his getting astray. They said his sense of direction and locality was very keen. He never had gotten lost, and I ceased to worry. It was not a difficult proposition he was undertaking, provided the sun was shining, and to strengthen my confidence, I thought he had been going over there occasionally and had a trail to follow.

I found later that this was not true. As the snow began to fall thicker and heavier, I was uneasy.

Possibly he was a little over-confident himself and did not observe as carefully as he ought; his direction, and very likely his mind, was preoccupied. But at last he awoke to the fact that he was taking a long time to cross the mountain. Also, the light-falling snow was loading his snowshoes, making hard traveling. He could see hardly a rod in any direction. After a time, he began to descend, but he saw no sign of cutting or roads and heard no sounds of men or horses.

Still, he traveled on studying the situation. At last, it dawned on him that he had slowly veered to the right and traveled the length of the top of the mountain and was now descending the southern slope into the Sandy Stream region. Here was where he stopped and looked for a sheltered place to spend the night, which was falling early and fast.

A few minutes previously, he had caught and killed a partridge, which had bounced up out of the snow almost under his snowshoes. With this in his hand, he turned into a thicket of spruce where there was shelter from the wind. He trod down the snow and started the fire with such dead, dry limbs as he could break or cut with his hunting knife from the trees. It was not much of a fire. Dry wood was not easy to get, and he was too tired to tramp much after it. He skinned the breast of the partridge and, breaking it from the body, tried to roast it. It was burned, smoked and half raw. Moreover, it was unsalted and rank of spruce buds. However, he got some nourishment from it.

Nursing his fire, he sat over it shivering through the long hours of the night. The snow ceased falling after midnight, the stars showing intermittently. He was too cold and worried to feel drowsy and too cramped to keep still. He straightened up now and then and stamped his feet to get the kinks out of his legs and beat his hands and arms to keep up the circulation.

When day dawned, he had his position quite well settled in his mind and knew in what direction to travel. About ten inches of light, dry snow had fallen, creating the very hardest snowshoeing. Seven miles, at least, lay between him and the south end of the mountain. His snowshoes went down to the old snow at each step and came up loaded, a condition to try any man's endurance. Add to it hunger and sleeplessness, and it takes courage to go on.

A bitter wind had arisen, showering him with snow from the evergreen trees. He trudged doggedly on, knowing his life depended on his keeping in motion, though he was ready to drop with weariness. In the afternoon, he heard the welcome sound of an axe and directly came upon some men loading logs. At last, he felt that he could safely sit down and rest. An hour later he opened the door of Robar Camp.

Never had any place looked so comfortable, so inviting, as those rough benches and the long board table with its frayed oilcloth covering. Even the scent of the fir boughs in the tiers of sleeping bunks drew him, for there was the smell of simmering meat in the great kettles on the stove and newly baked gingerbread and mince pies in the air. Robar sat by the table smoking. It was good to see him, old-timer that he was, looking like a bandit with his bowlegs, his fierce black mustache and his little sharp eyes.

He took his pipe from his mouth and stared at Ed. "Heavens, man! What ails ye? Are ye sick?"

"No," said Ed, "but I am hungrier than a bear. Get me something to eat before I die in your hands."

"Yer look it," said Robar, hustling wood into the stove while Ed removed his mackinaw and wet stockings and moccasins.

In a very short time, a steaming basin of hot broth and meat, along with a plate of bread, was on the table.

"There, set to," said Robar, "while I brew ye some tea."

As he ate, Ed told him of his experience of the last twenty-four hours. "

Well, yer mighty lucky ye didn't fall asleep and freeze to death."

"I knew better than to even shut my eyes," Ed replied. Fortunately a team traveling light came along, and Ed rode to his own camp.

Robar, an odd character, haunted the Wisattaquoik region with its lonely mountains and valleys, and fished in its lakes and followed its trails for many years. Nobody knew his nationality. Probably it was German. His chief business was hunting bears, but he also trapped all sorts of fur-bearing animals. He picked a spruce gum for market and often took strings of glistening speckled trout to the towns to sell.

At the head of the valley where the mountains are tumbled without order, yet not without symmetry, he had his snug log hut. He sometimes tended camp for those lumbermen who returned for successive years to the same locality and, consequently, stores of provisions left in camp through the summer months destined for winter use. He cooked for two years at a camp built by the Rogers outfit for the accommodation of toters and other men traveling to and from their camps. This camp was about half way up the Wisattaquoik Valley and was known as the Robar Camp.

There was one winter that has always been remembered as the winter of the deep snow. It as a very anxious, heartbreaking season, not only for those who battled with storms and endured the consequent loss, but also for us who bided at home and watched with apprehension and suspense.

It began in January with a heavy fall of snow; then one storm after another kept the roads in the worst condition. The toters steadily persued their jobs, for the men and horses must be fed; but their progress over the route was slow owing to the loose footing and the necessity of frequently shoveling through drifts. The horses slipped off the narrow tracks, and often the sled with its load slued off the road and time was consumed shoveling and skidding it back onto the track.

They also had frequently to leave a part of their load at the way camps to relieve the tired horses over the worst part of the trail. So it happened that at no time during the first two months of the year were there any provisions, hay or grain in the store at the camps for an emergency. This was true not only in the Wissattaquoik camps, but also in all camps far from settlements.

Whenever I went in the town, I heard it talked by the businessmen, and I knew just how anxious the bosses were at the camps. Still, everybody hoped that each storm was the last, and we all rejoiced when the sun came out from behind the clouds, thinking the trouble was over. No more than the usual amount of winter snow had already come.

To our consternation, then, the fifteenth of February it began again, and for thirty hours it never ceased its steady downfall. There was an addition of four more feet of snow when it stopped, and twelve feet on a level in the woods. In the camps were ninety men, and they had been working thirty horses. When the last storm got well under way, they stopped work and went onto short rations. No team ventured over the road. Ed told me that he secretly took a small amount of flour from the cook's barrel and hid it in his own camp so his wife and three-years-old child might have something to eat in case the food was entirely exhausted.

There were two or three pairs of snowshoes in camp; and, the last day of the storm, three men snowshoed to City Camps, where a part of a load had been thrown off, and brought back what they could carry of flour. That gave the men some bread, which was certainly the staff of life since they had little else.

When at last the storm ceased, the horses had been without food twenty-four hours. The Boss immediately organized their own relief party. Before daylight, they sent three men on snowshoes down the trail to Robar Camp with instructions to him to prepare food for the noon meal; they were to assist him as much as possible. Some job to feed ninety men and one woman and child, especially when they have been on short rations for three days. Nevertheless, Robar was equal to the occasion, as they all knew he would be. I have never heard it said that a man complained during those days, and only the teamsters knew how the horses begged and coaxed for their grain and hay.

There were shovels enough in both camps to man about half of the working crew. They were given to the men with directions to shovel one track, keeping to the tote road as much as possible. They shoveled as they walked. That is, the headman threw out a shovel full of snow, then stepped ahead and took up another. The man behind him did the same thing and so on down the line.

The last man finished the track. The remainder walked in single file behind the shovelers. When the latter were tired, they stepped aside and the others passed him taking their shovels. Behind the men came the horses single file, and bringing up the rear was a narrow handmade sled with a horse attached, and on it a chair made of a barrel. It was lashed to stakes. In it rode Ed's wife and the child well wrapped in blankets. Ed and one man walked with them to make sure the sled kept right side up.

It was rather past noon when they reached Robar Camp. They found a good, hot meal awaiting them. Though they had to sit around in any unoccupied spot, even out of doors, and perhaps use a spoon rather than a knife of fork, and drink from a basin because there was a lack of dippers, they didn't grumble.

There were ninety men to feed, but the stove was covered with great pots of boiled meat and baked beans. Gallon coffee pots of hot tea waited to be poured, and the long table was heaped with biscuits and gingerbread and mince pies. Robar and his helpers filled their dishes from the kettles. They helped themselves otherwise. The long benches which flanked the table were full. Some perched on the long row of bunks filled with spruce boughs and woolen spreads. The horses also got hay and grain.

The sun shone from a clear sky on the dazzling white snow, and before noon, several men became snow blind. Others dropped out for the same reason later in the day. These were all mounted on horses and carried to the East Branch. It was late at night when the long procession crossed the Penobscot and wound up the hill to the old East Branch House and its stables (headquarters of Ayer and Rogers operations.)

Mr. Rogers did not get home until noon the next day. They left the horses at the East Branch except two or three span. Many of the men came to town for a brief visit, for men and horses all went back to camp and finished the winter's work as soon as the roads were in condition to haul supplies over them.

Robar had a gift for story telling, and he always illustrated his stories by pantomime. The men delighted to lead him on to relate one of his many adventures hunting bears. The story was a monologue, but Robar assumed the role of the bear with as much ease as he did his own—even when the tale held a joke on himself.

He related how a toter was driving up the valley one day with a four-horse load. This meant that the long, heavy wagon, drawn by four horses, was filled with all sorts of goods to the height of at least three feet above the axles-often more, if the load happened to be light as, for instance, baled hay. The whole was solidly tied on with ropes, crossing and recrossing the load, and securely knotted. The toter had with him one of the men working at the camp.

From some side trail, they picked up Robar and invited him to ride. There was no unoccupied seat. The only place available was the top of the load. On account of the exceeding roughness of the road, the top would be a precarious position were it not for the ropes to which he could cling. But Robar was used to rides of that sort; he didn't for a minute hesitate, but clambered up and seated himself.

The men adroitly led the conversation around to bears, and soon Robar was relating with great gusto his latest bear hunt. In his own intense interest in the tale, he forgot where he was and got up on his hands and feet to show his hearers how bruin made his last charge. Just at that moment, a forward wheel dropped into a hole. The men had a vision of Robar shooting through the air with arms and legs outspread like a gigantic frog and disappearing head first into a clump of bushes. The teamster said later, "I couldn't have helped laughing if he had broken his neck." But his neck was intact as he crawled out rather shamefacedly and again mounted the load.

He was rather brigandish in appearance, and strangers traveling the road alone didn't enjoy meeting him. A messenger was sent from a distant city with a package of money amounting to several thousand dollars to be used in paying the men. Checks were not much in favor with operators. The men were to be paid off at City Camps, and the money had to be carried there by a messenger or by some member of the firm.

The man selected for the job at this particular time had very little knowledge of the woods and was not at all familiar with the class of men one meets up with in the lumbering camps and on the trails. He had read about them and gained the impression therefrom that, as a rule, they were wild, lawless, and often violent and vicious. Consequently, the care of the money entrusted to his keeping weighed much on his mind. He carried it in a small handbag along with his few personal effects, and he never let it out of his sight.

From the time he descended from the train at the station, through all the lonely ride to the East Branch where he was to stop overnight, his apprehensions increased. When he arrived, he was prepared to be suspicious of everyone he saw. The landlord, and even the men who worked about the house, looked to him as if they were part of a gang planning to rob him. Shown to his room, he hid the package in the bed; when sleep finally came to him, it was broken and disturbed. He was calmer in the morning, and his courage came back to him.

He had taken this job, and he intended to go through with it, if possible. A walk of sixteen miles was before him in order to reach City Camps, and he inquired if a guide could be obtained. "Oh certainly," was the reply. "There's a man here who is going to City Camps today. He can take you right there."

After breakfast, the messenger stood on the steps facing the river with his grip containing the package of money in his hand. He was waiting for his guide and to be ferried across the river. Around the corner of the house came the landlord and with him a man at the sight of whom his heart turned over. All his fears of being robbed, perhaps murdered, in this wild, God-forsaken country, were strengthened; and here, no doubt, was the man to do it.

He was of medium height, but stocky, powerfully built. His arms were long and muscular. He was very bowlegged which gave him, as he walked, a roll like a sailor on shore leave. His face was broad and weather beaten with small black eyes, a fierce-looking black mustache and powerful jaws. He wore an old slouch hat, a gray flannel shirt, trousers tucked inside coarse woolen stockings, and heavy shoes. But the most fearsome feature of his dress, which after all was that of an ordinary woodsman, was like the contents of the belt buckled about his waist. It consisted of a business-like revolver and a long row of deadly looking cartridges, a long hunter's knife in a sheath and a small axe, or hunter's hatchet. What was a defenseless man to do if attacked by a person so armed?

"This is Mr. Robar," said the landlord. "He will take you safely to City Camps, and you had better let him carry the grip. It's a long, hard jaunt for you. He is used to carrying packs."

"Yes, indeed. I can take it just as well as not," added Robar.

"Oh, no. I can carry it well enough," hastily replied the messenger. He decided he would take particular care not to walk in front of that man. He would not give him that advantage any way, so as they climbed the bank by the river, he fell in behind.

There seemed nothing premeditated about it; still, he couldn't help fear that the man was watching for his opportunity, and whenever it occurred, he expected a command to stand and deliver or a bullet in the head. As they tramped along the lonely road, Robar enlivened the way with stories of the woods, of his own hunting exploits, enlarging on his skill with a gun, his narrow escapes from enraged bears and other dangers. He was a good storyteller, and a great mimic, and would have been entertaining but for the money he offered again to carry but was again assured that "the grip was not at all heavy."

After several hours of this strained apprehension, the messenger's nerves were in a frazzled condition. They were still some five miles from City Camps and going through a stretch of fir growth so thick that it nearly shut out the sun. Robar had told him of frequently seeing deer in the road as he traveled it. A thought occurred to him.

"Do you think I could shoot a deer with your revolver if I should see one in the road ahead?" he asked a trifle faintly. "I have practiced shooting but never hunted."

"Perhaps you could," said Robar. "There! Take it, but look out. Don't shoot yourself. I'll walk along beside you. Probably I can see one quicker than you can. It takes practice to see a deer in the woods."

His mind was relieved. There was still the knife to reckon with, but he felt that at least he stood an even chance if matters came to a crisis.

The remainder of the way, the two walked quietly and peacefully. There were no deer in sight. There was no holdup or murder. When they stepped out of the forest into the fields about City Camps, the messenger found a rather foolish feeling creeping over him.

Still obsessed with the idea that his guide was a desperado whose courage had perhaps failed him, he unburdened himself of his apprehensions during the long talk with the operator over their cigars in the office that evening.

Somewhat to his amazement, the gentleman leaned back in his chair and gave vent to a hearty laugh.

"Wouldn't Robar chuckle if he knew that! There's nothing he enjoys more than to make somebody believe he's a desperate character. Oh no, he wouldn't hurt anyone, and there has never been a highway robbery in this valley."

What the operator said was true. Robar loved to pass as an unsafe man, especially if he was dealing with a group of strangers. He was generally able to scare Frenchmen, but he sometimes missed the mark when confronted with certain types.

There came into camp one day for dinner a man from Prince Edwards Island who was going to Rogers Camps to work. Robar put his dinner on the table and then proceeded to have what he called "a spell" to which he claimed he was subject. He got out his long hunting knife and a whetstone and began vigorously to sharpen the already keen blade, casting in the meantime black, scowling glances at the guest, who seemed to pay not the least attention, but went calmly on with his eating.

Robar tested the edge of the blade frequently as he ground it and at last was apparently satisfied with it. He got to his feet and began tramping around the camp flourishing the knife, gritting his teeth, scowling with eyes snapping. The man, having finished his dinner, rose and faced Robar.

"See here!" he said, "Cut out that funny stuff, or I will knock your damned head off."

Robar took a good look at the man and concluded he might try it. As he had never intended to press matters that far, he at once began to apologize, saying, "Don't mind me, Stranger. I wouldn't hurt anybody for the world. I have these spells that come on sometimes. I don't mean anything."

The man threw down the match with which he had just lighted his pipe and remarked as he shut the door behind him, "You had better not when I am around."

Robar's occasional visits to town generally resulted in a spree of several days' duration if the whiskey was to be had. When he could no longer pay for a bottle, he sobered up and took his way back to his shack.

One day, his road lay through a neighborhood in the country not far from the village. He came to the schoolhouse just after it was opened for the day's session. Some of the scholars had already arrived. He took it into his somewhat befuddled head to have a "a spell" and terrorize the school. The children fled to a house nearby when they saw him coming.

From that safe distance, they could see him in the doors or at the windows, flourishing his knife and gritting his teeth and looking ready to slaughter the first one on whom he could lay his hands. The men folk were all away in the fields at their work, and nobody dared go near him. The teacher, who had joined the scholars, counseled getting out of sight and waiting until he went off. The mistress of the house next door, however, had an idea.

She fetched the chairman of the school committee who lived in the village. Describing the situation, she asked what they should do about it. His reply: "Tell all the people to stay where they are. I'll be there very soon." He was well acquainted with Robar, and he went right after him. "Robar, what are you doing here?"

"Oh, Mister Howe, I wasn't doing any harm. I was just having a little fun. I wouldn't hurt the women and children."

"Well, you get out of this as quick as you can go. You know you have no business doing a thing like this."

Robar hung his head and walked off as fast as his bowlegs could carry him.

While tending camp one summer, Robar discovered that a bear was haunting the place, presumably looking for something he could eat, and he decided to set a trap. He got, from somewhere, an old, muzzle-loading gun—a small cannon, in fact. He loaded it, besides the charge of powder, with any iron thing he could find lying about that would go into it until it was quite full. He then set it in a frame on a stump, pointing it directly at a chunk of pork which he put where he supposed the bear would come into the camp yard. A string was attached to the trigger, also to the pork. A bear is very fond of salt pork. He will break in the head of an unopened barrel with one blow of his powerful paw and, after eating what he wants, will often muss up and destroy the remainder.

When Robar had his traps set to his satisfaction, it occurred to him that it would be a fine idea to test it, thus making sure it would be effective. So he began to play that he was the bear. He got down on his hands and feet and crept up to the chunk of pork. He didn't intend to touch the chunk of pork with anything but a stick, but somehow his foot slipped and he pitched headfirst straight at it. There was an explosion that shook him from head to foot. For a minute, the air around and over him was full of flying nails, bolts, nuts and other deadly missiles, and thick with smoke.

"Now I'm dead," said he with his eyes closed and waited for whatever should transpire next.

For two minutes, there was profound silence. Nothing happened. Robar opened his eyes. Everything looked as usual, no change in the world. He felt of himself and seemed still to be in the body. Then he asked himself, "Why don't I have a pain somewhere?"

He got to his feet and looked around. There was the gun lying on the ground. The pork covered with small pieces and so was quite an area of the yard. He finally went all over himself. Not a scratch or a bruise could he find. Only one thing about his person was damaged: He had lost the entire crown of his hat!

In one of Robar's hunting expeditions, he got possession of a bear cub, which he kept until it was nearly grown. It was always hitched at the end of a long chain and, as it developed in size, it became rather sulky and fractious. It was not quite out of control, however. Robar arranged for a den for its winter sleep in a small shop at the East Branch farm, and it remained there during the following summer. A pole was erected, also a small platform at the top where it spent much time beyond the reach of humans. A hogshead turned down on its side served for sleeping quarters. The chain with which the bear was hitched was long and afforded plenty of room for exercise.

One morning, Robar strolled across the yard to interview the bear. Robar was not in a pleasant mood, having just returned from town the previous night after a spree covering several days. He walked up to the bear and commanded it to go up the pole. It didn't go. Again and again he told it to go up the pole. No use. The bear sat sullenly on his haunches, watching Robar with a wicked sparkle in his eyes.

At last, in a rage, Robar picked up a club and started for the bear who made a dive into the hogshead. Robar promptly went in after him. His feet only protruded. But out of the great barrel poured the noise of a terrific struggle, intermingled with growls and strings of oaths.

The lunging of the combatants started the hogshead rolling down across the yard where several men were watching the proceedings. When it had rolled the length of the chain, it slued around; both Robar and the bear were thrown out, breaking their hold on each other. Robar's face and hands were covered with scratches and blood, and his clothes were in tatters, but scrambling to his feet, he advanced toward the bear with an oath.

"Go up that pole," he roared. The bear fled up the pole to the platform where it sat nursing its bruises until Robar moved on.

The boss for whom Robar had worked for several years persuaded him to bank the larger part of his wages until he had acquired a tidy sum. Instead, he invested it in a worthless enterprise that required his residence in the town. He did not last long. There was too much temptation for him. He became sick, and after lingering for some months, he passed on penniless and friendless. What odd characters in the Valley of the Wissattaquoik, most of them gone on to their final reward or condemnation—no, not condemnation—because they were mostly like children without real evil in their souls.

Ed was for awhile stopping at the Lunksoos House on the East Branch of the Penobscot where the firm had opened a camp for sportsmen. Among those who came for game during the season was a man named Craig who was hunting alone. He appeared to be familiar with firearms and the woods, but the most experienced men sometimes get careless.

One morning, he came in with his left arm broken near the shoulder by a bullet from his own gun. A physician was summoned from Sherman who etherized him and dressed the wound. Craig had already decided to go to a hospital and remain until he was partially recovered, and the most feasible route to the railroad was by canoe to Grindstone.

Ed made preparations to start as soon as the man was in condition to ride the twelve miles to that point. He engaged Wesley Butterfield for the Bowman. Wesley was a guide, a good canoe man, and efficient in any ordinary capacity. To carry a helpless man around the Whetstone River was a job for four men, but they would have to get along with two, as the canoe could safely carry no more besides the patient and his blankets and baggage.

The Doctor told them that Craig was suffering from the shock of the wound and the dressing. He was also quite sick from the effects of the anesthetic but was not so seriously ill as not to be able to make the trip, and he advised his getting to the hospital as soon as possible.

It was late in the afternoon when he was transferred by stretcher to the canoe where a comfortable bed of blankets was prepared for him. It was their purpose to reach Grindstone in season to take an early train in the morning. The fall rains had not yet begun and the water was still quite low. In order to steer the canoe among the rocks in the many rapids, they fastened a carbide light to the bow, where Wes stood with his long slender pole, Ed taking the stern.

Those who have never watched two men pole a canoe still have an interesting experience coming to them. When the water is so low that the canoe must be poled, one assures himself that, if he does upset, he will not drown. Perhaps not, though the current is still strong in a river of that size and there are many deep little pools where one would get wet.

Sitting helplessly as a passenger on the bottom of the canoe, you may watch the Bowman (the stern man being behind you) standing erect, swaying with the motion of the frail craft, poking its nose this way and that as he pushes, with first one end of the pole against a rock, and then the other end on the opposite side. It is apparently so easily done, with such quiet, deliberate poise one hardly realizes the constant, vigilant, tense muscle and swift action attending it.

When they reached the upper pitch of the Whetstone, it was already dark in the thick forest through which the river runs at that point; nevertheless, they decided to run the canoe through rather than carry around on the shore. The carbide light was a poor substitute for daylight, but it was some help. Craig was still too drowsy from the anesthetic to be really conscious of his surroundings, for which they were very thankful.

The Whetstone, at low water, is a wicked looking place. One can hardly conceive of getting any boat through it whole, let alone a canvas canoe. The bed of the river narrows at the upper pitch, and the channel, though rough and clear of rocks, is practically a falls and narrow. The bed of the river widens below the pitch into a small basin half full of boulders, around which this channel swings toward the lower pitch. The shore around the basin is not much above the level of the river but rises over a bluff around the lower pitch. The latter consists of a series of ledges over which the canoe has to be cautiously dropped from ledge to ledge by the poles.

Both men were familiar with it at all stages of water, but neither had ever run through it at night. The zigzag boulder-strewn chasm ahead looked dubious in the light of the lamp; neither was there any attraction about the carry through the rough dark woods. They reasoned that if they could safely run the channel, the wounded man would be in much better condition than if he were carried around the falls. They braced themselves mentally and physically and started. In the few minutes necessary to reach the foot of the pitch, they worked with taut muscles and bated breath, yet deliberately with quick movements avoiding each rock and keeping the bow straight until at last they plunged into the level water of the basin.

"I think we had better carry around the lower pitch," said Ed.

"All right," replied Wes, relieved, although he kept his feelings to himself. "We had better take Craig first and come back for the canoe."

Beaching the canoe, they lifted him onto the stretcher they had brought and started up the carry trail. It led over a bluff, which was fifty feet above the river. Two may carry a loaded stretcher for a short distance provided the path is smooth. To carry it under the conditions they encountered was another matter. The path is used but little, except in the driving season, and is often choked with fallen trees and brush. They found all these obstacles, and their way grew more difficult each moment.

At last, they ran into a tangle of fallen trees and brush. They laid down the stretcher and considered getting down the bank to the water. They were nearly at the top of the bluff, but the bank, though steep and rocky, was free from trees and underbrush.

"Do you suppose we can get down over this bank?" asked Ed.

Wes, after a moment's hesitation, replied, "I think so if we take time enough."

"We will try it," said Ed.

Slowly, cautiously, by the aid of the lantern, they picked their way among the rocks and brush, stopping to rest whenever there was a chance to lay down the stretcher. Craig complained fretfully, but they reassured him as best they could. It was a grueling task, and the perspiration ran from every pore. It was accomplished at last, and they laid the stretcher down beside the water and went back for the canoe. Before they had him comfortably settled in the canoe again, the light went out. It utterly refused to burn any more. There was nothing to do but make the rest of the journey in the dark. Undaunted, they pushed out toward the ledges of the lower pitch and began the second lap. It was much like the first except they were obliged to go more by a sense of feeling and their memory of each rock and turn.

It was no light task to hold the canoe against the force of the current and keep it straight while they carefully dropped it down from ledge to ledge. There were moments when it seemed that nothing could save them from being turned over or smashed on a rock, in spite of their efforts; but each time, by a quick thrust, they slipped past the danger. At last they were through and could draw a full breath while they sat down to paddle along a quiet stretch of dead water. There were Rogers Rock, Bear Rips and Dead Man's Point ahead— all rough water—but it seemed smooth sailing compared to the experiences of the last hour. These places were safely negotiated, and from Dead Man's Point to Crowfoot was easy. At Deer Island, they found a sportsman who loaned them a lantern. The remainder of the trip was made without incident. They were able to get Craig aboard the early train as he had planned.

The two younger boys [Luther and David] and I spent a vacation in Russell Camp among the mountains on the North Branch of the Wisattaquoik. Our headquarters was a little office, but we ate in the big cook room whatever the cook gave the men. It always tasted good, for we spent nearly all our time out of doors and were always hungry when we were called to eat. The boys chummed with the teamsters, who like to have children come to visit, and rode the loads to the landings and the empty sleds to the yards. We all had snowshoes and enjoyed hiking about in the woods. We often walked to some small ponds along the logging road to fish through the holes in the ice. We were successful, too. Fish are plentiful in that region.

One bright spring day in March, Ruth and I packed ourselves and some baggage into Mr. Rogers' pung and started out for a two weeks' stay at Pogy Camp. Ed and his family had come out to town for a much needed change and rest before he had to return for the drive. Mr. Rogers was going to Camp to boss the small crew remaining while they finished up the hauling. The sun was riding high in the heavens and the snow settling. The woods roads were still in prime condition, and it was hoped they would remain so until the work at camp was done.

Since we could occupy the cottage vacated by Ed's family, Ruth, just three years old, and I were delighted to go and keep house for Mr. Rogers. We had plenty of robes; there was a crisp, exhilarating feel to the air; all the firs and hemlocks sparkled, reflecting back the sunlight; and the mountains shone clear and blue in the transparent air. We drove one horse, Prince, to whom it was a delight to spin along over the road. There was no traffic to bother. We had the whole thirty miles to ourselves, excepting the squirrels and the winter birds. We spent the night at the East Branch and the second night settled in our camp.

The weather was perfect for a week. We lived, cooked and ate in our snug cot of two rooms, though we used supplies from the larger cook camp near, varying our fare sometimes with a plate of beans baked in the ground which the cook kindly gave us. I had some cooked food from home, so the work was light. Ruth and I spent much time riding with Mr. Rogers over the smooth, hard roads to the landings, the yards and the runway where during the winter logs had been sluiced from the top of the mountain to the road at its base.

We walked out to nearby shallow ponds and fished in what teamsters called water holes, cut by them to get water for their horses. We always got trout, though they were small.

At the end of the week, the weather turned much warmer. It no longer froze at night, and the sun beat down from a clear sky during the day. How that snow melted. Water ran everywhere. Pogy Brook, which flowed down into the Wisattaquoik Valley, began to rise. Fortunately, the camps were above the high water mark. The snow became so soft in the middle of the day that the teams were taken off for a few hours and were worked nights instead. All work was rushed to get done before the snow disappeared entirely.

From that time, the perfect silence of the night was broken now and then by the tinkle of bells, the clanking of chains and creaking logs as the loaded teams passed the camps on their slow way to the landings. Overhead, the stars flashed and sparkled in the clear atmosphere as the constellations swung across the heavens until they faded in the brilliant light of the moon coming over the mountains.

The melting of the snow was not the only trouble feared. It was also melting on the bare, rocky mountaintops and soaking down through the snow, letting loose little streams of water, which would directly overflow the flats. Before the second week was gone, the water was flowing over the little bridge, which had been weighted by two logs. The larger bridge below was in danger of floating off, and the road to the landings was filled to the top of its banks. No span of horses could take a load of logs over it. However, very few logs were left on the yards, and those must be abandoned. They now began to break camp and pack the stuff.

That night, the thermometer dropped down toward zero, and before morning, a sheet of ice formed over everything. Soon, all the stuff was packed on the tote sleds and the men were off, except Bill Fleming who was to help get Ruth and me to the valley. The road was still two feet under water, but the teams who preceded us had broken the ice that still floated there. Mr. Rogers walked on one bank and drove the horses, while Bill walked the other bank with the task of keeping the pung right side up.

The water had worn out the snow, and the bottom was rocks, mud and skids. Prince pluckily plunged along, stopping after each two or three leaps to get his breath. It was, fortunately, not a long stretch, and we were all relieved when we rode out of it onto the bridge—none more so than poor, frightened little Ruth.

The road for the remainder of the way to the East Branch, though more or less bare and rough, was nowhere very hard for a horse used to woods traveling. At a place called Rapi-de-fan, where the young spruce trees formed a close shaded avenue, the road was covered with water and broken ice. My husband then reined Prince to one side of the track to avoid wading it. A long log lay lengthwise of the road, and the horse stepped upon that log, walking it to the end, dragging the pung half sideways after him. At the end, he stepped down again with perfect unconcern as if "it was all in the day's work." We both laughed. We were used to Prince's little tricks to save himself.

We stayed that night at the East Branch, and next morning we began the last lap of our journey. It was clear and cold with a brisk wind blowing. For seven miles, our way lay through forest and the remainder through farmlands. There was still a fairly thick blanket of snow, in some places slushy with water.

Pete Sargery drove a span of horses and sled ahead of us, but we kept near each other in case either needed help. A mile out brought us to Dry Brook, usually containing so little water a bridge was never needed. Now it was full, being a drain for the accumulated floods from the high lands during the thaw.

Before we reached the brook, Mr. Rogers said, "You had better pull up your feet; the water may be coming into the pung."

I took Ruth in my arms and put my feet on the sideboard, which was low, but I had failed to grasp the situation and was totally unprepared for what followed. The stream was eight feet wide with the walls of the channel made by the water through the snow as straight up and down as the wall of a house.

When Prince stepped into the water, the pung followed until the front struck the bottom and I shot out into the stream my full length, on the upper side of the pung. My head did not go under, but for a moment Ruth's did, and I thrust her up out of it. At the same instant, her father grasped my shoulder with his free hand, and the horse dragged us all out onto the bank. Ruth was screaming with cold and fright, and we were both very wet although my fur coat had protected my body.

We were in and out so quickly, I hardly realized what had happened. I stripped off Ruth's outside wraps and, opening my fur coat, I buttoned her inside next to my body. My feet were in the worst condition. It was impossible to change stockings in the cold wind. We could only tuck the robes more carefully about them. I then stood up while Mr. Rogers took off his own long, thick fur coat and buttoned it around both Ruth and myself. Soon we were warm, though still wet and uncomfortable. Out of the woods on the country roads, we found the snow nearly gone. We had to pick our way beside the roads or across fields to find snow enough on which to haul our pung, and we were certainly glad when we drove up to our own door. For two months, Ruth cried with fright at the sight of a puddle.

The youngest children and I spent several days at the East Branch one autumn. We were always delighted with such an opportunity. The colors of the forest on the mountainside were a marvel, as if all the hot sunshine of the summer was concentrated and poured out in one last effort to fill the world with glory. Each sunrise and sunset was a magnificent spectacle—a combination of mountain grandeur and radiant, shifting colors. I beheld a picturesque scene in the early morning.

I was on the piazza when the four tote teams wound down the hill to the ferry. The old tote team was built to meet the needs of the business, the roads through the forests, (which were of the most primitive kind) and the economy of horseflesh (the only motor power.) Four horses to each team, weighing from fourteen to sixteen hundred each, was the rule. The wheels were built with the idea of combining the least weight with the greatest amount of strength. The body was buckboard style of double planks reinforced at the edges and set securely on the frame beneath which held the two sets of wheels together. There were no springs to the body; but when a seat was used, it had a wagon spring at each end.

These wagons weighed twenty-five hundred pounds. The height of the load depended on whether it was a lightweight substance like pressed hay, or barrels of flour. In the present instance, each load was hay snugly packed from front to end, five feet high from the boards and securely lashed on with ropes. This was also a trick of the trade which only teamsters knew. I always wondered why the loads didn't go bottom-up in some places on the mountains or the wheels drop into a hole from which they could never be extricated. I concluded long ago that the teamsters' business was a trade in itself.

Pete Sargery was ahead. I could hear him say, "Easy Rit! Mah Zole, what you trying to do!"

Then came Wes Crommett, Henry Blake and a man whose name I do not remember. Pete drove on to the ferry, half hidden in the mist rising from the river. The man who ran the ferry cast off the chains and began sculling them across.

Before the last team was over, the fog was gone and I could see the horses climbing the opposite bank and disappearing in the woods. I glanced up over the mountain. The sun was just rising, tearing the clouds apart, and the bare flanks of Katahdin were showing pearly pink in the first rays.

We were all much amused that night listening to Johnny Amboise telling the story of how he made the train that afternoon: Dr. S. proposed spending his annual vacation hunting on the East Branch of the Penobscot. He descended from the train at Stacyville, in due time was transported to Bowlin Camps by our team and, after quite a successful sojourn, was leaving for home.

Dr. S. was in a violent temper, however, when he landed with his bags of game from a bateau at our wharf. He demanded of Ed, who was in charge, why. In response to his message of the previous day, he had not sent boat and team to get him to the station in time for the afternoon train.

"Why," said Ed in surprise, "the man said it was tomorrow you were going."

"It was not tomorrow. It was today," was the instant reply. "I waited until the time when you should have been there was past, then had to hunt around for a man and a boat to bring me."

"Well," said Ed, "I'm very sorry, but I was not to blame."

"I want to take that train this afternoon," said the irate doctor.

"I don't see how you can," said Ed. "There isn't time. We have to allow three hours over those roads. There is not much over two hours till train time."

"You will get me there, or I will not pay you a dollar. It was the agreement when you brought me in to camp that you would carry me out, and I want to go today."

What he said was true, and his bill was of goodly size. Ed could not afford to lose it. He said slowly, "I will see what can be done."

He hunted up Johnny, the teamster. Johnny Amboise was an Arcadian Frenchman—a jack of all trades, but just now the teamster. He had learned his English on the New Brunswick side of the St. John River. He flung the letter "h" about with perfect abandon and sadly mixed his genders; nevertheless, he is a born philosopher and idealist, and cause and effect are closely related in his mind.

He delights in giving the youngsters wise advice in his quaint, broken phrases, and his descriptions are something to remember.

"Johnny," said Ed, "Dr. S. says he won't pay me a dollar on his bill unless we get him to the station in time for the afternoon train. Do you suppose you can do it?"

Johnny looked at his watch and considered. "Maybe I no make dat train. Perhaps I do. Me, I'll try, by Gee Willie Boy. See what I can do."

"All right," said Ed. "The horses are fresh, the load is light. Hustle them, and remember there's no time for careful driving."

In an incredibly short time, the horses and big buckboard were ready. A nice fat deer was carefully tied on behind the seats along with the doctor's bags.

He should have worn a more complacent expression on his face, one would think, as he took his seat on the folded blanket that served as a cushion on the wide middle seat. Johnny cast a critical eye over the outfit to make sure all was secure, then settled himself in the front seat, picked up the reins, swung his long-lashed whip curling with a whistling sound out over the horses' backs, and they were off down the hill at a rattling pace.

A whip was really unnecessary with the team; Johnny rarely struck them. There was only a message in that whistle and snap of the lash. Judy never needed urging, but Punch (Paunch, Johnny always called him) was perfectly willing Judy should do some of his share of the work; hence the whip. If he knew it was along, it helped matters.

For a mile, the road wound along the bank of the river. It was of rock foundation, rather thinly covered with the wash of the mountain. It was a mixture of mud, roots of nearby trees, rocks and poles to ease the loads over the holes, but it was level, and there being so few stretches where time could be made, Johnny drove them at a trot. Out of the corners of his eyes he saw the doctor holding on with both hands, sliding and bouncing from side to side.

At last he protested, "Johnny, drive more carefully. I'll be thrown out."

The only reply was, "Hey, she say make dat train for a possible. Git up, Paunch," and again, the lash whistled in the air, and the span sprang into their collars. The flat crossed, they began to ascend the mountain. Numerous spring freslets had swept this road clean of everything but bare roots, and stones from the size of a walnut to a half-barrel. It was gullied until a buckboard pitched down on one side and up the other like a boat in a gale until one not accustomed to this mode of transportation expected momentarily to see it all go bottomside up into the woods. It was too steep for trotting, but Johnny was not doing any careful driving. The horses were making the top too fast for that.

At last, the sadly shaken passenger cried, "Don't drive so fast, Johnny, I can't stand it."

The driver, without slacking rein, flung back over his shoulder, "Hed she say now no make dat train, Johnny, dat sport she say she not pay me one dollar. Get up Paunch!"

Reaching the top, the doctor congratulated himself that now there would be soft earth on which to ride. Alas! It was just here Johnny elected to make time, and the whirling whip again sent the team at its best pace. After two hours of bouncing over rocks, skid, into holes, through mud and all the other inequalities incident to a road where only the trees have been removed, the doctor, exasperated beyond endurance, shouted "Johnny! Johnny! Stop! I don't want to get that train. I don't care whether I get there today or not." Evidently his body was mellowed, if not his spirit.

Johnny, in his grimmest manner, delivered his ultimatum. "I make dat train for a possible, me!"

The doctor settled back in despair, and the remainder of the ride devoted himself to staying on the seat as much of the time as the erratic motions of the buckboard permitted; the remainder, he hung in the air.

When, at last, the steaming, lathered horses swept up to the station

Johnny, describing the ride to Ed that night, said, "She go in dat station and write on a leetle piece of paper, and she give hit to me and she say, "Give dat to Hed; but me, by Gee Willie, boy, I notice dat sport she don't sit down mooch!"

The work on Wisattaquoik was finished, though Ed still kept the Lunksoos Camp open to sportsmen, and his family lived there. During the previous winter, he managed a camp for Ross on Sandy Stream.

It was an early spring with no rain and very little snow to melt. May opened with weather hot enough for July, and what little moisture remained in the ground soon dried out. It was one of those times when it is not safe to build a fire outdoors unless one is prepared to set a guard over it with a barrel of water handy. Yet, there are always people who do not realize the danger. The spring is the time of year when the old stumps, brush piles and other clutter is disposed of by fire.

Sometimes, also, tops left from woodcuttings or "fell pieces" are burned then to clear the land. Many of the fires set for these purposes gave no cause for alarm at the time, but the fire smolders in the log or the very dry ground until a stiff breeze fans it into flames ready to do their deadly work.

The Wisattaquoik Valley changed. Nearly all the marketable timber originally growing there was cut, leaving behind a perfect tinderbox of dry tops. A fire sweeping across the country came over the mountains that hem the north side. For a week, the narrow stretch of land was a raging caldron of fire. There was no soil left on the tops of the hills on that side and no living trees left below except in one or two ravines near Robar Camp. Only bare standing trunks were left, like a huddle of sailing ships in a harbor through whose masts the wind eternally shrieks and whistles. Everywhere lay giant boulders with which the ground was strewn in prehistoric times, for this was a glacial region, undoubtedly.

The first fires of this particular time started somewhere in the Trout Brook region. They swept over Traveler and the smaller mountains across the west end of Wisattaquoik, the north end of Katahdin, and the South Branch Valley between Katahdin and Turner. The sky in the west was black with smoke.

It was at this time the fires began around our town. There had been three or four hot, dry days. On a Tuesday, we began to notice slight columns of smoke, every one within two miles and at all the points of the compass. On Wednesday, a strong wind was blowing from the northwest.

Within two hours, all those fires were burning as though bent on annihilating the country. Every man in the town was out fighting them and not altogether successfully; the fires raged over large areas in spite of them. The women stayed at home and packed their household goods and, in some instances, buried their most valuable possessions. At noon, a man from the East Branch brought us a letter from Mattie, Ed's wife, telling us that he had been sent with a crew of men to Hersey Dam on Sandy Stream to protect the camps and dam should the fires endanger them. When the fire crossed the Wisattaquoik Valley, Mattie became alarmed and sent a man to ascertain the situation and find out if he needed help. The man returned saying he could not get through to Hersey Dam because the forest was all ablaze.

I was aware by the tone of her letter that she was fearing the worst. She was afraid he would stay by the dam until they were surrounded and would perish. I feared it also, but there was nothing to be done in the way of rescue. My husband and I were alone there, and every able-bodied man was fighting for his own home. More than that, if the fire was still traveling as fast as it had for a week, they were already surrounded, and nobody could get there till it had died down.

While we watched the progress of the one fire that menaced us, we comforted ourselves with the thought that Ed was resourceful and experienced. He would keep his head, and there was always the pond at the back of the dam which one could not be burned even though the dam was destroyed. To this pond they would certainly flee if necessary.

All day long on Wednesday, the hot wind blew. Cinders filled the air, and the sun was obscured. Men fought the raging demon trenching, backfiring, clearing out bushes, tearing down fences and carrying water. At four o'clock, the wind suddenly shifted into the northeast, which relieved our anxiety for ourselves but only menaced the village from a new direction. The local train went to Sherman Station, a small town seven miles south, at two o'clock as usual. Soon after, a message from that station stated that the town was on fire and all messages ceased. It was greatly feared the local had been cut off by the flames and friends of the crew hung about our station in an agony of suspense.

About five o'clock, the train came whistling in, black with cinders, scorched with fire, and loaded to the steps with people. Not a house remained in the little village of Sherman Station and very little of their household effects. Our village people cared for the refugees as long as they needed shelter. Night fell, and with it a cessation of the wind. The fire died down for the night.

We were left in suspense for four long, hot, windless days in which we all fairly held our breath for fear it would suddenly begin to blow from some quarter. The sky was cloudless, but so thick was the smoke we saw the sun only about four hours in the middle of the day, and then its light was comparatively dim. We could see the stars overhead at noon. Even the air in the cellars was blue.

Sunday afternoon, there was a shower, which relieved the tension. Everybody became normal again and when, on Tuesday, we had a regular rainstorm, the last anxiety died a natural death. Before the storm was fairly over, we knew for certain that Ed was safe at home with all his men, and this is the story he told me:

He had with him one of the crew bosses, Bill Fleming. The other fifteen were axe men. I did not know any of them. There was no fire in the immediate vicinity when they arrived, but it was burning in two lines up the north end of Katahdin, one on the west side, the other from the north. The fires died down at night but breezed up with the wind each morning.

The camp was built on the shore of the small pond made by the dam and was situated at the southeast base of Katahdin. The little valley was surrounded by the foothills, which were not very high. They made their preparations for fighting the fire, got some food cooked, and all hands, except Bill Fleming, went to sleep.

About midnight, Bill woke Ed. The wind was blowing a gale, and the fire was coming down from the mountains through a slash (tops left from old cuttings), a solid wall two miles long, and seemed to reach a half-mile in the air. The wind, probably created by the fire, was blowing straight across the valley, and the fire was traveling as fast as an express train. The men were in a panic and, excepting Bill, were all determined to get out. The tote road was probably still open, but Ed pointed out to them that the fire would be across it before they could get out, and they would be caught in it. They would be much safer to remain and get into the pond if their lives were in danger. They cooled down and decided to stay.

The cinders were falling thick and fast as fires were starting, and everybody got busy wetting down the dam and the four buildings comprising the camps. It was no small job. The water was all dipped from the pond in pails and passed up to the men on the roofs which were low. The air became heated like an oven. The men had to plunge into the pond frequently to cool their own steaming clothes, and the intense heat dried the water almost as fast as they threw it on. The smoke nearly suffocated them but would have been intolerable if the wind had not been blowing so hard. As it was, they had often to lie on the ground for a breathing spell.

Morning broke, and the sun rose on another hot day. The fire began to burn, if possible, more fiercely. The cinders passed over their heads and set the woods on fire beyond them. It crossed the stream below the dam, and soon they were surrounded. During that day, they hardly took time to eat. By the middle of the afternoon, it had reached the edge of the pond; then, what seemed to those men like a miracle happened.

The wind stopped blowing. The fire kept on burning, it is true, but it now traveled very slowly. It was going from them, and there were no cinders from across the pond. They still kept the camps and dam wet and a watch on at night, but they were able to get their regular meals and sleep. It was not until the storm on Tuesday that it was safe either to leave the property or pick their way out through the burned section.

It is plain that a marked characteristic of the men who work in the lumber woods and on the river drives is their sympathy with the troubles of their fellows and their readiness to sacrifice their own comfort and convenience to aid those in difficulty. In the dangerous occupation of lumbering and driving the logs, tragic events are of frequent occurrence, and the men never fail to respond to the call for whatever help they can render.

I have seen men after a hard grueling tramp come from their beds in the morning unable to stand erect, so lame and sore were they in every muscle. Yet they chaffed and teased each other on their ridiculous appearance and, if I ventured a word of sympathy or admiration for what they had accomplished, then someone would likely say, "Oh, it's all in the day's work."

Gradually, life revived in the stricken land. Firs, spruce, cherry, white birch and poplar sent up their sturdy stocks, while over the ground amidst the bracken and hazel bushes grew the most luscious blueberries to be found in any country. The valley is very striking and impressive viewed from Easy Mountain which lies along the East Branch of the Penobscot and closes the valley on the east, except the narrow pass between it and Hunt Mountain where the stream flows out into the East Branch.

From this point, one can see the length of the valley, a distance of twenty miles. It is a scene of mingled beauty and grandeur and desolation. At the western end stands Katahdin, the mountain I have always loved, with its foothill, Turner, on the eastern side, Russell on the north, and stretching still further north are Pogy and Traveler. Over these can be seen the peaks of the Sourdnehunk Mountains, blue and hazy in the hot summer days.

A crew had been idling the spring days away in winter camps on Sourdnehunk, a small but rapid mountain stream north of Katahdin. For two weeks they waited for cold Winter to release his clutch on the icebound water and leave the sun to thaw out the snow and ice that held the big, long timber heaped on its banks.

At last, the time had arrived, and every man was out with his peavey, prying logs apart and rolling them down to the bed of the stream where the water swept them down on its strong current. It was the beginning of their mad rush to the city mills a hundred miles away. All up and down the line of landings there was the grind and rumble of moving logs and the roar of splashing water. The banks were high and steep; when rolled from the sleds in the winter, the logs were dumped over the banks without much order, though landing men straightened them after a fashion. A channel was first picked clear, and then they were rolled into it from the face of the pile.

They worked at each end and above, using great care in handling so that no one was caught below by the unexpected sluing at the sides. All went well for a time, but early the second day, without warning, a log swung out of its course. The men above shouted to those below, but one man was struck and thrown down by the timber. The men carried him into camp.

My husband, "The Boss," being the son of a doctor, had occasionally assisted his father in emergencies of this kind, so he proceeded to set and bandage the leg. Later, the physician found it in good condition and properly set. The situation was dubious. The injured man was fifty miles from his home and twenty miles from any habitation. Moreover, no team could take him over the road. He must be carried on a stretcher on the shoulders of relays of men for twenty miles. The Boss picked his men for the task.

"Steen," he said, "I want you to get Howes to his home."

"All right," returned Steen. "We will have to walk to Trout Brook. No team can get through now."

"Yes, you must make a stretcher of grain sacks. I will send men enough to help you. Get a team at Trout Brook to take him the rest of the way."

It would take four men to carry the stretcher containing Mr. Howes. He was a heavy man weighing nearly two hundred pounds. With the added weight of the necessary blankets with which he was wrapped, it would be a heavy enough burden for four men. Eight in all, stalwart men, were selected, seven besides Steen. They were to relieve each other at stated intervals, four in each group.

As the hours of preparation passed, Mr. Howes began to complain of a severe pain in his head. The Boss reasoned that the excitement, shock and pain of the leg had perhaps caused indigestion, so he said, "I'll give you a dose of Syrup of Figs," which was a mild laxative much in use in that period.

While he was measuring the dark liquid into a spoon, one of his men detailed as carrier came into the camp and asked for lanterns to take with them. "To be sure," said the Boss "Take three or four, and don't forget to take an axe and each man must take a lunch."

It was nearly night when they finally got off. They encountered small streams made by melting snows; hardly a rill in summer, now the water was up to their knees, icy in temperature. At the first change of carriers, they found, to their dismay, that Mr. Howes was unconscious. They could not rouse him, though they tried, and were much alarmed by the unexpected turn of affairs. Then the man who had been in the camp when the Boss gave the dose of Syrup of Figs spoke up.

"The Boss was giving him some medicine when I went in to see about the lanterns, a whole spoonful, and it looked just like the laudanum the cook had for his toothache."

"A whole spoonful!" exclaimed Steen. "That's enough to kill anybody."

"Yes, sir," said another, "He'll die before we get halfway there."

Worried and anxious, still they tramped on through the long hours. They did not talk much. Why waste one's breath when it was needed to keep up the weary march? The air was damp from melting snows, and the sky was overcast. There was a faint rattle of wind in the treetops. There was the tinkle of nearby brooks and the roar of larger ones plunging with full banks down the mountainside. Nothing else disturbed the silence, and not a star pierced the blackness of the night.

They followed the winter road, rough and uneven, winding through the forest over the low ridges around Traveler Mountain. The mountain seemed always to loom straight across their path.

They waded through water, picking their way over corduroy bridges and avoiding stones with care, but always with the thought that a man's life depended on their strength and skill. They had no light task to accomplish. The load was heavy; if one has ever tried to carry a loaded stretcher on his shoulders, he will remember that inequalities of the road's surface render the burden doubly hard. These men accepted the job cheerfully and made no complaint.

They examined Mr. Howes each time they changed carriers and found him warm and breathing, though otherwise dead to the world. After some hours, they reached Trout Brook, the largest stream between camp and Trout Brook Farm, the first dwelling place. It was a mountain stream, bridged for the autumn travel; but, to their dismay, the bridge was gone, carried out by high water and ice.

"Well, by George! " exclaimed Steen, "Look at that for trouble!"

The men stepped down upon the shore ice, which still seemed firm and solid, and laid their burden down

"We'll have to build a footbridge," continued Steen. "There's a couple of trees that will do," and he pointed them out to the men. "One will have to be lifted some at the butt. It's small, though, and not very heavy."

Two of the men stayed by the stretcher; the others joined the group on shore helping to pile away the brush and treading down the snow to make a path to the trees they were felling.

Suddenly, the man on the ice gave a shout. The cake on which they stood was swinging into the current. They jumped to the side nearest the shore and so shifted the weight that both men and stretcher were nearly precipitated into the water. They were only saved by instantly flinging themselves back towards the center when the cake righted itself.

They were now out in the current, which was strong but not rough. Two lanterns, fortunately, had been left beside the stretcher, and these served to light up dimly the shore beyond them. Of course, all the men ran down the shore, tumbling over logs, rocks and brush in pursuit of the stranded party—except Steen; he leaped to the bank at the first alarm and paused for a moment to grasp the situation and the prospect of rescue. He remembered that just below the stream made a turn and a point of land made out into the water. The current would set against that bank and form an eddy.

It all flashed through his mind in a moment of time. That was their chance, and he went on the run out to the half-dazed men afloat and galvanized them into action. They, by this time, saw the bank and the chance it gave them, and when the ice slid in under the overhanging bushes, they quickly grasped them. Little by little, working back, they got out of the eddy; but the bank was above them, and steep.

"Can you hold it?" shouted Steen, now on the opposite shore.

"Yes," came the reply.

"All right! We'll be there in a jiffy," and back he and his choppers ran. "Chop one small one," Steen told them. "It has limbs down the trunk, and we can cross on it."

In an incredibly short time, they went down the other shore to where, still holding a grip on the bushes, the stranded men waited. Steen swung himself carefully down on the ice, and adding his powerful grip to theirs, they moved the cake back to where the bank was more nearly on a level with the water and where they could easily carry the stretcher and its burden back to the trail.

Daylight found them very near Trout Brook Farm, and soon the welcome smoke from the chimney floated up the sky against the sunrise, cheering their hearts. They tramped in, weary and hungry, and laid the stretcher down on the nearest couch.

After a hot breakfast, Steen sent his men to bed, and producing a team and man to assist him, he carried Mr. Howes to his home (another day's journey).

Thus it was, without warning of any sort, that he was carried into his home. Someone was immediately sent some five or more miles to the town for a physician. His friends were much alarmed at his unconscious condition, especially after what Steen told them of the medicine the Boss gave him. There was much discussion about it. The doctor assured it could not have been laudanum. Such a dose would have killed him in a few hours. He said that this sort of a condition is found in certain cases.

Mr. Howes recovered consciousness after the third day and lived long years, possibly thankful he knew nothing of the hard, grueling journey home.

Away back in the early years, there was a Grange in the town that flourished for awhile, builded itself a hall and gathered a very good membership. It fell, however, upon evil days. By some mismanagement, it lost its hall; discouraged, it finally surrendered its charter.

The first year of this century, another grange was organized in the town. There were just sixteen charter members. Mr. Rogers and I were of the number. In a short time, many more were added. The insurance companies connected with it were an inducement to join, but the great attraction to join was the social gatherings from time to time. The meetings, some of which were continued all day, the bountiful dinners, and the discussions and business, were all good for the breaking of the monotony of farm life.

We bought the old hall, which was unfinished except the audience room, and finished and furnished it, using the lower floor for a store. After a few years, I was elected secretary and held the office seventeen years. Mr. Rogers was Master a number of years, and always one of the committee on finance.

As secretary, I came to know nearly every farmer, not only of our town, but also the adjoining towns. Through our Pomona Organization, we gained a wide acquaintance in the towns of Aroostook. We generally attended the State Grange meetings and came to know many of the people who were from time to time its officials. These friendships, and the helpful, interesting meetings we had together, are among my pleasantest memories. Our attendance continued until the closing year of Mr. Rogers' life.

CHAPTER 4
CHILDREN OF THE EAST

Mary Elizabeth reminisces about the children: During the growing-up period of the children, their school duties and social activities and the maintenance of health and vigor were an ever-present care. As their individual characters developed, I found they had in common only one predominating trait, and that was a love of the woods and all wild things.

Lore, though he loved to fish, called for a camera rather than a gun, and I believe a camera and a fishhook have always remained his only weapons. He early developed a liking for research.

Mamie *[Mary]* was decidedly domestic, with shrewd executive ability, and became my right-hand dependence.

Annie was born with a grievance; namely, being a mere girl when she would so much rather be a boy. She consoled herself with dressing in her brothers' clothing and taking a boy's part in all their games. One of their amusements was to stand her on an improvised platform and demand a speech, which she always delivered at length with unction and all the gestures.

She developed a taste for drawing, which, because of the daring way she sometimes used her drawings, was the bane of the teachers and the delight of her classmates. It was that love which finally took her out into the world and decided her life's work.

David had stronger social instincts than others. He cared more for music, dancing and the society of girls. He was a good athlete, as was Luther. Luther's favorite amusement as a child was forming a circus wherein potato bugs performed on tightropes, siphoning off the water from the kitchen reservoir through pipes made of dandelion stems, and building railroads. As all boys have this fad sometimes, I did not think it indicated much; but, as he grew older, he read everything he could find on electricity and saved up his money to buy textbooks on that subject.

When David finished the University, Luther entered it, and in due time he also graduated from the electrical engineering course. His abode for three years was in Pittsburgh and then he went to the New Haven Shops, later to Schenectady to do field work for the General Electric Company.

Edwin finished the high school and began work for his father in the lumbering business. The experiences he gained there in classifying and estimating timber settled his occupation for him.

Lore entered the University of Maine, graduating four years later, getting post-graduate work at Wisconsin and Geneva, and finally being listed as an expert in the government laboratories at Washington.

Mamie went away for two years of school training. Ed married and took his wife into a cottage in the woods near his work. After Lore graduated from the University, David entered. And now Mary married a schoolmate, also a graduate of the electrical engineering department, and they went to Boston to live.

The greatest wrench in the family came to me when Annie decided she must spread her wings and fly. Her love for drawing absorbed and held her as nothing else she did. She wanted to go to Boston and study. She had a little money of her own, enough for a start, but for the most part she must earn her way. We were not in condition to aid her much. I tried to dissuade her, to make her realize what a struggle she was up against. There followed years of self-denial, poverty and hard work before she was earning a comfortable living wage.

Mary's husband, who was in the employ of the Sturdivant Company, was sent by them to manage their business in Canada and moved his family to Montreal.

In 1912, Ruth (the baby who was "to be with us in our old age") went to live with them and attended the University of McGill.

The family was growing smaller fast, and their going was a sad trial to me. I spent many lonely, depressed hours, often anxious as well. I didn't want to keep my children at home, or deny them the privilege of following their chosen professions wherever they called them, but I missed them. The world looked rather gray without them.

Ten miles from the farm is a beautiful little lake dubbed long ago the very common, unromantic name, "Shin Pond." It is a lovely sheet of water set in among the hills, having very attractive shores and two fine sand beaches.

When the four eldest children were old enough to enjoy camping, we used to drive in there for two or three days after haying, usually taking some of the children's friends with us. We always used a canoe to get about the lake. We were the pioneers, but it soon became the fashion to drive there for picnics and camping. People began to build cottages in which to spend a summer vacation. At the end of five years, the place became quite a resort.

When the boys and girls began to leave home and could come for a vacation in the month of August, Mr. Rogers and I conceived the idea of making a permanent camp where we could all spend the time together in a way we all enjoyed. We bought land of an old hermit at the end of the lake farthest from the road and there we builded, mostly with our own labor, a rough but roomy camp. Gradually, as the different members of the family became established in their life work, more cottages have been erected and improvements made until our rather large group and their friends can be comfortably accommodated. It is the Mecca towards which all the cars turn when August comes.

There is one favorite spot at the camp. It is where each pleasant evening, when darkness falls, a fire of driftwood piled high is lighted. Around this, everybody gathers and stays until it is burned to a bed of coals. There are stories, songs, games, and specialties. The youngsters are adept at that—and some of the older ones also. Everybody departs reluctantly when the fire is out. No part of the camp life intrigues us, as does this campfire.

[Decades later, In 1998, cousin Elizabeth "Betsy" Elliott Rush e-mailed this note to me: "...Mum said that you would remember hearing of Great Uncle Luther...he was also quite the pilot and used to fly into the area and land in the field in front of the cabins at Shin Pond Village. Mum said the very first time she ever flew was with him coming out of that field full steam ahead, up over the firs and pines in an open cockpit!" —JM]

DAVID NATHAN ROGERS (goes West)

My first introduction into the Forest Service came during
the summer season of 1905 when I was given a student
assistant position under A. W. Cooper in connection with
the preparation of a silvicultural working plan for the
Delaware & Hudson R. R. Company in the Adirondack
mountains of New York.

Bob Stuart was in the party. He, at that time, was
about as "green," as far as woods lore is concerned, as
any city boy could possibly be and was usually lost
when out of sight of camp.

One day, when he and I were out on a cruise line together, we saw that the country was pretty rough with
brush tangles, swamps, and deep still water streams. We
came to one stream about twenty feet wide; it was too
deep to wade, and the only crossing to be found was a tree
about 10 inches in diameter fallen across but at a height of
some 3 or 4 feet above the water.

Having had considerable experience in walking logs, I made it
easily enough. But Bob, when halfway across, lost his balance and fell
into the water closing the door behind him. After trying it again with the same result, he
finally made it across by straddling the log and hitching along. I felt sorry for Bob in those
days because I couldn't see how he could ever hope to make good in the Forest Service.

I entered the Service under appointment as Forest Assistant in July 1907, reporting
along with C. M. Granger and Frank Kellogg to Forest Supervisor Greeley at Hot Springs,
California, then headquarters of the Sierra South. It was the policy to group the new Forest
Assistants for a short period of training before definite assignments. Kellogg and myself
were instructed to report to Bill Maule—who at that time was in charge of the Hume Sale
with headquarters at Millwood, a three days' horseback trip from Hot Springs, and no
horses.

We drove to Porterville via stage, then undertook our first financial dealings with the
Western public in the acquisition of horses and riding equipment. I was not so well off
financially as Kellogg, who made his purchases without any difficulty; my assets amounted
to only forty dollars and no credit. I succeeded in purchasing a forty dollar riding outfit for
fifteen dollars down but had difficulty in buying a one hundred twenty five dollar horse for
twenty five dollars.

I remember calling Supervisor Greeley on the phone and asking him for a loan of a trifling
hundred dollars, but I didn't get very far with that. I supposed then that Supervisors were
rich men. To prove how honest I looked even in those old days, I succeeded in getting the
horse for twenty-five "bucks" and my personal note for the hundred.

On the second night out on that trip, Kellogg, a California man, played a bum trick on
me. We were in the foothills somewhere north of Lemon Cove where the foxtail grows
rank and, at that time of the year, was quite dry and brown. Frank selected a bare spot and
rolled down his blanket in the dirt. I wondered why; but, without asking any questions,
selected the thickest mat of foxtail upon which to lay my blanket. By about midnight, I had
no occasion for further doubting the wiseness of Frank's dirt bed. The next morning, I was
just one hour picking the foxtails from by blanket; however, Frank was a good fellow and
helped with the plucking job.

We eventually found the timber sale headquarters, after considerable inquiry, located outside the town under some scrub oak. It consisted of a pup tent, bed roll, and combination grub box and filing case. Bill Maule, however, was all that we had hoped for with his dapper uniform and big Stetson hat. He was not long away from the Philippine Islands.

A couple of very interesting months were spent on sales work, and then we three new assistants drifted back to Headquarters at Hot Springs. We found upon our return that things about headquarters had taken on quite a festive appearance during our absence. Mr. Greeley seemed to have quite a number of his friends visiting him, among which was a very pretty and attractive young lady.

It was the custom in those times to have a big campfire each night out under the trees near the creek just back of the office. Everybody gathered around telling stories, singing songs, and making merry generally, and each night there was keen competition between Granger and myself as to which one would monopolize the charms of the attractive young lady. I remember that Supervisor Greeley seemed to be very attentive to this young lady's mother, and as the evenings passed would usually remain outside the gay circle entertaining her with what at that time seemed to us more-or-less gloomy discussion.

Suddenly one day, out of a clear sky, came orders from Greeley for Granger to go to the extreme northern end of the Forest and myself to go to another inaccessible section with sufficient schedule of work to last us until late fall.

Bidding fond farewell to our mutually attractive young friend, we sorrowfully departed, as was our duty. That fall, both Granger and myself received invitations to Bill Greeley's wedding—which, to our great surprise, involved the young lady whom both of us had attempted to win from him. I still think that Bill violated the regulations in using his official authority for personal gain.

As I reflect upon the action taken by Bill in effecting his plan to eliminate competition for the hand of his sweetheart, it would appear that he considered that I should be disposed of permanently, if possible. My passing out would be in the line of duty with no chance for him to become involved.

My instructions were to cruise, single-handed, some 12,000 acres in the high country, subsist myself, and if I became lost or anything happened to me, that would be just my hard luck. A ranger would come through the country once every week or ten days to see if my camp was still intact. I did get lost many times, but very fortunately never became injured in any of my hikes over the rough country.

I had no tent but fixed up a shelter made of poles and bark. I baked biscuits in an improvised reflector made of a coal oil can. I had no firearms but took my axe to bed with me every night for company. The coyotes made me nervous, and I had seen many lion tracks in my travels. I used to think many times that if I ever became a Supervisor, I would never send anyone out alone on any job requiring him to be out of touch with people for any length of time.

Another job in connection with the cruising assignment was the location of a road from the Tule Indian Reservation around the head of Cold Spring Creek and into Parker Meadows. Such a road was to be used for the transportation of the logs or lumber down to civilization. My ability as a locating engineer was either taken for granted or quite probably not considered. You were given jobs beyond your apparent qualifications to see just how much rope you would take to hang yourself.

Supervisor Greeley had notified the farmer who supervises the reservation that a road engineer would call upon him for any assistance that he could render in the location of this road, and, in due course, I appeared astride my trusty buckskin.

The farmer—so called—was absent, but he had evidently left instructions to the Indians that the visiting engineer from the Forest Service should be shown every courtesy.

Apparently they thought they were going to meet a very great personage, since, upon my arrival, they all turned out: bucks, squaws, and children dressed in their very best. I could see immediately, however, that something was wrong because they all began talking among themselves and made no attempt to conceal their disappointment in meeting a young kid instead of the big man with the proverbial long whiskers.

It was evening, and they did reluctantly carry out their original plan of honoring their guest by allowing me to sleep in the family bed in one of the cabins while the family slept on the floor. But the next night I was delegated to the stable loft which was used not only for hay storage, but a drying place for hundreds of strips of jerked deer meat. Aside from the smell of the stable, odor from the meat and buzzing of the flies, my sleep was quite uninterrupted.

I think it was the afternoon of the third day after my Indian guides had ridden with me pretty much over the reservation, and as far as I knew, all of the necessary information was available. I was piloted to the east side of the Reservation and told that if I continued straight over the mountain I would come out somewhere near my cruise camp. It was late in the fall, and the weather had been threatening all day. As I climbed higher, I was soon in the clouds, which later turned to rain and then darkness. There was no trail to follow, but I managed to keep working my horse fairly straight up until I had crossed the spur of the ridge, and then we traveled down into a meadow.

About halfway across this meadow, my horse dropped into a sinkhole. In those days, such places were usually fenced or obstructed, since if animals went, in they seldom ever came out. That night I shall never forget struggling with that horse. Sometime along toward morning we got out. When daylight came, I recognized the meadow and the way to my camp.

During the fall of 1907, instructions came from Washington for our permanent assignments to various Forests. In spite of the hardships, I had become very fond of California and asked Bill Greeley to try and obtain an assignment for me in California. This he succeeded in doing, getting me placed on the Inyo.

I reported to Supervisor Hoge at Bishop, the headquarters of the Inyo during the first of January, 1908. The office consisted of one fairly large room with a small room in the back used for sleeping purposes. On one side of the main room, there was a typewriter and filing case. On the other, a drafting board; in the back was a pile of miscellaneous service stuff, and in the middle a table.

As I entered, Supervisor Hoge was sitting in a chair with his feet on the table reading some Forest Service bulletin. He continued to read without looking up, and when finally I interrupted him by attempting to introduce myself, he cut me short by saying that he knew all about my coming and considered my assignment to the Inyo as a waste of good government money.

My first job was to typewrite a longhand letter that he handed me. I never did finish that letter; after the fourth attempt, he told me to go out behind the office and I would find some wood that needed splitting.

My crowning achievement on the Inyo was the reconstruction of the Round Valley Ranger Station house. I somehow acquired the position on head carpenter on that job, my assistants being Paragory, the District Ranger and Glen Crow, detailed from another District. Our problem was to enlarge the then present house with dimensions 12 x 12 to a house that would be 24 x 24, and still remain quartered in the existing building. This called for considerable group consultation.

The final plan agreed upon was to build out from the end and side leaving the old building to become one corner room of the new four-room building. Everything went along OK until it came to cutting the rafters. I couldn't find any literature on this subject, and my assistants didn't offer any suggestions—perhaps for good reasons of their own. This situation might have been my most embarrassing moment.

The Rangers had a habit of leaving for town right after dinner in order to get the mail, or so they said. Not wishing to have to admit that I didn't know how to cut those rafters, I resolved to take advantage of their absence and try to work the thing out.

For various reasons, the pitch of the new roof had to be the same as that of the old building, which was still intact. I placed one rafter on the old roof, spiking the lower end, rigged up a gin pole, hoisted the opposite rafter in place, then shinnied up the pole and marked the two rafters joined at the top. By the time the boys returned in the evening, I had all the rafters marked for cutting, and it would surprise you how well they eventually went together. I explained to the boys that cutting rafters to any pitch was a mere mathematical calculation that any one ought to easily figure out!

My last important achievement on the Inyo was the establishment of an interior boundary of the Forest extending from somewhere north of Round Valley to Benton some 25 or 30 miles. With the government team, Glen Crow as horse wrangler and cook and another assistant, we put in over three weeks retracing the old section lines and marking this boundary. It was all more or less open sage brush and lava country with innumerable low ridges crossing our line at right angles.

Upon the top of nearly every ridge we erected monuments, on line, from 3 to 6 feet in height dependent upon the flat rocks available. It was a beautiful job; one could follow that boundary with the eye for miles. We had the job just about finished when we received word from Supervisor Hoge that this boundary had been changed and no further work on this line was necessary.

In the spring, I was called back to Washington, D. C., to assume charge of a proposed branch of the Division of Silviculture that was to be known as the section of bug control— or something like that. The activities under that branch were to be started in the Black Hills of South Dakota. I reported to Nick Carter and told him that I didn't know anything about bugs and wasn't interested in that kind of work. Nick, in his very characteristic manner, said, "That doesn't make any difference whatever. You have been selected for this job, and you are going to do it."

I remained in Washington most of the summer writing practice letters in the "bull pen," none of which were ever satisfactory. One day, late in the summer, I happened to be in Bill Greeley's office. Greeley by that time had been made Chief of Silviculture in Washington. He said to me, "How would you like to go to the Stanislaus Forest as Forest Assistant."

The proposition affected me as a ray of sunshine affects one after a storm. I said, "Gee, nothing would suit me better, but Nick won't stand for it." Bill advised me to say nothing about it to Nick, that he would arrange everything. In due course I received my transfer orders.

To get even with Nick, I walked into his office the morning of my departure, and said, "Well, Nick, I'm off for the Stanislaus."

Nick looked at me for a moment and then said, "The hell you are!"

The Forest gave me a choice of the route West, so I selected the Canadian Pacific through Vancouver and, naturally, all my baggage except suitcase was checked straight through to San Francisco. Somewhere between Vancouver and Seattle, a couple of Priests got away with my suitcase. I stopped off in Seattle in an unsuccessful attempt to locate the suitcase, bought an umbrella to keep the rain from spoiling my new straw hat and was unable to connect with my trunk in San Francisco.

I finally walked into Bummer Ayers office in Sonora on a typical hot, sunshiny day, carrying my umbrella and all my earthly possessions tied up in a handkerchief. It seemed to take several months to live down the impression that I made on that bunch in that office. I remember the first job Bummer gave me was a review of one of his timber sale cases. After I had worried over it for a couple of days, he came around to me and said, "Say, how long does it usually take for you to familiarize yourself with sale cases?"

My stay on the Stanislaus was more or less uneventful from a personal standpoint. Officially, I managed to make myself sufficiently useful to secure—justified or otherwise—an appointment as Deputy Forest Supervisor.

During December of 1909, I was instructed to report to Quincy, California to assume charge of the Plumas. I was out calling the night that official notification arrived. Bob Ayers, who happened to be in the office that evening looking over the mail, was immediately on the phone and said, "Say, Dave, you have been promoted to Forest Supervisor in charge of the Plumas!" Well, I can still recall with vividness the sensation that this news gave me. I turned cold and the shivers ran up and down my back, I couldn't believe but that Bob was playing a joke on me. I had hoped that some day I might become a Supervisor, but this was so sudden!

I arrived in Quincy a day or so before Christmas, 1909, and put in a very strenuous winter of office research trying to rediscover whatever it was that a Supervisor should know in running a Forest. I never did find out very much, but my efforts did lead me to one conclusion: There were too many no-good Rangers on the payroll. With very little knowledge of the regulations affecting Civil Service employees, I immediately started firing these "inefficient birds" right and left. Then the war was on! Broadsides came from the dispossessed, bouncing off, hitting San Francisco and finally reaching Washington. Investigators arrived and investigations were made and finally peace was restored, but the status of the fire-ee's remained unchanged.

LORE A. ROGERS

Dr. Lore A. Rogers

He came to the University of Maine at Orono as a freshman back in 1892 and was a member of the first "Black Bears" football team. After graduation in 1896, he worked in his father's lumbering operation in Maine; then, in 1898, he began a distinguished career in the new science of bacteriology. After graduate work at Wisconsin and the New York State Agricultural Experiment Station at Geneva, he served for 36 years as chief of the dairy products laboratory, U. S. Department of Agriculture.

Dr. Rogers retired in 1942 from a professional life that had seen him the creator of the preserving process for butter and dairy products, the initiator of hundreds of agricultural achievements, and the recipient of honors and awards. In the World War II years, he served as an advisory on secret biological work for the American government.

When Lore came home to Patten with his [second] wife, Katherine (a graduate of Cornell who found a niche as the town's librarian), he started a dairy business. He built a small quality control laboratory for testing milk supplies and processed products. But his searching mind reached beyond his own daily bread to the history of his native region, and he began to collect material and data on the Maine logging and lumbering past.

Patten, a town of 1,266 persons in the northern Maine woods, is not exactly a place to be heard from, but Dr. Rogers had had the acclaim in his earlier years, so that in his 50's and the 60's, satisfaction of his curiosity was his motivation, along with the desire to preserve for others the history of an era gone.

At the age of eighty, he put together a small museum in the back of a local store. It soon moved to the town library and then out on its own. Summers, over 10,000 people trek to northern Penobscot County to see Lore's museum. In his nineties, he met visitors personally at the door, anxiously wanting, as one visitor put it, "for you to see and understand," as he understood.

ANNIE LUCASTA "LOU" ROGERS

It is sometimes thought that those most intent on social change are discontented radicals, outside the dominant culture, who have little to lose by protest. Nothing could be further from the truth in the case of suffrage artists. Most, like Lou Rogers (probably the most prolific American suffragist artist) came from long-established families.

Annie was the fourth of seven children. The siblings, four boys and three girls, formed a close-knit family in the rural lumber town. Her images of her childhood remained intense and nostalgic. She wrote, "In all the woods life—from the winter camps

Annie "Lou" Rogers

with their vigorous activities to the spring drives of logs with crashing white waters, log-jambs, the ringing bing of cant dogs, dams with their roaring sluiceways—we children belonged. Not so much as looking on, but as feeling part and parcel of it."

After attending art school in Massachusetts, she moved to New York City and lived in Greenwich Village. It is here that Annie changed her byline to "Lou" Rogers. Lou became a cartoonist by 1908 and became the earliest American woman to produce a series of suffrage cartoons.

In 1911, at the New York offices of the National American Woman Suffrage Association, she displayed a cartoon sketch that was too controversial to publish, even for these radical women. It was a caricature of a proud-chested man with asses' ears and a paper crown, asserting his monopoly over the ballot box by standing on it and saying, "The Ballot Box is Mine Because It's Mine!"

"The Ballot Box is Mine Because it's Mine!"

I. I.
Lou Rogers, "He Does the Family Voting."

Another classical image she created was that of a crowned goddess in drapery seated upon her throne, shackled by "disfranchisement" and "economic dependence." Her technique was hybrid, combining an allegorical meaning with socially constructed shackles symbolizing specific conditions. She used this as a physiognomic perception. That is, a direct communication of feeling through posture and dynamic qualities.

Annie married artist Howard Smith and settled down on a farm in Brookfield, Connecticut. She began publishing verses for the Ladies Home Journal about little people called "the Gimmicks." In the 1930's she hosted a radio program, "Animal News Club" that entertained a child audience. She also wrote two books that were based on the tales that she told to her nieces and nephews at Shin Pond.

MOORE, Mary (Carr) (mŏŏr), composer; b. Memphis, Tenn., Aug. 6, 1873; d. Byron O. and Sarah (Pratt) Carr; musical edn. under Emma Dewhurst, Louisville, Ky., John Haraden Pratt, San Francisco, Calif.; also voice under H. B. Pasmore, Mariner-Campbell; Mus.Doc., Chapman College, 1936; m. J. C. Moore, M.D., Feb. 15, 1898; children—Byron Carr, Marion (Mrs. C. M. Quinn), John Wesley, flight surg. (killed at Port Moresby, New Guinea, 1944). Concert and church singer until 1928, in charge theory dept., Olga Steeb Piano Sch., Los Angeles, since 1926; teacher at Chapman College; former prof. theory, Calif. Christian Coll. Mem. numerous orgns. Founder Mary Carr Moore Manuscript Club, having mems. throughout U.S. and in foreign countries. Composer more than 300 songs, 10 operas, several orchestral scores, concertos, quartets, quintets, sonatas, choral works, instrumental solos. Conducted own orchestral scores, Intermezzo from opera David Rizzio with Ford Bowl Orchestra, Aug., 1936, and Indian Idyll with Federal Symphony Orchestra, May 1937; during the period 1938-40, Dr. Moore conducted programs of her works performed by the Bay Cities combined orchestras (90 members) at Oakland and San Francisco; also conducted own works performed by San Francisco Symphony Orchestra at Treasure Island, Golden Gate Internat. Expn., 1940. Awarded David Bispham memorial medal for "Narcissa," 1930, and 9 other prizes since 1927; 1st prize for chamber music from Nat. League Am. Penwomen 3 times in succession. Home: 4037 Leeward Av., Los Angeles, Calif.

Mary Louise Carr

CHAPTER 5
CHILDREN OF THE WEST

Mary Louise Carr: The boys had cholera and so did Mother *[Sarah Amelia Pratt].* And one stormy afternoon when a caller stayed and stayed, waiting for the storm to clear, Mother just managed to get herself upstairs and to bed. One boy went for the doctor, another for the nurse—for this cholera attack seemed worse than before!

Finally, the nurse arrived and decided against cholera. "But," she said, "you must be very brave, my dear; it will be hours before you can really expect the baby!" So she blithely went downstairs to get ready for the doctor. Some fifteen minutes (or years) later, she came up to see how Mother was getting on. Mother said weakly: "Nurse, the baby's here..." That old nurse began to scold my mother and tell her to be brave—and I got so mad, I yelled right out: "You bet I'm here, and don't you scold my mother!"— And the nurse was surely sorry! That is how Mother and I took care of that first situation—just between ourselves!

It seems I was rather puny, and Mother wasn't a very good provider in some ways; so, when Yellow Fever began to menace the city, my father hustled us all out of there and on the last boat before quarantine. Paradoxical! Although he was Supervisor of River-going Vessels, there was not a reliable craft available; all the others had gone out ahead. Our boat broke down, and no milk was to be had. The Ship doctor didn't seem very enthusiastic about me; I'm sure I didn't look worth saving. But Mother got her "dander" up and decided I was going to survive.

We got over into Illinois, and when Papa's mother saw me, she said, "Poor little thing; she's starved to death"—and gave me a nice juicy piece of steak, which I sucked until it was white. That, I believe, was the beginning, although I still remember old ladies clasping their hands over me and saying to Mother: "She looks delicate, my dear. I'm afraid you'll never raise her!"

We went to live in Jeffersonville, Indiana. Father's *[Byron Oscar Carr]* headquarters changed to Louisville, from where he commuted. My first positive memory must have been when I was about two years old! Sitting in the sunny bay window of Mother's bedroom where my "Aunt" Minnie Groseider and Mother, who looked relaxed and "different," not my usual lively Mother! I stood at Mother's elbow, feeling quite one of the group. As they talked, Mother reached over and WIPED MY NOSE FOR ME! Right before company! I remember feeling utterly crushed and insulted, and the day was spoiled! Mother later recalled that this must have been about the day before my little brother Georgie *[George Pratt Carr]* was born.

About Georgie's second year, we moved over to New Albany and lived in a big stone house on a wide shaded street. Georgie and I used to run and cling to the iron fence every noontide, for "Papa Day" was sure to come by with peppermints in his pockets. Georgie would say: "Tanny, Papa Day? Oo dot tanny?" Georgie was one of those glowing, adorable children—everyone loved him on sight; and I was his adoring slave. Sunshine and sparkle were in his blue eyes—and even then, there wasn't one of the nursery rhymes he couldn't rattle off at stop speed, though I had to translate to make them intelligible to the uninitiated.

At Christmas, the long drawing room was heated early so we could go down and look at our presents. A chair for each of us, a little red bureau and a solid black walnut bedstead for "Miss Tyree," I remember vividly! Miss Tyree was number one of my doll family whose composition head and cloth body rotated from time to time when either an unusually hard bump or a sawdust wound made it necessary to add "spare parts." From her first mishap, it was seen plainly that I would never be able to survive without her! She was still head of the doll family when I was sixteen, though really outclassed by more modern successors.

Georgie and I used each to draw up our little chairs before the grate fire in the library on winter evenings, and he would help me sing the dolls to sleep. Soon it would be our turn, and I in my father's arms and Georgie in Mother's would grow drowsy, listening to "There's a Land that is Fairer than Day," and "Listen to the Patter of the Raindrops on my Cottage Chamber Roof." I always wondered if a "cottage chamber" was different from the one under my bed, but never stayed awake long enough to ask.

Father had a beautiful baritone voice and was asked to sing a lot. Mother was very proud of him, but she sometimes worried because she couldn't sing at all and the choirgirls were so pretty and full of fun. But she must have learned soon that my jolly and adorable father, whom everyone loved, was entirely bound up in her happiness and welfare. His early, tragic loss of his first wife in childbirth made him a tender and devoted husband.

I was taken to a church social, and Aunt Minnie Poseider took me off to one end of the long Sunday school room where Georgie and I went on Sundays. She told someone I could sing, and before I knew it, I was stood on a table with a sea of faces around me and besieged to sing. I was frightened to death, but having been accustomed to obey, I started in a high, quivering little voice—something about a "Robin." Far off, I saw my father and mother turn and look at me and drift over nearer. I was no longer afraid, and Mother says it was really my debut! At any rate I remember the applause was terrifying.

Mother invited Father's only sister *[Grace D. Carr, half sister*, the youngest of the family*]*, to come on from Illinois for a visit and sent for her own sister, Hattie *[Harriet Emily Pratt]*, a sweet young girl of seventeen or eighteen, to come East so the two might be company for each other. It was a gay time. I remember a gorgeous heliotrope taffeta, ruffled and draped, and with a real train, which was to be a part of Hattie's trousseau, as she was to be married on her return West. Auntie Grace's new dress was blue.

As the two girls tried on their dresses, my father walked in, and seeing Hattie glance over her shoulder, called out, "It's all right, Hattie; your train is just as long as Grace's. Perhaps a bit longer!" Poor little Hattie, easily teased, blushed furiously. She was always so sweet to me! During that visit, I slept with her, and no matter what emergency arose (and there were a few), she was always gentle and patient.

One Sunday, we all started out for a walk. Georgie wore a sash of vivid blue, like his eyes. My sash was of dark brown. I felt so <u>terribly</u> about it but couldn't express my feeling. I thought, "I am so spindly and ugly—a <u>red</u> sash would be something pretty to look at." We walked on slowly, as Father had been delayed. Then as he came breezing down the street, shoulders back, his long golden-brown beard blowing to either side as he walked, he came straight toward me! Stooping, he picked up my handkerchief, which had fallen, handed it to me with a courtly little bow, and we all four moved on together. Father loved me—even if my sash was brown! "God was in His heaven."

A little later, there was candy in the library—a lot—white taffy candy (not the sticky kind), wrapped in white paper from the candy store. How well I remember that package! Father and Mother were going to Louisville to the theater. Georgie and I could have "so many pieces," and when that was gone, I was to put the candy away on a certain shelf. And this I did!

Hilma put us to bed. She was a big, stolid looking girl, who was there because our dear German Rosa, who loved us, had to go home for awhile and help her Mamma in some business about a stork. However, Hilma wasn't so bad; she told us some different stories! But next day! There was no candy left—not even any paper! Who had eaten it? Georgie had gone up with Hilma the night before, but I had lingered. I was the culprit! But I denied it. Mother, who hated a lie, threatened, and finally, as was her stern duty, spanked me. I still denied it, yet terrified for fear I might have eaten it and forgotten—but no, I hadn't. Another spanking, and still no confession. I was sent to bed, and when Father came home, he almost broke my heart telling how much he loved me and not to be frightened but to tell the truth.

I know the doctor came that night, for I have learned since that I was a very sick child—temperature and delirium. But during the next few days, real trouble was in the house. Georgie, my beautiful Georgie, developed brain fever. Nurses and doctors came and went, anxious-faced. One dreadful morning, Mother took me into the big living room to see once more my little brother, lying still and white in his little casket. I bent over and kissed him. I shall never forget the shock of his cold, marble lips. Soon the room was full of friends and neighbors. The minister came and "had church." Still, I didn't understand. We drove to the cemetery in a long, slow procession. Someone took me to see funny little shrines with dolls in plain sight behind the glass over in another part of the grounds.

Then we were driving home again, Mother holding fast to Father's hand. A big, gloomy house! Georgie was not there, anywhere! The neighbors looked sad. Everyone had loved our boy. Mother got quite desperate and decided to move over to Louisville. Hilma must have gone, for Rosa came to help us move. And then, while dismantling the house, high on a shelf in Hilma's closet was *the paper—the white paper*—with the candy man's name that was around the taffy. Even some little crumbs clung to it!

I was there and saw it, clapping my hands in ecstasy that I really wasn't a liar! But my poor mother! Though I never saw her tears when Georgie went—always a brave little stoic—now she wept torrents and clasped me in her arms, sobbing "Never again shall I whip you, my child." And though I needed it many times, Mother always arranged her discipline some other way.

In Louisville, we had a studio-flat. Mother took up her struggle with something of the courage of despair. I was four and a half, a delicate "only child," for the darling big brothers were now in college and only visited at holidays. I always gave them adoration, mingled with awe. Eugene [Eugene Merwin Carr] and Thorpe [Byron Thorpe Carr], fifteen and thirteen years older than I, were men in my eyes, as they were even then over six feet. They treated me to a judicious mixture of teasing and affectionate toleration; and, all in all, I believe were more devoted than if we had been "full" brothers and sister. Mother bent over backward to do the right thing by them, and they always treated her with the utmost consideration.

"Aunt" Hannah, a former slave, was my "Mammy"—my especial property. But Hannah went home nights, the little grate did not burn so cheerfully, and there was only one chair in front of it. There were no more evening songs, for Mother's lap was empty. Louisville, to me, after our quiet, spacious home across the river, seemed fraught with unknown terrors from which only the police could rescue me. (Father had warned me of the busy street below.) One evening, a deep sigh caught his attention.

"Well, Chickabiddy. What seems to be troubling you?"

"Oh, dear!" I wailed, "Only one God and more 'n a hundred thousand policeman!"

There was a friendship with Zona, the brown-eyed girl above us. I was frail, and yet she would generally tire before I did. Her mother, a semi-invalid, soon won Mother's interest and concern. The two families became intimate. The custom rapidly became that every evening, either at the Carr's or at the Howlett's, supper was served when "the paper was put to bed." Colonel Waterson often came, Colonel Howlett, my father, of course, the current colobritios, and a little coterie of close friends. Sometimes they met at some of the other houses for a "special," but usually with us.

At this time began the Bohemian hours which have always seemed so natural to me. In our tiny flat it was much easier for me to be around at night, as I was always willing to sleep *hours* in the morning. Zona and I had lots of fun. One Christmas Eve, I got myself thoroughly disliked by cutting my own mouse-colored locks, and before I was caught, one or two of Zona's lovely brown curls, to send up the chimney with a letter so Santa Clause would send us dolls with real hair!

Another time, we masqueraded as little beggars and went out begging for pennies. I wore a braid made of bright red worsted. One of our victims happened to be a friend of the family and recognized us. We were, of course, promptly discouraged from this practice, even though we were planning to give our pennies to the really, truly poor little girls!

Which reminds me of other "stunts" when we lived in the Studio Flat. The entire block was one building, and in front of each flat was an iron balcony, connected by a lodge as wide as the length of a brick. Mother used to tell how she would be sitting by the window, sewing or reading, when she would notice some lady on the opposite side of the street stop and gaze at our building in horror. She would then realize that I was doing the "human fly" act, and would step out on the balcony and gently remind me to step inside at the next balcony. It seems that it was an almost incurable habit with me, and I really needed, as Papa would say," A little of the oil of spank."

The Eastern winters, the coal soot and Mother's empty arms conspired to develop in her more than a hint of tuberculosis. The first winter, my father sent us West to visit my grandparents, with brother Thorpe as our courier. A late reservation at Chicago found Mother consigned to an upper berth with me. A courteous passenger exchanged his lower for her comfort; the next morning, in the men's washroom, he asked Thorpe how his wife and little daughter slept! Thorpe was much set up and bribed me a dollar to call him "Papa" the rest of the trip.

Later, I ran across a serio-comic letter of sympathy to Father, that his attractive young wife had allowed another man to pose as her husband clear across the continent! Thorpe remained in the West, under the general supervision of Grandfather, and took up train dispatching. Being always an independent youngster, he wouldn't let Father put him through college. In time he would require an account of his eye trouble, and the dispatching seemed a means to an end.

On one of those many trips across the continent for Mother's lungs, I almost put an abrupt termination to my career. I was always inclined to walk about in my sleep, and I remember being startled into full wakefulness by the exclamation from the porter, who was awakened by the draught as I opened the door onto the platform which was not enclosed. He reached me in one bound and caught me in his firm grasp just as I prepared to step off the fast-moving train. He guided me back to the middle of the sleeping car and told me to "Climb in wid yor mudder, Chile, and don' you climb out again."

In my confusion, I climbed into the wrong berth and was very embarrassed and apologetic when the nice young man across the aisle from us gently, but firmly, inserted me between the curtains of Mother's berth. She, not having missed me until then, was thoroughly frightened; and then, and later, she tied my arm to hers whenever we traveled. It was a vivid recollection—that sleeping porter startled into instant action as the snowy landscape rolled swiftly by.

Dear little Aunt Hattie had been in Arizona, bravely earning her living by giving music lessons, while her little son was either with Grandmother or with us. She now came engaged to be married to the grandest man—we all adored him! He proved to be the kindest of fathers to the little stepson, adopting him and showing him almost more devotion than to his own two baby daughters who arrived during the next few years, and made little family stair-steps just younger than my baby brother.

I could write reams about the holiday trips. One Christmas, it was down to Phoenix, Arizona for our entire family, on Grandfather's special car. Then there was an extension to our trip for my young Uncle Newcomb [Bradley Newcomb Pratt] and Aunt Carlin, [Carlin Louise Pratt] who was only six, and two years older than I.

Then we went on to New Mexico, to Fort Wingate, where we were the guests of Father's oldest brother, General Eugene A. Carr, then in command. There I saw a sham battle, heard the blood-curdling Apache war-whoops (which in later life I have tried to re-create in the last act of my opera, Narcissa), and had a brief and thrilling glimpse of Army life.

Uncle Eugene's wife [Mary Maguire] was said to be the most beautiful woman in the regular army at that time. Once, when she was out rifling with a small party of officers and her own sixteen-year-old son, they were surrounded by Geronimo's party of braves. Only by dint of extreme bravery and good luck they were able to get back to the Fort. Shortly after that, Geronimo went defiantly on the warpath. A tragedy was averted by Eugene's foresight, which was to evacuate camp under cover of darkness. They traveled on a rough "short-cut," at "double-quick," and re-occupied the Fort a scant half-hour before the Indians made what they expected to be a surprise attack upon the women and children of the

Fort. Shortly after this, Geronimo was taken prisoner. The papers were full of it at the time, and the play, *The Girl I Left Behind Me* was founded upon this incident.

Thanksgiving of the following year, the "Clan" gathered at the hospitable Rancho home of Captain Lillis, the husband of Grandfather Pratt's sister, Lucy. For several days, we feasted and visited, driving all around the enormous length and breadth of "El Rancho Laguna de Tache." There, Uncle Lillis told us he would show us a swarm of fish turned out to graze. Of course, we thought he was fooling, but driving around through pasturelands, which had been overflowed from the nearby creek, we could see little twitches of a grass blade, and looking closely, saw the fish swimming about. Alas, poor things; when the water receded, they were left high and dry. It was at that gathering that little cousin Helen Lillis asked her mother this poser: "Mamma, where is a fly's bosom?"

Naturally somewhat puzzled, Aunt Lucy said, "Why, Helen, what are you talking about?"

And Helen very literally replied: "Why, Mamma, you always sing, "Let me to thy bosom, fly."

One of these trips, when I was about five and a half, I took a set of dishes out to my Aunt Carlin. It was a bitter pill to have to call that young harem-scarum "Aunt!" Grandmother was always my champion and thought Mother was far too strict with me, but Mother was equally sure that Grandmother was too "easy." One never-to-be-forgotten day, when we children were temporarily alone, a caller came. In those days, a caller was not to be treated lightly. My Aunt Carlin and I perched on chairs and prepared to be entertaining, as the caller decided to wait. All went well for a few moments, although the conversation was spasmodic, when Carlin turned to me, and in her most grown-up voice remarked, "Now Mamie, you may go out and play!"

Oh, but was I furious! I, who at home in the East was always included in Mother's company. But I hadn't the courage of my convictions, so I got up and meekly went out, and then performed the meanest revenge I could possibly imagine: I buried those lovely dolls' dishes under the sand pile, here and there, close to the surface, so that by the time we went East, only a few were left. Needless to say, Mother made me save from my allowance the price of a new set, which was promptly sent back.

This time, on our return, Father had taken a house out on Broadway, which was then quite fashionable part of town, though not one of the large mansions. Our house was the usual style, four stories, the upper a manard roof, marble steps, kept shining by constant scrubbing. The household consisted of my beloved Hannah, the old-style type whose "fambly" was her chief concern. Hannah presided over the kitchen. Then there was Lucy *[not Lucy Pratt]*, a new style housemaid, with immeasurable scorn for Hannah! Lucy was tall with a narrow pointed head, and voluminous skirts, so that she "sloped out" from top to bottom. Hidley Reed, the boy of general utility, hitched the pony to the phaeton, kept the stoves filled, ran errands, and waited on tables in a starched white coat!

But, saving the best to the last, Father had persuaded Miss Emma Dowhurst, a well-known piano teacher, formerly assistant to William Mason, to make her home with us and undertake my education. She was a middle-aged lady with curly gray hair, nose glasses, a sensitive mouth, tall and robust in appearance, who took me at once into her heart and arms. She taught me my notes (but not my letters. There was a standing threat that anyone teaching me to read would immediately be discharged—the aftermath of my little brother's death from brain fever.) She taught me to love music, spoke a little German with me, and read me lovely fairy tales and poems. Sometimes she just sat and held me in her strong arms—a refuge against loneliness for both of us, I suspect.

When Mother "wasn't so well," Miss Dow would often go to market and take me along. Poor Mammy Hannah used to be dreadfully distressed by Mother's manner of marketing; to Mother, it was a business matter, and she went in the phaeton (with Ridley to carry the basket) in the simplest of morning costumes. Hannah would protest, "Mis' Cyarr, efn yo all go lookin' like that, they'll think yo're nothin' but po' white trash!" But Mother just couldn't see silk and ostrich plumes with diamonds in a market of a morning and stuck to her own ideas.

Sometimes, a very magnificent colored funeral would pass by our house. (All the funerals came out Broadway on the way to Cave Hill Cemetery.) Hannah would snatch me up and rush to the front gate where she perched me on a pillar, herself swaying to the music, sometimes singing along, "Go chain de lion down—"

My religious education was no longer neglected. Poor Mother had been reading some of the dark philosophies of Schopenhauer, and for quite a while after Georgie left us, was in a sea of doubt and misery. Now I began going to church, occasionally with Miss Dow who was a devout Episcopalian. There I first experienced the sorrows of unrequited love. One of the choirboys, so angelic looking as his voice roared heavenward, never glanced my way! But I saw "curruptitious" games of jacks when the choir-director wasn't looking.

For a change, I sometimes got permission to go to church with Hannah, where it was very exciting, as so many took part. "Yes, Lawd." "Bross do Lawd." "I'm acomin' to Jesus, Lawd, sho' as yo' is bawn." And then, at other times, I went with Lucy to her stylish church, where the service by the old colored pastor was formal, and the utmost decorum was observed. Then, sometimes I was sent to drive with Ridley Rood for the fresh air. Ridley knew many exciting tales, invented for my exclusive consumption. What affection I recall for our devoted Southern help!

One of my first ventures out among children of my own age proved disastrous. I was a guest at a birthday party and the partner of a very sophisticated little boy. When the ice cream was served, I remembered that Father had told me the recipe for making it a few days before. Hoping to appear more important before my young partner, I announced that I knew how ice cream was made. I was instantly the center of attention. "First you find a cow," I quoted, "then you feed her all the sugar she can eat, then you freeze her, and then milk her."

The wild hoots of derision that greeted my remarks sent me flying to the dressing room, where I wept inconsolably, until what seemed centuries later, Ridley called for me. I was almost sick, and the worried hostess drove over later to inquire for me, telling Mother of the whole affair. That night at dinner, Mother fairly pounced on Father for filling my head with such stuff. For some time afterward, I would continually ask Father if this was a "true lie, or only a joke."

Louisville at that time was winter quarters for several big circus companies. I remember so well the snowballs and sleighing. Zona had a little sister by then, but since we lived so far apart, our visits were fewer. Sometimes Ridley would take us on a picnic.

One day, when there was to be a first performance of the circus season, Father bought tickets with instructions for Ridley to meet him, bringing Zona and myself for the afternoon show. When Ridley arrived with Zona, I was missing. Inquiring, Father learned that, at the last minute, "Mis' Cyarr kep' Mamie at home."

Father arrived at our home a little later in a state of wrath such as I never beheld before or after, and in his turn, "pounced" on Mother. It transpired that I had done something or other that Mother had strictly forbidden.

Father said, "Why didn't you spank her and send her along?"

But Mother answered, "You know, B. O., that I will never spank that child again."

"Well, I will," said my splendid Papa, suiting the action to the words and turning me across his knee. A few rather mild spats, and he stood me up and told me to get my hat.

I've never forgotten his oration to Mother: "Madam, it is the inalienable right of every American child to attend the circus whenever it is available; and we will understand, here and now, that if punishment is necessary, some other means are to be found."

Father hurriedly drove us back to the circus himself, deciding against a return to the Custom House, and personally supervising the "tour," even to peanuts and elephants and a visit to the famous Mr. and Mrs. Tom Thumb.

Mother was strong enough to go with Father on one of his many trips to Washington. Garfield was President. Mother had a gorgeous brocaded black velvet dress, draped and caught up here and there with huge ornamental hooks and eyes of blue. A fan-like train of plain velvet, edged with fine black lace, was buttoned on. Down the front panel was fan-like pleating of plain velvet, while black satin pleats outlined the jet button on the basque. Another item, special for this trip, was a beautiful brocaded blue and gold "rodingote" to be worn with a plainer velvet skirt. Fur-lined "circulara" were then in vogue and floating ostrich plumes.

I went with Mother to one of the fittings, and the fashionable "modiste," finding that she must once again take in her seams, said; "Madame, where do you keep your organs?" Mother was no longer buxom but incredibly slender, with a crown of bronze hair that fell several inches below her arms' length. She could easily have been one of the "Seven Sutherland Sisters."

While Father and Mother were gone, "Miss Dow" and I were "glad to have each other." When they returned, my reward for "being good" was a beautiful new bisque doll, "Fanny Lillian," with eyes that closed, real hair, and a face that soon became known to all the family. She was always mentioned as an individual and, until I was quite grown, was a real member of the household.

One night I awakened late, and hearing merriment below, I slipped down the stairway, and peeking over the newel-post, saw a very gay company just rising to go into the dining room for supper. One gentleman, glancing into the hallway, spied me, and at once claimed me. Of course, Mother thought I should go back to bed, but Father thought I could stay awhile. So I was wrapped in a shawl and spent the evening on the knee of "Colonel" Barnabee, later of "Bostonians" fame as the "Sheriff of Nottingham" in Robin Hood. His clever comedy amused many an audience in later years. So many notables shared pleasant evenings.

Among Father's close friends were General *[later President]* Grant, General Sherman (whom I called Tooumsoh), General Logan, President Garfield, Colonel Watterson, Robert Ingersoll, and so on. *[The list certainly reflects B. O.'s interest in Republican politics. It could be that he may have entertained political ambitions beyond his current appointment. At any rate, Mary Louise was aware of her position as a member of a family that was a part of the social and political aristocracy that the visitors represented.—JM]*

One of these evenings, at midnight supper, the butter was frozen too solid. Ridley passed it first to Mother, who was always deft. To her embarrassment, in her effort to dislodge her little mould, it bounded off the plate into Colonel Hewlett's lap! Mother, crimson with mortification, started to apologize, but Colonel Hewlett said gravely: "Ladies and gentlemen, why is Mrs. Carr like a cocoon?" When everyone started guessing, he finally announced, "Because she makes the butter fly!"

Mother's uncle *[John Haraden Pratt]* returned for a brief vacation from Leipzig, where he had been for several years studying organ and music theory under such men as Richter, Roinecko, Jadassohn, and Rubinstein. Being an amateur penologist, he felt my "bumps" and concluded that I was destined to become a musician—and Mother was to leave no stone unturned. In this opinion, he and Miss Dow were in accord, together laying plans for my future.

Inch by inch, I learned to read, spelling out the words of newspaper headlines from the reverse side of Father's paper. I asked judicious questions, which Father unsuspectingly answered. Eventually, I was given the coveted permission and was provided with *Little Prudy Books*; Charlotte M. Xongo's *Histories of Greece, Rome, Germany*; *Tales from English Literature,* and Charles and Mary Lamb's *Tales from Shakespeare,* whereupon, I began to feel more at home with the grown-up conversations.

Miss Dow played accompaniments for Father, and the evenings were lovely. Father's rich baritone in Mozart's "In This Celestial Dwelling;" "Oh Hush Thee, My Baby;" and "It Will Be Summertime, Bye and Bye," and Miss Dow singing a capable alto.

I had a bad fall and began to limp. Dr. Long, of the Marino hospital, decided that I was threatened with hip joint disease. Then began those dreaded treatments, to which I undoubtedly owe my escape from crutches! When, during a period of about six months, a very few days my left hip was pierced to the bone by a set of fine needles, released by a spring as part of the treatment. Dr. Long was very gentle and suffered more than I did, I'm sure; but often I awakened from a dream where the dreaded needles are about to be released! Whenever possible, Mother and Ridley would drive into the country, taking Zona along with me for a day's sunshine and open air.

Finally, the danger was averted. I was allowed gentle exercise, and later was sent to a dancing school, which I loved. As the term wore on, there was to be an "Exhibition." Mother had a sweet little dress made for me, fine lace and tucks over silk, with a red sash. One would think I would have been satisfied! But when we arrived at the Hall, to Mother's amazement and my consternation, the little girls wore tights and tarlatan ballet skirts, with stage makeup, diamonds in their hair, and some with wings and bow and arrow. The annoyed Maintresso do Ballet would have gladly left me out, but would have spoiled the number of a "set;" so, utterly miserable, I had to dance my part, being like Barry's heroine in "What Every Woman Knows," frightfully overdressed!

We spent the summer at a watering place, Lake Elmo, where Father was with us as often as possible. I remember his strong swimming and how I went clear across the lake on his shoulders. He had once made a record, swimming the Ohio River over and back just above the falls, being carried by the current some three-quarters of a mile from his starting point. On Sundays, the country people used to come in for picnics.

The hotel clerk came to Mother about eleven in the morning and asked her to visit the athletic field with him. There, on the highest of the horizontal bars, I hung, head down, modestly holding my skirts with one hand, while the other stuck out approved circus fashion, and a crowd of picnic folks applauded. Seeing my Mother approach, I slid down the upright, afraid of the scolding I knew I deserved. But Father, strolling up in leisurely fashion, with a twinkling glance at Mother, said: "Takes after you, doesn't she?"

That summer was the year of Giteau's dastardly shooting of President Garfield on July 2nd, although the President lingered until September. A time of great concern for all his devoted friends and adherents.

On our return from Lake Elmo, we went to the Galt House for the fall months, and only Hannah came with us. Our rooms were on the sixth floor corner, overlooking the river. They must have faced the West, as I remember the sun pouring in one warm afternoon, and I decided to let down the awning myself. I climbed up on the deep windowsill. I must have felt a little dizzy and sick, for I can't remember how I finally wriggled back to safety, but my acrobatics must have come in handy.

The following winter, Mother's lungs got to a point where the doctors could give no hope. Dr. Long felt that if she went to California she might live six months or a year. Father applied for a leave of absence and took us West himself.

At Sacramento, consulting with the grandparents, he decided to investigate Napa Valley where they had recently bought a country home. We three went to Saint Helena, stopping at the hotel there. We drove around the valley, and finally decided upon a place which pleased both Father and Mother: A large, old fashioned house on a knoll, with wooded hills behind, and the valley rolling away in front past a little brooklet. Mother was delighted with the possibilities of the place. It had been formerly a summer resort, and four cottages surrounded the larger place which was then occupied by a family of father, mother, and four children—the youngest a boy about my age. One of the cottages was fixed up cozy and comfy for Mother and me, while Father went East to settle up his affairs.

The family in the big house was to attend to all our wants. It was then that Mother went through a dreadful trial. I promptly got the measles, and in my way, was very sick. The family in the big house had never had them so could only bring mail and supplies to the door. The doctor, who became our fast friend, came as often as he could, but it was two and a half miles from town on horseback; as for a nurse, there was none to be had. My eyes were badly affected, and most of the time I was "out of my head." What Mother went through, those lonely nights in the little cottage, only she can tell. At any rate, spring came, I got well, and Mother had been feeling better from the time we struck California.

Father had put his affairs in shape and sent in his resignation. Some of the finest letters of regret and the most gratifying columns of praise from all the papers as to his efficiency and integrity that any daughter could hope to own are among Mother's papers. Fortunately, Colonel Hewlett sent them on, or Father would never have exhibited them—he was not of that sort, being altogether modest and loveable.

Arthur was President.

Then began the building of the new house. Mother drew the plans, utilizing the original house as a nucleus. The family went away, and a hired man, instead, took charge of the outside, with a Chinese cook for us. All the cottages were requisitioned. Father always said the big house was "built upon honor" by honest day's work. The dining room was paneled in carved black walnut and Fort Orford cedar, the sideboard and mantle place of the same. The sideboard rose to the fourteen-foot ceiling and was big enough for a playhouse. Around the fireplace were tiled scenes from the stories of Sir Walter Scott. The library, in carved oak, had titles with scenes from Shakespeare. Up in my room, they built a doll's closet and a chest of drawers for the dolls' belongings. And later, I was given one of the cottages for my playhouse.

In the midst of the building, dear little Aunt Hattie was in great trouble. She had, by then, been married two years and had a six-month-old baby boy. Her husband had developed a tumor in his arm, which, after being removed, appeared again. Finally, the arm was amputated.

Mother sent for them to come to our place, where they lived in one cottage, and we supervised the baby—a beautiful, high-strung boy, who, of course, missed his mother. I used to play the "Flyaway Waltz" by the hour trying to distract his attention—but only succeeded in distracting everyone else. For weeks, Uncle Henry steadily grew worse and finally died of the tumor which had formed in his throat. Poor little Auntie—so small and pitiful in her black dress—a bride, a mother, and a widow at twenty. Father had stopped the army of workmen during the worst of Uncle Henry's illness, keeping the men on pay, as per contract, until they could proceed.

Finally the house was ready and furnished, and we moved in. I remember the solid black walnut dining set that came from Kentucky and the thrill of my own room, with the evening star and the little crescent moon rising above the hill behind the house, toward which some of my window looked. I had a "three-quarters size" bedroom set, and how I loved that room. And how I accumulated possessions, until at one time I had to have all my meals in my room for three days while I decided what I could part with and make the room livable again. That was a trying decision.

I was eight-and-a-half years old when we came to California to live, having made eleven times the overland journey, and was almost nine when we got settled in the new home. Of course, I had teachers at once—several changes before Uncle John returned from Leipzig to take me in hand. Mother took charge of my history, and I took charge of my reading. One time Senator Perry was visiting us, and while the family was assembling, he commented on the library titles.

I piped up and said, "Oh, yes, this one is from *Merchant of Venice,* and this from *King Lear,* etc., etc.—and he said,

"You seem pretty familiar with Shakespeare, young lady."

I replied, "Of course; I've read him in the original." I never heard the last of that.

I began to be seriously interested in singing. Uncle John brought me some Roinecko songs for children. One, "Spin, Lassie, Spin," Father liked especially. I was terribly timid before people, and I remember once singing before relatives, the tears rolling down my cheeks. Father had threatened to stop my lessons if I declined or had to be unduly coaxed to sing when I was asked. After all, though, he was wise, for I could never have overcome my natural stage fright otherwise.

Brother Thorpe, being very grown up at twenty-two, took his vacation from hot Sacramento and went up to the mountains for a two weeks' stay at a summer resort. While there, he met the sweet young daughter of the owner, a lady who had married a second time and whose husband was most unkind to the daughter. It was a case of love at first sight between them, and Thorpe finally persuaded the harassed mother to allow them to marry so that he could be in the position of protector.

I shall never forget the night Father got the wire: "Was married tonight; please wire congratulations." Not even the bride's name. Father was inclined to be dreadfully cut up, but Mother calmed him down and insisted on the telegram being sent. Father was sure Thorpe had been ensnared by some adventures. However, later we three took the train to Sacramento and visited the bride and groom in their modest housekeeping rooms and fell in love at once with the shy and lovable little Amy. Many visits back and forth followed, and the time came when Mother insisted on the frail bride coming to us to stay while Thorpe visited us over the weekends.

Amy was terribly lonely and very shy; if visitors came, she vanished. She was a tiny doll of a bride, but as time passed by, I saw her unaccountably growing plump. Her pretty dresses no longer were in evidence, and she wore loose, dark housedresses. She was still lovely, but I wanted everyone to know how pretty she had been.

One morning, a distant cousin came unexpectedly. Amy was in the library. I, the ten-year-old diplomat, introduced the gentleman, saying; "This is my sister Amy. You should have met her last winter when she was wearing all her pretty dresses, but she has outgrown them all."

Amy fled. I would never have recalled my remarks, except that in the evening Mother and I had a quiet little talk in the garden. She told me that God had planted a little baby under sister Amy's heart, and that, like the rose-bud, it must grow awhile before we would have it for our own.

Dear "rosebud" was born—a fine boy, far too large for the little mother; he was badly hurt and lived only four days. For four, precious days, I had a baby nephew.

Poor brave Thorpe—then came the dark days. Little Amy lingered for months, blood poisoning finally taking her; a sweet flower faded too soon. My brother was bereft of wife and child within a year and a half of his marriage.

Thorpe was transferred to Wadsworth, Nevada, where a few months later, a fire destroyed the rough, pine village in two or three hours, burning his trunks, his keepsakes, a lock of Amy's dark braided hair, and the beautiful quilts made with her tiny stitches. Father was very tender with Thorpe, then, whose birth had deprived Father of his own young wife.

During these months of illness and anxiety, Father and Mother were on a great strain in regard to Eugene *[Eugene Merwin Carr]*, the older son *[of Mary Buck]*. He had finished his course at Norwich University, graduated from Columbia Law School, and settled temporarily to practice law in a small Arizona town when the "Alaska fever" broke out. With some other young friends, he ventured into the interior of Alaska where, for many months, we had no news of him.

The discovery of a party of six starved and frozen prospectors in the newspaper headlines terrified us; but finally, when suspense was almost unendurable, Eugene returned. For weeks he had tramped over the snowfields, his dog, Snydor, being his only companion. Finally, he neared the coast, joined a tribe of half-famished Eskimoaux, was picked up by a fishing vessel and brought to Seattle; from there, he wired his safety and came to us at once.

The months sped on. I had my playhouse. There, with Miss Tyree at the head and Fanny Lillian, the darling of my heart, my thirteen dolls held sway. The little red bureau, the black walnut bedstead, were there. And there stood the little "Saratoga" trunk which, on so many of our "trial trips" of new vessels, was checked with Mother's trunks in the baggage room, and which I would importantly unlock, toward dinner time when Mother and I went for our dinner clothes. For you must know, Fanny was a very grand doll, with a large wardrobe, and was the official traveler of the doll family.

One special trip stands out in my mind, the ill-fated "Steamer Donnelly" from Louisville to New Orleans and return. Such a jolly party—the owners, and their guests, my father, the "Inspector," the Negro band every evening at dinner, with dancing. But, of course, all this was several years before, prior to our locating in California. The Donnelly was sunk by an explosion and the beautiful river-palace totally destroyed.

By this time, Grandfather *[Robert Henry Pratt]* had been transferred to San Francisco where he was Assistant General Superintendent of the Southern Pacific Company. Our visits were now to the City of the Golden Gate instead of the Capitol. I missed the Capitol grounds and the hide and seek games we children had on warm evenings. However, I was beginning to get acquainted in St Helena. The Grahams were great friends, and there were several concerts and church Cantatas in which I took part, which were great fun. Oscar Weil's *Three Little Kittens from the Land of Pie* was one; another, a *Flower Cantata,* when I stood in a bower and sang "Touch Me Not," rather scared, but living through it. Besides the dollhouse, there was the Library, and before I was eleven I had read all the novels of Dickens, Sir Walter Scott, George Eliot, the full set of Shakespeare, and all of Thackery and Jane Austin.

One day in July (Mother's birthday), we drove to town for the mail, and when I brought it to the carriage, there was a package for Mother. Naturally, thinking it was for her birthday, we opened it—and in it was a dear little baby-bonnet and saque. I exclaimed; "Oh, they don't know we lost the baby. But then, glancing at the card which said, "For dearest Sarah, with a welcome for the little stranger," and one look at my mother's face, I almost died of joy. Mother hurried the horse along toward home embarrassed 'most to death.

As for me, I was in seventh heaven; and from then on, I was allowed to plan, to cut and to do all the machine sewing on that wonderful little layette. It was a marvelous time. I was eleven when the little brother was born. I wrote letters to all the family, a "poem" to Grandma Carr about the new brother, and sat up half the night, frantically finishing a scrap book made of all the brightest cartoons and flowers from seed catalogues. No one can realize how crest-fallen I was when little Wray Torry failed to notice the book on his second day in our house. I was such a mixture of old woman and child.

Well, here was Mother, sent out West to die, surviving three deaths in the house, and having a fine baby after the doctors had entirely given up hope. Father fairly glowed. Everyone loved him, and he took his place naturally as a leader in the G. A. R. and Loyal Legion doings. Every Memorial Day we went to town early. Mother, an active member of the Woman's Relief Corps, later State Inspector, would go to the cemetery laden with flowers for the soldier's graves. Father, on a dashing charger, always led the procession in full regalia. How proud I used to be as his horse danced up and down Main Street as the march was forming.

After the exercises at the cemetery, there was always a formal program at the Turn Verein: usually an oration by Father, (and he was <u>eloquent</u>!) generally one or two songs by me; of course, "The Star Spangled Banner," and usually, "Tender and True, Adieu."

Now that I was eleven and a half, I was allowed to start the winter term at Vineland District School. Mr. McCarthy, a one-armed veteran of the Civil War, taught this school, which consisted of a one-room building set in a large yard filled with beautiful oak trees. What an adventure! For the first time, I could really mingle with human beings of my own age. My nearest neighbor, Etta Moacham, two years older than I, was my sponsor and protector. I was probably spared much that I might have suffered otherwise from being such a mixture of knowledge and vast, abysmal ignorance.

Also, Mr. McCarthy, who had been in frequent conference with my parents, kept a watchful eye upon me. In Arithmetic, I was with the babies; in spelling and reading, with the big boys and oldest girls. I couldn't sound the states and name the capitals, but hardly a city or state could be mentioned but that I'd pipe up, "Oh yes, I remember when we were there; we stayed at such-and-such a hotel;" or "There was where we saw Mary Anderson and Salvini in *Ingomar!*

One momentous morning, on my desk were sprays of lilac and bridal wreath, wet with dew. Every morning, for weeks, the flowers were waiting. Finally, I came to know the donor—James—a big overgrown boy of fourteen, looking like his Spanish mother, with even then a soft down on his upper lip. Love came into my life; my heart would beat, and my cheeks would flush if our eyes met. (We never spoke during those several weeks.)

One day, he wrote a note to me saying that he was going to town at noon (about a mile) and asked me to wait for him under the big oak. Of course I would! I took my lunch basket out there—all the other girls brought theirs, too. Finally, James arrived. Kittie closed her basket and said to the girls, "Come on, let's play tag; James want's to talk to Mamie."

I sat rooted to the spot. James, it seems, had brought me a ring—a gold one with two hearts on it—much too large, even for my thumb. I said I didn't think my mother would let me have it.

James said, "Don't tell her, then."

But I said I always had to tell Mother everything.

Then he responded, "Well, <u>tell</u> her then! But tell her not to worry; we won't get married for two or three years yet."

So, with many misgivings, I took the ring. It was easy to imagine the cyclone my news caused at home. I must be taken from school at once and be sent to boarding school. Finally, Mother's confidence reasserted itself, and she made me promise to return the ring and to have no more talks with James.

"But we never did speak until today."

Mother made a brave effort to conceal her amusement. The next day, I returned the ring, with Mother's edict that I was years too young. James was hurt and angry; he thought I could have managed better. His own parents were married at eighteen and fifteen, and they owned a fine vineyard and wine cellar and had a big family. What more could anyone ask? Alas, no more flowers. James never spoke to me or looked my way the rest of the term! I suffered acutely with disappointed love.

On the day of the final exercises, when we all did something to be conspicuous, I recited "Maud Muller," with feeling (especially, "it might have been"), and sang, with poignant grief, "Bid Me Goodbye and Go—You Do Not Love Me—No!"

Driving home from school that day, James, who was ahead of us, turned around and threw me a kiss, which lifted me above the clouds. However, that was the last time I ever saw him, for in the fall I didn't return to Vineland School.

Home was a very happy place that summer. The baby brother [Wray Torry Carr], who had at first been delicate, grew and thrived. The sunniest smile, the sweetest nature. I could never disentangle my feelings toward him—part sisterly pride, part maternal. I was twelve, and the lady who had been Mother's nurse came to stay with us while Mother took a short trip with Father. She had a little six-year-old son, a manly little chap with big brown eyes. One evening we were all in the living room when, encouraged by his mother, he asked me if I would marry him when I grew up! Feeling like a grandmother, I told him that when he was as old as I, we'd be married!

During the autumn of my twelfth year, I went to Armstrong's Academy in St Helena. Once a week, with an older friend, I made the afternoon trip to Napa and returned, taking my first vocal lessons from Professor Walter B. Bartlett, whose musical enthusiasm and confidence in my future lent great zest to my studies. My voice, in spite of my delicate appearance and small stature, was very mature—a brilliant soprano. No one doubted that I had an operatic future.

After Christmas, Mother installed me as a boarder in Miss Darling's "Young Ladies' Seminary" at Napa. Miss Darling was a charming lady of the old school and had a flourishing establishment. I was, with one exception, the youngest of the boarders, and utterly homesick. Several of the teachers I loved very devotedly, but much of the talk was unintelligible to me; I must have seemed to them an unsophisticated young prig. But they all spoiled about my singing, and my practice periods were more or less of a private recital.

Being already able to handle almost any accompaniment, I was unhampered by the need of an "assisting artist." I gaily warbled "l Bacio," or the "Waltz Song" from *Romeo and Juliet,* and other numbers, high and loud. My other studies were Robinson's *Higher Mathematics* in review with the other girls. I had the uncanny ability to do long problems in mental arithmetic and arrive at the right conclusions.

[In home study, the subject of mathematics was largely ignored. Early in formal schooling, Mary Louise started with the youngest children. It quickly became evident that she was a lightning calculator; she digested all the arithmetic offered in that earlier school by the end of a single term. — JM]

My other subjects were English Literature, Mythology, Poetry, and Word Analysis.

All went well every day until toward six when the train would whistle up the valley toward home. Father and Mother and my baby brother! How many times I have lingered in the garden, torn with the desire to run for the train and be "AWOL." The conductors all knew me; we had our annual passes. It was only my fear of being ridiculous that withheld me. But oh! The emptiness of the evenings! It seems the evenings were not empty for all the students. There came a time of half-veiled hints and secrecy, and then the chagrined relatives of two of our liveliest girls came to take them home, expelled in disgrace for slipping out after hours and going for walks or drives with the boys! Poor Miss Darling! Poor "the rest of us"; our daily walks were more than ever like a chain gang.

I remained at the Seminary two-and-a-half terms, with a blessed summer vacation in between. When the school was closed on account of an epidemic, I was sent over to Santa Rosa to finish the spring term at Miss Chese's Seminary, where my great-aunt Alice *[Alice Edwards Pratt, Ph.D., sister to John Haraden Pratt]* was teaching. I was assigned as her roommate, and Aunt Carlin was there, also "finishing." She was a great favorite and a leader among the girls.

Uncle John came up once a week from San Francisco for a harmony class among the teachers, and I was the only student pupil. The barrels of tears I shed, because try as I would, the parallel fifths and octaves <u>would</u> creep in. I worked very hard over my theory, but I had no vocal teacher there, to my sorrow.

However, I was promptly put into the choir, and of all the busy days, Sunday now was the busiest. Sunday school was at ten, church at eleven, and then back to the Seminary for a cold Sunday dinner. Bible study was from three to four, Young People's meeting from six-thirty to seven-thirty and church afterward—getting home late to bed and pretty tired. I sang in every session, of course. There were no weekends at home, as Miss Chase did not approve of interruptions in study.

Then Moody and Sankey came to town! All during one rainy week, as soon as school was out, down town we went to the revival. It was my first experience of such intense devotional strain. At home, in St. Helena, I had gone to church when and where I pleased. One Sunday, perhaps I went with Katie to her Catholic Church where the organist always took me up in the choir loft, and generally I sang an "Ave Maria." Another Sunday, I went with Bruder, the hired man, and his wife to the Lutheran Church. Next, I would go to visit Aunt Emily at the Baptist Church and help in the choir; and still another time, I would go with my friend, Etta, to the Presbyterian Church, in the Bible class.

Once, at dinner, I astounded my parents and the guests present when I responded to my father's question as to the subject of the Bible lesson by saying, "Oh, we had the seventh commandment, Thou Shalt Not Adulterate." I thought it was only recently that they began putting sand in the sugar and trying to cheat people, so we had to have the PURE FOOD LAW. Mother, in her most severe tone said, "<u>Mary</u>!" and changed the subject. Later I was given orders not to discuss weighty problems in public.

To get back to Santa Rosa and the revival—I poured my whole soul into that revival, being thoroughly converted. I caught cold, got wet feet, but continued my classes by day and my singing by night throughout the week; but on Sunday night, when the revival was over, I was "finished" too. I couldn't speak. I wanted to die. I asked to telegraph home, but Miss Chase thought it was only a cold and would soon pass away.

Finally, my sensitive mother sent Father over to see me. (He crossed my heart-broken letter on his way: "voice is gone forever!") Father was one very disgruntled man when he found me voiceless and hysterical. He told Miss Chase that if she would confine her attention to her pupils' health and education, he felt sure their parents could handle their "immortal souls." He took me home with him, and that ended my education in schools.

Then began the tedious process of coaxing back first my speaking voice, then a faint, whispering ghost of my singing voice. Only one who has sung with such freedom and joy—and then cannot—knows what I suffered.

With the voice apparently lost, I redoubled my efforts at the piano and began some little experiments at composition. They were very crude and annoyed Uncle John, as he felt I was neglecting my Harmony and Counterpoint studies. However, it comforted me to write a few songs with the despair of one who has "lived and loved and lost."

I was almost fifteen then. Mother tried to keep me out-of-doors a good deal, and took me driving or sent me to town for the errands. I loved driving our spirited gold-colored Ned, who would dance on his hind feet if the train came by, but was gentle. We were good friends. Torry used to come along, and we always weighed him. Otto, a fair, blue-eyed lad, clerk at the general store, always weighed me too. Katie, our Irish cook, always teased me about him, and taught Torry to say: "Sister, how you' dot?"—which, of course, always made me blush.

Being very romantic, I got to thinking a good deal about Otto, although our acquaintance was strictly limited to the errands and the weighing. One summer afternoon, Otto asked for leave, borrowed his employer's surrey, and drove out the two-and-a-half miles to our house. From our hill, I could see him coming a half a mile away. In a quiver of excitement, I ran upstairs and told Mother. She whistled down the tube to Katie to make some lemonade and cut some fruitcake. Mother was always hospitable.

The surrey arrived, and as Father was sitting on the front porch, I waited bashfully upstairs for Father to call me. After what seemed an enormous time, we heard the surrey driving off, crossing the bridge, and going back toward town. Mother and I came downstairs, and Mother said: "Where is Otto?"

Father's eyes twinkled, and he said, "Why, he just left."

Mother demanded the rest of the story, and Father said, "Well Otto drove up, and I asked him if he had a telegram—and Otto said, No—he just came out for a drive. I told him it was a nice afternoon for a drive, and then he asked if he could have a glass of water. Of course, I gave him one, and then after a pause, he said he guessed he'd have to be going!"

Mother burst out: "Papa, I think you were mean; of course, he came out to call on Mary Louise."

But Papa said, "How could I know—he didn't say so."

Well, I was rather deflated, and wished for once that Papa wasn't such a joker. However, once in awhile, I was allowed to go to a dance in town with Father and Mother, and Otto always danced once with me (more would been too pointed)—but we always spoke of the weather.

Father began to be terribly worried. His coal mines in Iowa, the source of our very ample income, leased for twenty years to come, abruptly ran out; or rather, the vein turned at right-angles off of Father's property. For several months this possibility loomed and then became a fact. One by one, Mother reduced the servant staff. But, of course, our lovely, big home and the thirty-five acres, most of it grounds, some in vineyard, was never income property, only an expensive luxury.

Mother had, by then, become amazingly well and energetic and took an active part in much of the town activity. She wrote and staged several plays, of which *Kentucky Belle* was performed many times. Father, whose rich baritone voice was always in demand, comes back to me vividly as he portrayed King Ahesueras in *Esther, the Beautiful Queen.* With his flowing robes, his naturally kingly aspect and his royal gestures, he was a vast success. There was much doing in little St. Helena at that time, in a musical and dramatic way. Some of us younger ones gave many scenes from Shakespeare, using the landing of our spacious hall and stairway for a stage—a regular *Romeo and Juliet* balcony.

A final blow decided our future. Father, with three others, had signed security on a friend's bond. Through large-hearted hospitality, a wife whose understanding of financial problems was nil, and a swarm of children, the poor man had defaulted for an enormous sum. Father and three others had to make it good, or the penitentiary loomed for their friend. Naturally, with Cleveland in the White House and Father a staunch Republican, their was no government appointment to be thought of. So, at fifty-six, having retired from active business, Father began life over again, obtaining a position as cashier in a large San Francisco bank.

We moved to San Francisco and sold the lovely Napa Valley home for about one tenth of what it had cost. From that time on, Father's gaiety and spirit gradually lessened, although he gallantly tried to hide his anxiety. He felt himself a failure. He had always thought only of his family. It was chiefly because of my future that he grieved; he had planned to take us all to Europe to "finish" my musical education. I have always felt, and many times told him, that had he kept his money, I probably wouldn't have been worth the powder to blow me up."

I was almost sixteen when we moved to San Francisco. There we took a large house, and Grandfather and Grandmother Pratt and Auntie Carlin, who had graduated from Santa Rosa Seminary, left their quarters at the Lick House and came to live with us. I began intensive vocal studies with H. B. Pasmore, and after having been a "prima donna," began the laborious and discouraging task of building back, note by note, the ghost of my former voice.

Many of the friends of Carlin, with whom I had before had only a slight acquaintance, now became friends. The Balch family, especially Maude, Carlin and I were fast friends. George, a great tease, was like a big brother. Bert, the next brother, a big, silent, shy boy, exceedingly handsome and totally unaware of it, became my ideal of all a man should be. Now, Mother began allowing me some part in a few social affairs—always in a "foursome"—with Carlin and one of her several escorts, generally Bert for me. When the boys came to call, Carlin, who was eighteen and "going in for society," could stay up; but I, with a career planned for me, was promptly sent to bed at ten o'clock.

I had become subject to inexplicable fainting spells, and Mother was anxious to build up my health. One evening, when Bert was one of the callers, I was sent upstairs as usual at ten. I felt very much upset about it, and as a child in disgrace, I started upstairs—and the next I remember, I was being choked with whisky, my hands being chafed, and a general hubbub surrounded me.

Around midnight, when the callers left, all the family gathered in the hall; the grandparents, with Father and Mother, finished off the evening with a game of cards. I was discovered halfway up the stairs, head downward, in a dead faint. How I ever failed to break my neck is a mystery. I was always, it seemed, "coming to" and finding myself the center of an excited group, without the slightest memory of having fainted. Later, doctors diagnosed it: a sudden excitement causing an accelerated pulse, which receding, left the pressure below normal and failed to pump the blood to the brain fast enough.

For years, I was subject to these very exasperating occurrences, from over-fatigue, emotional excitement, or from nobody knows what.

My oldest brother, Eugene, became engaged to Alice Preston, the lovely young sister of his law partner, Harold. She and her mother came to visit us, and I promptly fell in love with her; she seemed more and more like a real sister.

Eugene and his partner, soon to become his brother-in-law, had located in Seattle, and had, together, weathered through some serious difficulties. During the Chinese riots, Gene, Captain of Company E, State Militia, had risked his life over and over. He was badly wounded in his efforts to give the Chinese safe conduct.

These inoffensive and harmless laundrymen, cooks, and railroad gangs who had been victims of the most dastardly attacks by so-called "white labor," most of them foreign, many of them darker than the Chinese, and none of them so cleanly and law-abiding. Suffice it to say, the best that could be done for them was to safe-guard their exodus. Poor Seattle! She has been victimized by the lawless elements far too long! *[Eugene Merwin Carr was one of the five men arrested and charged with murder for their part in facing an angry white mob and protecting some hundred Chinese as they were being evacuated from the city...The charges, brought by the police officers in sympathy with the mob, were never pressed — JM]*

Then came the Seattle fire, which resulted in havoc and a very slim practice for two young lawyers. So Eugene, being the larger and huskier, decided to take a pick and shovel and go out on the railroad, earning day wages, while Harold kept the office open and took care of what little business there was. Eugene was only three days with the "gang" when he was made "section boss" and later put in charge of construction and finally returned to the office with some accrued savings. All of these hardships behind them, their law firm was one of the most successful, and their friendship firmly cemented.

The marriage was a very happy affair. Alice did some of her shopping while with us, but the wedding was consummated at her uncle's large ranch, one of California's historic old places. The bridal pair returned to Seattle, where they occupied a pretty home that Eugene had built and furnished as a surprise for Alice. Also a Swedish housekeeper had been installed. If Alice ever had a lurking regret that she hadn't a hand in the planning and managing, she never mentioned it!

That summer, during my vacation, I was their guest; never could a full-fledged young lady have had a grander time. I was almost seventeen. Mother had made me some of the prettiest clothes! One costume of dove-gray cashmere (heavily embroidered by Mother) in shaded gray silk, had its own little embroidered shoulder cape, a gray net hat with pink roses, gray gloves, and so on, and was quite admired by Eugene, whose observant good taste was the final seal of approval. Also, I had quite a grown-up tea gown and flowing sleeves. That was Mother's one concession to my desire to be grown-up.

When I left San Francisco, Carlin and all the young friends "saw me off" across the Bay and to the Oakland 16th Street Station. I was inclined to feel very homesick. I was going to miss Bert terribly, even though I seldom was with him—and always in company—but his fathomless eyes were always on my mind. He never gave me the slightest sign that I held any interest for him; it was presumption on my part to love him as I did, absorbingly. I was only sixteen, and he was twenty-one, with an important position in the Railroad Offices at Third and Townsend! However, my heart always behaved in a queer manner when I saw him unexpectedly.

The excitement of my first long trip, alone, soon dispelled my homesickness. Eugene met me at Tacoma, and when I reached the pretty house on the Lake with a balcony leading from my bed room—and a <u>moon</u>—I was entranced.

Alice treated me like a young lady and as a dear sister as well. Several teas in my honor increased my "grown-up" feeling. Then we went to the State Militia Encampment over at American Lake, where Eugene was now Adjutant on the Governor's staff, and for General Carr [*"Uncle" Eugene A. Carr*]. About five hundred militiamen were encamped on the lovely, rolling, wooded grounds near Tacoma. In 1690, it was called Camp Curry for the Governor.

Eugene's bride, another bride and I were, for the greater part of the time, the only ladies in camp. Eugene's two tents and Colonel White's tent were pitched just outside the lines in deference to the ladies. I was given my brother's former Captain's cap and sword and immediately elected "Honorary Captain of Company E" (made up largely of young lawyers and professional men of Seattle), and then began my first experiences of a grown-up sort. Seattle was new, and young ladies were at a premium.

One morning, a young lawyer Lieutenant came over to our tent quite early and accompanied us to breakfast; then he invited me to look around the campgrounds. In the afternoon he chartered a motor boat and took me around the lake where, to my amazement, he asked me to marry him. I was so astonished that I gave the old bromide that I would have to think it over. After dinner in a Washington drizzle, hardly more than a mist, he called for me again with an umbrella, once again to show me around the camp. Under the shelter of the umbrella, he kissed me, and I suddenly decided that we weren't well enough acquainted for an engagement, so suggested we be just "friends." I think he was fully as relieved as I was.

The two weeks passed in a whirl, and we were back in Seattle. Next door, our neighbors were expecting the first baby. I was hoping it would arrive before I had to leave. I was to be the godmother. Night after night I would get up and look out of the window to see if there were any signs of excitement, but no!

All the Militia boys vied in showing me a good time. A young minister took me canoeing on the lake and brought me rare specimens of forest flowers. Seattle was carved right out of the luxurious forests of evergreen with tangled undergrowth of mammoth ferns and twining peavines, almost impassable. Next door, the very good-looking and sophisticated brother of my new friend planned several nice parties and was my escort to my first real ball at the Rainer Club. We drove down with Eugene and Alice. Learning through his sister the color of my party dress, my escort gave me my first corsage. My, but wasn't I a real Society Lady! At the ball, I saw for the first time ladies dressed in the extreme decollate of that time and was mortified almost to death!

The following evening, the last of my visit, Eugene was detained at the office. Alice had a headache, and I was left alone to entertain nine farewell callers bearing candy, books, and flowers. Among them were the young minister and the escort of the previous evening. Brother Eugene, returning home about ten, was rather aghast at the crowd. He had the housekeeper serve lemonade and sweet biscuit, and one by one, the callers finally faded away.

Eugene read me a brotherly lecture, telling me it was time he sent me home to Mother, and never again to have quite so many callers at once, nor to receive them in a tea gown, which, although the fashion, he considered too intimate. All in all, I felt rather a little girl again, and suddenly remembered how, when I was about ten and he had returned from Alaska after his hazardous trip, that he used to offer me a nickel for every time I would refrain from kissing him. He branded me with the horrid nickname, "Kissy Carr." At any rate, we had a fine talk, and he told me he had enjoyed letting be a young lady just for vacation, but that I must be a good girl and go back to my studies and not grow up for several years to come.

That was a never-to-be-forgotten summer, and when I started home the next day, I was filled with gratitude for the good times, though also eager to get back to home and studies. Father met me, and I was never gladder to see him. I probably didn't stop talking for weeks! And the next time Bert called, with his brother, I realized that no one could ever take his place. I found it difficult to obey mother and start to bed at ten o'clock, but I did, and both boys came into the hall and watched me upstairs, to be sure I didn't faint!

I had been home about a week when a telegram announced the birth of my little godson, Ben! I sat right down and composed both words and music of a Lullaby for him, which is my "Opus 1, Number 1, it being the first of my compositions approved by Uncle John. It seemed very simple and old-fashioned, but I could never get through a recital or concert without singing it as an encore, and usually had to repeat it.

My voice, by now, had become more dependable, and I secured a position as soprano soloist in the large First Baptist Church on Eddy Street. Once Dr. Henry, after a fine sermon, invited all who would to meet him for further talk in the crypt of the church and asked me if I would remain and help.

About fifty or more gathered the impassioned plea of this sincere Evangelist. I sang "Tho Your Sins He Is Scarlet," and one or two other songs. Most of those present came up and confessed their conversion. I was very serious about this and felt my responsibility deeply. Imagine how startled I was when Father (who would cheerfully joke on any subject without in the least intending any blasphemy) replied: "Congratulations to you and Dr. Henry for bagging so many sinners with song."

I began to realize that I should assist my father with the expense of my education. The choir position helped some, but the fact that Mr. Pasmore had several times employed me when Mrs. Pasmore, his regular assistant, felt ill, or when another of the Pasmore babies was imminent, encouraged me to feel that I might start a little class of my own. I wrote to friends in St. Helena and Napa, and in each town a class was arranged. Then I told Father and Mother. They were dubious, but finally consented.

So, just after my seventeenth birthday, I began going to Napa Valley for two days a week, staying overnight with a school friend in Napa, whose father was editor of the Napa Register. How kind those people were to me! Giving me their living room and piano for the lessons, for which, of course, I taught their daughter in partial return. She was the only pupil in my two classes who was as young as the teacher.

My long piano study was a great help, of course, as accompaniments were no problem. My repertoire was large and varied, for at Mr. Pasmore's studio we not only took our own lessons, but listened to the others. Often I was allowed to accompany, and Mr. Pasmore's own excellent musicianship was an ever-present inspiration. My voice was improving, and I was having more confidence; it seemed that probably my voice would regain its earlier promise. I was studying operatic parts and was prepared in ten roles.

Father had a fine offer to take full charge of one of several banks in central California owned by Uncle Lillis. Then came the problem of interrupting my studies. But finally my grandparents, Uncle John, and Mr. Pasmore persuaded Mother into leaving me in San Francisco. She, my father, and Torry moved to a little town in San Joaquin Valley, and I moved in with the grandparents and Carlin to the Bella Vista Hotel, on Taylor and Pine Streets, one of the best family hotels in the city. There, the kindly manager, Mrs. Spaulding, allowed me the Ballroom, with its fully equipped little stage, for my classes in return for a monthly recital, free to the guests.

Grandfather and grandmother had a large suite on the sixth floor, and Carlin and I had one adjoining. I was the guest of my grandparents. While I paid my board and other expenses, I could have never afforded a room of the style and size that Carlin and I shared. But Grandma always seemed like my second mother, and Grandfather, in his quiet way, really approved of my efforts at earning my own living.

Now came a time of hard work—many concerts, large classes, and constant composing. In spite of all this, I had many good times. Our suite and the hotel ballroom became headquarters for the "What's Up" Club, so named because Grandfather would come to the open door between our suite and theirs and say, "Well, what's up tonight, girls and boys?" No hour was too late for them to be up, joining in, and interested in our fun. We had many theater parties, picnics at the beach, and hikes over into Marin County, always "Dutch Treat." Most of the group lived in our hotel and a few at the Colonial a block away.

Grandfather decided to take a family party East to visit the Chicago World's Fair and to tour the Eastern States in his private car. Of course, he invited me. That was my first difficult decision to make. It was right in the middle of the season. I actually prayed over that problem. If I went, I would have to give up my church position, and how could I ask my pupils to discontinue their lessons for six weeks or more? But, oh, how I wanted to go!

I went to Grandfather and talked it over with him, hoping that he would not think I was silly. I told him that I thought it was my duty to remain, and that, if I wanted to be a musician, I must expect to make some sacrifice. I know now that he was very proud of my decision, but at the time, he told me I was the one to say. Since I could not accept his invitation, then he would appreciate it if I would keep an eye on the rooms, and that since he had planned to have me as his guest, he would instead see that my board was paid during his absence. It was all as business—as if I had been another businessman! What a grand person he was!

The son of family friends, a young medical student, asked me to marry him (of course, at a far distant date, after his graduation.) Always of a romantic nature and being much in love with the idea of love, I accepted. Of course, as it was in one of the hotel parlors, there was no further "demonstration." No "lady" living in such a hotel would receive any gentleman alone. The bellboy always brought up a card, and you went down, except when the family was at home. So the best we could do in the way of visiting was for him to call for me at church Sunday evening and walk the few blocks up the hill to Pine Street.

In the meantime, he addressed a letter to my "parents, in Tulare County," asking permission to become my suitor. The telegram in response—addressed to me—was a thunderous "NO! Your mother will arrive tomorrow."

Poor Mother, having to take that tiresome journey! She stayed with me for several days, talking to my would-be fiancé very kindly and sensibly, saying that we were both too young to know our minds. But she said if we would wait <u>four</u> years, until he had graduated and established a practice, and still wished to marry, she would withdraw all objections. So, while my first engagement lasted through an afternoon, the second was of two days' duration.

I was much distressed a few days later by receiving from my erstwhile fiancé a tragic letter saying that he hadn't the courage to face the next four years without me, and that by the time I read his letter he "would be no more." We had no telephones. I hardly dared write a letter to his address, fearing publicity if he had "destroyed himself."

I scanned the paper fearfully every morning—until several days later, I received an exact replica of the first letter, only evidently recopied and neater and with no misspelled words. I could only conclude that he was still alive, that he had mailed the first letter and then finding the good copy, concluded that he had not mailed his letter to me at all.

Quite relieved as to his suicidal intentions, and somewhat disillusioned, I finished up my spring classes. Upon return of the family from their wonderful trip, I went south to spend my first vacation in San Joaquin Valley.

The days were indescribably hot, but the nights were heavenly. It was wonderful to be at home again and to see how Torry had grown. Like many small towns, people here were well acquainted, and the social life had a far more intimate quality. Informality was the rule, and everyone set about making me welcome. I sang at a lot of gatherings—never professionally, but with a nice feeling of friendliness about it.

Mother had started a girl's club called the "Alpha Club." She had obtained a grant of land, about four square blocks near the Railroad. With two or three other ladies, all influential in the town, she had planted a park, "a grateful shade in a desert land."

All too soon, it was time for me to return to San Francisco and my fall classes. Grandmother and Carlin were still in their Napa Valley home. Grandfather went up for weekends, and there were many jolly house parties. I had to forgo these, as my church position kept me busy. To save the expense of the extra suite, I took a room near Mr. Pasmore's studio with one of his pupils, Mrs. Middleton. Her husband was often away on business and disliked leaving her alone; also, she needed coaching and assistance with her vocal work, so I was able to earn the greater part of my room and board.

There were two young sons, eleven and ten. This was my first introduction to real live boys of that age. They led their mother a great life. I believe she was only sixteen years older than her oldest son.

One night, after the boys had spent the day at the beach, Mrs. Middleton and I were awakened by stealthy sounds. I listened awhile, breathless with terror. Finally gaining courage to go into her room, I found Mrs. Middleton also nearly hysterical. The sounds came from the long front stairs leading down to the street entrance. After awhile, we risked lighting the gas in her room. Nothing happened! The queer noises continued. Together, trembling, we lit the hall gas jet and discovered the midnight marauders. About twenty or more tiny soft-shell crabs, which the boys had corralled in a dishpan in the kitchen sink, had, one by one, climbed out and dropped to the kitchen floor. They made their way along the hall and dropped step by step down to the front door where they could get a whiff of the salt night fog, reminding them of their "home on the beach."

I kept receiving letters from a young journalist named Louis, assistant to his father, who was editor of the town paper. We had had many interesting talks, en famille, during the summer evenings when our families exchanged visits. His letters were gems. Imperceptibly, we drifted into an "understanding" by correspondence. I had great dreams of life in the country, wife of an editor, until I would come to a sudden obstacle—what would become of the music? Well, I could always teach. However, a very good-looking young baritone, son of one of the G. A. R. men, whose wife and family I had long known, began studying voice with me. I had quite a few men pupils, most of whom took their lessons in my ballroom studio early in the evening.

On one of the occasions, Roscoe's lesson fell on the night of the weekly hotel dance. I invited him to remain for it. During the course of the evening, I danced, as usual, with all of our friends, while Roscoe danced only with me. I was cross about it, but didn't know what to say. Finally, during one of our dances, he decided to "sit out" the rest of the dance. The only place to sit was either in the overcrowded ballroom or in the stairway, people coming and going all the time. He chose the latter and managed, between interruptions, to make me a very formal proposal.

Well, his voice, his good looks, and his obvious devotion were too much. But, I was engaged to Louis! Later that night, I wrote to Louis asking him to release me, a difficult thing to do—doubly difficult when another lovely letter came the following day. But this time, I felt the really <u>right</u> person had come. (Of course, each time I had felt the same thing!) However, with Roscoe I thought love would go hand in hand with music. At his next lesson, I gave him his answer, in the meantime having received the letter from Louis releasing me, but telling me he would always feel the same. Of course, I cried over it and reluctantly returned the large packet of letters. Those letters were very unusual. I had read a great deal, and I could not be lightly moved by trivial conventionalities. It seems as if the boy who wrote those letters should have become a great author.

Roscoe took our engagement very seriously. It wasn't a week before he asked me to give up dancing because it made him suffer to see me in the arms of another man. (I was never in <u>his</u> arms, by the way, for there could be no tête-à-têtes in a big hotel. I lived the life of a goldfish.) It wasn't proper to drive unchaperoned, and San Francisco was not a happy climate for driving. Nor could a nice girl venture into the Park and sit upon a park bench. The actual extent of most love-making in those days was a furtive pressure of the hand or a rare and hasty kiss, snatched at the risk of being observed and "talked about." I am sure there <u>was</u> lovemaking, but it never came under my observation. During my stay at the hotel, one sweet-faced lady, about thirty, was requested to leave because she received a caller, alone, in her sitting room. Although they were engaged to be married shortly, after the marriage came off as scheduled, there was always a shadow of scandal about the affair.

Very soon, Roscoe began to feel qualms over the fact that I had other men pupils. (All of them antedated his own term.) I felt that was unjust, as no one, by any stretch of imagination, could think of a no tête-à-tête in that wide-open, well-lighted ballroom. I was rather shocked, and felt under suspicion.

I had been commissioned to arrange a little operetta near the holidays, so Mother arranged to have a duplicate cast rehearse the music and planned to present a performance during my vacation for a Park benefit. As my leading baritone could not leave San Francisco at that time, I had Roscoe understudy the part for the home performance. The San Francisco affair was a great success. It was a miscellaneous program, followed by the cunning little comedy by Frank Walkerk, *Penelope, or, The Milkman's Bride.* I was Penelope then, and for many subsequent performances. After the performance, I left for the Valley having been able to arrange a substitute at Church for part of the holidays.

I was nineteen, and this Christmas I was able to give real gifts to the family. Father refused to get himself the new overcoat he needed, so I ordered a really nice one from his old tailor; for Mother, a new set of dishes, and for dear little Torry, some books and toys. I had not always been so "flush." Lessons, music, dentist bills, concert dresses—it took all I could earn. Church salaries in the West were not large. Several extra concerts had brought up the exchequer. Father had often had to come to my rescue.

When I reached home, there were many intensive rehearsals for *Penelope.* Roscoe came down the night before the performance; although the rehearsal was terrifying, the performance went well, with a big crowd and a large sum netted for the park. Everything seemed rosy.

The next morning, Roscoe and I took the tiresome day train back to "the city." During that trip, I heard a good deal about my behavior on the stage. My acting was too convincing. It wasn't necessary to be so realistic. I reminded Roscoe that, being the Milkman and the successful suitor, he should not object. But he did object and had "suffered" at the San Francisco performance and hoped I would not seriously think of going into grand opera. (What had I been studying for all that time?) I had not spoken of our engagement at home, as Roscoe did not want it announced until he was in a position to marry.

That evening, upon reaching San Francisco, I found Grandfather alone, Grandmother and Carlin having taken a party to Napa Valley for the holidays. I made a complete confession to Grandfather, and instead of treating me as a silly child, he talked it all over quietly and reasonably, and I came to realize that a great deal of unhappiness and frustration might result. So I wrote a letter that night, breaking my fourth engagement!

That weekend, Grandfather, too, went up to the Valley. I went as usual to my choir rehearsal and found Roscoe waiting to take me home. He stormed a good deal on the walk up the hill, and I felt terrible, but I did not ask him in, and instead of using my latchkey, rang the bell. Of course, when the bellboy answered my ring, I said goodnight, and Roscoe could only leave. Three times the next day, the bellboy brought his card up and took back word that I was out. On Monday, I got a dreadful letter, denouncing me as a flirt—four pages of it. Carlin was home by then, and finding me in a dead faint, read the letter, and as my "Aunt," and natural protector, wrote him what she thought of him. (Doesn't this sound like *The Duchess* or some old fashioned thriller?) I had really been very fond of him, and it was a difficult experience. I worked hard at my music and wrote several rather lurid songs about that time.

I had taken on a new class and had given up the Napa Valley class, which had become somewhat irregular. I was gradually learning to demand more of my pupils. The new class was in a thriving little town in the Santa Cruz Mountains; from the outset, it was most satisfactory. Among my pupils were the wife of the hotelkeeper and her grown daughter, the principal of the school, the Presbyterian minister, and other talented residents. My headquarters were at the Morgan Hotel, and nothing was too much trouble to do for my comfort. The kind-hearted hotelkeeper and his wife and daughter saw to it personally that I had the juiciest steaks, the richest cream, and that the parlor was entirely at my disposal for my lessons.

A newspaper account recalls the time; "The Drawing Room of the Morgan House was filled with the crème de la crème of Boulder Creek, with here and there a representative from Ben Lambent and Santa Cruz." Mentioning the dignified school principal, the article continues; "He sang 'Love's Sorrow' in his usual happy style." And again, "Let Me Love Thee.' as sung by Miss Carr, was immense."

I took an early morning ferry from San Francisco on Wednesdays, arriving in Boulder Creek about noon. I would then teach all that afternoon and evening, and the following morning leave for San Francisco at one o'clock, arriving at six. The Santa Cruz Mountains were noted for their rainfall. The inhabitants measured it "by the yard," instead of by inches. Several times during my period of teaching, the stage met the train at Ben Lambent—and once at Felon, ten miles away—because of washouts. On that trip, we had to alight from the stage at several narrow places while some of the men steadied the stage as it crept past a narrow spot with one wheel over the bank. But it was exciting. Much better than remaining safe at home and missing classes!

I was a member of the "Progressive Club," founded by Mrs. John Farnham for young people. It was a place where they might meet to dance, play cards, enact plays or give musicales, under proper sponsorship. The club met monthly at Golden Gate Hall on Sutter Street. Many of the young people of the club have since become noted in their various professions, such as the talented young artist, Bertha Stringer, whose engagement to her future husband, George Lee, was first announced there. I treasure a lovely painting of hers, given me as a prize from the California Contest of 1933, National League of American Penwomen. Although I won first prizes in cash at the National Biennials in 1932, 1934, and 1936, I still have this picture while the money has, of course, evaporated!

Mrs. Farnham startled me one day by asking me to write an operetta for the club! I was sure I was intrigued by the idea. I was nearly twenty at the time and busy with my Boulder Creek classes, San Francisco pupils, Church position, and concert engagements. But during the long trips to the mountains, I thought about it more and more.

Finally, I concocted a silly plot about an Irish policeman who left New York and went to Athens, where he re-opened the Oracle at Delphi. He installed his pretty New York bride as the High Priestess, engaged a lot of Athenian girls and boys as vestal virgins and priests, and himself became the Voice of the Oracle. Through some ventriloquistic feats, he maintains a great air of mystery and secrecy until his employees become convinced of the authenticity of the "revival." There was a young Athenian heiress whose "rapscallion" of a guardian wanted to marry her (and her fortune), although she was in love with a nice, young "out-of-a-job" dry-goods clerk. Her young companion, attending her mistress at Delphi, struck up an acquaintance with a travelling salesman for a wholesale cigar and liquor store in Rome. Altogether, with a combination of misunderstandings and complications, the "plot" was ridiculously funny.

I began burning midnight oil on the music. There were several choruses, solos and duets, and finally it was completed. The young people at the hotel helped with the chorus copies, and it was put into rehearsal. I was in charge as musical director, and the hotel ballroom with its well-equipped stage was turned over to us.

Work began to pile up overwhelmingly. I was chosen to sing Cleo, the heiress, and although I protested that I should not sing the lead in my own opera, I was overruled and secretly delighted. My childhood friend, Virginia Graham, who had taken her first lessons from me in the Napa Valley during my first venture as a teacher of singing, and who was now in San Francisco studying with Mr. Pasmore, was given the difficult role of Aurora, High Priestess. Jolly Will Fine sang opposite her as the Policemen, and Patrick O'Shay, alias Laecterian. His Irish brogue was quite ridiculous! Frank Coffin, a well-known young tenor, sang Claudium, the traveling salesman from Rome, and Father Neadham was the flirtations Doris. The cruel guardian, Droteus, was essayed by Orlo Eastwood. He was all sorts of a friend in helping me with the chorus costuming and training.

Through Mrs. Farnham's influence, E. M. Rosner, director for years of the Orpheum orchestra, was prevailed upon to conduct our orchestra. Although he must have felt annoyed at being dragged into an amateur job of that sort, he was always kind and never ridiculed my work.

At the final stage rehearsal with orchestra the day before the performance, as I was rehearsing my first aria, the kindly old double-bass player looked up at me over his glasses, saying: "Vel, I can't play vat you write, but I play vat you mean, hein?" (I had, alas, though better taught by Uncle John, written the bass parts down on pitch!)

We preceded a few bars, when a terrible sound came from the clarinet player. Not so patient, he declared the stuff was impossible. We discovered, through Mr. Rosner's investigation that, I had carefully written the B-flat clarinet a major second below instead of above its actual sound. (How many times since have I sympathized with young orchestral students making the same, very natural error.) No one can guess the depths of my humiliation. I sat up most of the night and re-copied both the bass and clarinet parts, and the performance the following night went without a hitch.

It was in invitation affair, and invitations were at a premium. It had been "front page stuff" in the *Examiner, Chronicle,* and *Call* for several days, with reporters and photographers at dress rehearsals. I was amazed when I found my own picture on the front page. I went to my room and actually wept, feeling a complete disgrace at being so "public"—as if I were a criminal.

Uncle John had supplied my picture, which I had refused the reporter who had come to interview me some days before, saying I did not care to have my picture in public prints. Mrs. Farnham had tried to shake my decision and in the end had phoned Uncle John. Papa had come up from Lemoore to attend, but Mother could not come. The "What's Ups" were out in full force, and society with a capital <u>S</u>. The papers were very kind afterward, as well as before, and devoted columns to it.

After my disappointing experience with Roscoe, Carlin, as ever the moving spirit, paired me off with the young brother of one of our older girls, excepting the times when Bert could come. But his increasing responsibilities at his office and rapid promotion kept him busy. As I look back over these years, I realize that had he ever asked me, I would have said "yes." But, although he never took anyone else out and frequently arranged a theater party or a dance or a jaunt with the "What's Ups" for Carlin and her current escort, with me for his guest, yet I never knew whether he really cared for me.

So young Frank became my escort. He was almost a year younger than I. Gradually we drifted into a real friendship, which imperceptibly took on the status of an engagement. The whole group took it for granted, and so did we. I shall never forget the sweetness of that friendship which lasted for about two years, and during all the busy "Oracle" time, he was my "right hand man," helping with copying and in every way he could.

Carlin announced her engagement to Orlo Eastwood, and we four were a happy group. The strain of "The Oracle," its compositions, preparation and performance had taken a good deal out of me. I gave up my Boulder Creek class and finally my church position in order to cope with my "city" classes and increasing concert engagements. I took a brief summer vacation in order to rehearse with an opera company, which was preparing for a short summer tour. I was to sing Maraguerita, Hosina, and Mincaola.

As rehearsal went on, toward the final time for departure it happened that I was called to rehearse two operas on one day and three the next. I fainted in my dressing room but was able to keep the matter quiet. The next afternoon, I had the bad luck to faint in rehearsal. The kindly director, although very sorry for me, took a firm stand saying that he could not risk taking me out on the road and having me die on his hands!

Although I was promised a part with the company the following year if I would rest and get strong, my heart was quite broken. I struggled through the fall months, my fainting spells more and more frequent. When I went home for Christmas vacation, Mother had the family doctor give me a thorough going over. He laid my nervous condition to overwork and ordered me to rest. Half glad and half sorry, I returned to "the city." I bade goodbye to Grandfather and Grandmother and went home to Lemoore to <u>rest</u>.

Also, in my heart, I bade goodbye to my young sweetheart, for I had begun to realize for the first time that our boy and girl friendship could not stand the test of poverty, delicate health, and responsibility. I began to think of entering a convent, feeling that life was quite over for me. Bert evidently did not love me, my career was at an end, and there was nothing else worthwhile except to devote my few remaining months, possibly a year or two, to God.

I think I would call this point the close of the first Movement. There followed a sweet and pastoral theme. Friendly calls were made upon me by the Alpha Club girls, women who wanted to like me if I did not turn out to be too "citified." There were the little socials, the musicales, when Lynn Fox, a really gifted violinist, and my fingers at the piano, would play a Deriot, or Wioniawski Concerto.

The fainting spells persisted, and our old family physician had sold his practice to a young graduate of Cooper Medical College (the forerunner of Stanford Medical College) who soon became a welcome member of our little group. We were a "sextet," consisting of Lynn, his sweetheart, a young schoolteacher who boarded with the young doctor's mother *[Amanda Jordan Hall]*, the Doctor *[John Claude Moore]*, his brother *[Fred T. Moore]* and myself. Mother never thought of permitting the "young doctor" to attend me during a fainting spell, even if he were present. An old retired physician was always called in, greatly to the chagrin of the neglected young medico.

One evening, after a long musicale at home, I "came to," finding my feet propped up on pillows, my wrists being rubbed, and amazing to say, found my hair and forehead quite dry. Usually, some well-meaning soul had managed to drench me with cold water, which always resulted in a chill, took the curl out of my hair, and made me feel utterly disgusted and disgraced.

This most ungraceful position was bad enough, but was mitigated by the fact that only Mother and the young doctor were present instead of the usual excited and curious group. It seems the "old doctor" was known to be out of town, and Mother had to accept the ministrations of the "young doctor." He was a sturdy, broad-shouldered farmer-boy, with fair hair and clear blue eyes, strong features, and although not handsome, was very attractive and dependable looking. He was less than two years older than I. He had managed his widowed mother's farm at fourteen, had borrowed money from a family friend, had put himself through medical college, and was practicing medicine before his twenty-fourth birthday!

The lovely spring months were my first taste of leisure from teaching, concerts, and church choirs since my early girlhood. I rapidly gained in strength, and we six had marvelous good times together. Nora, the teacher and several years my senior, became my bosom friend.

As we four (the Moore boys and Nora) often drove over to the county seat to attend a play or a social, we paired off as it happened, equally friendly. Fred Moore had a beautiful baritone voice and took lessons from me—while the Doctor, eager to sing, had a sweet tenor voice, but no idea of pitch. He would sing quite cheerfully during the hymns, a perfect fifth above the soprano, or vice versa, as he felt in the mood. I struggled with his musical education, and in time he improved. But Fred was the real singer.

My mother, having studied intensively, was ordained into the ministry and accepted a pulpit in the neighboring town for Sunday mornings, taking the train on Saturdays and returning Sundays after services. Sunday evenings, she conducted an informal young people's group in the hall above the bank where Father was cashier. As Mother's denomination was Unitarian, some of the other churches looked upon her as almost godless. But before long, she won the warm co-operation of the other ministers, for while they did not approve of her label, they liked her and admitted that she was reaching many who had not been regular church attendants before.

June came and the wedding of my dear Carlin. We all went to the Napa Valley home. A special train was sent up from San Francisco to bring the guests from "the city"—about two hundred. Orlo's brother was best man, and I was maid of honor. Bert was there—he and his brother were ushers, and their sister was one of the bridesmaids.

Such a wedding! Carlin had planned to come down the winding staircase as the old clock struck nine. The last few minutes seemed to creep. I learned later that a delay had been caused by a slight accident, breaking of a shaft, I think, to one of the carriages bringing guests. Father had thoughtfully turned the minute-hand back, a bit at a time, for nearly a half-hour until the last guests had arrived. So Carlin came down the stairs to meet her Orlo as the clock was striking the ninth chime. Mother performed the ceremony, which was sweet and impressive.

Before I returned to Lemoore, I visited a few days in "the city." Bert's sister gave a party for me, and I stayed all night. After the company had gone and we were about to retire, Maud teasingly dared Bert to kiss me goodnight, which he did, after some hesitation. I remember blushing until it hurt. The next day I went home and three weeks later I learned of Bert's brief illness and death. His poor mother and family were grief-stricken— I was stunned!

When, a few weeks later, I received the entire contents of his private box, consisting of my picture (given long before to his sister), a lock of my hair, a few letters, dance and theater programs—then I knew. His dear Mother, who followed him in less than a year, told me that I had always been the "only one." How different my life might have been. But, my life has been the life I needed, or it would not be mine!

Back in Lemoore during the hot summer, the "young doctor" took me driving a great deal. Darling Father was friendly to a young man calling on his "only daughter" and failed to refer to him as a "young cub." My little brother, Torry, adored him, as in fact, the whole town and countryside did by then. When school re-opened and our teachers returned, the pairing off was the educational department together, with music and medicine allied.

After I had taught a year and had lost weight, it seemed that I needed a cooler climate for the summer. So again I visited Eugene and his sweet little wife in Seattle. Brother Thorpe was by now married again, having spent eleven years remembering his young wife, Amy.

His second wife was a distant relative of his own mother and bore her name, Mary Buck. They lived at that time in the mountains on the Great Northern Railway where Thorpe was Chief Dispatcher for the Division. It was decided that I should spend the first part of my vacation with them.

The scenery was wild and beautiful, a narrow gorge with a wild mountain torrent dashing through. Thorpe had a Great Dane, "Rustler," to protect his wife, as there were many tramps along the tracks. I used to take some walks, with Rustler always accompanying. If any stranger came in view, the growls and rising hair of my huge protector were warning enough to make the bravest keep distance.

The Ladies' Aid Society invited me to give them a concert, offering as accompanist a young German pianist (married to the daughter of the town butcher and trying to support a rapidly increasing family by playing nightly at the "Red Front," and on Sundays in church). He was thoroughly familiar with the numbers on my suggested program and happy to play again the familiar German liader and operatic numbers known to him in his early musical environment. The date was set, and we rehearsed daily in the Knights of Pythias Hall. Rustler attended all rehearsals, his favorite position being to lie so close to my feet that I could hardly move without stepping upon him.

The night of the concert arrived. Rustler was shut up inside the house, which was surrounded for protection from possible marauders by a six-foot barbed wire fence.

To quote: "The Knights of Pythias Hall was crowded," says the article headed, 'An Elegant Affair,' and the audience was composed of citizens both capable and appreciative."

The program, which had opened with "Kaernthner Dieter March," played by Professor Max Kringle, was proceeding auspiciously through several groups of songs and piano numbers when a disturbance occurred. Rustler suddenly arrived at the concert, heralding his approach up the narrow stairway leading to the hall with a vigorous tail thumping on each wall as he ascended. He marched up the aisle, and with one bound, mounted the platform and laid himself at my feet just as I concluded the recitative introduction to "Una vooo poco fa." During the wild applause of the audience for this addition to the concert troupe, I had time to control my giggles and felt more nearly like the Mischievous Rosina probably than ever before or since. During the balance of the program, Rustler escorted me on and off the stage to the entertainment of all.

To return to the mentioned article: "It is not the intention to enter into detail but simply to speak of the entertainment in general terms. Miss Carr has a wonderfully sweet and flexible voice, which is in perfect control, and that a brilliant future lies before her was at once apparent to all who sat enraptured as she rendered number after number on the splendid program. Her voice was just as clear at the close as at the beginning. There was no affectation whatever. It is simple, at the same time grand, and well does she avoid plays upon quavers, although her voice is capable in that direction."

Unlike many recitals, this was a financial success, and both the Ladies' Aid and Professor Kringle netted a nice sum.

The time came all too soon to leave for Seattle—to the beautiful little town of Leavenworth in its mountainous setting as the overland trains pass through at night. This Seattle visit was quieter than my first for two causes. Dear little Alice was in very frail health, owing to a serious operation. In fact, most of her young life was marred by delicate health. She and Eugene continued to adore each other.

A group of friends made camp at the head of Lake Washington for several weeks in a beautiful grove of evergreens where there were several lawyer friends of Eugene's and their families. They called it by the romantic title of "Lawyer's Roost." It was often my privilege to paddle one of the canoes over to the Madison Street wharf for our own use after the lawyers had gone to business. That meant, of course, returning for them in the evening. My fainting spells subsided—only one or two during the summer. But one was a near tragedy. Every evening we had a huge bonfire, and all of us sat around and told stories or sang before separating for the night.

One evening, Gene asked me to sing my "Lullaby." For some reason or other, I did not feel up to a solo but felt ashamed to admit it, so I started to sing. All I remember was a sudden palpitation of my heart, and the next thing I knew, I was being dragged away from the fire, Eugene carrying me to my tent. It seems I had fallen, face forward, with my hair almost in the fire. As for me, it was only another of those mysterious blanks which seemed no longer than a blink of my eyes. But in reality, they often lasted minutes, or even half an hour, with no apparent heartbeat or breath.

Our camping came to an end with the Gold Excitement of 1897. Eugene, always adventurous, decided to go back to Alaska where he had not so long before tramped alone with his dog over the gold fields. Dear little Alice was aghast. My brother, Thorpe, also decided to go; his wife was enthusiastic over the venture.

So the day came when the "Portland" pulled out, loaded to the gunwales with equipment and wildly excited passengers, while anxious wives, sweethearts, and mothers waved farewell. Alice was in near collapse. We took her home as soon as I could get her to budge from the spot; her father, mother, and two brothers trying to cheer her up. She was a brave soul, but worried night and day and lost weight.

I returned to San Francisco by boat, and by train to Lemoore. As I neared home, I felt more and more depressed. This time it was not: "had I changed my mind?" but "had the Doctor become indifferent?" (He was always a most unsatisfactory letter-writer!) However, when he boarded the train at Hanford, having gone over earlier on business, I was soon encouraged.

The fall term began, and I started my classes. I learned for the first time that the Doctor's mother seriously objected to his marrying me—or anyone. She thought a physician should remain single and devote himself to his profession. She sent for me one day and told me she thought seriously that I should break our engagement, but not ostensibly for that reason. I returned home, terribly crushed. I thought the Doctor was probably tired of me and that his mother, realizing it, was trying to spare my feelings. So I wrote a letter, saying I had become convinced that our engagement must be broken, and sent my dear little brother to the post office with it. He, realizing that I had been crying, asked me and felt dreadfully when I admitted the truth, as he was devoted to the Doctor and already looked upon him as a big brother. About an hour later, the Doctor, with the letter in his hand, insisted upon knowing my real reason, which of course came out. Then and there, he set the wedding date for six weeks later.

The brief period was filled with trousseau and wedding plans, added to my already full schedule. I had one elaborate suit made in Visalia. Some things were ordered by mail from Chicago, and Carlin shopped for me in San Francisco. It was to be a family wedding at home. I taught my classes as usual, returning Friday before the Tuesday wedding to find Mother Moore sick in bed with "La Grippe," and the Doctor also confined to his bed with the same ailment. It did not look much like a wedding! However, Mother got better, and the Doctor recovered. Carlin and Harriet came from San Francisco and took charge.

Our house was one with a spacious living room on the first floor. Upstairs, reached by a wide stairway dividing half way up, was an old-fashioned "parlor" and the bedrooms. The wedding ceremony was solemnized in this parlor with my mother performing the ceremony and my father giving the bride away. I had planned to wear a beautiful white pina cloth, embroidered in pearls, which had been purchased several years before from Mark Twain's far away Moses of *Innocence Abroad,* by Uncle Clarke Carr, for the first bride in the family. Because of lack of time and a suitable dressmaker, it was decided that I should wear the "elaborate suit" from the Visalia moilate. It was made of peacock blue and black braided silk and wool material, with lots of black satin pleating, a crinkled crepe front, with a pink velvet collar and crepe rushing! It was very stylish.

My grandparents, all of our family connections in the West, the Doctor's mother, brothers and three older half-sisters, with their families, attended. The place was a mass of violets—never have I seen so many! Boxes of them came from my pupils in neighboring towns, from San Francisco, from everywhere. And the wedding presents, so many and so beautiful, the family concentrating on silver. It was a lovely February day, the 15th, being the anniversary of my parents' wedding.

At four o'clock, after the wedding breakfast, the Doctor's youngest brother drove us the ten miles to Hanford to catch the evening train for Los Angeles. We had stopped just outside of our town, and Doctor had removed the old shoes and satin ribbons bearing various signs from the back of the carriage. But rice fell out of my hat and coat when we boarded the mainline train, and reaching Los Angeles the following morning in a pouring rain, I opened my umbrella only to be deluged with rice!

We found from the headlines that on the day before [our wedding day] the Maine had been blown up in Manila Harbor, and there was great excitement. We were met at the train by an uncle whose carriage was waiting. He took us to his hotel where our suite had been engaged. We were his guests during our stay. We went to Catalina, visited Mount Lowe—all the things customary for newlyweds—and had a happy week.

The ten days we had allotted were shortened—as is the case with most Doctors' plans—by telegram from home announcing several serious cases among his patients. In the meantime, my father and mother had moved to the hotel, turning over their house to us. Doctor's mother, a good friend, his younger brother, and mine made up our family.

I went on with my teaching and kept my mother's maid to relieve the Doctor's mother, and also in order to help with the expense of the family while the Doctor was still in debt for his education. I have always feared that, although my intentions were of the best, Mother Moore would have been happier to manage things by herself. However, it was a happy and a busy time. I was away three days a week at my classes and always eager to get home. It seemed at the time that Fate persistently sent emergency calls for the Doctor and long confinement cases during my brief stay at home. But it wasn't always so, and we had happy times.

School vacation came, and Mother took Torry to Marin County for a camping season with the rest of the family at their permanent summer camp. Lots of the young cousins were there, and he had a grand time. Doctor's mother and brother went to visit one of her daughters, our schoolteacher went home, and Doctor and I were alone for a few weeks. My father went up to Camp during the Fourth of July holidays. Before he returned, Doctor and I went up to San Francisco so he could take advantage of some special lectures at "Cooper."

We had been there only a week, at the old Lick House, when a telegram arrived alarming me greatly about my father. I sent a messenger to the college, packed our belongings, and both of us caught the night train for home.

We found Father apparently well but greatly alarmed because he could not add up a column of figures or recognize by name any of his friends or business acquaintances. On his trip north, he had gotten into a heavy fog, was unable to get a Pullman reservation, had gotten terribly tired, and had taken a heavy cold. Returning to Lemoore after the brief holiday, he had found scorching weather and had suffered sort of a sunstroke.

Although he improved under Doctor's care, he became more and more fearful of making some serious mistake, and during the fall, he resigned his position. He and Mother went to Seattle to make a long deferred visit to Eugene and Alice.

Never again did he resume active affairs. Torry remained with us and finished grammar school. He was a great favorite among his teachers and fellow students, and, of course, I adored him.

The Doctor's business was improving constantly. He was busy day and night and had paid off all of his indebtedness. We decided we could afford a baby. All of my life I had looked forward to a family of my own. I had even invented a mythical family of six during my lonely childhood, of whom I recall that the two oldest were to be named Jasper and Hildegarde!

Everything seemed very rosy. I gave up my out-of-town classes at the end of 1899, retaining only a few students in my hometown. Mother Moore was with us again and was teaching me to sew. How I loved making these little garments.

Back Row: Sarah Amelia Pratt-Carr, John Claude Moore, Mary Louise Carr-Moore
Front Row: Byron Oscar Moore, Byron Carr Moore, Louisa Merrill-Pratt,
Robert Henry Pratt, Marian Hall Moore

John Wesley Moore — 1909

Marian Hall Moore

In March, we went to Napa Valley to attend the Grandparents' golden wedding anniversary. Such a re-union! Seventeen children and grandchildren, including husbands and wives, besides brothers and sisters and their descendants. Up to forty-six relatives celebrated that event in the lovely Napa Valley home.

Afterward, Doctor and I traveled up to Seattle by steamer with Father and Mother to visit my brothers and to look over the city. Even then, the Doctor was thinking of accepting my father's suggestion that he locate in the wide-awake young city. Returning to Lemoore, I went on with my sewing when I felt able.

In June, Torry graduated from grammar school. The morning he left, I was unable to be up. I shall never forget his dear young face as he bent over me and whispered, "Take good care of yourself, Sister, and be good to that little stranger!" It was the first time he had mentioned my plans.

Mother Moore again went to her daughter, and Doctor and I were alone. A very hot summer culminated in three weeks of "116 degrees in the shade," following which my twelve-pound boy was born in early September. Aunt Hattie came down to be with me. It really was a difficult affair. I, who had never owned a corset, weighed 97 pounds at the time of my marriage, and with a seventeen-inch waist, accomplished the birth of this "man-child" without any of the modern helps. An anaesthetic was impossible, partly because of my heart, but chiefly because the big boy was disinclined to leave his abiding place.

A Cesarean was indicated. Doctor had performed one before upon a colored mother, two months overdue, and had saved both mother and child. But our old family physician, who was in charge, demurred. After many hours of pain, when they decided I could stand no more, I heard them discussing the necessity for removing the baby in sections, so I just "got busy" and had him.

Perfectly conscious, I saw that lovely little human being as soon as the Doctors did. He looked three months old, and when later, bathed and dressed, he was put on the pillow by my side, he turned his head and looked over at me, as much as to say: "Hello, Old Dear; we managed that job, didn't we?" When the old doctor asked me if I ever cared to have another baby, I declared I'd have another one next year—it was worth all the trouble!

Oh, that first child of mine *[Byron Carr Moore]* —what a joy, and what a problem! So far as food was concerned, I was a good mother. When my baby was only six weeks old, I took in another little fellow of three months and nursed him through the crisis of his mother's attack of typhoid. My little fellow seemed to understand and was always smiling and gurgling when I looked into his bassinet.

As the weeks flew by, my boy grew so fast I could hardly "tote him." I was so afraid that he wouldn't get enough sleep that I gave him a nap morning and afternoon, with the result that he kept us awake most of the night. Doctor and I both got very tired. Mother Moore returned, and our mutual understanding and real affection came about through the baby she did not think we could afford. After this, we were in entire agreement, and she became my staunch, true friend. Those were rich days. Life seemed very complete.

My baby was three months old when one night I simply couldn't quiet him. He cried and cried. I was sure he was sick. Dr. Moore, tired out from many calls and anxiety over an epidemic, said I was spoiling the child. Mother Moore sat and crocheted but did not interfere.

Finally, the Doctor took the baby from me and spanked him—hard! I was suddenly a tiger. I jumped up and slapped him full on his cheek. With the baby in one arm, he took my wrist in his free hand and twisted it until I sank to my knees. Such a terrible show of the primitive! But dear Mother Moore just sat and crocheted and never then or later commented. But the next day, when the baby's abscessed ear broke, she was silently, but unmistakably, on my side.

A very beautiful, vivid brunette, with her husband and son by a former marriage, arrived from New York. The husband had been through the Cuban war, and finding his law practice disrupted and his health not of the best, decided to locate in Lemoore where he took a clerical position in the large general store. All the town vied to make the beautiful New Yorker, with her charm and style, at home in our little Western town. She was at once the leader in clubs and styles. I, who had tried to submerge my urban ideas and conform to the customs so I need never be considered "citified," began to feel a certain "uncertainty" about myself. My baby had exhausted me, and I wasn't up to my usual enthusiasm.

As the weeks went on, we had the visitor to dinner several times. For one of the dinners, my nice Doctor, who never drank, ordered champagne, with claret to precede. This, for a mid-day Sunday dinner, seemed unsuitable to me; and when he iced the claret, I, who had been brought up to the proper serving of wines with our meals, was rather aghast. Before long, Mrs. S. seemed to be suffering from some unexplained trouble and spent her days on a couch. She wore gorgeous kimonos and invalid gowns. We all tried to relieve her loneliness and boredom. Doctor was much worried over her. Mother Moore was much worried over him.

I recall how utterly without guile was my young husband at this time. Mother Moore asked me once if it did not trouble me to have the Doctor spend so much time with Mrs. S. I remember replying, with some heat, that I would not insult my husband by suspecting him of any but the finest motives. But it was difficult to silence the lurking germ when, in the cool of the evening, Doctor felt obliged to take his patient for a drive, leaving Mother, the baby, and me at home.

My first active temptation from Beelzebub toward jealousy came one afternoon when the Doctor had been suddenly called to Hanford on business. Friends of ours, who were driving over, invited me to go along and return with my husband on the evening train. Mother added her voice to theirs, and so I went. When I boarded the train in the evening, eager to surprise my husband, I saw him up toward the front of the coach, his arm over the back of the seat, with Mrs. S. beside him. I didn't know what to do, but it was too late to escape. I tried to assume that I would be welcome and made my presence known. It transpired that the Doctor had accompanied his patient to a dental appointment, and the natural assumption was, of course, that I had been spying on him. So I was treated with appropriate coolness.

Months went by. The hot summer came, and Mother Moore went North again to her daughter. One morning I found a scorpion in the baby's bed, and later a black spider crept across the floor to meet him. When I told the Doctor, he suggested that I go North and spend a month with my family at the Marin County Camp. I gladly agreed. Byron was then eleven months old. He had weighed thirty pounds at seven months, and since, I hadn't the courage to see how much he had grown.

When I reached the camp, I realized for the first time the difficulties. The tents were all on a steep hillside, hard enough to climb up and down with safety for even an active person. But with a heavy child, too young to walk and with no chance to use a baby buggy, I found myself a complete wreck at the end of the week. A family council was held, and it was decided that it would be best for me to go over to the city, find a room for awhile until the worst of the Valley heat was over, and then return to Lemoore.

We had all overlooked the fact that this was the great celebration year of the Native Sons: 1900. California was celebrating her fiftieth anniversary of Statehood. None of the hotels where I planned to go were available. Finally, I found a queer little hotel on Market Street, which was decidedly second class. It had a pleasant enough room and bath, although the furniture was shabby.

I felt terribly alone, but an Oriental house-boy became very fond of my baby. He kept telling me about his own fine family at home—a boy of six, a girl of four, and a baby boy of two.

I asked him when he had last seen them.

"Oh, never," he said. "I not go back for twelve year. My bludder, he live there."

I asked no more. It was a queer San Francisco. All my old friends were at their summer homes, and the city was filled with strangers there for the celebration. Finally, I could stand it no longer, so I wired the Doctor that I was returning on the ninth, which was Admission Day. It was almost impossible to reach the ferry, for the crowds in the streets. Not a cab was allowed in the crowded thoroughfare. I finally walked the entire distance, pushing the baby in his little go-cart, leaving my baggage to be shipped the following day; but after reaching the ferry, it was easier. I was practically the only person leaving San Francisco that day. The baby was so good all the way. It was a twelve-hour ride, and we arrived hot and tired at nine o'clock in the evening.

The Doctor didn't seem very glad to see us, but I hoped it was because he was tired. The next day, he told me he had arranged to take another course at Cooper and was leaving the following day. Of course, I felt very lonely but was glad to be in my own home again.

Later, I was disturbed upon learning that Mrs. S. had also gone to the city. Her son, a precious fourteen-year-old, began calling upon me. Little by little, he gave me his life history. He was devoted to his stepfather, who had been the attorney for his mother when she had obtained a divorce from his father. Subsequently, his stepfather had married his mother, and later had gone through the Cuban War. He had returned to find his wife very popular with many gentlemen; so, instead of re-establishing his law practice, he had brought them out West to this obscure country town.

He astonished me by saying very earnestly: "Mrs. Moore, you mustn't blame your husband. All men are fascinated by my mother." To have it brought out in the open like that frightened me.

The Doctor came home strange and changed. Mrs. S. remained in San Francisco. One terrible day, the Doctor didn't come home for lunch or for dinner. The office and the house were full of waiting patients. Finally, the druggist telephoned me to send the patients home, that the Doctor was away on a "long call." I presumed I knew what that meant.

After dinner, the members of the choir came over for rehearsal. About nine o'clock, we were interrupted by Mr. S. who rang the doorbell. It was clear that he was not quite himself. Seeing that I was busy, he said he would return later. After they had gone, not Mr. S., but the young son came, saying his father had decided not to disturb me further that evening. Woman-like, I sent the boy home to demand an immediate explanation. Returning, Mr. S. told me that he had suspected a correspondence and had wired his wife, signing the Doctor's initials, asking her to write him at such-and-such a box in Hanford—of course, he collected the letter himself. He asked me to read it. I refused. He claimed that the Doctor was meeting his wife on the Overland and was eloping with her. I lied. I told him the Doctor was on a confinement case. He demanded, "Where?" I replied, "Do you think I would tell you in your present state of mind."

He finally left, and I immediately telephoned our good friend, the druggist. We could not discuss matters on the local telephone; so, when he had closed the store, he came to the house and explained some matters to me. He said he had been receiving letters addressed to him with an enclosure for the Doctor. Not knowing from whom they came (although probably suspecting), he had delivered one of them to the Doctor in his office not long before when Mr. S. was present. All day, Mr. S. had been drinking heavily and threatening to shoot the Doctor on sight. The druggist had been able to warn the Doctor, and he had gone to our old friend in Hanford.

I could not think what to do. First, I thought I should take the baby and go to my people in Seattle. But, in considering this, I wondered when my boy grew older what I could tell him? For a little while, I thought hard and fast. Finally, I told the druggist that I would drive to Hanford and talk with my husband first. So, as obviously I could not go alone, the druggist offered to take me and notified his wife. My dear little pupil, Beulah, soprano in the choir and old beyond her fifteen years, was still in the house and offered to stay with the baby. It was unthinkable to let her stay alone. I went to my good neighbors, awakened them, and told them a few words of what they knew far better than I. They dressed and came over to stay the night, the husband having first gone to his store and brought back fifty dollars for possible expenses. Deeply touched, I kissed my baby goodbye and drove out into the night.

On the ten-mile drive, I learned much, and I felt both despair for myself and sympathy for my young husband, fascinated by the sophisticated charm of this vivid beauty. We reached Hanford at midnight only to find our doctor friend out on a call. I think the longest hour of my life was spent awaiting his return. But he was spontaneous in his welcome. He, who always had seemed to me like an older brother, felt that my coming might prevent a great mistake. He had heard the whole story from my husband, who was already disillusioned and uncertain what to do.

He said my husband had gone to his brother's house in Fresno for safety and to avoid a "shooting scrape," and thought if I could go to him at once, it might be the solution. He telephoned the livery stable for a fresh team, casually giving his errand in an entirely different direction (in case Mr. S. was following.)

We left Hanford at two o'clock in the morning. We lost our way several times in the heavy fog but finally reached Fred's home at seven o'clock. My husband was expecting us because of a telegram sent earlier, met us and carried me into the living room. There, alone, he took me in his arms and told me if I would forgive him, he would never give me another moment's unhappiness. I not only forgave him, but vowed to myself that I would erase it from my heart and never in the future judge him by the past. We went home on the train, and the next day I forced myself to go downtown to be seen with my husband and to be cheerful and gay.

That Sunday morning, we had both slept late. When I came downstairs, I noticed that the old Carr clock had stopped at twenty minutes before eight. It was fully wound. I told my husband of the old tradition that this clock always stopped when some member of the family died. It seemed such a foolish superstition!

The next evening, Monday night, news came that my darling Torry, my baby brother, almost sixteen, had been drowned sometime Sunday morning, together with his cousin Clarkie Carr. They had been in a canoe on Lake Washington. For one terrible week they dragged the lake and finally found first Torry, then Clarkie!

My poor Mother and Father! My poor Uncle Clark and Aunt Grace! My poor brother Eugene who had lent him the canoe! And oh, poor me, who had lost my faith and my darling brother, all in two days! How did we ever get through that time? I was so stunned that Torry's death didn't seem real. I could only think of Father and Mother. After the funeral, they came to spend the winter with us. It was a sad homecoming, back to all the scenes of Torry's boyhood.

Mr. S. began to drink heavily, and one dreadful night, after he had threatened the Doctor in town, a telephone call came which was urgent. I went out to the carriage with my husband and made the trip with him, feeling that he was safer with his wife along. We learned later that it was as we had feared. Mr. S. had been very close to the house, concealed; but a friend, seeing him there, had taken him home and persuaded him to forget the matter.

More and more, we began thinking seriously of Seattle. We talked it over with Father and Mother who, of course, knew nothing of what lay behind the decision. Almost immediately, Father sold the house to the young bank assistant whom he had trained and who was now my father's successor. Father and Mother went north again, and the Doctor, baby Byron, and I took rooms at the hotel until he could settle his affairs.

Spring came, and my fine healthy boy had an attack of malarial fever. Doctor was busy day and night. I sat up for nights and nights wringing out wet sheets and wrapping the baby in them, until the fever was reduced. He finally got better and was almost well when suddenly, up went the temperature again.

I was packed in a day and off to Seattle on the first of June, 1901. That trip laid the foundation for years of invalidism for me. My heavy baby was almost two years old, too heavy to carry and too sick to walk. The many transfers, the scarcity of "Red-caps" in proportion to the travelers, all conspired to exhaust us both. When my big brother, Eugene, met us at Tacoma, took the baby, and ordered the "Red-caps" around, it was like waking up in heaven.

The visit with Eugene and Alice (this time Mother and Father there, too) was sad. The lake, beautiful and tranquil, lay just below us—the scene of our tragedy. The big hunting dog who had gone with the boys in the canoe and who had reached Mercer Island, where he was found later, was quite beside himself. He would come in and put his head on Mother's lap, gazing at her with sad eyes, which spoke more eloquently than words. Our boys, both excellent swimmers, had been stunned that early October morning by the icy waters of the lake, which was always cold, and in places had never had its bottom sounded.

Mother found a large house, unpacked her stored furniture, and made a home for us. The Doctor came up in July to take the State Medical Exams, then he returned to collect bills and sell his practice.

The weeks and months went by. I lay on a couch, trying to recover from the physical strain of a ninety-five pound mother attempting to carry a thirty-five-pound baby for so many weary hours of journeying.

Fortunately for our finances, I was known to be a musician. Few teachers at that time were available, so I had as many pupils as I could handle. Most of the time I was drawn up before the piano in a steamer chair, playing what I could maneuver of the accompaniments.

It was fine for my morale that our teacher friend from Lemoore came North and obtained a teaching position in Seattle and a room at our home. Her strong arms were often around my big boy when I had not the strength to hold him. "Auntie Nora," came right next to his "Mama."

A little later, my dear friend of St Helena days, Virginia Graham (the "Aurora" of The Oracle) came to join us, and we three meant much to one another. Mother had a fine housekeeper but was still active enough to keep her mind occupied. Poor Father had not that release, but he devoted himself to his first grandchild who was named for him.

One day, two perfectly fetching young matrons came to call, and one of the girls brought Byron in from his sand-pile to meet the "pretty ladies." He stood just within the doorway, gazing at us each in turn, and finally said, "Where are the pretty ladies?" So tactful!

Not until January did the Doctor finally come! It had seemed like years!

I was up and around. I had been invited to produce for charity my opera, "The Oracle." I had gone over the score and added a little here and there. We had a fine cast. A young postman by the name of Frank Coombs was the tenor. Beautiful Della Spray was his "Doris." Virginia was, of course, "Aurora," and I again essayed "Cleo." Frank Atkins, with a beautiful high baritone voice, played opposite me.

That third act scene was again a problem. I, a married woman with quite a bit of professional operatic experience, wanted everything to move smoothly. Mr. Atkins, a married man, courteously but firmly refused to embarrass me by rehearsing the embraces. He described where we should meet and after which note we should melt into each other's arms.

Well and good; but in the excitement of the first night, he sang his impassioned love song over the footlights, and I had to improvise. Before the matinee next day, I asked him if he intended to carry out the original plan. Much surprised to learn that he had forgotten it the night before, he told me to depend upon him. Well, the same thing happened again.

Making no further mention of the matter, imagine my astonishment at the final performance when my stage lover raced to my "spot," grasped me so firmly in his arms, and almost collided with my "finale" with his ill-timed kiss! Since then, I have believed even more fervently in rehearsing all details. At any rate, the production was pronounced a success, paid its way, and netted some money for charity.

After the Doctor's arrival, he found offices in one of the early medical buildings. We continued to live with Mother and Father, and our two friends, Nora and Virginia, remained as well. We had jolly times together. In the spring, Mother decided to leave the house to us, and with Father, she returned to San Francisco. She was interested in a new study of a religious nature, and her teacher was frequently in San Francisco where Aunt Hattie and Carlin were living with their families.

Owing to the very high rents in Seattle, Doctor decided to put his savings into a home. Following my plans, we were soon the owner's of a pretty and comfortable two-story home. I took Mother's Norwegian girl with us, for she was devoted to my Byron who was growing so fast into a big boy.

My classes had increased to such an extent that I rented a studio in the old Holyoke building. Some busy days, when I was trying to coach a timid young voice, with a loud pianist on one side and a violinist on the other, all of us in different keys, it seemed a warning of what I might have to endure. It was fatiguing work and difficult days.

It was naturally galling for my husband, whose profession had to grow slowly in a large city, to spend many hours in an empty office those first months. He chafed, as any strong man would, at the thought of permitting his wife to earn the major part of the income while he found his bank account dwindling. I see clearly how restless and discouraged he must have felt. But it was not for long. His own ability and likeable personality very soon won him friends and patients.

I was invited to join the "Seattle Conservatory of Music," jointly owned by Frederick William Zimmerman and Vaughn Arthur. Mr. Zimmerman was a tenor of the old German School, and Mr. Arthur was a violinist, both highly respected.

Sometime in the early fall, we had our first burglar. He bored a hole through the kitchen door, turned the key, and efficiently relieved us of all our silver! Seattle was a very wide open city, and there were many robberies. I was always a light sleeper, and when the Doctor was out, I always had the pistol under my pillow. I took it with me when I went to see if Byron needed covering, but on this night the Doctor was at home and I slept soundly.

In the morning, we found there was not even a spoon left for breakfast. I had no kitchen spoons, as we had such a lot of silver. My lovely wedding silver was gone and some of the family heirlooms too. I felt sick about it. Several other houses in our vicinity had been ransacked the same night.

As my brother Eugene was important in the State Militia and a well-known lawyer, the police department made an extra effort. The burglar was rounded up in Portland the following week. He was selling some small articles, coffee spoons and other little trinkets, to a pawnbroker. The wily shopkeeper induced him to bring him some more of the loot, and upon his return, he was arrested and brought back to Seattle.

He confessed to the place of his cache as being at a spot on the Willamette River, which had risen during the past week several feet as was usual in the fall. He thought it could be located in the spring and was sent to prison for a five-year term.

The next spring, very early, instead of at the spot indicated, a farmer several miles on the other side of Portland discovered all the silver in a hollow stump, wrapped in a Seattle newspaper! We recovered all but a few of our precious wedding gifts. After that, we always burned a night light in the upper hall. I was convinced that we were spared the loss of other belongings, to say nothing of a bad fright, by that means.

In 1904, Easter Sunday, I received a most precious gift—my dear little daughter, Marian *[Marian Hall Moore]*, who was a joy and comfort to me. I can think of no greater blessing than children. Now I had a sturdy little son, almost five, and a little daughter in my arms.

Byron had been very impatient about that Stork. For some weeks he had gone the first thing every morning to look in the "guest room," to see if the Stork had kept his promise. He was becoming very skeptical. The next morning the baby was there. Easter was a pretty good day to celebrate after all. When Byron woke up and padded into the room, not observing me at all but standing on tiptoe to look into the bassinet, his startled exclamation and the look on his face made us all shout with laughter! The Stork had finally kept his word. That was a happy year! Byron adored his baby sister and was her willing slave.

We had a gay time. Financial anxieties were not harassing the Doctor, and our circle of friends included several young doctors and their wives—also a number of lawyer friends, and their wives. Seattle was a very gay place with receptions, teas, dancing and composing. I never seemed to escape that necessity for spoiling a lot of perfectly clean music paper! Toward the end of this happy year, though, I was quite ill, and it was discovered that there was to have been another baby, but it was not so to be.

Then, I began to realize that one of the most beautiful girls in our group of friends with whom we associated so constantly was becoming very dear to my husband. I had begun almost to feel secure, and I tried to assure myself that it was all my imagination, but I knew my fears were true. We were very good friends, this lovely girl and I.

One day when she came to see me, as she often did, I told her that I knew the Doctor was deeply devoted to her. If it were for their mutual happiness, I would be the one to go away. She hotly denied anything of the kind, and told me that she cared nothing for the Doctor and would never see him again. As it happened, she went directly to his office, for when the secretary telephoned me later about some matter, she interrupted her conversation with me to greet the girl by name and to tell her the Doctor was expecting her.

For awhile, I tried to carry on—but with my recent illness, and my grief over my inability to make myself beloved by my husband, I brooded too much; I kept thinking of the children's future if I took them away with me as a "divorced woman." Few can imagine the effect of that phrase upon many of us in those days; particularly, I was prejudiced, and loathed the idea for myself. Yet I could not ruin my husband's life by clinging to him. I began to reason that the beauty and culture of this really lovely girl would make her a better companion for my children, and that I could be grieving, delicate in health, and looking forward to a life of bitter loneliness.

One night when the Doctor had to go to an emergency operation at the hospital, and I had a very severe headache blinding me with pain, I took from my box of strychnine tablets (which were always near at hand, owing to my sudden fainting spells) and over-dosed—deliberately.

There was no excuse for me, whatever; except that I thought, sincerely, it was better for the happiness of all that I should go. Had the Doctor been gone as long as he expected, I would have been dead long before his return. As it was, he found me in the frightful convulsions. I was terribly remorseful.

The final result was a very real re-union between the Doctor and myself, which lasted longer than I could have dared to hope. Without these growing pains, we would be like jellyfish; it takes "trial by fire" to develop that spinal column which enables us to stand erect.

Not long after this, the Doctor was offered the medical contract for the building of the Chicago and St. Paul Railroad. He was to be in charge of a chain of hospitals, sixteen in all, along the right-of-way. It seemed a fine time to take a complete rest and give the children some out-of-doors life.

So, near the main hospital, a few miles from North Bend, a little cabin of pine boards was built with the most primitive arrangements: a cheerful living room, a bedroom, a bunkroom for the two children, and a lean-to wash room. The partitions only ran up about nine feet, and the only doors were the front and back doors. I hung cretonne curtains at the other openings, and altogether it was a delightful camp. My only concession to civilization was the small upright piano that Doctor was thoughtful enough to have sent up. Establishing ourselves in the little cabin, with our meals at the hospital about a block away, we all found this free, open-air life, delightful—"roughing it," without any of the hardships.

Byron was almost seven and Marian two. I outfitted my pretty little daughter (much to her big brother's disgust) in overalls and a sunbonnet. She followed Byron around all day long. Our cabin was on a plateau, and just below we could see the men working along the roadbed of the new railroad.

One day, I allowed Byron and his sister to go down closer and watch the workmen. I could see them down the winding road every step of the way. As I watched, one of the men turned from spiking a rail and began to talk to Byron; several of the others gathered around. Then, to my astonishment, Byron turned and started back up the road, his little sister's feet flying to keep up with him.

When he reached me he was crying. I said, "What is the trouble Byron?"

He replied "Well, they said is it a him, or a her?" and I said, She's a boy. Then they asked, What's her name?" and I said, Her name is John, —'nd then they all laughed! And no wonder, Mamma, with overalls on one end of her, 'nd a sunbonnet on the other." Poor Byron!

I found lots of time and much inspiration for composition in this beautiful, wild country. The Doctor had a beautiful bronze mare—Belle—who bore him on his trips to the various hospitals. She was devoted to him, but on the few times I tried to ride her, she resented my presumption. So the Doctor, finding a magnificent black horse at one of the camps, had him brought down to our camp. We had many fine rides together—he on Belle and I on my "Black Beauty."

One day, we rode into North Bend, some two and a half miles. As we rode up to the hotel veranda and dismounted, the man who had the contract to supply horses jumped up and said, "By God, Moore, how do you dare let your wife ride that horse? He's a killer!" I spoke up and said he was perfectly gentle, and I loved to ride him. The man replied that he had sold the horse because none of the men at the camp would go near him because he was so vicious. He added that he could have gotten a much better price had he been able to say a woman could ride him! Which goes to show that "temperament" extends to others besides musicians.

Here was Doctor's Belle, quite willing to carry his two hundred odd pounds, but strenuously objecting to my ninety-five, running under hanging branches to brush me off, or prancing on hind legs—while the vicious Black Beauty, was gentle and "simpatico" when I was in the saddle.

Mary Carr Moore's writings end abruptly at this point. I, John David Moore, a grandson, can only try to fill in the blanks.

The authors of Mary Carr Moore, American Composer suggest that if her voice had fulfilled its earlier promise, she would have been heard widely as a singer; but as a composer, she faced insuperable sex discrimination obstacles. She was powerful in her integrity, commitment and achievement. A pioneer in music as her grandfather had been a pioneer in railroading and her mother a pioneer of domestic feminism. She was granted an honorary Ph.D. in music.

My father, John Wesley Moore, was born in 1907. He was named after his grandfather and was called "Wes." His older brother, Byron, picked up his nickname "Dinty" as he pursued a career in aviation. Wes loved airplanes, too, but concentrated his studies in the medical field, graduating first from the University School in Victoria, British Columbia, with scholastic and athletic honors, and later earning his M. D. at the State College of Washington.

Eventually, Mary and John Claude were divorced.— JM

In 1927, Wes wrote to his grandmother, Sarah [Sarah Amelia Pratt]:

Dear Nanna,

At last the "spirit" has moved me! And here's the long-awaited letter.

School closed with a flourish and I came over to Seattle with four other fellows in a rattlesome Ford. It is a great relief to know that the summer is mine—that I don't have to move at the beck and call of some fussy professor or write agonizing French themes!

Seattle is the same old town. I'm rather fond of its winding streets and steep hills. It has always held a certain charm for me. Then, too, the odour of the dusty woods is just great after the dismal rolling plains of eastern Washington. The evergreens are hard to beat.

I'm just in the process of making my summer plans. I expect to be in Los Angeles within the next two or three weeks for a short visit. Then I shall go to work for the remainder of the summer. I think I'll choose some sort of out-of-doors work for a change—to put a little brawn on me and to give me a man-sized appetite. Mother used to tell me I had a canary bird appetite!

Byron was here just a short while ago. He is a regular aviator now, right up with the best of them. He has changed a great deal lately—became very much more serious. He seems well on his way to that eventual success. I'll be happy when people say that about me. I'm anxious to pull out of the doldrums of "youth" and find my stride with the rest of the world. I suppose, though, that I'll soon be looking back and wishing for those "dear old college days" again! So many people seem to. One of my fraternity brothers who just graduated said the other day, "Well my playtime is over. I'll have to break away from this four years vacation and get down to labour!"

I hope this sudden burst of penmanship (?) won't prove too much of a shock for you, Nanna. Perhaps I should have started in easier, say with a post card!

Lots of love to you—as ever,

Wesley

William Watson was born in England within a few years time of Sarah Amelia Pratt and Mary Elizabeth Barker's births. A surveyor by trade, he arrived on the East Coast of America and traveled via train to Quincy, California. There he met his bride, Mary Kanaday, a schoolteacher at the nearby Meadow Valley School. Their wagons met on the narrow road, and while their horses maneuvered around each other; apparently Watson did some maneuvering of his own. They were married soon after and produced a number of children, one of whom was Edith.

Mary Kanaday

Watson became involved with Arthur W. Keddie who explored the North Fork of the Feather River for the newly organized Oroville and Beckwourth Pass Wagon Road Company. Not even a footpath existed. Later, work began to construct a railway bed for the Southern Pacific. Surveyors often hung suspended from the sheer Mesozoic granite walls above icy waters that could fluctuate as much as seventy-five feet. Field parties sometimes were forced to resort to rafts to get through "shut-in's." During the construction stage, men and work animals were killed with accidental blasting and rockslides. Poison Oak and drunkenness were problems too.

In 1941, William Watson was pictured in the Feather River Bulletin among "Quincy's Finest" with other locally famous names such as Moncur, Robertson, Gray, McLaughlin, Payne, Jeskey, Welden, Flournoy, Williams, Giffoed and Swingle.

[In 1909, rails met from Nevada on the east and from Oakland on the west at a bridge over Spanish Creek located downstream a few miles from Quincy. That same year, David Nathan Rogers, son of "Down East" pioneers Luther Bailey and Mary Elizabeth Barker, took over as Supervisor of the Plumas National Forest. William and Mary's daughter, Edith, married D. N. Rogers. Together they produced David Harold Rogers and Frances Gail Rogers.

John Wesley "Wes" Moore became a partner with his father in Seattle for a time. His father, John Claude, won medical acclaim for inventing a new surgical procedure in 1938.

Wes moved south to Quincy where he established the Plumas Industrial Hospital. He was the physician-in-charge of the California Conservation Corps camp nearby and became acquainted with D. N. Rogers, who was in charge of the camp.

In 1938 Wes Moore and Gail Rogers were wed. Their union produced me—John David "Johnny" Moore.—JM]

David Harold Rogers
Uncle, Pilot

PART II

AVIATION LOVE STORY:
A World War II Drama

Wes and Gail — Wedding Day
January 30, 1939

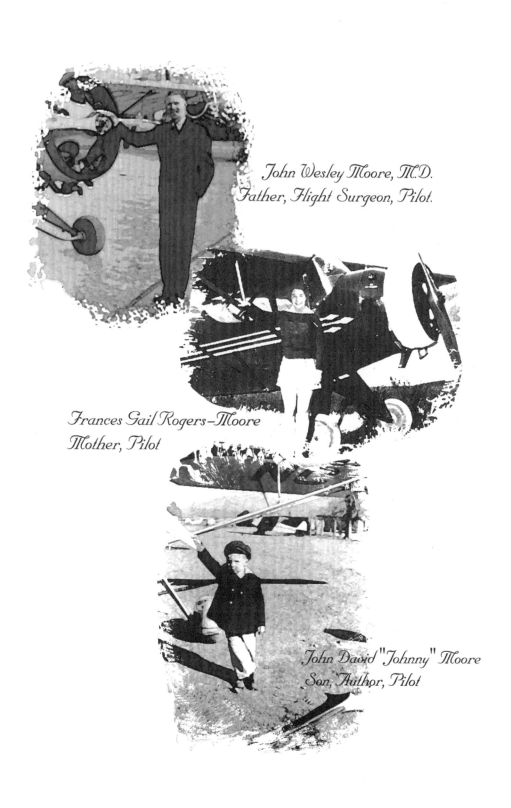

John Wesley Moore, M.D.
Father, Flight Surgeon, Pilot.

Frances Gail Rogers-Moore
Mother, Pilot

John David "Johnny" Moore
Son, Author, Pilot

CHAPTER 6

BEFORE

University of California, Berkeley, The Woman's Athletic Association awards membership in the "All California Swimming Team" To Frances Gail Rogers in 1934, and "All California Basketball Team," in 1937.

APRIL 24, 1937 SAN FRANCISCO EXAMINER

ROGERS TO STAGE COMEBACK

Dave Rogers *[David Harold Rogers]*, University of California pole-vaulter, gets his first test of the season Saturday against the Olympic Club. A promising 13-footer last year, he nearly ended his track career when he suffered a broken leg playing football last fall. Now he hopes to break records instead of legs.

JANUARY ? 1939 SACRAMENTO BEE

GERALDINE ABBOT WAS HOSTESS AT SHOWER

A charming afternoon tea and surprise linen shower was given Saturday afternoon at the J. M. Haun home when Mrs. Geraldine Abbott entertained in honor of Miss Gail Rogers, whose marriage to Dr. J. W. Moore *[John Wesley Moore]* is to be solemnized January 30th.

Those invited to the affair enjoyed the afternoon in the spacious living rooms of the Haun home into which Mrs. Abbott, recovering from a confining illness, had been moved for the occasion.

Mrs. Abbott greeted her guests and presented each with a plain hemmed dish towel. Making a contest of the affair, each guest was presented with needle and thread and requested to embroider her name and nickname in the corner of the towel. Mrs. C. R. Schott was the winner of the event, and received three sets of bridge score pads and tally cards; Mesdames. W. C. King and L. H. Thayer, who tied for second place, were given dainty bouquets of baby roses; Mrs. A. J. Watson, last to complete the task, received a pretty corsage. As a special treat, a draw prize was offered, with the honoree, Miss Gail Rogers, holding the winning ticket, and receiving a potted pink geranium. All of the prizes were made by Mrs. Abbott, whose clever fingers, since her illness, have manufactured realistic flowers and favors, which have delighted an ever-increasing number of friends

During the tea hour, Mrs. Abbott was assisted in serving by Mrs. H. C. Flournoy, who poured, and Mesdames, H. S. Watson and E. D. Baldwin, who served the guests.

The buffet table from which refreshments were served carried out a spring theme in pink. A tablecloth of Chinese silk in pink was an appropriate background for the fresh pink carnations in their bubble bowl, centered on a mirror centerpiece. Tall pink tapers at the ends of the table further carried out the color scheme. Guests were served tea and cake on individual trays, on which dainty pink dishes and fragile China teacups complemented the buffet.

Following the serving of refreshments, a knock on the door revealed Dr. Moore who asked for his fiancée and presented her with a well-filled laundry bag, with the remark that "here is the laundry for the next fifty years."

Opened, the bag was found to contain many lovely gifts of linen for the home of the bride-to-be, complete down to the large package of Lux Flakes in which they should be washed. The last gift in the well-filled bag was that of Mrs. C. J. Lee's who had included the newspaper clipping telling of the wedding of Miss Roger's parents, Mr. And Mrs. D. N. Rogers, and also a picture of her parents.

Miss Rogers, the daughter of Forest Supervisor *[David Nathan Rogers]* and Mrs. D. N. Rogers *[Edith L. Watson]*, is one of the popular members of Quincy's younger set, and a graduate of the University of California. Her betrothal to Dr. J. W. Moore, local physician, is being made the occasion for several social functions.

Those who greeted Miss Rogers at the invitation of Mrs. Abbott were: Mesdames. L. L. Clough, L. H. Thayer, F. R. Young, C. R. Schott, L. M. Olsen, George Cotter, L. C. Remick, C. J. Lee, C. L. Peckinpah, J. N. Stephans, E. D. Baldwin, A. J. Watson, J. M. Haun, H. L. Cate, H. C. Flournoy, F. G. Gansner, W. C. King, Miss S. Faye Miller and Mrs. D. N. Rogers, mother of the bride-elect.

Mesdames C. T. Bedell and E. D. Bordwell, also invited, were unable to attend owing to illness.

Gifts were received by the honoree from Mrs. J. O. Moncur, on vacation in Los Angeles, and Mrs. W. J. Miller, unable to be present for the occasion.

JANUARY 9, 1941. PAGE 3 OF LETTER FROM GAIL TO ?

[First part of letter missing] ...slept in, then went up to the Parker Café for our bacon and eggs. Waited around for the mechanic and poked about the engine—didn't sound any better this morning. In testing the compression in the different cylinders, Wes noticed the rocker arm lift the whole cap off the valve box. There was the trouble—a cracked head. We got busy taking the cowling off, nuts and bolts (I was custodian of the latter) and had everything off of the head but the cylinder when we heard the welcome sound of the 65 Porterfield and the mechanic arrived. Too bad we had taken all of the nuts off between the head and the cylinder—the darn thing had to be shrunk off and on again to the new head. Because there were no Warner 90 parts in Phoenix or Bakersfield, the nearest spot was Glendale. The flying weather was very poor and finally the arrangements were made for the mechanic to fly to Blythe (50 miles or so) because the stages went out of there more often and pick it up there when it returned. Just before the mechanic left, an Ercoupe dove into sight, in a few minutes Fred Russell was telling us that he'd heard we were down over here in Parker and was expecting us to be about ready to go on with him to Miami—Fine thing. Fred wanted to make Phoenix tonight but by the time he had gotten gas and considered the hour change in time, he decided to stop over with us. Marion took us into town in the pickup and we moved over to the other auto court, which was nearer the airport, and nearer to town and was patronized by our new-found friend Mr. Hubbell (Standard Oil), who helped us find the source of our misery. We all spent quite a calm evening—took in the movie and the weekly screen. *[missing]*

JANUARY 16, 1941 FEATHER RIVER BULLETIN

This picture of Dr. John W. Moore of Quincy and his wife, Gail Rogers Moore, was taken at Oakland Airport as they took off in their airplane for Miami and Cuba. It was published by the Oakland Tribune, by whose permission the Feather River Bulletin reproduces it here. Their plans were altered when motor trouble forced them down at Parker, Arizona, and it is believed they will now spend their vacation in Mexico. F. L. Russell, another Quincy aviator, and Mrs. Russell stopped at Parker also when Dr. Moore was forced down. Both couples will be away for a month.

APRIL 3, 1941 Dr. MARY CARR MOORE TO JOHNNY
(For our very precious grandson, John David Moore)

Dear John David-

A very happy first birthday to you. Perhaps you <u>are</u> just a little young to read *When We Were Very Young* by yourself, but I wanted you to be sure to know about Christopher Robin and "The King's Breakfast" and "Teddy Bear" when you get a little older, so in the meantime this is for being read aloud to you when you get to be about half past one.

Love from Mary

DECEMBER 1941. BYRON C. "DINTY" MOORE WRITES:

I couldn't explain—what motivated me to leave a soft airline captain's job right after Pearl Harbor to start as copilot (I had never before flown as second-in-command) with the airplane factory that built Catalina Flying Boats and Liberator bombers in San Diego. Shaking down those unpressurized bombers at 26,000 feet was tough enough. Still more grueling was delivering Catalinas to Pearl Harbor; flights in which the airplane became our home for eighteen to twenty-four hours; a noisy, drafty home, that would make our ears ring and our skins tingle from the vibration for days.

I couldn't tell you what I was trying to prove when I volunteered for one of the survey flights to Australia; flights that resulted in a civilian-operated military schedule that reached from California halfway around the world. There was no time for immunization shots, uniforms, passports—not even identification cards. We pushed right on through without any rest, catching a wink while refueling at some atoll, at other times throwing ourselves on the flight deck and sleeping from sheer exhaustion.

Nobody knew where the Japanese Fleet was at the time, but we flew mostly at night, or when we could, on top of a cloud deck. We took turns as lookout in the greenhouse, but none of us had ever fired a machine gun. Of course, without uniforms or military identification we'd have been promptly shot as spies if captured.

A crew member on one flight mistook Venus rising through a cloud deck for a Japanese fighter dropping a flare. In a fine panic, he blazed away with his double fifty calibers. He missed Venus but shot away a portion of the airplane's stabilizer.

Dinty Moore

CHAPTER 7

1943

<u>JUNE 29, 1943 WES TO GAIL</u>

Darling,

This being my first try on V-mail, you must let me know whether I write plainly enough. Sure wish you were still with me. It's funny how much I miss you! Golly, if it's this bad now, it's going to be really tough by the time it's all over!

Thank you for the new wings, Dear. They were quite favorably commented upon. Hope you are wearing yours for me.

The weather is wonderful—seems to be getting warmer all the time. It can't get too hot to suit me.
Saw Al Ulshart the other day—said to send his love. There are a couple of my schoolmates here. You don't know them.

Not much more to tell you, Darling—and not much space. I love you. Tell Johnny *[John David Moore]* "hello" for Daddie, and my love to the folks. I am wondering if you are home yet.

Write soon, Darling—   Wes

P.S. Just noticed I had all this space too! Will try to do better next time—Bye, now

JULY 6, 1943 MARY CARR MOORE TO WES
(4037 Leeward Avenue, Los Angeles, California)

Wesley Darling,

I cannot begin to tell you how I felt on hearing your voice over the telephone on June 16th and that you were so near and "yet so far," and that you had to go right back to San Francisco. I have still a feeling of futility that so many people called me that afternoon and talked so long (each conversation I cut short, because I had a pupil waiting); but all those calls might almost have prevented me from hearing you at all.

I do not know whether my letter in care of Gail, at Quincy, was in time to reach you before you left. Marian *[Marian Hall Moore]* had left your long numbers of the address at the office and so couldn't give them to me. And behold, now that I have them, they are the same you sent me from Spokane, before you left there. So had I known it, I could have written directly to S. F.

I have not written since to Gail, although I enclosed a brief note to her, in with your letter. I will soon, but have been frightfully busy. Tied up with some things I have promised to do for others, in the way of correcting and arranging; besides a full orchestral score of "Brief Furlough," of which I am now making the "Master" copy for reproduction, so I can have more than one conductor's score. There is a possibility of its being used if I get it finished in time. Thirty-eight pages of 24 line paper; some job—and then, the masters for the partitures being a composer entails an awful lot of drudgery in copies, or else an enormous expense.

You are on your way to a very far distant place, and I am trying to send my heart a-journeying with you. It is a strange country to me, when I try to reach either you or Byron. In his case, he seems a little nearer, as I have had several letters from him, which came through in a week. I have written him often too, as by sending care of American Airlines, I know they will be passed from pilot to pilot and not in so much danger of going astray.

I composed a song, by request, a short time ago, with poem in English by Patrick McAuliffe (Irish-born American citizen) translated into French by Professor Ferand Baldensperger (pronounced the French way), temporarily Professor of French at UCLA (stranded here on account of the war) and dedicated to General Giroud. My setting was necessarily to the French text, as it is a very beautiful French Poem (the Professor is quite a noted French poet), and so the English verse is printed on the front page. The poem is very inspiring— "O France vaillante, O France intr'epide," etc; and it has been sent to General Giroud; whether it will be to his liking, I cannot tell. I will mail you a copy in a short time. You will enjoy the beauty of the French poem, I know.

Marian and Cy *[Cyril Quinn]* are having a bit of a belated Honeymoon, as the boys left a week ago for Seattle where they are to spend the summer with "Grandpa" *[John Claude Moore]* and "Esther." *[Esther Sax]* Of course Marian misses them, but it will be a nice quiet time for the two who have so long been part of a family—first here with me, and then, with those nice young "wild Indians."

The boys are getting quite manly. Clyde *[Clyde Benton Hudson, Jr.]* graduated in spite of our fears to the contrary. Bob *[Robert Wray Hudson]* has another term to go; of course, this is <u>Junior</u> High.

Marian just called me on the telephone, which she does every night before she retires and which I think is mighty sweet of her. Of course, she says she does it to check up on me— whether I am gadding about very much, as my right ankle is badly swollen much of the time. A touch of arthritis. Lewis is giving me hypos and some Bicarbonate crystals (I think that is it—the package is down stairs and too much trouble to go down and see if I am telling the truth). Also, I soak my feet in Epsom Salts solution, and then use Imadyl Unction, very gently. I should, I suppose, keep entirely off my feet; but who would feed the dogs and cats, and water the lawn? It will take care of itself before long, as I am only a young thing of seventy (lacking a month) I need something to keep me from acting too young and gay.

I am getting lots of quiet and freedom to work at my composition, but miss my College work. The private pupils are so irregular although sometimes I am rushed to death, and others, an arid space.

Marian says to tell you "you are a big egg" not to write before you left—I asked her if she thought Cy would spend his last moments writing to his sister when about to leave—and she said, "Oh, that's different—Wesley is my little brother!" Well—I realize, at any rate, how hard it is to get letters written; I am always a "bad egg" and owe everyone I know letters by the dozens. My desk is such an accusation, that I have moved my music copying into the room which was Cy's, so that I can orchestrate in peace, without being confronted by the piles of letters which I have marked, "immediate reply." So, you see, I know how you feel.

I must stop now and get some rest—for tomorrow, I am to have a busy day; several pupils—and when they come to the house, they NEVER go—until the next one drives them out; at College the bell rang, and that was that.

It is a year now since I have been without a regular job—and, at my age, I do not know where to get another although there is such a shortage of men, I should be able to find plenty to do in my line. But I am not good at hunting them out; my standing is of the highest in my profession, and where there is an opening, I think I could have it—but where? I am at a loss where to apply. UCLA has Dr. Arnold Schoenberg; and USC has Toch, and with those eminent foreign Jewish refugees, there is no room for an American female. So—of course, not all Colleges give the Bachelor and Master of Music degrees; in fact UCLA and Berkeley do not—only an AB with Music Major.

Well, anyway, I have news from a fine conductor in New York that he considers my LEGENDE PROVENCALE superior to Massenet" MANON—that is going some; but of course, the usual reluctance to put money into anything by an American is a hindrance. I am not surprised, or indignant; it is the attitude of the public in America; but I have no doubt that some of my things will be going well when I am exceedingly dead, and so I don't mind the state of affairs. I have taught too much Music History not to know that this is nothing new. All that concerns me is to make my music GOOD ENOUGH—and some of it is—I know.

Well, Dear boy—I run on, and on. I am thinking of you—and Byron too, very steadily these days, and wishing you both the highest joy in service to your country—and feeling very strongly that you will both be home with us, in our own country, before too long. God go with you, my Darling.

With my deepest love and all my good wishes   Mother

JULY 6, 1943 GAIL TO WES

Darling—

Haven't written you for a few days, but I just wonder if any of these will catch up to you. I'd certainly like to know where you are about now. However, I suppose you might be wondering that yourself. Don't forget to tell me about the trip—as much as you can.

I just finished washing the Gold Lake dirt off of John. We came home last night, but he was asleep when we arrived so I just tucked him in. He was really worn out but did he ever have a good time!

Del and Ken and Pop Small and his son, Bill, drove into Gold Valley on the 4th in one of Del's old Packards. Outside of having to climb over a few fallen trees and a flat tire and having to push the Packard out over the hill, their fishing trip was a success. They each came home with a limit. They didn't do much fishing on the 5th. We all missed you, Pop, and I know you would have enjoyed the fishing trip.

Last Friday George C. *[George Cotter]* took John and me for a plane ride about dusk. When we came in for a landing there were two little boys sitting in the runway. George had to go 'round and boy was he mad! It was getting darker every minute. Course Mom and Dad were having ants, so Dad hops in the car and races down to run the kids out of the field so we could get down.

We had an announcement of the graduation of Howard Kohler from Advanced Training in Litus, Oklahoma. He is now a Lt. I wonder what has happened to Chuck Grace.

I received a letter from Doris Hansen and she told me the whole story about Chris. She said he was pretty low and expected him to come back to Illinois after his operation. Doris also said that the Meyers are still in Pendleton and have had no further orders about school. Colonel and Mrs. Moore are back in Texas.

Honey, I've found out that I can't send you anything unless you specifically ask for it. Some people have said that the request has to be autographed by your commanding officer. So—if you want a birthday present, you had better make your request early.

Nine p.m. Dad has the news on and there seems to be lots of unfinished business in the Solomons. Darn this old war!

Helen Bailey is having Supper Club tomorrow evening down at Paxton. I guess I will go with either the Dellinger's or the Cotters. They are having it early this month so Margaret Hays can get in on it.

She has rented a house in Woodland and sold their house here to the Chester Hards.

Guess I'll turn in early tonight 'cause my weekend at Gold Lake was a strenuous one—

All my love, Darling   Gail

JULY 9, 1943 GAIL TO WES
(11pm)

Darling,

I certainly wish that I would get a letter from you, although that it will be at least a couple of months before I do. It would help so much just to see your writing!

I've had a big day today. San and Elda *[Cotter]* and Sue and I took all the kids swimming today and did we have fun. Johnny had a marvelous time. He was directing traffic and telling the kids to keep out of the deep water and quit splashing, wash off the mud etc. I put some coconut oil on him but he came out of it with pretty red shoulders. I went in and shook him for his nightly watering and he didn't even sigh so I gave it up.

This evening I have been flying Nan's ship—was up about an hour and a half. Outside of a tight bushing in the tail wheel and stretched shock cords, a bum cylinder and bad brakes, the ship seems to be in fairly good order. She rented it out to a mess of CAP's *[Civil Air Patrol]* last weekend and they didn't help things a bit.

Last night I went to the Wed Club party for Marg. Hayes—Alga was there and she said from Barney's letters to Melly she expects he may move into port any day. Alga made no bones about saying that Barney told Melly to be sure she could get a week off any time now.

Dad got a wire from David *[Gail's Brother]* tonight and he said he'd be in for dinner— there would be two of them. We are trying to decide whether he is flying or driving and whether his passenger is a bride, a girlfriend, a boy friend or the Colonel. It would make a great difference in *[the rest of the letter is missing]*.

JULY 11, 1943 GAIL TO WES
(Sunday evening)

Dan Baldwin was down to dinner tonight and he says that Bunky Parker didn't make it at O. C. S. Poor Bunky—I'm afraid it will be quite a blow to him. I imagine because of his nervousness and personality he probably was not considered good officer material. I'm sure that Bunky has plenty upstairs and that scholastic grades wouldn't have much to do with it.

Clarence *[Clarence R. Schott]* and Bud G. *[Freeman E. Grover]* are going up to Bend in the morning. I tried to tell Clarence where the Airport is. I guess they are going up to see Itchy *[Douglas Redstreake]* who is about 15 miles out of Bend. George Cotter and Elda went up to Klamath Falls last evening and came back this A. M.

Johnny seems to be growing awfully fast and everyone thinks he looks like you. He keeps pretty busy around here with his tricycle and the swing. He builds roads out in front and runs his little red truck around over them. When you ask him to do something it is usually "I can't." He changes his mind rapidly when I drag out the switch.

We've been having some pretty hot days but gee, Honey, the nights are balmy. We could do so many things if you were only here! We should be out flying this evening. You would certainly enjoy it. Bill Bailey is just roaring over. Seems like a perfect evening for galli-vanting. David and another Lt. flew in yesterday and were they glad to get somewhere that they didn't feel all sticky. I think David is getting itchy feet to get into combat. It seems that they have been sending some of the boys away from Luke into combat. It seems like it's about time for some of them to decide he needs a change.

David didn't do much fancy stuff as he left here—guess he didn't want to frighten the natives again. He did do three slow rolls and an Emelman before took off for Ontario. John was very impressed by the exhibition and said "Isn't that good?" He also took out his gun and went boom boom as David came around. When I asked him what he was doing, he said he was "shooting Uncle Dave down."

This afternoon, I went swimming out at Oakland Camp and it was wonderful. It was so warm that even you would have liked it. They have put up a diving board that is really a peach. I almost broke my neck but had a good time anyway.

Nan and Bob Peckinpah, Clarence Schott and Lee DeCamp all went to Klamath Falls. It seems that Nan has a case on Bob now—it's quite a budding romance.

Monday: Darling, we had a little excitement out at the airport today. A 2nd Lt. came in with an AT and ground looped it to keep from hitting the line of cars and planes. He dragged the field a couple of times from both directions and then came in from the North like a shot. The old ditch scared him, but he didn't set his wheels down 'till he was way past the barn. I didn't see it, but they say he did a beautiful ground loop. He dug the right wing in and the tire on the right side must have rolled way over 'cause there was gravel in behind the hub. They took the tube to town and patched it up and he's on his way back to Hamilton. He had been scouting a fire over around Inskip and the Plumas had asked him to come up to take Keith McDonald over this forest. Mac was certainly disappointed when the fellow went off without him. I think on the strength of this episode, Dad is going to put in a permanent white line and a wind tee facing South. He's worried about the reputation of our field in the eyes of the Army.

Guess I'd better go put the car around in the back. I still have no garage for it. Guess I'll have to put it down in Nebel's. All my love Sweetheart—   Gail

JULY ? 1943 WES TO GAIL

Darling,

Please excuse the typewritten letter. I understand that this the safest way to insure V-Mail being readable. This is my second V-letter. I will try to keep the numbers in mind so you will know whether any are missing.

Of course, when it gets into the hundreds, I won't guarantee my memory. I am not writing frequently on the trip for the simple reason that there is extremely little I am allowed to tell you. When we are more settled, I'll do better.

The weather has been exceptionally good all along. Even you would have enjoyed it, and the meals—man, are they good. On two occasions we had rare roast beef every bit as good as we had at John's Rendezvous not so long ago, and both times I had two helpings. They especially are not stingy in that respect. Accommodations and such matters I cannot discuss as yet.

We are now all proud possessors of ShellBack cards, having crossed the equator. Considerable sport was had by the crew members with a few of those who had not been across before. Of course, we didn't know what day we crossed—in fact, this letter is undated in order that I may even mention the fact of our crossing. Ordinarily, all passengers participate in the ceremony, but owing to conditions, only ship personnel had that dubious pleasure. They had the boys stripped to bathing trunks, covered with designs and writing, apparently made with gentian violet; such decorations as bed pans bandaged onto their heads and urinals slung around their necks prevailed. Most liberal use was made of paddles, and they sang songs and did dances for the passengers along all the decks. Several parted with their hair and not a mustache was allowed to remain.

Speaking of mustaches, I'm sure you will be proud of the foliage which is getting more rank daily on my upper lip. It really is going to be a dandy—aren't you glad you don't have to suffer through this one? I'm not sure but what I'll come home with it if it seems to be successful!

I don't mind shaving with my new razor nearly as badly as I thought I would. I waited about three days before getting courage to whack them off, but it looked so horrible, I finally gave in. Perhaps the years I put up with the other gave my face a chance to toughen up, or maybe I am just growing up. I had a haircut the other day, and asked for just a little off the top. The barber apparently had his own ideas, because it now sticks straight up, regardless of the amount of gunk I layer on. Maybe I'll just get it all cut off later, then I won't have to worry about it any more. Certainly, my patients won't object!

The water has been beautiful and there have been loads of flying fish. No porpoises or whales, though. I've sure missed you, Honey, on these beautiful warm nights at the rail. Sometimes, we'll take a nice long sea voyage together. It is most wonderfully relaxing to me. My worries have just sort of melted into the passing waves.

How is Johnny getting along? Is he minding Grandpa and Grandma, not to mention Mama? Sure wish I could see the little Guy. Tell him Daddy loves him. Hope I can find something new and different to send him. Honey, be sure to send me pictures of all of you occasionally, so I can see the changes occurring. Tell me what he is doing. And tell me how you are getting along with your flying. I hope you are keeping it up, Dear. I see the end of the paper in view.

Loads of love, Dearest, and my best to everybody.   Wes

JULY 13, 1943 WES TO GAIL

Dearest,

Can't get a typewriter today so you will have to struggle through my scribble. I cabled to you, so you should know that we arrived safely. It feels good to live on land again, much as I enjoy travel. The last few days were rather monotonous.

We are in Australia—right "down under" you. The country is nice, and the "winter" apparently quite mild. Camp life is more or less rugged—a la Long Lake R. S., but with less refinement. The candlelight is romantic if nothing else! I can see that my Boy Scout training is going to come in handy. I haven't any decent table to write on, so that this doesn't look very legible. Hope you can read it—Honey, there was no mail waiting for me here. Please write always by V-Mail, as it has priority over all other and comes quite quickly. Capt. Van de Carr had several letters waiting for him, all V-Mail.

The liquor situation is pretty rugged—in fact, nil, so far, although we did manage a couple of glasses of beer. It's pretty good but not quite as good as what we had in Canada.

Bud Rolnbaugh is behaving pretty well since we got here. I guess we'll make out O. K.

All my love, Sweetheart—kiss Johnny—and write soon. Use same A.P.O. #. until further notice.

Wes

JULY 15, 1943 MACKAY RADIO TELEGRAPH WES TO GAIL

DARLING. ALL WELL AND SAFE. ALL MY LOVE

John W. Moore
859P13

JULY 15, 1943 GAIL TO WES
(Thursday night)

My Darling—

Nan has been staying with me while Mother is away. She is out with Bob Peckinpah, however, so she isn't much protection. Bill Bailey took John and me for a ride over Pilot Peak this evening and the air was grand. John enjoyed it for awhile and then almost settled down to go to sleep—it being just about 8:15 and he hadn't done any sleeping when I put him down this afternoon. It was awfully hot—we went swimming this afternoon. John has a great time in the water but he isn't learning much about swimming. I think that time will take care of that so I'm not forcing him. Guess he's kinda' young for that anyway.

Gee, Honey, I wish I could think of something less than 8 oz for your birthday. It would probably be like your Christmas present and get to you about New Years. Anything that I can think of to send you weighs more than the allotted 8 oz.

Nothing very exciting has taken place so there isn't much to tell you—'Nite Honey!

Saturday—I got a radiogram from you today, Sweetheart, and was I tickled! We've been trying to figure where it came from and we all came to the conclusion that you are still on your way. I have a feeling that you have been where that radiogram came from a couple of times before, but of course there is no way to tell. It was mailed to me from San Francisco. Everyone is glad to know that I have had word of you. I was hoping that you might be able to get a letter off too, but I guess that is one of those things that just isn't being done.

Some Army Air Corps men have been in here surveying the valley and looking up records and stuff and we have all been worried for fear they might decide to stick a runway in here somewhere and run us out. Maybe they are just practicing and will find similar conditions overseas.

Last night, we had a meeting of the CAP. It seems that since the government has taken it over they have decided to reorganize the Quincy Flight. Last night the suggestion didn't meet with much enthusiasm. The boys seem to think that they want to reorganize us so that the Oakland and Sacramento flights can come here and use our planes. Bill Meyers who is now a Captain in the CAP and our group commander is supposed to be here tomorrow and I guess is going to give us all the details at the meeting in the Fire House.

After our meeting, CA [C. A. King] and Irene [Irene Lund] took me down to the Sump and insisted that I become a short snorter—so I bought drinks for about six of them and in return got about 6 signatures on my fresh new dollar bill. Maybe you should have initiated me long years ago, Honey. 'Cause maybe that would have meant that I had just that much more time when I could get caught without it.

CA has taken one of the Forest Service radios up in his plane and it works beautifully. He was certainly thrilled when they could hear something over it.

Guess I'll sign off now, Honey, and see if I can find someone to go swimming. Gee it's hot!

All my love   Gail

JULY 16, 1943 WES TO GAIL

Dearest—   #4

I received your letters 1 and 3 today. Believe me, Honey, it was wonderful to hear from you. Whoever said that mail call around camps on foreign soil was the most important time of day certainly knew what he was talking about. It is a real disappointment when nothing shows up.

Gold Lake sounds mighty good to me—I could go for a little Gold Lake dirt myself. Hope that Bailey *["Bill" Bailey]* or someone can get the gun fixed up for you. Del *[A. C. Dellinger]* must have been awfully lucky to find it.

Don't let Dr. work you too hard up there at the hospital, Hon. A little of it should be good to keep you busy. Give my best to Dr. *[Laswell]* and Margarite *[Mrs. Laswell]* and tell them I will write when I have time.

I'm sure getting a kick out of Australia and the people. They are most gracious toward us, and I could listen to them talk for hours. The money is really tough to get use to. The one pound note looks like a dollar bill, and the tendency is to spend them about the same. The rate at present is $3.27 per pound sterling, so it suddenly seems gone faster than one realizes, if one uses them as dollars. We haven't been paid since we left the U. S., but are hoping to get it by the 21st. I haven't received any dope on the Flight Surgeon status or promotion as yet. However, our temporary flying status (flat $60.00 per mo.) is automatically continued until such time as the other goes through. They tell me it will probably take about three months. I can't wear my wings now, but I did have the fun of wearing them on the boat.

I am sending along a purse for you, its only distinction being that it was manufactured in Australia. I wanted to get you a kangaroo skin one, but they are not manufacturing any non-essential items. These people really are feeling the pinch of lack of import and no luxury production. Every article of apparel is rationed by coupon, even hankies. We are going to be issued seventy coupons, but we cannot send out any manufactured garment. I don't know what we can send, but am going to try to get some hankies, etc. We received tobacco rations which allows us 1 pkg. cigarettes per day. However, no matter what brand you buy you must take an equal number of Raleighs! All cigarettes are two and six—that means two shillings, six pence—per carton—about forty cents.

I see that I am getting toward the end of this sheet so I will continue this on another sheet, which will of course be in a separate envelope as a separate letter. I asked in the last letter that you use all V-mail in writing to me. The reason is that your airmail only goes as such when there is room on a plane. Otherwise, it is carried by ship and will be two or three weeks longer in arriving. That is why your no. 2 letter didn't come through with 1 and 3. Captain Van received a letter (V-mail) today, which was mailed in Oakland on the 12th—4 days.

I am mixing my topics up badly. I'll go back to what I am sending along under a separate cover. I found an illustrated ABC book for John on Australian animals. Wes *[continued]* I love you—

Sweetheart: This is a continuation, and doesn't need the salutation, but gives me a good excuse to be mushy—There's something about you, you know, that keeps me longing for you, my Dearest.

To go on about the animals: tell John that Daddy saw all of these (almost) in Australia, and that he will come home and tell him all about them personally some day before very long. There is also a map of the Solomon Islands for Dave, which I am hoping will be allowed through. It has no significance whatsoever as to where I am, because I am in Australia. But I thought it might supplement his group of maps. So far, I am sorry to say I have found nothing specifically for Mom, but will have another opportunity to shop, I am sure.

There are so many interesting things I think of to tell you about, but many of them escape me when I come to write them down. I like Australia and the people. Oh—I spoke about cigarette rationing for us. We obtain ours through the Army. It seems practically impossible for the Australian civilians to get cigarettes. Cigars are even more scarce. A tobacconist told me that Australia only produces three million pounds of tobacco annually, whereas, they consume about nine million pounds yearly, and of course importing is pretty tough these days. About 75% of the women wear no stockings, so I guess they are as scarce as in America.

Now, you asked about my birthday. I think I would love to have a couple of boxes of cigars—Corona Larks would be fine, if you can get them. I request that you send me two boxes of cigars—John W. Moore 1st Lt. M. C. Above request approved: Lt. Col. George J. Benoit—Commanding Officer 63rd Service Group.

Ask Mr. Barr whether it is necessary for officers to obtain the approval of their C. O. on these requests. We weren't sure, so got it to be on the safe side. Hope the request doesn't turn out to be too big an order…I didn't ask for cigarettes, as I already stated that we could get a package a day, which is enough, especially as some men don't smoke. I could sure go for some good bourbon whiskey, but I doubt that you could send that particular item. If you find you can, I'll certainly send you a request for it.

I am using my footlocker set up on a box as a desk and have two candles on each side. It works out very nicely, although I see I have made a few mistakes. This machine is a pretty well beat-up article, though, and causes some of them.

By the way, I just remembered, I want some fishhooks about #6—larger than trout size, leaders and a line—no reel or rod. Perhaps this request will serve. If not, let me know, and I will get a formal one as above. I don't want to bother the Colonel again tonight.

Well, enough for tonight Dear. Sweet dreams. All my love—and I too am FOREVER yours — Wes

Dear Marian and Cy:

I am addressing this c/o Mother, having lost your address. Please send it to me when you write. Is Dinty's address: Capt. B. C. Moore, c/o Amer. Airlines, LaGuardia Field, N. Y.?

I am sorry I was a "bad brother" and did not write to you before leaving. So many things must be done at departure time and the few days preceding that one's time is not always one's own—I certainly did intend writing you, Honey. However, seeing that you have a nice soft job with Hills Bros. Coffee Co. and nothing better to do, see that you write me frequently. Mail call is a mighty important time of the day in Army life, and it is mighty nice to have lots of letters coming along. I'll do the best I can to answer.

Australia is a swell country. A lot of the boys gripe because everything is bas-ackwards from the good old U. S., but me, when I think of how people lay out lots of hard cash for the privilege of seeing new and different countries, I'm tickled to death to be here. Not saying I probably won't be damn glad to get back before it's all over. They do have many strange customs here, new to us. I went to Masonic Lodge last night at a nearby town. Afterwards refreshments were served. No one smoked after eating, I noticed, as I was about to light up, so I waited, and pretty soon some bloke gets up and we all have to sing God Save the King. Then we all raise our glasses and, TO THE KING we says, draining the beer to the last drop. After being seated, then, this bird says, "Gentlemen, you may smoke." Another thing I noticed was that there was no clapping after entertainment and speeches. The Master says "All right, Brethren, one, two, three," and with that, he bangs the table, and everyone else gives the table a terrific thump with the end of their knife and that's that. I had to give a response to the toast offered to visiting Worshipful Brethren, me being a Past Master, as it were. Boy, did I lay them in the aisles. Well, some fellow liked it so well, he invited me and one of the Officers with me to dinner tonight, so I'll find out what life is like at home in the Great Australian Commonwealth.

I'm sorry I can't tell you where we are or what we are doing. Suffice it to say, we can see the Southern Cross. Not being anything else I can say in that regard, I'll try to think of something else.

Slang here often has a quite different meaning than at home. When one feels rather tired, they are apt to say I feel a bit knocked up. To dance with someone is to jazz them, consequently the following conversation may even fail to elicit a smile: "Pardon me, would you care to dance?" "No thanks, I'm knocked up; go jazz my sister." If you are someone's good friend, you are their cobber. The "straight McCoy" is "Dingus Oil" down here. The money is a little tough to catch onto—I believe I explained that in my letter to Mother.

Life isn't so bad in the Army. I kind of enjoy it although I miss Gail and Johnny quite a bit. I don't think I'd ever want to make the Army my career though. We have a good healthy life with regular hours and plenty to eat—so far.

Oh yes—I am raising another moustache, and it's really a beauty. Bet I'll sure make the girls swoon when I swagger down the street. You can see it if you get the right light.

This is the end of the paper. This V-Mail is hard to get. Wish you would send me a few forms. Just stick them in an airmail envelope when you get a chance.

Lots of love,   Wes

JULY 18, 1943 WES TO GAIL

Gail Dearest: #5

Cozily seated on my bunk in my tent I can glance up and see your sweet frame as I write. It has been before me all the way, and I love to look at you, but I wish I had the real article. It's going to be a lonesome life without you, my Darling; I wish you could be seeing this different country and people with me. Some day, maybe we'll come here together—'til then, you must see it through my eyes.

I had a grand time last night. One of the boys found a Masonic Club where they actually serve scotch. He became acquainted and learned of some degree work going on, so we took it in last night and saw two first degrees. Afterwards, we went upstairs to the refreshment room and had some sort of cold sausages, green peas (a considerable treat here as fresh vegetables are practically impossible for these people to obtain) bread and butter and all the beer we cared to drink. Being a Past Master, I was seated in the East of the Lodge and addressed as Worshipful Brother Moore. A seat of honor was also accorded me at the refreshment table along with other Past Masters and I was called upon to make a response to a toast to the visiting brethren. When we had finished eating, I noticed that no one was smoking, and faintly remembering an English custom, waited. Sure enough, the Master soon rose and called the group together, whereupon we drank a toast TO THE KING, sang God Save The King, and after being seated, were permitted to smoke. I enjoyed the whole proceedings immensely.

One of the Brothers invited us to dinner and is to meet us tonight. We also made a date to see an Installation Monday night, which is said to be a most impressive ceremony over (down) here. I don't doubt it, as the work last night was accomplished with considerably greater flourish and fanfare than I have ever seen before. Their work is at considerable variance with what we are use to at home, much of the wording both in the esoteric and written work sounding entirely different.

Apparently one time there were Scotch, Irish, and English factions here, each following their own particular ritual. I do not recall dates, but at a later time, Masons in Australia consolidated and all now conform to the English version. However, every once in a while someone would slip in a Scotch or Irish bit and everyone would grin, and the old boy next to me would lean over and say, "I'll wager you the Grand Lodge would gi'us 'ell could they 'ear that!" All this would probably be of considerable interest to old Masons like Dr. Charley Kerr and Judge Moncur. If you should have a chance to, read that bit to them. While having refreshments there were a few soloists for our pleasure, and these and all speeches were applauded, not by clapping, but by the Master saying, "All right now Brothers, one, two, three." On the three he would bonf down his gavel and everyone would strike the table once with the butt of their knife or fork! It was really a kick.

There is something you could do for me, and it would be more than welcome, and that is to send along the funnies each week. You can put each sheet in a separate envelope, it would be a wonderful homely touch I would enjoy. The papers here carry one or two strips but that far from satisfies my Sunday morning urge to relax! As they come, I'll save them up for Sunday.

Please let me know whether you receive your allotment check for each month, so that I can check on it if it is delayed. On requests by officers for packages to be sent over, it is not necessary that the C. C. approve the request. If you have any difficulty, let me know. On these bankruptcy proceedings, re: Foster, just send the referee a statement of any charges against her. I have not received any other than your letters 1 and 3—maybe more today, I hope. Keep 'em coming. Give John a big kiss from Daddy.

All my love, Sweetheart.   Wes

JULY 19, 1943 GAIL TO WES
(Monday night)

Hello Honey—

You are sitting here in your picture and smiling at me. What I'd give to see that smiling face talking to me or be able to touch it in the flesh. Keep on smiling Honey, 'cause I don't want you to have forgotten how when you come home!

I went to the show tonight—it wasn't so hot. "Forever and a Day" they called it, and it taxed me too much to keep up with what was going on. I ran into CA and he left in the middle of it.

The papers I sent in for the traveling expenses came back and they want your signature on it or mine with a power of attorney and I can't figure out where to sign it. I have plenty of powers of attorney if I could just figure out where your name belongs. I'll see if some of the family can figure it out.

I'm afraid that the CAP isn't going to make a go of it—the enthusiasm isn't running very high. Myers didn't have what he wanted to say very well organized and the crowd was pretty restless during the meeting. Nothing was settled very definitely. Wish I had something of interest to tell you but everything is getting pretty routine and there isn't much news.

Tuesday—just heard downtown that the boys have bombed the tip of the Island of Japan— Hoorah for our side! I hope they give the little devils something to remember us by.

Golly, it's hot here today! We are due for a thunderstorm from the looks of the sky. Johnny has been waiting for the lightning to wake up. I expect he'll see some before this day is over.

Johnny is growing, Honey, and getting fat and sassy. You would probably say he's spoiled but we are doing our best.

All my love Sweetheart—   Gail

JULY 22, 1943 GAIL TO WES

Are you off the boat yet? (Silly question #999!) I wonder how long it will be before we get each other's letters. After hearing Rule Bar tell about the letters that are stacked up in John Redstreake's department down in the city, I wonder if you will ever get any of them— Here's hoping.

Bert Dale said he wrote you about some insurance on the hospital but Dr. and I will take care of it. It seems to be a matter of $9.00 coming due to protect the hospital from a bomb or something.

I went up to Edna Lee's last night to Wednesday Club and won the high prize. I was so elated. Then I came out and got in the car only to find I had a flat tire. Stub *[Lee]* changed it for me and I took it down to George *[Cotter]*. There was a tack in it. It didn't hurt either the tire or the tube fortunately. George said that I had a few miles more wear in the tires and not to get them recapped yet.

Honey, how's about putting your name on some foreign currency—a dollar—and starting me out a trans-ocean short snorter. I think that that would be a pretty good deal. Have you had to start a second dollar yet? Ken *[J. K. Metzker]* and Del seem to be getting along pretty well with their sawmill enterprise—I can't remember whether they had already purchased their mill at Grays Flat when you were here or not. It is keeping Ken pretty busy.

Helen tells me that Gladys Pierce is going to gave a baby in November and I guess Janet Finnegan is due sometime here about then. I noticed a card for Jan at the hospital so maybe she is coming in here to have it.

Dr. delivered a little one yesterday for some friends of the woman who had the crippled baby. Margarite gave the mother gas most of the morning. I think Margarite would like to make a nurse's aide or something out of me. I don't know whether she can or not—that's a big order!

All my love Sweetheart, and I hope to hear from you soon!

Always your Gail

GAIL TO WES

[First page and date missing]

…the sleeping arrangements.

Pop Small said today that he had gotten himself in Dutch. Dr. B. came in <u>hot</u> on his trail and said that Pop's article put him in a bad light. Some how or other Pop has gotten on the other side of the fence and is now pulling for <u>us</u>. San was telling me that she got in on Dr. Blank reading the riot act to Dr. B.— accusing him of not having a case history in the joint etc. San said it was embarrassing for her and she almost walked out of Dr. Blank's waiting room. Dr. B. came out of the session sweating like a porpoise but he didn't have a word to say in his defense. And so it goes on. Pop thinks the whole matter of Dr. B. is coming to a head directly, the coyote!

Dr. Lasswell is doing a grand job with the Industrial business. Everything is running smoothly at the office and everyone is cheerful. The new secretary has made a few blunders such as sending a final report on a man that's still being treated but Dr. Lasswell said he'd take his loss out on my hide. I'm pretty thick skinned so I guess it won't hurt much. I'm pretty pokey learning but I hope to improve—Yesterday, I slammed the car door shut on my little finger so my typing wasn't so good today.

Got a letter from Esther yesterday and she said your Dad is coming along just fine. She is pretty busy though with the boys there.

Had a cute letter from Mavis and she wanted to know what I'd heard. Haven't written her yet but expect to shortly.

All my love, my sweet—   Gail

JULY 24, 1943 GAIL TO WES
(Saturday)

Darling—

I received a card giving me your correct address, which is the same as the one I've been using. I'm hoping that the fact that they've sent the card means that you have landed at your destination safely. Dr. and I have it all figured out that you are in Australia. But then maybe you aren't settled yet. Wish I were along, Honey, I'll bet the moons are beautiful down there!

I had quite a talk with Dr. Fletcher a couple of weeks ago—I didn't tell you about it because I didn't want to worry you. Now I'm afraid you will get the paper and wonder what is going on. Dr. Batson went up to Two Rivers with me—where Fletcher was staying (I had gone to see Batson the night before when the report got to me that Dr. B. was stirring the Industrial business out at Mt. Hough.) Fletcher was very sympathetic and said he would do everything he could. He came to town the next day and talked to Dr. L. and also to B. Dr. L. agreed to have Dr. B. come to work for him and I think he's going to pay him $200.00 a month.

(As Dr. L. says, the devil you know isn't half so bad as the devil you don't know.) All his private patients are <u>supposed</u> to come through the Plumas Industrial. Dr. L. thinks he will have the whip hand and be able to control him. I hope he can stand up to it. If he can't, Margarite and I can!

I think that Fletcher really gave Dr. B. a working over, but that slippery Hebrew smoothed him over a lot 'cause Fletcher was almost ready to send him in as a buck private if he didn't mind his own business and he also told him that the California Medical Society disapproved heartily of his actions in this community. I know that Fletcher is well acquainted with the conditions here and the principals in the case and that if we have any more trouble, he will be glad to help us. Dr. B. starts to work on the first of August, so I'll tell you then how it works out.

Dr. L. told me this morning that he was going to put him on a salary basis so he could fire him if he tried any funny business. Also, he will have no reason to stick his nose in the books. We are going to try to arrange for one of us to be around whenever he's in the office.

I talked with Ken about the whole affair and he thinks it will work out OK. At least there isn't another <u>new</u> doctor to get a foothold. Dr. B. has gotten a certain following, but I think he's going to stick his neck out too far and gag himself. I suppose this is all just about as clear as mud to you, Honey, but don't let it worry you. We all have gotten over that stage and I guess we are in the stage of expectancy.

The airport is having a chicken feed out at CA's tonight. He rounded up 20 chickens. I guess there will be 30 or 35 there. It should be fun—wish you were going to be in on it, Honey.

By the way—last night I flew Dicky's Porterfield—no, not solo. My first takeoff from the front seat was a dinger—I might easily have been Charlie Thompson from the course I took. On my 3rd trial—from the front seat—I did lots better and even painted on a landing. I haven't done much flying lately. CA and Bill Bailey flew to Klamath yesterday and had a grand trip. CA borrowed your maps.

We had a CAP meeting last night and it seems to be getting along OK. Maybe we can make a going concern out of it yet.

Darling, I wish you a happy birthday—this might get there by Aug 2nd —I certainly hope so. Wish I could give you a great big kiss, but there seem to be difficulties.

All my love my sweet.   Gail

JULY 25, 1943 WES TO GAIL

Dearest Gail:

I sure hope you are getting my letters, Dear. I will be glad when I get your first in response. I can see that our correspondence isn't going to be very intelligent, considering the length of time it takes for our letters to go and come.

We really have a fine outfit; everyone gets along well with everyone else. I'm glad of that because I've seen some outfits that don't do so well. There is only one bad thing about the Australian theatre, and that is a matter of promotions. The way it looks, I'm just as likely to come home a 1st Lt. I guess you practically have to be decorated for bravery or something to get a boost. They tell me it takes actual combat service, and about a year of that. I talked with a fellow the other day who had been in New Guinea (no, I'm not up there) for fourteen months. He applied for a twenty day leave to start when he arrived in the U.S. Instead of that, they gave him a week to start when he arrived at *[censored]*, Australia. So you can see I probably won't be home for supper very soon!

Today (Sunday) I went to see the Koala bears. They are cute little devils—definitely the original teddy bear. There were about half a dozen little fellows about a week old. They have faces like little old men, and they are no bigger than a small rat. I'd sure love to bring one home to John for a pet. They seem to spend most of their time curled up on the limb of a tree—you can see the little fellows heads popping out of the pouch. They let us hold them and take your picture, for six pence. I will be able to get the picture in a day or so, and will send one to you if it is allowed. They had all sorts of animals in this place; kangaroos, wallabies, wallaroos, dingoes, Emu's, and what have you. We could get the wallabies up to the fence and feed them grass and pet them. They look for all the world like an overgrown jackrabbit. All this for a sixpence!

Boy! It sure is dusty in these tents—guess I've mentioned that before. Everything is layered with it. I don't think I'll ever get it out of my B-4 bag. But nobody cares much about fancy clothes down here anyway, so what the 'ell, Bill.

Tell the gang I am going to Rotary Club tomorrow. Some day I'll be able to send home a makeup card. I'll try to give them a report on what goes on. I suppose, like everything else down here, they'll do it backward.

My Darling, you certainly are getting dirty down here. I have to wash your face every day—maybe sneak in a kiss, too, when no one's looking. Hope you don't mind. Boy, Honey, how I could go for one of the real article. I love you so much, my sweet. When we get this job done I'll bet it will be a long cold day before I leave home again. Send me a kiss by airmail, Darling—a la Hollywood—so I will remember how sweet they look. As if I could ever forget!

I just took time out to watch a lad wringing out a 38. Boy, what a circus those kids can put on. It's really beautiful. By the way, where is David now? Bet he would like to get hold of one of those babies. They tell me the boys have to spend six hours just sitting in the cockpit learning the instruments and controls by heart before they are allowed to fly them.

Well, Darling, here's the end of the paper again. All my love, Sweetheart, always

Wes

JULY 26, 1943 ESTHER TO WES

Dear Wes—

Suddenly realized your birthday is just a few days away—hope you know we are all thinking of you. I hope next year you'll be with your family. Now that the Italian rat is out of the way, maybe it won't be long ere we can get the other two on the run.

Had a letter from Gail today. I'll plan to get up to see her when I go south either in September or October. I am so anxious to see Johnny now that he's talking and so very grown up.

Good luck, Darling! Dad is fine—he's better than he's been for a long time.

Much love from us all.   Esther

JULY 27, 1943 WES TO GAIL

Darling: #9

I am keeping a little record of the letter numbers—being overseas hasn't improved my memory in the least. How am I doing? Better than when I was at Randolph. I know I haven't written every day by any means, but am trying to write as often as possible. Conditions are not exactly conducive to writing all the time. It is particularly miserable today, as the wind is blowing and it is cold and threatening to rain. This old tent is flapping around like it was ready to take off. I borrowed another typewriter today—from Capt. Van de Carr. It writes easier and blacker, although I notice the margin seems a bit *[unreadable]*. From some of the V-Mail I've seen, I imagine you will have to have a magnifying glass to read these.

I enjoyed Rotary very much. It was about the same as any club in the city. The President gave a very gracious welcome to the American visitors, of which there were five or six. An R.A.A.F. pilot gave an interesting speech on pilot training in Australia. Capt. Knight and I attended—and the Parson, Chaplain Cooper. They said it would be about three months before they would be allowed to send through my makeup card, in order not to reveal my station at the present, so you can tell Dave to tell the gang I made up "somewhere in Australia."

Last night I took in a movie—saw Moscow Fights Back and Pittsburgh. Both pretty good entertainment. I'm getting to be quite a movie fan. You used to have trouble getting me in to a show!

I really had a treat. The boys set up the portable generator which goes with our x-ray machine, so I had an electric razor shave. My face gets pretty sore after a few straight days of shaving, so it really felt good. I usually let it go every three or four days but if they keep this up I'll be able to use my razor every day. I'm glad I brought it after all. I couldn't use it at all on the way over.

Still no letters, Sweetheart. Boy, will I be happy when I get one. All the boys are getting V-Mail pretty regularly, and a moderate amount of airmail. I know it isn't the change of APO numbers, because all that would do (sending it to 4584) should be to hold it up about two or three days, because it means an extra sorting. I told you in letter 7 that no. was changed to 923. I am repeating it in the event that no. 7 might not have reached you. I also said that it did not indicate any change of station. We are still in the same place.

Boy, how I do run on. It's pretty hard to write when there are so few things we are allowed to talk about. I'd just keep saying I love you, Dear, but I guess you would get tired of that sort of a letter. When I hear from you, I'll have something to write about—provided your questions are answerable. Tell me how Clarence and Ole's baby is getting along. I'm going to write soon to Dr. B. and the *[unreadable]* and thank them for being so nice to us.

I sent along a purse for you and one for your mother. It probably will take six or eight weeks for the package to get there. Anyway, it will have to do for your birthday present, sweet. Maybe this will be too early, but many happy returns of the day on your 27th birthday (Aug. 19—see, I do remember). My, but you are getting to be a grown up lady, almost, aren't you?

Well, Darling, I guess that's all for today. I do love you tremendously and miss you badly. Tell John to be a big boy and look after his mother. Daddy will take over again when he licks the Japs. *[censored]*

JULY 27, 1943 GAIL TO WES

Hello Honey,

I have visions of a V-Mail catching up with you, 'cause I got my first one from you today, written on June 29th. Were we all thrilled! I've written airmail until today. Rule Bar told me all the rules and gave me this paper. We have you all landed and located now but of course we could be wrong. CA had a letter from Julian *[Atkins]*. He had a leave and went to Australia. He says he's going to retire when the war is over.

We are all fine and Johnny is getting husky and pink cheeked. He has quite a tan and is about to become a swimmer. You should have seen him pouring over your letter. He was thrilled to pieces.

Have flown the T Craft and done a little dual work in Dicky's Porterfield. The CAP is beginning to flourish again. I am working about half a day up at the hospital and am learning how the place is run. We are getting along fine and seem to have no major problems at the moment. Your V-Mail letter was easy to read—hope mine is the same. We miss you an awful lot Darling—Clean 'em up quick and come on home!

All my love   Gail

JULY 29, 1943 WES TO GAIL

Darling—   #10

Can't locate a typewriter today—all seem to be in use. Anyway, I'm likely to forget how to write if I don't occasionally. Perhaps you will enjoy my scrawl for a change.

All continues quiet. Movies are about the only excitement—saw "First of the Few" last night. A marvelous picture—Leslie Howard. Capt. Giles and I took on a feed before the show. Had a porterhouse for two that must have weighed ten pounds, including bone, fat, etc. It was all we could do to polish it off. Beer before and during dinner (it's customary here) and whiskey after—the paint remover kind.

I am still looking for letter #4, Darling. I'm beginning to feel a little worried about you, it seems so long since I heard anything. I do hope you are all right, my sweet. You must take good care of yourself Darling, because I could stand almost anything but to lose you.

My love to Mom and Dave, and a big hug and a kiss for John.

Always yours—Wesley

JULY 29, 1943 GAIL TO WES

Darling,

I tried to send you a wire today to wish you happy birthday, but it was no go. The operator didn't have an APO # that went up as high as yours. I guess you won't even get a written wish, let alone a present. Anyhow, Honey, you know we are all thinking of you all the time.

I've gotten 5 V-Mails from you so far. The last was written on July 13. Needless to say I was awfully thrilled to get them. You do an awful lot better than I do with the typewriter. The typewritten one really puts out the news, and was interesting to the whole community. I'm glad that you enjoyed the trip, only wish that I could have been along although I probably would have had a couple of wobbly days.

About the mustache, I don't know. I'll bet it's a Honey! Is it blonde or brunette? The sun will probably turn it a golden yellow. By the way—how many times have you peeled? You should come home with a healthy coat of tan. I don't know whether you could best Johnny or not. He is doing pretty well—'course some of it may be the good earth showing through. He manages to get pretty black by the end of the day. But does he have fun! He scares people to death with his bicycle. He goes tearing down the sidewalk, right up to people and then kicks right or left rudder or puts on the brakes right at their feet. His little old legs go around like a whirlwind. His latest accomplishment is bonking. He comes up to me all squared off and then starts in with arms flying. He thinks that is great sport.

Yesterday I put in about an hour and 45 minutes flying the Porterfield 95. It is awfully hard on the controls but is a lot of fun to fly because it is so different from any of the other ships that I've flown lately. To make a good landing in the thing you have to set it down at about 65 mph. Then you can paint them on. If you come in any slower, she drops out too fast. It has a 32 foot wing spread and slotted wings like the Stinson Voyager. We went over to Susanville and landed. They are having an awful time over there getting enough ships to keep their Navy program going. They say that the government wants everything they fly. There wasn't any activity there at all when we came in. It was about 1:30. It was so darn hot yesterday that we had a dickens of a time getting any altitude. I guess another reason that it was so hard was because I was flying and I didn't know the ship. I guess that I won't get a chance to fly it much more though, 'cause the Government has phoned Dickey and told him that they want it. Nan's plane is grounded. A bulletin came out on Continentals and after so many hours, the motors have to be magnifluxed. Hers comes in for that. CA's and Fred's were out of it. No, I guess Fred has already had his done. They finally got Lee Jorganson's Ercoupe put together and it seems to fly pretty well. We now have three Ercoupes on the field. I guess the Government doesn't want them.

Mother and I are having a bridge party tonight and John is heckling the dickens out of us. I hear big screeches from the back yard and fear that John D. got his pants warmed for sprinkling the swing. His favorite pastime is playing in the water and he thinks that it is his duty, when he gets his swimming suit on, to sprinkle everything and anything. He can't seem to resist the hose, somehow. Wow, it is hot today. I don't blame him for playing in the water. I think this is one of the warmest summers that we have ever had. I certainly would like to be out swimming.

Honey, I'm so sorry that you didn't have my mail waiting for you. I wrote at least three times a week so some should be coming in soon.

All my love, Sweetheart   Gail

JULY 30, 1943 WES TO GAIL

Darling—   Letter #11

I was sure tickled to get a letter from you today. I'm going over to send you a canned telegram in a while. It wasn't numbered, so I don't know whether it came in between. You dated it July 15 and it was postmarked July 17th. I do hope you are writing oftener than this indicates, as the last postmark was July 7—a whole week in between! My first letter in 15 days!

I was amused at your deductions about my wire. It was sent from Australia the day of our arrival. The first land we saw after leaving S. F.

So John is going swimming. That's swell. I'm glad he's not afraid of the water. He'll learn to swim all right in due time.

Are you doing any flying for yourself? Be careful, sweet—don't take any chances. I guess you've had my request for cigars by now. They should come under 8 oz. One would sure taste good. I hope your purse gets to you before Christmas, Darling! Hope CAP can function and do a little Forest Patrol. Don't let these Bay boys ruin your airplanes.

All my love, Sweetheart   Wes

JULY 31, 1943 GAIL TO WES

Hello Darling,

No more V-Mail from you. I hope you haven't become discouraged about my letter writing because they should be arriving in droves shortly. I can't understand what has happened to all of those Airmails that I sent to you.

Last evening I had a grand time out at the airport. I went up with Dicky for an hour and ten minutes during which time we called on the lookout on Mt. Hough and dropped him the morning papers. I gave them a good toss and they lit down in the brush at the foot of the rocks. He had quite a hunt for them, but he finally found them. When we got back about 7 o'clock, CA was out there and he wanted me to take him for a ride. So, I did it. We went out to Payne's and I showed him how you used to land in the Porterfield. When we got down fairly close, he said that he'd had enough so we went on upstairs and he gave me the equivalent of a private test. Apparently, I passed with flying colors because he said to go and take the plane any time I wanted. I think that he had been worried about my ability to go from one ship to the other and he wanted to give me a check ride first. I hadn't been in his ship since you soloed me in it before you left. That was the first time that he had offered it to me and I didn't ask him to fly it because I wanted him to offer it.

Johnny is really getting to the climbing stage. This morning he climbed the new green fence and proceeded to fall off smack on his tummy. He knocked the wind out of himself and got white around the gills, but apparently didn't do any serious damage. His latest version of where you are is out in the big water and he is going to pull you out.

I'll give you the local gossip in one paragraph. Joe Nebel has pneumonia and is out at the county hospital. Roseamond had a baby girl over in Greenville. Marjory Richards was committed to Napa. She disappeared for four days and they found her in one of those rooms over the Stone House drunk. The paper says that Blankenships have bought the laundry and are taking over the last of Aug. I'm glad for Etz's sake. She had been sick and looks like a walking ghost. Evelyn Clevenger says that Ray is in the Navy hospital down at Corpus Christi. He was in an automobile accident 5 years ago and some internal injuries are catching up with him. She is leaving this week. Roy Brown and Charley Haggerty bought a 50 T Craft and have it out on the field. Bud Moore went down below to bring up another Cub. Myers left a Club Coupe here on the field last Sunday. Business is picking up. The Club Coupe is suppose to be a CAP ship, I think.

Yesterday Ken and Dellinger hauled brick for their new mill. They were certainly industrious to go out on a day like yesterday to pitch brick. Ruth *[Dellinger]* said that before they could get through, their outfit in going to be bigger than Quincy Lumber. Ken seems busier than a bee these days. Dr. Lasswell had a rattlesnake boy in the hospital and he is doing OK. I think he is one of the Blister Rust boys. Today five of them came in covered with poison oak. Monday, Dr. B. comes in to work for Dr. Lasswell part time. I think that Dr. B. can handle him. In case you haven't gotten my other letters on the subject, Fletcher was here and looked the situation over and he and Dr. L. decided that was the best thing to do. I think that it will work out if we can get enough people around the hospital to keep an eye on him. I think they are going to move Mrs. Ruth Stuart to Westwood. Dr. Blank operated twice on the bowel and now the latter is leaking out through the incision. We have a few troubles now and then. Please tell me all you can about your work and are you in a station hospital.

All my love my, Darling, and take good care of yourself.   Gail

AUGUST 1, 1943 KATHERINE WATSON *[Katherine R. Woods]* TO WES

Dear Wes

This is to wish you a happy birthday. I am writing it the day before your birthday and goodness knows when it will reach you, but in time you will know that we are thinking of you here and wishing we could help you celebrate properly. We will look forward until the time when we can. Seems to me Johnny is growing every day. Edith comes up here now and then for vegetables and Johnny comes along. He likes Uncle "Doc's" *[Arthur J. Watson]* wax beans. You know he calls "Joe" Uncle "Doc" instead of Uncle Dot. I really prefer it!

We are very well, but we feel safer when you are back looking after us. I think my knee is getting better all the time. I didn't have to have an operation. The trouble seemed to be in the muscles and not in the cords. I don't have to go back to see Dr. Haig unless I want him to operate after another few weeks but I am sure I won't. I am still taking my exercises faithfully and my slight limp doesn't cramp my style much.

Arthur *[Arthur R. Watson]* is still in Africa we think. Heard from him last week, and hope we continue to hear frequently. Virginia is coming down for a few weeks' visit the last of the month. We are counting the days until she arrives. Edith and Gail had a lovely bridge party last Thursday night. Imagine Gail keeps you posted on all the local and family news. There isn't really much to write. No family barbecues this summer but Tiny had a dinner at Rainbow's End for Anne *[Anne Blench Lepley]* on her birthday. We are planning to have one there for Virginia too on her 21st birthday. The dinner last Monday was very successful as the Watsons were all able to have steaks! We think of you often. Uncle "Doc" wants to be remembered to you!

Affectionately, Katherine

AUGUST 2, 1943 WES TO GAIL

Sweetheart: #11

Happy Birthday from you to me, and again, Happy Birthday from me to you! I wasn't able to send you a wire the other day in honor of the first letter in fifteen days, so did today, including possibly a premature birthday greeting. Wonder if you will ever receive the purses I mailed? I also wired Birthday Greetings to mother and sent her a purse (purses seem to be my long suit in the gift division). Her birthday is on the 6th. My first telegram to you was on the [censored] of July.

It sure takes a long time for our letters to go through. Captain Giles just got a wire from his wife dated the 29th stating she just received his first letters mailed the 13th so you must have some of mine by now. It is a bit unsatisfactory, isn't it, Darling? But then, it is simply marvelous to have a letter from you at all. I got another postmarked July 22. Your question, of course, is answered—I am off the boat!

I am familiar with that war clause on the insurance policy, having paid it on existing policies before I left.

Don't wait too long before recapping the tires. Do you have plenty of money? How much have you been getting from Dr. and are you receiving your 217 dollars? I sent you $50.00 the other day (Saturday), feeling that I would only spend it foolishly if I kept it around. I have sufficient for my mess and liquor, smokes, etc. There really isn't much to spend money on outside of those things and an occasional feed downtown. I am planning on going out with Capt. Giles tonight to have a big steak and beer dinner in celebration of my birthday. Wish you could be with me, sweetie—would we ever have fun?!

It is windy as the very devil. They say the wind blows around here all during August, and I really believe it, because it started blowing yesterday morning, and hasn't stopped yet. I sometimes wonder how these tents ever stand up.

Oh, I nearly forgot. I bought myself a present yesterday—an air mattress. They got a bunch of them in at the PX—an English kind, for two pounds ($6.46). They are quite an improvement over the GI cot and straw tick. I also succeeded in getting a pillow a week or so ago (or did I tell you) so now have nearly all the comforts of home—except a wife. Come on over, Honey, and keep me company?

Congratulations on the first prize at Edna Lee's—only you didn't tell me what the prize was.

I have a few extra names on my Short-Snorter bill. I haven't started one on an Australian bill, but will do so. However, I can't start one for you and send it to you, as we are not allowed to send any Australian money out of the country. You'll just have to wait, I'm afraid, and I'll bring one home for you, Darling. I didn't know about Ken and Del's venture. They must have gone into that after I left. I hope they are making a pot of money and can retire and go fishing after a while: I'm afraid that sounds sarcastic—I don't mean it to be, and do wish them all the luck in the world, as they are a couple of swell fellows.

Keep up the good work on the letters, Sweetheart. It's sure wonderful to hear from you. All my love to you and Johnny. Sounds real cute in all his antics. Give him my love, Dear.

Wes

AUGUST 2, 1943 GAIL TO WES

Honey,

I hope that you are having a happy birthday, despite being so far from home. I tried to get your cigars today and Bill said that he didn't have any Corona Larks and hadn't had some for ages. He has some Corona Sunsets that cost the same and he says should be as good. He is going to help me pack them all together and I should get them off to you in a day or so. I can't imagine you smoking cigars but maybe if I'm not around you will enjoy them. Will try to get the fishing equipment in same package.

I got the second half of your 4th V-Mail letter yesterday. So far the 1st half hasn't shown up. Guess it will be along in a day or so. I forgot to ask if the request has to be signed by the CO. I'll do that and let you know in my next letter.

Well, we completed our first day at the hospital with Dr. B. It was really a panic. He came in like a whirlwind and started in by following Dr. L. and Margarite around most of the time. Finally Margarite sat on him, but not before he had watched Dr. through an industrial case. He can't seem to keep his nose in his own business. I'm afraid that he thought that his reception was anything but warm. I'm hoping that Dr. L. and Margarite can get along with him and that Dr. L. will be able to get away occasionally, which is what he needs very badly. I think that if he can do that, he will last the war out. I hope this situation isn't worrying you, Honey, because I feel that between us we will be able to manage it.

I have decided that I won't attempt to get Johnny's tonsils out this year because the Polio seems to be raging in all congested areas and I don't want to take the chance of taking him into the midst of it. Today I heard that there was a case in Greenville. It's getting pretty close to home. Johnny seems awfully well and looks very husky—you probably would say that I am silly, but it seems too bad to risk the other when nothing is bothering him.

One of Dr. B's patients, a woman of about 60 or so, Mrs. Cunningham from Meadow Valley, who was slightly crazy before she came to the hospital, was sent to the insane asylum just about three weeks after Dr. B. did a complete hysterectomy on her. Oh boy are we getting some dillies You should be around to see the fun, my Dear, you'd probably blow up on the average of three times a day.

I just came in from the airport and taking CA for a two-hour ride. We didn't go anywhere special but we had fun. I did a couple of lousy spins to lose altitude but came in and did one of his favorite "scootin'" landings so was back in his good graces. Today the Supervisors were forced into considering doing something about the local airport. Harley Flournoy and a few of the old timers were again' putting out the taxpayers money on this airport, so Bill Bailey got up and gave the old timers a fine lecture. He said—it won't be you old boys who will be paying the taxes, we're the ones who represent the future and it's just fine for you to want to sit here and hold down what you've got.

This airport won't be just for Quincy people, but for the whole county and for outsiders as well, start the ball rolling. I guess it made headway because they appointed a committee—Bill Bailey, CA and Dad to look into it and drew up rules and regulations and a contract. Looks like something may come of it.

I guess you must've gotten some of my letters, Sweetheart, there seem to be no more complaints. We miss you lots. Johnny sends his love and would like very much to take a couple of punches at this typewriter. Good night now and please don't like those Australians too much.

All my love,   Gail

AUGUST 3, 1943 MACKAY RADIOGRAM WES TO GAIL

VERY GOOD TO HEAR FROM YOU DEAREST. AM FIT AND WELL. LOVING BIRTHDAY GREETINGS. MY THOUGHTS ARE WITH YOU.

John W. Moore   222A/3

AUGUST 4, 1943 GAIL TO WES

Darling,

I haven't been numbering my letters but write every other day.

I got your July 18th letter today and read the Masonic part of it to Dr. He got quite a kick out of it as did the rest of us. Your 1st edition of #4 arrived yesterday. There seems to be no rhyme or reason to when they get here.

Bill B. and I got the cigars and fishing stuff wrapped up and sent yesterday. Hope it gets to you OK. I couldn't buy you any good line so took one off of an old reel around here. I don't think that it will be stout enough for your purposes but you can pinch hit with it until you can get a better. The leader and #2 and #4 hooks are presents from Bill. The package turned out to be just the limit to what I could send—36" around. The limit in poundage is 5 lb. If you want something bigger, Bill and I will have to get together and send it in sections. About the funnies—I'll wrap them all at once and send them each week. I was going to do that when I got home from Piedmont and then decided that you would probably be kept too busy to get a chance to read them. When I told Del about your request for bourbon he said that he had some Canadian Club that he was saving for when the boys come home. So at least you have a trust in store for you when you get home. He said if there was any way to do it that he would be tickled to send you a bottle, however, I think that is entirely against the rules. You can't buy quarts now—it's coming in half pints. It isn't putting any hardship on the local drunkards though because Emile *[Austin]* still puts a little jigger in his drinks.

Last night I went down to Paxton with the Dellingers and the Metzkers for dinner. It was Ruth's birthday. I raised a Benedictine to you, my Dear, and wished that you might be drinking it instead of me. Tonight I am going to the Wednesday Club as a member. It is at Betty Peckenpah's. I have been filling in at Wednesday Club for about 4 years now, and as long as you aren't taking Wednesday afternoons off any more, I might just as well spend my time playing bridge as any other way.

My allotment seems to be coming along OK. I haven't gotten any notice for this month yet, but it seemed to come through all right in July when the change was made. Can you tell me yet if the Government income tax is deducted from your salary or is that going to be due the first of the year? I'll probably have to have some coaching on the income tax situation. Honey, why the dickens didn't you make me do a few of those things so that I would know what they are all about. You should have given me the office books once in awhile just to let me know how the thing was done.

We seem to be getting along pretty well at the hospital. The latest squabble came when Margarite told Blank that she couldn't bring a Sacramento woman in and do a complicated operation on her and expect the practicals to take care of the patient. Blank went up in the air and we haven't seen much of her since. Bill B. told me that she wanted to build a hospital and he was pretty worried about it. Let the old bag go ahead and do it (says I) if she thinks that she can. In the first place she would have an awful struggle getting materials to build or equip it. When I told Bill the situation, he said there wasn't much could be done about it. You'd be proud of your friends, Pop, they have stood by you. They are doing everything in their power to keep things under control. Ken, especially has been a great help to me. I feel that I can tell him things and he will advise me and that they will get no further.

I have been wondering why you can't wear your wings down there. I thought that once you put them on you could wear them all the time. I am going to send your mother a check for $5.00 for her birthday today. I hope that that meets with your approval. I couldn't think of anything to *[unreadable]* that anyway.

All my love, my precious Sweetheart, and keep up the good work on the writing   Gail

AUGUST 5, 1943 GAIL TO WES

Dearest Wes,

I have several things to send you so I guess that I'll have to write you airmail and hope that it gets to you eventually. I got your V-Mail of July 20th today and also a birthday greeting by Mackay radiogram. It certainly did get here in plenty of time and I thank you my Darling! As much as I appreciate that, I certainly would give a lot for a great big smacker from you. Delivered in person, of course. We all find your letters very interesting and informative—keep up the good work. I read the Masonic part of that letter to Dr. and he got a big kick out of it. Bill B. heard the last one and he enjoyed it a great deal. 'Course his comment was that you were a lucky devil to be a Mason. I liked the little episode at the police station. They must be quite a bunch. Bring me home a horse, Honey, one of those tall graceful creatures. I'd certainly like to have one.

The card that you find enclosed (if I remember to put it in) is for you to sign—under my signature. It is for a savings account that Dr. is starting for you so that when you come back and no one has any money, you'll have something to keep going on. Dr. gave me a tidy little sum of $1574.00 that he has saved up for you while he has been there. You understand, I hope that it isn't being put away to buy airplanes, speedboats and the like, I hope! Please sign the card and return it to me as soon as you can because Raynor wants his banking procedures to be correct. I thought maybe we could surprise you by having something put away to go on when you came back, but as long as I have to have your signature on the card it kind of put the kibosh on my brilliant idea.

They are burning the grass off the airport tonight, so we went out to see what went on. The inspector has been over all day inspecting ships—O'Brien. I still don't know whether he is the same O'Brien that we know, haven't seen him. They all seem to think that he is a good guy. Speaking of airports, etc. guess who I saw while breezing down the main drag tonight? None other than the great McCurly and bride. I didn't get a chance to talk to him because I was with Dad and he wouldn't stop. I'm dying to know what he is doing here. Maybe it's just a visit. We have an A and E on the field for a month or so, so maybe we can get all of the airplanes in <u>legal</u> flying trim for a change. He just got his E rating today from O'Brien so he hasn't had a chance to do much yet.

David writes that he is back to instructing again after taking some kind of an instrument course. He also says that it is 145 on the flight line. I don't know how he stands it. I'd be wilting long before it had a chance to get that hot. He bought the new Ford convertible he was talking about and thinks that he is pretty smart. He still would like to be doing something besides instructing, but can't do anything about it.

What's the matter, Honey, did you run out of pajamas? Do you miss what little warmth my anemic self gave you, or are the nights just too cold down there? Ours are getting a little on the chilly side now too. The wind has been blowing all afternoon and I mean blowing. You shouldn't stir it up so much over on your side of the world. I wish I knew how long you would be there and what is next on the program, but I guess that is one of those unmentionables even if you did know.

This is Friday the 6th — ran out of things to tell you last night, so am starting in again today. On my way to the office this morning, I met McCurly and his wife. Mac looks fine and he seems to have a very nice wife. I think that she has done wonders for him. They were just here overnight on a visit. Mac says that he has been flying the Pacific. He has been in Africa and down to Natal. I told him about Dinty thinking that he might possibly run across him. The McCurlys have bought some kind of a place down at Paradise, he's just about due to go out again now. He's been flying B-26's and he said that he has just been taking a rest. He seems to like it. I took them out and showed them the airport and Mac spotted a Cub Cruiser out there and had to look it all over. He was trying to figure out how you could convert one of the things into a rice sewer.

The latest dope that I have heard on the Polio cases around this vicinity is 3 cases in Greenville and 55 in Reno. Hope it doesn't get here. Dr. B. took Bunky and Rosalie Niehous' tonsils out this morning and apparently did a good job of it. He was telling me that he was using your method of taking them out.

I guess that I will lose my renters next month. I have been wondering what to do about the house. I'd kind of like to move back there if I could get someone to come up and live with me, but I don't know who I would get. I have a pretty nice setup here, with mother to take care of John while I go up to the Hospital, and I don't think that she would like for me to bring him down here every day. She doesn't seem to mind having him here all of the time, so—I guess I'll just have to find another renter for the winter, if there are such things around here. The Hoods have really taken good care of the house and the yard. I kind of hate to see them go because they have been such good renters. I am going to have to spread a little paint around by the doors where the snow and ice have exposed the wood. I'm 'fraid if I don't that the boards will rot away. I'm hoping that maybe I can get Everette Wilsey to do it for me, but he is pretty busy. The thing to do would be to paint the whole house, but I'm afraid that I can't afford it. I'm putting what extra I have away for the lean winter months. They are liable to be pretty lean this year.

Can you please tell me Honey, why they gave me your cable address as Amabor and yet every cable that I get from you has Amlois on it? Neither of these has you're APO number for it.

Mother and Dad want to know if you would like *Time* sent you for your birthday or if you would rather have some other periodical. They are going to have to have your request for it to be sure to send it along. Mother also says that she intended to write to you, but she has just been too busy.

I was going to cut any interesting articles that I could out of the Bull and send them to you, but as far as I can see, there just aren't such things in it.

Hope that this gets to you eventually, Sweetheart. All my love, forever your   Gail

AUGUST 7, 1943 WES TO GAIL

Darling—   #11

Typewriters all busy again, so must write long hand. We have been busy with field work for a few days, and I have been unable to write since Aug. 2. Hope you get the telegram all right, Sweetheart. I have two more letters from you, including the most interesting clippings. Dr. B. would have his trouble getting into the Army under Limited Service with his eyes. Any man that can carry on a civilian practice is most welcome in the Army. All he needs to do is sign a waiver for the depot—tell him for me!

I find in going over your letters I have the following postmarked June 30, July 2, 7, 10, 13, 17, 20, 22 (8 in all). As you aren't numbering them, I don't know whether any are missing. Won't you start numbering them, Sweet, so I'll know? They come very much out of order, you know—the last 2 were July 10 and 22. I haven't quit smiling yet—as a matter of fact, I'm getting a lot of good laughs out of Army life. There are lots of silly inconveniences. It's raining like hell today; muddy, and I'm in O. D.'s and have to tramp around in it.

Sorry about the CAP. Guess the set-up isn't right for it in Quincy now. Nothing like that here, as private flying since the war, although there is a Civil Air Guard in England. Wish I could tell you more of what goes on here. No can do!

We are all watching Italy with deep interest, and there are some good blows being dealt in the South Pacific, too, we are glad to see. Just getting anxious to get actually into it. Hope it won't be too long, now.

Darling, I love you more than anything in the whole world—did I ever tell you?

Always your own—   Wes

AUGUST 7, 1943 WES TO GAIL

Darling Sweetheart—

I've already written you a V-Mail today, but it's been so long since I wrote, and this was longhand, that I wanted to talk to you some more. Because I love you so, and wish I could see you. Then, too, I guess you get tired of the V-Mail which doesn't seem quite like a real letter. I mean to say, you probably will get tired of them _after_ you get a few. You hadn't heard from me as yet (except for the telegram) up to July 22. You say you were anxious to see my writing even though you couldn't see my smiling "puss," so here goes.

You will notice that I only use one side of the sheet, because when they censor our letters, they cut the objectionable part right out. You needn't worry on yours as they aren't censored.

Honey, I hope the finger is all well that you caught in the door of the car July 9th. Seems some time ago now, doesn't it! And by the way—see that Nan gets her ship in ship-shape—or you see to it—before you go flitting around in it anymore—do you hear me now? I won't have you risking that Darling little neck of yours—at least, not without me around! And another thing, Sweetheart. Don't take John up alone. In fact, you should have someone along with you in case he should become panicky or unmanageable.

You know, I'm glad if you are spoiling John a bit. It will be good for him. I was too severe with him most of the time, poor kid. He probably thinks of his Daddy as a most ferocious sort of a guy. I'll remedy that situation when I get home. He's a good boy, and you are much better with him than I. I rather suspect that Grandpa and Grandma are the spoiling element and you are the balance wheel!

I do hope you aren't kept so busy at the office that you don't have plenty of time for him. He needs you, Darling, more than anyone, to guide him in these extremely formative years of his. Keep telling him Daddy loves him, Dearest, and always know that I love you completely and hopelessly.

I told you that I wrote Barney. It was interesting to hear of that order for Melly to "stand by," in case he should come ashore!

So you think Pop is swinging over on our side—well that should help. I made further remarks about Dr. B. in letter, so won't repeat. But I don't know how he can smugly sit at home these days—so matter of fact, though I wouldn't be surprised if the Army wasn't better off without any more of his type. Lord knows, there are plenty of them all around us.

Ask Pop where in hell my newspaper is. I haven't had a copy in ages. Ask him if he has my address now, please Dear, and give him my regards.

I had a letter from Esther, in case I haven't told you, and was happy to hear that Dad got along so well. I've written them, and Mother, and Dinty, and Marian—am I not a very good boy?

Well, Sweetheart, I must go and attend to a few duties as O. D. I enjoy your letters so much, and you have been good about writing. Give my best to Mom and Dave and to Dr. and Marg Hard, Dearest Darling.

Always loving you,   Wes

AUGUST 8, 1943 WES TO GAIL

Darling—

Two V-Mail letters from you—one yesterday afternoon and one this morning. It's wonderful! The dates are July 29 and 27. You should turn the papers the other way, though, like this. They are quite readable, but you do need a new ribbon on your typewriter as it is dim in spots, and don't write in the red rectangle at the bottom, as it turns out perfectly black.

I just got word today of my promotion to Captain! Maybe you noticed at the top? It took effect July 13th. 13 must be lucky for me. I got a bottle of scotch through the Masonic Club about a week ago, in anticipation of this—six of us just did a neat job on it, in record time—and I mean neat!

I'm glad to hear you got to fly the Porterfield. I would have loved to get my hands on that little baby. I'll bet you could really wring it out if you tried—the 90 was that way.

I'm not getting particularly tan here, as it is winter in Australia, you know, and all too cool most of the time. But we have fun. You remember what I said about Bud Ralnbach? He's sure done well, and I'm pleased!!

Dearest, I wrote you twice yesterday, so this is really just a note to let you know of the raise. I'm really very pleased, to say the least, and I appreciated the birthday congrats. You can send wires to my APO NO. 923 now and 4584 as before; your telegraph operator hasn't anything to do with addresses—just tell him to do as he is told!

All my love, Darling—   your Wes

AUGUST 9, 1943 INTERNATIONAL TELEGRAM GAIL TO WES

DARLING. CONGRATULATIONS ON YOUR PROMOTION. LOVING GREETINGS FROM ALL OF US.... GAIL MOORE

AUGUST 9, 1943 ESTHER TO WES
(Seattle, Washington)

Dear Wes—

I can't tell you how pleased we were, and a bit relieved, too, to get your letter. We did so appreciate getting so much of the local news. It was all most interesting and very new to us.

The most important piece of news we have now is that we've sold our house, and now that we've done it, both Dad *[John Claude Moore]* and I are ill about it. Reason we did it, of course, is that it is quite impossible to get help and I was working much too hard to keep the house going and yet be down here at the office practically full time. We must be out by September 15th, so we have another month to enjoy our victory garden. We are going to the Camlin Hotel where we will have a fairly nice apartment and I hope we may furnish it with our own things, but as yet we have made no definite arrangements. Dad is hoping that after the war he may have someone here in the office so he will not need to be here full time, and if so, I suspect we will buy something out in the country, and a very small place.

We had such a nice letter from Gail. We are so very sorry she couldn't manage to get up here with Johnny while we are in the house, but of course that was something the government couldn't plan to suit us. I have promised Gail that when I go south in October I will do my level best to get to Quincy for a few days, but it is so out of the way. However, it may be that Fred, or one of his men, may be going that way and I can drive up with him.

The boys are still with us. We had rather planned to keep Mick and send him to school up here, if Marian approved, and I rather suspect she would, but now that the house is gone such an arrangement doesn't seem feasible. I'm rather sorry because I believe it would be a fine thing for both the boys. Marian and Cy could do more for Bob while we took care of Mick. They are grand youngsters but have their own way which is understandable with Marian working and away all day, but in spite of it they are ever so well mannered.

The news coming to us seems better and better, but I hope our people do not get too optimistic too soon. We have a long way to go even with the collapse of Italy. Even after the war is over there will be so much rehabilitation to be done and the peoples of Europe will be in such a pitiable state that for sometime to come they won't be able to take care of themselves. However, we are hoping for a speedy end to this ghastly holocaust so you boys may come home to your families.

Do you need another sweater or socks or what else may we send you that you really want? Dad is fine but terribly tired. He is going to rest up toward the end of September, 1 hope.

Lots of love to you from us both, and we'll write you again real soon.   Esther

AUGUST 9, 1943 GAIL TO WES

Sweetheart,

Received your July 24th letter yesterday and was distressed to find that you had not gotten more than the first three letters. Hope the rest come in soon 'cause I know what the physical routine in the Army is giving you! Have you gained any weight?

Dan Baldwin came down with the news yesterday that Hersh Laughlin was killed last week in Aukland, New Zealand. He was taking a bomber off and crashed on takeoff. Apparently he was off of the transocean flights and was on inter island service temporarily. They were all very stunned by it. So far they haven't gotten any details on it.

Saturday, Metzkers, Dellinger's, Cotters, Bailey's and the Moore's took a picnic lunch out to the Forest Service campground and we had a swell time. John had the time of his life and the next morning the first thing he said was " I want some more picnic." After the picnic, we, the Dellinger's and myself, took in the sump and proceeded down the canyon to take in the dance at Paxton. (A very elegant rat race). Bill Dixon was dealing at the 21 table and a man and a woman had a very high powered battle out in front. I guess the worst of it was the beer bottle smashing the windshield—no one got particularly injured. Del did himself proud and danced practically every dance. We got home about three.

Yesterday the CAP from Oakland practically took over the airport. There were only two close ones—one fellow decided to go around in Beattie's 50 Knocker when it was almost too late. They said that he was practically stalled all the way from the wires over past the Stone House. They told me the wings were fluttering to beat the wind. The second episode was when Schneller took off in his 40 Cub right in the face of a landing Luscombe. Mother was there and said they were waiting for the crash when, zowie, Schneller pulled up and played a little game of leap frog and then settled back down again. I guess it must have been a thrill. It was apparently Schneller's fault because mother says that it was still light enough to see. Lots of the boys have illegally qualified for night flying, 'cause the lights are on when they finally put little kites to bed. They tell me that Bud is just about to take a powder. He has a couple of propositions that he is working on. I think the gang has someone to replace him with though so we won't close up entirely. The airport would be better off without him, from the viewpoints of most of the gang.

Last night Ken and Helen came by and asked John and me to go up to John Verdonagn's to dinner, so we piled in and went along. It seems like the rest of the town decided the same thing 'cause before long the Dellinger's came in and then Charlie *[C. T. Bedell]* and Openshaw, then the Larison's. On the way back, we stopped in to see the Finnegans and you should have heard Janet holding forth on what would happen if Dr. B. ever came close to her when she had her baby. I am sure that Dr. Lasswell would see to it that he had no part in it. She is apparently fine and in much better spirits than when you were here last—she can smile once in awhile now—Baby Ann is walking.

The letter that I wrote Thursday, I sent Airmail because I had to send a card on for you to sign. I hope it gets to you eventually—you undoubtedly will be tickled to see what it is all about. I'm going to wrap up a package of funnies for you today and send them on to you. I hope that they don't decide that it is a non-essential article and dump it in the bay.

I'm going to try and send you a wire today, to let you know that we are all right. I think that with the new APO # maybe I can do it. It won't be much, Sweet, but at least you'll get some word of us.

Had a letter from Mavis and she seems to be working right *[unreadable]* Chris didn't get to go home to recuperate and Mavis thinks that he might be able to rejoin the outfit. Hope so. She says that *[unreadable]* Clare, where is he?

All my love, my Precious, and we are sure always thinking of you.   Gail

and Johnny

P. S. I called W. H. and he says your APO is listed so maybe I'll get through this time—I certainly hope so.

<u>AUGUST 10, 1943 BOB HUDSON TO WES</u>
(Seattle, Washington)

Dear Wes,

I intended to write you in time for your birthday but completely forgot, so I hope this will do.

I know it must be lonesome up or down, wherever you are. Mick and I have been up here in Seattle nearly all summer and have had a really swell time. We have been working around the house and in the time that we don't we caddy and we have been getting ourselves filthy rich because there isn't any place to spend it and Grandpa is saving it for us and when I go home I am going to buy a war bond and give the rest to mom.

Golly, I sure hope you can read this now that I hold it out in front of me. By the time you get this I will probably be home in good old Los Angeles. Well, better close now.

As ever   Bob

P. S. Take care of yourself.

(Wednesday night)

Dearest Gail—   #14

I'm a little short on V-Mail, and some of the boys seem to think their airmail letters get home faster than V-Mail, although V-Mail makes better time over here. So, I think I'll use airmail for awhile. Besides, it seems a better medium to talk to you there—something sort of automatic about V-Mail. Maybe it's the typewriter!

Honey, please get a new ribbon on your machine. I could hardly read your letter of July 31—was terribly difficult to read. I got it all, finally. I was very much interested in your air exploits and so glad to know you are flying frequently. I have every confidence in your ability, Dearest, and I don't worry about you. I'm happy CA was so pleased with your air work.

Darling, we should be able to save a fair amount of money, because I'm going to be able to send you more as time goes on. I'll be getting better than $400.00 per mo. with my Captain pay and flying pay, and will send you as much as possible. If we ever get away from here, there will be very little need for money, and you can save it for us. Then maybe after the war, we can buy a real good ship. You will have to keep your eyes open for us and see what looks good among the new models!

I read a nice letter from Katherine today, too, in honor of my birthday. She is very thoughtful.

I have to date your V-Letters of the 27, 29, and 31ˢᵗ of July. They seem to come through pretty regularly. Keep using the V-Mail but be sure your machine is writing black and clear, but scatter in a few airmails, because it's good to see your unadulterated handwriting.

Johnny's exploits and doings sound wonderful. How I wish I could watch all this. He'll be almost grown up when I see him next!

I will be most interested in hearing how things work out with Dr. B. in the office. I hope Dr. can keep him in hand. I am glad that he will be there to relieve *[unreadable]*.

Honey, do give Dr. and Margarite my news, as I don't have a lot of time to write, and I must depend on you to be my emissary. I am so appreciative of the fine thing they are doing for us. There would be nothing left, I'm afraid, without someone like them to look after it, and of course I should have had to go eventually, even tho' it was voluntary at the time. I am much happier being in it than at home, because I just couldn't have lived with myself, nor could you have stood me either, Sweetheart! You've been such a wonderful pal about it all and so unselfish. I appreciate that as much as anything you could do, Darling—do you know that and I love you very, very much too *[end cut off]*.

AUGUST 11, 1943 GAIL TO WES

Darling,

I received your letter written July 25th today—three days after the one written on the 24th. I was thrilled to pieces to see it there because they usually come in the morning and this one was in the box this afternoon. Don't worry about the promotions, Sweetheart. I'll be glad to see you come home even if you're a Buck Private! We all miss you so much, and the old gang—it's just not the same around here since Wes left. How little they know about that! In your letter, they blacked out where the fellow from New Guinea's leave started. All they left was Australia. Your description of the animals sounds very interesting. It sounds as though you have seen some unusual animals. Wish I could get in on it.

In answer to your one question—David is still at Luke and groaning about his students. He says that they get worse with each succeeding group. His latest grievance is with their formation flying. In fact his last letter, today, was one big groan. He seems to think that you are having a lazy time of it if you have time to drink whiskey and such. 'Course he is just grouchy 'cause he can't be over there too. Have you gotten in any flying, Honey? I'll bet that you have missed it if you haven't. I got up again last night. Haggerty (he has a student permit) asked me if I would like to fly his 55 T Craft, and of course I told him you bet your boots! So we kited around for a half hour or so and he told me to go ahead and take it any time. Somehow, I just can't seem to take people up on propositions like that. If they ask me while they are on the spot that is fine and dandy, but I can't see taking other people's planes when they aren't around—especially in these trying times when if you break something it is broken for the duration. However, his partner, Roy Brown, has about two dual hours and thinks he can learn just about as much by just going up and flying around. (I just left you for a few hours Honey, had dinner and Roy called me so I went out and went upstairs with him.) You should see me in the role of instructor. Maybe I'll learn yet. At any rate, I can build up my hours. I wish I were as good at it as you were my Dear. Got in :45 minutes tonight.

I hope that you can get a picture or two home to us, Honey, 'cause it would bring you a little bit nearer. I certainly hate to have you so darned far away. I guess you're better off away from me, though, or I'd be trying to tag you around. If I were just given the opportunity to do so now, I don't think that I would crab about anything.

Thank heavens the news from Europe sounds encouraging. I hope that they smoke them out soon so the boys can all concentrate on the yellow bellies. Would it be too much against the rules to tell me what you do all day long? Do you ever get any surgery? Have you applied your Randolph training? Do you have any pilots to look after? Please tell Al and Capt. Van hello for me. I guess that you see them all of the time. Mavis writes that Al hasn't seen anything of Jack. Isn't he with your outfit?

It has been getting colder and colder around these parts. We've had frost here already, and last night there was ice up at Mohawk. It's been too darn cold to even go swimming. I had to buy a new sweater to wear over my white uniform, because it is so darn cold up at that office in the morning. I hope that it doesn't ruin our tomato crop before we get anything off of it. We have some beauties, but they don't seem to get red. We've been eating fresh vegetables out of all the relatives' gardens, and boy are they good! I think even you would like vegetables if you could get that kind all of the time.

You should see Del and Ruth's garden—it looks as though they had gone in for truck farming. The Metzkers have chickens, you know, and today they caught "The Black Terror," a black pooch from up the street, stealing his 7th from the chicken coop. I tell you, that dog's life certainly isn't worth much at this point! All the little Metzkers came out loaded with clubs.

One of these days, Johnny is going to write you *[unreadable]* read it.

All our love my Darling—   Gail and John D.

AUGUST 13, 1943 RUTH AND DEL DELLINGER TO WES
[Ruth Gaulden and A. C. Dellinger]

Dear Wes:

Was sure glad to get your letter, as we all miss you as much as you do us I guess. Del and Ken are busy as bees with their saw-mill, it should be operating in another 6 weeks. Both are too cranky and busy to be human, but guess it is a worry wondering if it is going alright.

See Gail nearly every day as she comes by the garage. She and John were on a picnic with us the other night, and did John have a grand time. He won't be a little boy much longer.

Bob's *[Robert Gaulden Dellinger]* arm is all out of the splints and all OK—straight as a die. He learned to be very ambidextrous while in the splints. Back riding his horse again, so don't know how long it will be before he has another one.

Your gun will be OK; the little spring is broken but that is easily fixed. Was odd how Del found it just from a map that Ken drew for him. He found the two rocks and saw where your feet had slipped on the rocks.

I guess Bunky will be on his way soon. He phoned Sunday to Dot and said his address would be changing. I haven't heard from Barney, either, but Melba had a letter stating that he wasn't due home for at least six months. You know he thought he would be coming back this month some time, and had told her to be on the lookout for him. Really so little to write about as everything is awfully quiet.

Alvin Ellis has quit the Forest Service and is taking over our garage in Greenville. He came over last night to start cleaning it up. All three of his boys are now in this country so they are resting easy.

Del hasn't been fishing at all to speak of this summer. I think only a couple of times since you left, and it soon will be hunting season and he wants to go hunting, of course. He has too many activities for the amount of time he has to spend doing it.

Del drove to Portland and then to Seattle about two weeks ago buying mill equipment, said he enjoyed seeing the country all over again, and that it was a shame that it was raining when we were there as it was such pretty country. He is in San Francisco all this week, so I am really not much better off than all those 1A widows. I don't even have that glory.

Would like to talk Gail into going to the city with me in Sept when I take Bob to school, but she doesn't seem to think so. Dot may get off and go. She has been saving her leave in case Bunky got leave but looks as though she might as well use it with me. Not much excitement in going to the city, but it is a change.

Do write us soon again, and I'll really try and locate some scandal to tell you next time I write. This is sort of a messy letter, but I have been trying to talk to customers and write to you too. Right now there is a very drunk man trying to get my attention and he is a nuisance. Well lots of luck and—   Regards,   Ruth and Del

AUGUST 13, 1943 GAIL TO WES

My Darling—

I was dismayed to find in your letter of July 29th that you still haven't received any more than 3 of my letters. I received a $50.00 check yesterday from the finance Dept. and decided that it must have come from you. I don't believe it is the travel money.

If you are wondering why the scrawl instead of a typewriter, it is because the one at the office is haywire and I took mine up to pinch hit until we can get the noiseless fixed. Hope you can read this—if you ever get it. It takes about 17 days for your letters to get here. I have received 10 V-Mails.

Bud Moore is leaving Quincy—I guess for Alaska. I think that the committee has us all fixed up for a new instructor and managed. I hope so.

John is getting so big, Darling, and is really a lot of fun. I wish you were here to enjoy him. He talks about you quite a lot and says he wants to come and help you get a couple of Japs.

I love you, Pop, and just because the mails don't bring you my letters, don't forget that I'm loving you the same as always and am terribly lonesome.

Forever yours

Gail

<u>AUGUST 14, 1943 WES TO GAIL</u>

Darling—   #15

It was sweet of you to wire me—just received it last night.

We were out in the country yesterday with Headquarters Squadron. The boys had a lot of money in the Company Fund, so they put on a beer bust out in the woods. They had <u>12</u> ten gallon kegs, for only 110 people! Boy, did they ever get in good shape. I had to sew up two boys—one got into a barbed wire fence and the other put his face into a fist. They only drank 9 kegs—the rest they used up today. Fortunately, I don't like beer that well. I had three canteen cups full all afternoon, so was in perfect order.

You know, Darling, I haven't had any trouble about drinking—guess I'm getting some sense in my head at last. I've hurt you so many times, and I never want to again, believe me, Dearest. You're the most important thing in my life, Dearest Gail—always!

I haven't had another letter from you since yours of July 31st which I mentioned in my last letter. Hope tomorrow is a letter day!

Saw Bowman Grindele the other day. He's looking fine. Always wants to be remembered to you or something.

Wonder where in hell Julian is these days. Have you sent me his address yet? I'd like to drop him a line. Did Barney ever show up in S. F.? Wonder if he got my letter.

It's raining like hell again. Cozy in the tent with a nice oil lantern, etc.! We don't mind it at all, and the cot is really quite comfortable with the air mattress I told you about. You asked if I were in a Station hospital—the answer is no. I described our surroundings in a previous letter which you undoubtedly have now. We are more or less in training, as I said.

I hope that you will let me have Julian's address, as I would like to write to him.

Dearest, if at any time you don't hear from me for three or four weeks, don't be alarmed. Military secrecy prevents me from explaining.

I ran into Norman Gimble the other day—remember him? He's a sergeant now! It's certainly a small world, isn't it?!

Well, it's about time to crawl into my little cot. Hope I dream abut you, baby. Gee, it would be nice to have you in there with me—I wouldn't care about the bed being too narrow! Captain Van de Carr just came in, so guess there'll be a bull session for awhile. Good night Sweetheart.

All my love
                              Wes

AUGUST 15, 1943 MARY CARR MOORE TO WES

Dearest Wesley—

You have been so good to write me so often; I received the Cablegram for my birthday, and two letters (V-Mail), and it is such a comfort to hear so directly from you. Gail has been such a Dear little daughter, and has written every week with news of you (when she had it) and the cunning sayings of little John. How much like you he is!

Marian and Cy are well and enjoying their home; the two boys in Seattle—but you know all this. For the past two weeks I have had Mr. and Mrs. Vernon Steele in the house (occupying Marian's former room) while they waited for their apartment to be vacant and ready to move into. It is almost impossible to find living quarters here. I have enjoyed them, as they have been very considerate, and we have not collided in kitchen privileges. But I would not want to have strangers in the house. Mr. Steele is Editor of the Pacific Coast Musician, and an old friend.

I came near selling the house last weekend and buying a small 5-room cottage, one floor, but the price was so ridiculously high for the bungalow that I could not bring myself to make the change, and have only a small lot and house at the end of the war. So will stay here, unless some very attractive alternative is offered. Apartments are out of the question with my music.

I have just completed a full orchestral score to the BRIEF FURLOUGH, and I have added a more interesting close—and am now making the partitures. It _may_ receive a hearing—I will not say until I am sure. My Festival Chorus, recently completed, to John Steven McGroarty's inspiring poem, THERE IS A DREAM, is to be performed at Emmanuel Presbyterian Church, early in October, with their 50-voice choir. Mr. McGroarty will be present to hear it. You know, he is our California Poet-Laureate.

My family consists, you know, of the two Persian cats and Whizzer and Daisy—(Jakey lives with Marian and Cy). The dogs are so cute and such individuals. Whizzer is full of life and fun; gobbles everything in sight, and is too fat—while Daisy—when I give her dinner—always waits to thank me, and lick my hand if she can, and looks at me with her soulful eyes before she starts. Dear me—here I am at the end—will write more soon.

O—good luck; there is more space. Well, my Dear, I will tell you again what you already know so well—what a comfort you are to me, and how Dearly I love you. And how I am hoping that the experience ahead will be valuable and not too difficult, and that you will VERY SOON be home with us, who love you, again. My thoughts are with you constantly—and also with Byron, of course. I have not heard from him for several weeks, but have news about him, and feel that he is well and working hard. At least working hard when his flights are due; the waiting between trips, I imagine, must be tedious.

Ever so much love, and my faith in your protecting, and guiding POWER.

Devotedly XX

                    Your Mother

AUGUST 15, 1943 GAIL TO WES

Sweetheart,

I expected a letter from you today, was disappointed. I hate to think of how many mails have disappointed you! But believe me, Darling, I've done my best to get them to you. You must have had a big letter writing day on July 30th, everyone I've talked to has said they heard from you.

Last night we celebrated Dad [William] Watson's 91st birthday by having all the Watsons to dinner. Dad W. is percolating even better than when you were here. He certainly looks healthy. In fact, he doesn't seem to have as many ailments as the younger Watsons. After dinner I went out to join the Supper Club. They were having a picnic dinner out at the Forest Service campground. It was a beautiful night—one of those mellow harvest moons that looked as though it were right on top of you.

George Cotter was telling me that he flew up to Lakeview—Louie Olson had told him that there was a designated airport there—and George found out that they were just building it. He managed to get down and get enough gas to come home on. He also told me that an Army trainer had landed on the highway at Portola—they said that it was coming in from Mexico. The boys didn't get a signal from Beckwith to come in so they decided to look Portola over and ran out of gas. When they landed on the highway, a car that was coming along was so dumfounded that it didn't get off the highway so the plane had to take to the ditch. I guess they banged up the wing a little on a tree. George said that the trainer was going to Beckwith to be used in the training program. Yesterday, I got out the two radios that were up at the house, and we have been trying the Ranger out in CA's ship. It works swell on the ground, but didn't do a thing in the air. I guess what it needs is a ground. He's going to fix it up. CA took the batteries out of the Lear radio and is going to try to get some new ones. He was thrilled to pieces when I came out with two of them [unreadable] Out of the bunch, we should get one that will work.

Now I'll start in on Johnny. Some of his pals have taught him to swear. When things don't go the way they should, he comes out with Damn it! Grandma is very shocked. They have also taught him the art of being independent. He takes off and gets on the other side of the block now. I expect it won't be long before he decides he's big enough to go up town alone. The other day he was out on the picnic table with his "machine gun" shooting Japs—all at once Dad heard a big squall and went out to see what was going on. During his big battle, he had fallen off the table. When Dad asked what had happened, he pointed at the flower-pot and said that damn Jap shot me. You see, he's growing up pretty fast.

Mother had a letter from David this morning and he said the rumors about their leaving Luke were getting pretty hot. He wants someone to fly me to Phoenix and bring his car back, if he gets shipped off. Dad has it all figured out that he'll hire Fred Russell to take him down and he will drive it back. If it turns out that way, I'm going to try to talk CA into making it a foursome. I think that CA would jump at it if he can get away this time of year. It would certainly be good experience for him and for me too. I don't think that CA is too sure of my ability as a navigator. If Fred were along too, I think he would enjoy it.

I expect that you have been moved along by this time. I wish that I knew where to. Hope you manage to find as much entertainment in the next spot, Honey, as you seem to have had in Australia. Needless to say, I envy you, my Dear. Wish that I could be doing something too. I guess we'll be doing pretty well though if we keep the Hospital ticking. We are getting along OK, but it's a dull place without you.

Margaret Hayes is up over the weekend and I have been trying to talk her into taking our house for the winter. It might work out. By the way, I'm 'fraid that I am going to have to [unreadable] fall— there are lots of boards with no paint on them.

No more [unreadable] news, so I'll send you all my love,   Gail

AUGUST 16, 1943 WES TO GAIL

Dearest Gail   #16

Well, Sweet, another day, another dollar! I spent the day "sweating out" an airplane ride so I could collect my $60.00 this month on Flight Pay. What a job—I waited for 3 hours at one field and finally gave up—then 2 and a half hours this afternoon and finally talked someone into a short hop in a C-61 (Warner Fairchild). He was in a hurry so I didn't even get to fly. Will I ever be glad to get home and do some flying again for a change!

Your letters of Aug. 2 and 4 came yesterday. Thanks for getting my pkg. off for me, Dear. I will enjoy the cigars—I know I don't smoke them at home, but that's because you don't like the taste or smell of them. Furthermore, one has to do something with spare time in the Army. I'm even enjoying my pipe these days, sweet.

Again, I fervently hope things aren't too hectic with Dr. B. around. Hope he doesn't drive Dr. nuts! I think you are very wise about Johnny's tonsils, Dear, with meningitis about. However, when conditions seem ideal, do have it done, because the proper time is when he is healthy. Dr. Morrison will be very good to him, Darling, and you needn't have any fears about it. He will get over it much easier, the younger he is.

The committee to improve the airport sounds promising. I expect to find a beautiful municipal airport with three daily flights through on United Airlines.

(Honey, stay out of the red at the bottom of the V-Mail—it doesn't show through).

Don't send any extra line, the one off the old reel will be swell. Just want it for an emergency in case I ever get stranded on a deserted island!

Tell Del I'd give L10 (pounds) for a bottle of that Canadian Club right now—but I guess it can't be
sent. This Australian whiskey is sure horrible. I hope he keeps his promise and saves some of it 'till after the war. I'm afraid I'll be awfully thirsty for some of that good old stuff!

You said "an allotment" came. Please let me know how much—it should be $217.50, if I'm not mistaken. As far as tax goes, I don't know. The tax should be paid by me on all that, your earnings from the hospital included, because it is money from an investment and theoretically earned by me. So don't render any tax return—I'll take care of it all, after the war, and there won't be any accrued interest. Furthermore, they may forgive taxes to servicemen.

The Wednesday Club is a good idea for you Darling. By the way, have you given any further thought to occupying our house? Or are you comfortable where you are? I kind of hate to think of strangers in our little home—but I want you to do what is best and easiest for you. You are right, Dear—I have some very wonderful friends in Quincy—Ken, Del and Bill—and Dr. —I don't know what we'd do without them, and CA. Wonder if CA ever got the letter I wrote him. Has he had any trouble with the Silvaire *[Luscombe]* yet?

I worked hard making a new box for myself—or did I tell you? And in my spare time cut out a stencil of a caduceus, about 8" high, to put on it and my footlocker and my B-4 bag. I'm quite proud of it.

About the wings—there is some screwy ruling down here which reverses the regulation in the States about putting them on as soon as Foreign Duty starts. They require 3 months' service plus the recommendation of the Flight Surgeon who is in charge in the particular area. So-o-o, will just have to be patient for awhile.

Thanks for sending Mother the $5.00. I sent her a wire and a purse, but have no idea when she will receive the latter—got a letter from her today and have heard twice from Esther.

Well, Sweet, guess this is enough for tonight. I love you so very much, Dearest girl—be good—

Good night, Darling—   Wes

AUGUST 16, 1943 WES TO BILL BAILEY
(c/o Quincy Drug Store)

Dear "Old Bill Bailey"—

Have waited so long for a letter from you that I've finally given up in despair and decided to write you. However, I do know through Gail that you participated in my *[unreadable]* in the matter of *[unreadable]*, and thank you, whether I receive it, or not!

I'm glad to hear you boys got hot on the airport and decided not to let Schwarner get everything in the county. Hope by the time you receive this that a beautiful million dollar municipal airport will be well underway!

You can thank the Lord you are home with a nice busy little Drug Store. This damn country is sure a pain in the neck—and I'm sure getting tired of G. D. gold bricks. If we don't get someplace where there's some action someday, I'm going to die of boredom. Ah, well, such is Army life. By golly, I'm even smoking my pipe and enjoying it, I'm becoming so placid.

Bill, thanks for being a good pal to my little family. Gail says that you and Ken and Del and the rest of the gang are <u>real</u> friends to a fellow who's away and can't mind his own business at home

Say, I'll sure be glad to get home and get some flying again. I'm getting damn little of it here, I'll tell you.

Drop me a line when you get time. Best Regards, Wes

P. S. Four bits for the advertising on the address—pay my agent.

AUGUST 16, 1943 GAIL TO WES
(Monday night)

My Darling—

Today was a big day—I got three letters from you! One V-Mail written July 27 and one July 30th and your airmail written on the 7th. Nine days for the Airmail so it looks as though Airmail is fastest from you to me. I imagine that they have better facilities for photographing in the States than they do over there so the airmail comes faster. I don't have to use a magnifying glass for your letters and Darling, your writing is very legible—I don't need an interpreter.

We haven't seen anything of the purses, Honey, but I imagine that will take time to get through. I gave up numbering the letters long ago and wrote you that I would write you every other day. The most it has ever been between letters is 2 days, and that I believe was over the 4th of July while John and I were up at Gold Lake.

I don't know why you should be so amused at my deductions on where the cable came from—it took us a week to get to Honolulu unhampered by a convoy and it's about twice as far again to Australia. By the way—at the moment, we have you well situated in or around Brisbane. I won't ask you is this right or wrong 'cause I know you can't tell me, but I'll just let you know what we are thinking. I guess that can't do any harm can it—for us to guess as to your whereabouts?

Don't get excited about the planes I'm flying; I'm very careful and only choose the best. If they don't sound good, I don't get in them and Johnny has only been up twice since you left. I'm not one of those people, my love, who takes chances unnecessarily, and I'm telling you I'm taking care of this neck of mine 'cause they say when you lose your neck you are a sad pigeon.

My finger was nothing to scream about—it's still discolored, but the nail only loosened up on one side, and if I cover it up with polish it doesn't look bad at all.

Your son John is getting to be a hellion, my Dear, I'm 'fraid he's getting a sadistic streak—he's always pounding Grandma, Grandpa, or he's trying to make us squirm or shout. He's definitely decided there will be no more naps and he spends his nap hour tearing the back room to pieces. Tomorrow he's going to meet with a great surprise and come out of it with a red rear.

We are getting along fairly well with Dr. B. He brings in a few tonsillectomies, but his private practice is negligible—I think that he steers them away from the office and tells them to come out to the County. I wouldn't trust him as far as I could see him. I do believe, however, that his enabling Dr. L. to get away every so often makes his presence and double dealing an awful lot easier to bear. I hope you understand, Darling, that I did everything I could to get him "fixed up" and keep him out of the Plumas Industrial. However, that was Fletcher's solution and it seems to be coming out OK. If it will relieve Dr. L. enough to help him last the duration, we can stand anything. I wasn't going to tell you a thing about all of that because I was afraid you might sweat and stew about it—I'm certainly hoping that you aren't, 'cause it's really nothing to stew about.

Dorothy Parker is pretty low these days—I guess Bunky left from the East Coast sometime last week. It's a mighty awful feeling when our boys go sailing away from us.

One of Johnny's newest stunts is to get out of bed in the wee hours of the morning and crawl in bed with me. I guess he gets cold. He certainly can cuddle—with his knees right in my back!

All our love, Sweetheart   Gail and Johnny

AUGUST 17, 1943 ESTHER TO WES

Dear Wes—

My, but we were glad to get your letter dated July 30th. It arrived a few days ago. Undoubtedly by now you have several V-Mails from us and one from Bob. The boys are still with us and will likely leave two weeks from today unless we decide to keep one of them, but Dad is still mulling the thing over in his mind.

In my last note to you I told you we had sold the house. We thought we had a particularly attractive apartment at the Camlin, but when I went to check it over I found something had gone amiss and all we could get was a wall-bed apartment. It just didn't seem fair to put Dad into anything like that regardless of how hard I have to work, so after much thought on the subject we decided to do a bit of forfeiting and we are to keep the house. Both Dad and I feel so much happier although it was a bit expensive to do it. I've decided I would prefer to be a workhorse in nice comfortable surroundings than a gilded lily in a wall-bed.

Dad is about completely over his operation now. He isn't having any more treatments and he sleeps through the night with very little disturbance. Last Sunday he took the boys out with him to run the dogs and the three of them had such a good time. We are going to miss Mick and Bob horribly when they leave. The first few weeks were hard on both Dad and me and I guess a bit difficult for the kids, but since then we've all had a complete understanding and the boys seem to be having a glorious time, making money in the meanwhile, and we are enjoying them.

Tonight we are going to the Adams' for dinner. You recall they live right on the lake and have such a nice beach. I may go in too. Jean lives in San Francisco, as you recall, and has two children—both girls.

News from abroad improves with each day, and we pray the end will come much sooner than we expect. Just doesn't seem fair for so many families to be separated and so many children to grow up without the guidance of their fathers.

Your letters are most interesting. We too are being rationed more and more on liquor. Up here we are entitled to only a pint of Scotch or Bourbon a week, and we take what we can get—not what we'd like. However, if it were possible to send ours to you, I assure you we would do so without a murmur, because those of us who are back here have nothing to complain of when we know what our boys at the front are putting up with, and what the conquered peoples are experiencing.

We are expecting Fred up here very soon and hope Dora will come up with him. Mert has been down with a heart attack but has been very docile and followed Dad's instructions to the letter, so I suspect he'll come through very nicely if he continues to be a good boy.

Do write often, Wes, and if there is anything we can send you, let us know. Am hoping to see Gail either in September or October—will depend largely on what Dad does for his vacation. Am sure it will be a spot of hinting, but am not sure where he will go or when. The important thing is for him to get away and get some rest.

Your letters have been most interesting to us and our friends too. I'm going to take them over to the Adams tonight. They want to read them.

Lots of love from Dad and the boys as well as myself. Do take care of yourself.

Esther

AUGUST 18, 1943 WES TO GAIL

Darling,

Am writing V-Mail this time as I have only a moment to dash off a note.

I received your very newsy V-Mail of Aug. 11 and will answer that in a day or so when I have more time. I want to get this off now to get my new APO number to you so there won't be too much delay in future letters. I love you, Darling, so very much and I want you always to know that your sweet letters are wonderful, particularly because you are such a dear, cheerful little soul and not a sob-sister. I know how much you long for me because it works both ways, Sweetheart.

Tell Johnny that Daddy says "Hello, I'm thinking about you, little man—Don't be too grown up when I get back," and kiss him for me, Dear—Don't worry if there should be a delay in mail one of these days—all is well.

My love to Dave and Edith. All my love, Dearest   your Wes

AUGUST 18, 1943 GAIL TO WES

Sweetheart,

No letter today, darn it all! I go to the post office about three times a day, so that I won't possibly miss one. I was just talking to Pop Small and he has a renter for the house. He says that the Ray Smith's are anxious to get it. I am going up this afternoon with Laura to show it to her. They would like something permanent but I will make her understand that we want it back when you come rolling in, Honey. She has some furniture and that may cause complications, but I think that we can compromise on that. Winter is about to set in, I'm 'fraid, and I don't want the house to be unoccupied again during the cold months. They should be good renters and they say that she is a good housekeeper. I guess they can afford the oil too. Gee there are a lot of things to take into consideration in renting the house. The present tenants haven't done a good job on watering the yard, but other than that I have no complaints—yet. They will probably leave it in a mess when they leave.

I was suppose to go to Susanville today in the Luscombe to take a girl on a cross country and see about the Freedman Burnham prop, but my girl friend got the intestinal flu so we didn't get to go. Maybe I can go next week—I hope. There seems to be quite a struggle going on over who is to get the airport. I have heard rumors that Stu wants it, and also that the A and E *[FAA—Certified Airframe and Engine Mechanic] who* is here would like to have it. I think that Bud has made a deal with a fellow by the name of Draper who is an instructor. Whoever gets it will have to live up to the rules and regulations set down by the committee—Dad, CA and Bill Bailey. I believe that they are going to keep the interests of the private flier at heart and see that we get to fly as usual. Bud says that he is through here the 1st but is going to stay on a while longer to see that the guy gets going all right. Bud plans to go up into Alaska and fly for an airline or else get a bigger plane of his own and do freight work. He said that he would like to come back here after the war.

Do you remember the bowel operation that I was telling you about that Blank did? The one that ended up with such a mess and is still draining out the skin into the dressing? Well Margarite told me yesterday that Blank fainted during the last part of the operation and Sally had to sew the woman up. Some fun! I can see now why Dr. L. didn't want to have her operating up there. She had told Margarite that she has heart trouble. Recently, all that we have had has been maternity. Today, we had quite a struggle with Juanita Stevenson's mother. She didn't want to pay. They took Jaunita home after about four days because Juanita's mother couldn't come in and pick up the baby any time she wanted. Boy oh boy! What a headache that place is. I don't blame you for getting lines on your face, my love! I guess that it is worse now than when you were here though.

Johnny just woke up and is out by the car waiting for me to take him for a ride. I guess that I'd better hurry up. I have the doors locked and he is having a fit because he can't get in. I am going to Wednesday Club tonight. They asked me to join last time, so I guess I am a regular member. Did I tell you that I won the prize last Saturday night at Supper Club? I'm getting to be quite a card shark.

Well, Darling, I have to go—behave yourself and have a good time! As always, all my love,

Gail

AUGUST 20, 1943 GAIL TO WES

Sweetheart,

I wired you congratulations on your new commission yesterday and I hope that the wire got through to you all right. We were certainly thrilled to hear the good news! I'll bet you were a little tickled yourself—wish I'd been at the party.

Doris Hansen called me this morning and she wants to come out to work. She said that Chris hadn't been able to come home and that she hadn't heard from him for several weeks and she thinks that he is on his way over. I hope that he gets back with your group. I talked to Dr. and Margarite about her and they told me to tell her to report the 1st of October. She has to complete August back at Davenport at St. Lukes because she told them that she would. It makes it pretty difficult to know just what time she will be able to get here. Margarite is having a time because she wants to give the girl she has a month's notice because she has been training her and the girl needs the money. I hope that Doris doesn't get upset because she is being put off a month. Over the phone she said that she would like to spend the winter in California. Do you think that I should offer to pay her train fare out here? I don't think that Margarite would do that! Margarite is thrilled with the prospect of having a graduate nurse, but Dr. is a little skeptical about whether she will stay or not. He wanted me to have definite information that Chris was over—anyway; I wired her to come out by the 1st of October.

I had a very fine birthday party over at Marg. Morris' last night and ate up some of her chickens. Everyone was so nice to me and I got loads of nice things, slips, nighties, blouses, etc. The relatives all kicked in and it was just like Christmas. CA was going to take me for an airplane ride, but it just happened that the mechanic got around to giving the plane its hundred hour check yesterday, so we didn't get to go. He gave me a box of candy instead.

I have quite a time with your letters. Sometimes I get more recent letters first and I get all mixed up—you talk about things you have written about and a few days later I get that letter and find out what it is all about. Julian's address: Lt. J. R. Atkins, HQ. 5th Air Force Service Command, APO # 929 (I guess you, c/o Postmaster, S. F. would you)? If you should happen to see him, tell him hello for us. Also you might look into the matter of his riding in jeeps the round about way to the Club with a certain Lt. Bartholomew (a nurse). CA seems to think that he is very interested since he jerked her away from Little Jack Little's jokes. Norman Gimble sounds like a red-hot these days, hope he keeps the bullets headed away from him. Be sure to tell him hello for me—wish I could perch on the bars of your cap when you tell him!

Your airmail letter of the 11th reached me the morning of my birthday and that was all the birthday present I could have asked 'cause it was certainly a small one—all about the new commission. Course some of it didn't sound so good, but Darling, I know that you are happy so I'm not complaining. Please be careful and take good care of yourself.

Mother is writing you Airmail today so I am giving her that picture that Bill B. took of you and me down in front of the Drug Store. I haven't any others to send you, but am going to try to get Bill to take some colored stills of John and maybe I can get a good one to send to you. He looks the same, but he is growing up so in words and actions. The other day when Owen's *[Owen Morris]* roosters were crowing he said that they said, "Hello Johnny," and Mother said, "Johnny, what is your last name?" Johnny crinkled up his eyes and his face and said, "B.!" He knew he was going to get a rise with that one. I guess that we have been talking too much. He certainly doesn't miss very much.

We are planning a trip to Reno next Tuesday to do a little shopping. I have to have some white flats—I'm practically barefoot as I trudge up about the place slowly.

Must go to CAP now, Sweet, so all my love,   Gail

AUGUST 20, 1943 WES TO GAIL

Darling—   #18

I lost the little record of letter numbers, but think 18 is right—at any rate, this is the first letter since the V-Mail which gave the new APO NO., 928, Unit one. I am permitted to say that I am somewhere in the South West Pacific area—that certainly is definite, isn't it? However, I am enjoying myself immensely.

Your letter of Aug. 11 hasn't been answered as yet—well, Darling, I don't think you'll have to worry about my coming home as a Buck Private! Could be, though, if I'm real bad.

You can tell David, if he thinks I drink "whisky and such," he ought to see how the pilots handle it over here—wow! I couldn't stand up to those fellows, not halfway! They really go to town on their liquor.

I've managed to get a very little flying so far—just enough to ensure my flying pay. I've had to fight for it so far. Hope that it won't always be so difficult for me. Once I got to do some of the flying myself. Darling, I'm glad you are keeping up your air work so thoroughly. You'll have to give me lessons when I get home!

I had a picture taken by one of the fellows a couple of weeks ago. When it will ever be developed, I don't know—but if and when, you shall certainly have it. Oh yes, and the picture I had taken with the Koala bear should be on its way to you in another week. These people are so *[unreadable]* and so darned slow about everything. It's just impossible to rush them.

So far my training taken at Randolph hasn't been of much use to me. I used it more back at Great Falls than any time since. Better luck in the future, I hope.

Jack isn't near us at present. That's all I can say about that. Nothing wrong—it's just a normal course of events.

I didn't know you were wearing white uniforms, Dearest. Please send me a picture of you in it—with the white sweater on—right away now, Honey. I want to see <u>how sweet</u> you look. Don't let any of the patients make love to you, now—or anybody else but me! I'll promise I'm not worried about that, though, Dear.

Just took time out for chow—breakfast, and at 9 a.m. We had some delicious pancakes and syrup (I could only eat eight) fried beans, stewed peaches, and a whole canteen cup full of real good coffee—yum yum! My appetite picks up under favorable circumstances. I've started living in shorts, but can't manage it very long as I got sunburned yesterday—it's hotter than h——. Guess I'll have to break in gradually.

Darling, again, may I request that you do not write on the red square (rectangle) at the bottom of the V-Mail—it doesn't show through! You said something about one of these days Johnny was going to write me—blank—blank—blank—"can read it"—So do I. Will you help him write?

I got a nice note from Bob Hudson, written from Dad and Esther's in Seattle, also a letter from Marian and one from Esther. Marion and Cy are apparently very happy in their little home, and had a nice Honeymoon with the boys away. I'm glad they can finally have some peace and happiness, which they so richly deserve.

Sweetheart—write to Mrs. Francis Van de Carr, 51 Prospect Road, Piedmont, Calif. She has some interesting things to write you about her children.

Did I mention talking to Norman Gimble? He said George Osborne was [censored] I don't know what sort of outfit he is in nor could I discuss it if I did know! What a life. There are so many interesting things I would like to tell you, Dear, but cannot. After all, censorship is for the common good of all concerned and one must abide by the rules. I am at a loss to know what it was they blacked out in regard to that fellow from [censored] I discussed— you said it was the time his leave started—I'm surprised I even mentioned that and don't even remember the circumstances now.

This letter has to meet a deadline on mail pick-up, so I'd better stop meandering around and tell you how much I love you. I'm completely yours, my sweet and love you with every bit of me. Wait 'til I see you again—mmmm—

Give Johnny my love, and tell him to hurry and write Daddy—Goodbye for now, sweet

Wes

AUGUST 20, 1943 FRIDAY EDITH TO WES

Dear Wes,

I won't write V-Mail and deprive you of a look at your mother-in-law's handwriting. I have been a long time getting a letter started, but I know you hear all about us from Gail and she reads us all the news of you so I don't expect a personal answer to this.

We were all very proud yesterday when your letter came saying you are a Capt. Congratulations! We sent a wire off yesterday which I hope reached you before you started anywhere.

Gail's birthday was well celebrated and your letter was the best present of all. Margaret had a lovely dinner for her. Just CA and family. We dined on Maggie's home raised chickens.

Our little treasure is supposed to be napping but he is having a fine time from the sound. I was plucking eyebrows and gave a big squeeze and out popped John saying, "you scared me awful." He always works the bathroom gag when things are too dull.

Gail is at the hospital this afternoon as she stayed home to help me this morning. She doesn't feel too well. Her eyes are puffed and her head aches. I think it must be sinus. She keeps pretty busy. Everybody has been so nice to her. There are more things to do than she has time for. She has done quite a little flying and would have gone to Susanville this week but the girl she was to take was ill. Thank goodness CA insisted that she take his plane instead of going cross country in those old Cubs. He doesn't think they're safe for cross country. They certainly look like junk.

We tried having a girl to take care of John while we went to dinner last night but he knew where we were and over he came. The poor little girl couldn't do much and was quite embarrassed. I was negotiating with Lena Haun to take care of him for a day next week while Gail and I go to Reno to shop. As usual Gail's feet are bare and she can't get shoes here.

It was awfully nice of you to send me a purse too and I do hope they get here all right. Many thanks.

David thinks there will be a move for him quite soon. Now he wonders what to do with his new car.

From the noise upstairs, I'll have to go and tend to John. Hope you get home before he is too grown up. He gets off pretty cute things now. John shook the bed the other night but we can't decide who was to blame. He is on my back now so goodbye for the present.

Love from Edith

P. S. Julian seems to be quite interested in a nurse down there!!

AUGUST 22, 1943 GAIL TO WES

My Darling,

There have been no letters for a few days, so I take it you are on the move. Hope everything goes all right.

Today has been a busy day. I got up early and went out to the airport. We had a mission to perform for CAP. Each of us had a different one. I flew in the Silvaire and my objective was Meadow View over near Doyle. I drew an observer that hadn't been up much and knew nothing whatever about maps. I didn't know much abut the Forest Service map either, but we finally found it and scooted for home. CA was the only one who didn't score 100%, and he had to locate a burn and tell the acreage. He felt pretty bad about it.

I took Orville Brown up in the Luscombe for his first ride around here and he certainly enjoyed it. Yesterday, I got a half an hour in the Luscombe and today 1¾ hours. I'm building my time up slowly you see—but at least I'm building it.

Helen called me today and wants me to go to dinner at Mt. Tomba with them and the Dellingers. Mom and Dad have taken off for Harvey West's X-mas party at Forest Lodge. Sounds kind of crackpot to me.

Ken just called and we are going now, so bye now my love—Gail

AUGUST 22, 1943 CHARLIE BEDELL TO WES
[Composite Letter]

Hi Wes,

No one else would start his letter. Gail says you won't be able to read the first of this. This is all the space I can have, so will console the other war widow, Dottie. We surely miss you and wish you could be with us. Nevertheless, we appreciate all you are doing, and we're "hitting the ball" at home too.   Charlie

Hurry and finish the job so you can come home—   Leila *[Bedell]*

Wish you were here to eat chickens and have a drink. So hurry and finish it off and come home to the gang. *[Anonymous]*

Hi Wes, I just want to let you know I am still kicking. We are parked up at Mt. Tomba just about to chow down on a steak. Sorry we can't enjoy your company—So long —   Bill.

Waiting for you to come home before adding the fourth and last addition to our family—of course I mean the delivering part — Helen. (P. S. Watch out for those little brown girls out there).

Bill: Best regards Wes, wishing you all the luck in the world and bring a *[unreadable]* not in the party!

Ken and Charlie are waiting for me to write something. I don't know just what to write about. If you were a logger I could tell a lot of problems Metzkers and Dellingers are about to run into. We expect to blow the whistle between now and X-mas sometime. Hurry back. P. S. Saw mill depends on future fishing.

Del

[unreadable] $1.00 a month went into effect for M and D August 1ˢᵗ. Another quart or two consequently means nothing for a M. C. Captain. *[unreadable]* for the house was just like you did when nothing came in. We are looking for you home at an <u>early</u> date to help *[unreadable]* the *[unreadable]*. Please do not disappoint us.   Ken.

Hello Wes, old boy. We all miss you more than anybody I know of. Metzkers and Dellingers are trying to build a sawmill and are getting along good. So hurry home and *[unreadable]*. C. T. Bedell. P. S. Ken says this is all H. S. but I'd call it B. S.

Anyway, Sweetheart, wish you were here—Love, Gail.

AUGUST 22, 1943 WES TO GAIL

Dearest little Gail—   #19

When I wrote last, I overlooked your letter of the 9ᵗʰ of August. By the way, I now have 15 of your letters. There is a gap from Aug. 4ᵗʰ to 9ᵗʰ—one or just possibly two—letters missing. Sounds (in the letter of the 9ᵗʰ) as though the CAP put on a regular air circus. Hope no one gets in trouble over that dusk flying. I wish you would try to be out of the air before that, Dearest, because there is such an added collision hazard at that time. It isn't that I'm afraid of you—it's some of these numbskulls you associate with!

Wish I could have taken in the parties at Paxton and Verdonaga's, not to mention the picnic. I can just imagine John had an elegant time. I'm looking forward to the time I can take him fishing with me. I'm glad that Ken, Helen, Del, Ruth and you see a lot of each other. They're swell kids. Tell them to write to me—and Bailey, too. They all owe me letters. I'd like to hear a little of Ken's dry sarcasm for a change, and roll him for the drinks at the Sump!

Say, I'll bet Jan is happy now that Anne is walking, and she should be happier in her new pregnancy—It's a good thing for a gal like her—takes her mind off her troubles.

You, you little monkey, are so busy jumping from this to that, you shouldn't ever have time to brood! I love you for being such a wonderfully versatile little creature.

Did you write Mrs. Van de Carr yet—51 Prospect Road, Piedmont? Well, you'd better do it pronto—after this, you mind the boss and do as he tells you—or have you received letter #18? I haven't received the airmail letter with a card for me to sign which you sent Thursday, and I certainly will be looking forward to those funnies.

Did I tell you Chris is here? We were certainly delighted to see him. He survived his operation very well and made it over just about a month after we did. Again—I can't tell you where Jack is—we may see him again later but I don't know—he is with his squadron.

Say, Honey, I'm enjoying my pipe a lot these days. Wish you would send me two tins of Velvet smoking tobacco about once every two weeks. It's very hard to get smoking tobacco, although cigarettes are plentiful—it would give you something to do!

Ole says Mavis mentions hearing from you right along, too. That's a good idea, because you can possibly get news from one another when letters are held up—he is right along with us—haven't lost him yet!

I was sorry to hear about Hersh Laughlin being killed. Who is he? I dimly remember the name but can't seem to tie it up in my mind.

I must write to Marian, Bobby, Esther and Dad now. Am I not the ambitious lad?

All my love, Sweetheart.   Your Wes

AUGUST 24, 1943 WES TO GAIL

Darling Gail—   #20 (Sounds like you are the 20th Gail on my list! You are the only one).

I'm writing V-Mail for a change. There wasn't much to tell you about at present, nor was there much in the last two letters. But I love you, Darling—I can say that again, can't I? It is simply beautiful Darling. Wish I could tell you all about it. Wonder if this will beat my airmail letters of the 20th and 22nd, or vice versa? Guess you can't make much sense out of all my jargon, but one of these days, I'll be home and tell you all about it—in between kisses. Could you go for a nice, long, breath-taking kiss right now? I could. Gee, I sound like a lovesick schoolboy, don't I. Do you mind?

It's been several days since I had a letter from you, and it will be several more before I get any. Not your fault, Sweetheart. Hope you're writing me lots of letters, Darling—I'm going to be needing them.

All my love to my little Gail and Johnny—   Wes

AUGUST 25, 1943 WES TO MARIAN

Dear Marian—

It was swell to hear from you. Received your Aug 10 V-Mail on the 22nd— good time. I have no typewriter available so you will have to struggle through my scrawl. Please note my new APO NO., and use it soon. Don't take me seriously, Honey—I know you work hard. I feel sorry for all the civilians because in many ways things are much tougher on them than us. You have to double up on work and fight for ration points. Although we have to go without luxuries and may be lonely, we get plenty of good food and don't work too hard—sometimes! You don't need to worry about your letters being censored, by the way.

Had to take time out to cut a cast off a boy's arm. It wasn't due to come off for a week, but its been bothering him so long, I gave in. You can't beat these GI soldiers.

I hot a real nice letter from Bob. Guess Mick was lazy. He's more like me. I would never write a letter unless I was driven to it. Of course, now that I am becoming old and sage— ahem!

It's hotter than hell. Am living in a pair of shorts. Had a GI haircut—down to about half an inch. We are somewhere in the Southwest Pacific and that's as much as censorship will allow me to tell.

I'm awfully glad you and Cy had a little Honeymoon all to yourselves, in your new house. I can understand you both enjoying walks about the place, loving to work on my very own house so much. It's grand for you, Honey, and I know you must be happy. I do hope Cy doesn't have to go—and doubtful that he will.

Honey, if you get time, send me a couple of tins of pipe tobacco—I like Velvet—or any kind. I seem to enjoy my pipe more these days and tobacco is hard to get. Have plenty of cigarettes. Write again soon. Thanks for Dinty's address.

My love to you and Cy and the boys and Jake!   Wes

AUGUST 26, 1943 GAIL TO WES

My Darling,   #1

I am starting a new number sequence because I got all off on the other. I'll try to keep them all numbered. If I keep a list, I think that I can keep them in order. Yesterday, before we took off for Reno, I got your airmail letter written on the 14th, and was I tickled to see it. I had the idea that you had departed for parts unknown and was expecting that I might not be getting any letters for a few weeks.

It sounds as though the boys really put on a winging with their 12 kegs of beer. I'm surprised that only two had to be sewed up.

I've been wondering if you are getting in any flying. I expect that your association with Norman Gimble would practically require some flying, wouldn't it? Speaking of flying— I took the registrar, Barbara, over to Susanville the other day in the Luscombe. We had a swell trip and got in about an hour and forty-five minutes of looking the country over. It was lots of fun. Clyde Deal jumped me about the Freedman Burnham [Propeller] and said that it went with the Aeronca. I told him that was ours and that it did not go with the ship. He has been offered $2100 for the ship, so I told him that he certainly shouldn't feel cheated. I think that he cooled off a little then. They seem to have a pretty big program under way over there and the boys are pretty busy. Bill was trying to solo a boy who had been in the Solomans as a rear gunner. I don't know how his air work was. Bill had to wash him out.

To answer your question—I don't think that Barney ever got to S. F. I haven't heard that he did. I guess Melba is still waiting!

We wore ourselves out in Reno yesterday—I had an awful lot of shopping to do and was certainly a tired chickadee when I got home. Lena and Dad had John yesterday and as far as I know they got along OK. I tried to get the gun fixed, but the gunsmith was so busy with pre-hunting repairs on rifles that he couldn't get to the .22 for some time. So I brought it home with me. We had a terrible time trying to find anything for John to wear. I have to buy size 6 for him now. There isn't very much to choose from, and we were lucky to get anything at all.

Everything is running pretty smoothly up at the hospital. This morning we took out a couple of tonsils. Barbara Lee was one of them. Night before last, Dr. Lasswell operated on a strangulated hernia and everything turned out swell. Dr. seems much more cheerful lately, and I think that it is because he can get away every once in awhile. I read him the letter where you told me to tell Dr. B. how to get in the Army, and I asked him if I should read it to the man. Dr's response was "Women sure are vindictive." He wouldn't let me read it to Dr. B., and I was just dying to do it.

I guess the Smiths are going to move into the house. Ray would like for me to do something about the floors—I've been trying to find someone that would sand them, but there just aren't such around these days. They really are in an awful mess. The walls are pretty dirty, too. Well, I'll do the best that I can about it, and if they don't like it after that then they can just lump it. I'm afraid the chimney needs cleaning too.

I've got the loan to Occidental Life Insurance paid up, even got an $8.00 refund from them. I guess that I paid them too much. Now I'm going to work on the other Insurance loan. Please don't forget to answer my question on whether the Income Tax is getting deducted from your salary. I'm 'fraid that I should be laying away for that too.

Darling, I love you so much and miss you so much, I'll keep busy and cheerful and trying to grin so my face won't be full of so many lines that you won't love me anymore. Johnny is heckling me and kissing your picture—he says that you must have washed your teeth because they are so white. He's a very observing young man.

All my love, Sweetheart   Gail

Dearest Darling—   #21

Another delightful day of sunbathing. I am enjoying this phase of our work immensely and will be almost sorry when it ends.

Do you know, I only have 15 letters from you, and here I am on no. 21—but no doubt if I had all you had written to date they would total over 21. I guess you can tell when I don't have much to do—I start yowling about the number of letters you've written! Really, Dear, I am pleased, though you wouldn't believe it, at your very good work on correspondence.

How is John these days? Can he swim yet? Does he like flying pretty well? Does he do what he is told any better? How's about a picture of him? And one of you in your white uniform. Tell me about Dr. L and Dr. B. How are they hitting it off? In case you can't think what to write, there's some good leads.

Honey, I should have taken your advice in pajamas. One pair is shot and thrown away and the other ripped clear down the back. I bought two pair a couple of weeks ago but will be unable to buy any more for about a year—maybe. If you think I am worth it and can manage to do it, how about sending me a couple of pair—just as simple as possible, and without buttons on the top—I'll be sleeping in them *[unreadable]* blankets.

I put out quite a laundry today. As I said before, I am emulating your Mom in the matter of washing my way around the world. Boy, what I'd give for that Bendix!

Not much else to tell you today, Sweet. Be a good girl and don't work too hard. Love Johnny for me—

All my love, Dearest.

Yours always—

Wes

(Randolph Field, Texas stationery, name crossed out)

Darling,

This little ring was made for me by one of the boys out of an Australian Shilling. If it is too small, have it enlarged by a jeweler. Some day, if you are near a <u>good</u> jeweler, you might have it engraved with a G on the center heart and a J on each side, for your two John's—as you like, Sweetheart.

I love you, Dearest

Always, Wes

AUGUST 28, 1943 WES TO GAIL

Darling,

I'm getting a lovely tan and my moustache is flourishing. Maybe I'll let it get real long and twirl the ends. Would you like that? *[drawing of nose, mustache and lips]* Some artist!

Yesterday I sent you in an airmail envelope a little ring made from a shilling, and a note. Hope it gets to you OK. The ring is made by tapping the coin while held on edge, rotating it, so the edges are gradually flattened. When the desired diameter is reached, the center is cut out and the whole thing is polished. The design of hearts was cut with a file and the whole thing narrowed down. If it were left wide, you would see all the writing on the inside, but it makes too broad a ring for a dainty little girl's hand. I'll make one of the ordinary ones one day and send it along so you can see how it looks.

Remember the tall fellow with glasses and his blonde wife who used to stay at Staukey's? We often saw them standing across the street waiting for a bus and I remarked about her good looking legs? (I'm not allowed to mention fellow officer's names now.) Well, he's a buddy of mine, sort of, and has promised to bring his wife and visit us after the war. He's a lot of fun—he is our Intelligence Officer (S-2) and has slept next to me in all our various situations since coming to the South West Pacific.

I'm reading "The Silver Spoon" by Galsworthy. Not entirely certain whether I can read a lot of such high class literature, but maybe this life may actually have some beneficial effects on my coarse and untutored mind—

I had a gorgeous swim today in the South West Pacific area. First dip in a long while, and it certainly did feel good. I hated to get out. Got in some good high diving, too.

I'm glad this is Saturday—don't have to eat any fish for another week! We had lovely fried eggs and beans for breakfast today, too. Nice fresh eggs. Boy, what a job of fried egg eating I'm going to do when I get home, and Honey, be sure and have plenty of Cokes on hand!

Darling, it will be so wonderful to see you and John again. I've always known, Dear, what a wonderful little wife you are, but it takes a separation like this to drive it home to the fullest realization. You are the most wonderful person I know, Sweetheart and I love you so much.

That's all for now, Darling. I don't know how many weeks this will take in reaching you, and the last few, too—but all my love goes with these pitiful scrawls of mine.

Wes

AUGUST 28, 1943 GAIL TO WES

My Darling,   #2

Letter #16 arrived yesterday—It was a swell, big, long one—sounded as though you really were having a struggle to get any flying. I took Virginia Watson up in the 55 T Craft last night for her first ride. It was suppose to be in the Luscombe, but it had the tail off getting new tail pins. Haggerty is going in the Army and wants to sell me his half of the T Craft, but I told him I had to paint the house so couldn't afford it. I can fly the Luscombe practically any time, I guess, so why fool with a T Craft?

Our CAP is doing OK. We are suppose to be reviewed by Bertrand himself tomorrow—Some stuff. The kids all look swell in their "Mexican general" uniforms. I haven't had all of mine on at once yet. We did a little drilling for the first time last night and Oh, Honey, but we were lousy. I'd even forgotten how to right face.

Tonight we are all going up to Mt. Tomba to celebrate the Dellinger's anniversary. Del has had people reminding him all week. Wish you could be here, Sweetheart. I miss you so!

Would very much like to see the new stencil you cut out—must be a [unreadable].

Be sure to start writing about the things you would like to have for Christmas, 'cause people will want to know and there are so few things we can send—would like a few suggestions, Darling. I hate to think of another Xmas without you!

All my love   Gail

AUGUST 30, 1943 MONDAY GAIL TO WES

Darling,   #3

I've been doing a bit of house cleaning this morning—have the upstairs cleaned at least.

Every little bit helps. I'm sending along some excerpts from the Aug. 26th Bulletin that I thought you might be interested in. I sent the one of Patty Kerr along to show you that Emailing [Blank] is making a hospital out of her home. Virginia said Blank didn't give Patty gas or anything. I guess she's not equipped for that. I guess she's sending most of her OB's up to us. We're glad she's given up the operating—Thanks to Dr. B. The Shaw boy was over in Reno and Creveling sent him to SF when he stuck a knife in his throat and he had a time with the bleeding. I guess he sewed him back together and shipped him off to SF.

By the way, Floyd Shaw has bought Haggerty's part of the T Craft and I gave them part of the Hangar space for a little flying time.

The CAP was up over the weekend—about 75, or so. There was really quite a parade around here. I guess they all had a good time.

Sat. nite we went up to Mt. Tomba to celebrate Ruth and Del's anniversary and had a swell time. Only one missing was you, Darling. Wish you'd been there. Last night the Metzkers, Cotters, Bedells and Johnny and I went out to the Forest Service Camp ground on a picnic and did the kids have fun! Johnny had been to a party *[Sandra Lee's birthday]* all afternoon and he finally gave out about 7:30 and went to sleep in the car.

I got another letter from Doris Hansen yesterday and she is leaving home about Sept. 21st. I hope she likes it here! She says that Chris' APO # is 848, New York! I guess he's going the other way. She hadn't heard from him for 5 weeks and then finally got a cable.

I'm going to try to get the floors up at the house sanded and varnished before the Smith's move in, and do a bit of cleaning up. I think that they will be good renters and will take care of things nicely. I have been consulting Ken about what should be done and he has been a big help.

Gee, Sweetheart, more people have told me to send their regards that I can't remember them all. All my love, my precious—Have to get cleaned up and get to the office.

Your Gail

AUGUST 31, 1943 GAIL TO WES

Sweetheart,   #4

Wrote you Airmail yesterday. I was struggling through the 9 o'clock news (the station was very noisy) when Johnny came stumbling in and announced that he was going to sleep with me. Right now he's in his crib howling for all he's worth. He's gotten an aversion for his own bed and seems to think it is his duty to come in and keep me company.

There was a case of Polio brought down from Portola and Dr. L. spent most of Sunday night out at the County giving her artificial respiration. Dr. B. took her down to U. C. to put her in an iron lung yesterday. She's about 21 years old. Don't know her name.

Dr. L. seems to be thriving on his work and, if anything, looks younger rather than older.

This evening I went out to the airport and took Floyd Shaw for his first ride in the ship he is part owner of. He said he guessed I'd be pretty busy giving both Ray Brown and himself dual. Neither one of them know how to fly. Their ship is in our hangar now and I get flying time in it.

Dad and his committee wrangled a little more of Harry Lee's orchard away from him and they are going to move the office and the gas pump over.

Ken went up to look over the house with me yesterday after work and said if he were in my boots he wouldn't paint the house or sand the floors. Just clean the latter up a little and maybe put out linoleum in the back entrance.

No letters since the 27th. Am hoping tomorrow!

I love you, Darling

                                        Gail

NO DATE. MARIAN TO WES
(5656 Marburn Ave., Los Angeles 43, California)

Dear Wes,

I have been trying to write you for several weeks now, and can't seem to get to it, so today I'm going to start and then continue writing a little each day.

We are now on a 44-hour week—we were working only 37 ½ hours, so we have only half an hour for lunch each day and also have to work from 8:30 to 12:30 on Saturdays. I yipped and yelled that I would never work on Saturdays, but I'm doing it with all the rest of them. We started only last Saturday, and I haven't had a chance yet to see if it's going to be very hard. Formerly on Saturdays, I did my shopping for the entire week. It takes a long time nowadays to get through the line at the checking stand—with all the complications of rationing and counting the correct change. Guess the boys will just have to help me a little more and I'll have to worry less about the way the house looks, seeing as how I can't quit right now.

Gail sent Mother excerpts from your letters and Wes, I've never read anything more fascinating. You write very well and your descriptions are vivid. We were so interested—in fact, everyone I've let read them has felt the same as we did. Needless to say, I have not passed out the copy of the excerpts indiscriminately.

Bob and I each received your letters, and we were so glad you had finally gotten some mail from us. We were very interested in hearing about the eye training you are to get. I didn't know you like eye-work so much. While I think of it, your letters smell just like a hospital—imagine that fragrance (to me it's a fragrance, to most people it smells like a bad word!) persisting in all the miles it travels!

My paragraphing and punctuation is terrific, but I hate to waste precious space, so please forgive my apparent ignorance on such matters for this time and every letter that follows.

Dinty at the present is in New York. He expects to make one more trip to Africa, and then thinks he will be stationed in N. Y. We are wondering where he will be flying next, but if he knows, he hasn't told us yet.

I see Butch *[Richard Carr Moore]* very seldom to never. I'll try to write her soon though, and give her your address so Butch can write. He's a darling boy and she is bringing him up beautifully.

Bob made the first string at school in football. He plays right end, and got a very nice write-up in the school paper after the last game they played. Both boys in fact, all three of my boys, are darlings about helping me with the work. We are thriving on our vegetables, Dr. Moore, but right now there's very little left in the garden. Some late corn we can hardly wait to get ready to eat, and some chard and celery.

By the way, the description you gave your wife, and the one you gave Bob of the native women don't tally. What I'd like to know is, are you still <u>smoking</u> your cigarettes? I'm really worried about the pipe I sent you and the package of Sherry Pralines 'cause they were addressed to APO 928 without the Unit One. What should I do?

Much love
Sis

SEPTEMBER 1, 1943—SOUTHWEST PACIFIC THEATER OF OPERATIONS (Fifth Air Force): In New Guinea, 70+ B-24's and B-25's hit the Alexishafen-Madang area, dropping 201 tons of bombs (heaviest by Fifth Air Force to date). Other B-25's hit Iboki Plantation in the Bismarck Archipelago, barges on the Bubui River in New Guinea, the Rein Bay on New Britain Island area and several villages in New Britain. B-17's bomb Labu Island, New Guinea. B-26's attack Cape Gloucester area on New Britain Island. B-24's and B-25's strike targets in the Lesser Sunda Islands. The 68th and 69th Troop Carrier Squadrons, 433d Troop Carrier Group, arrive at Port Moresby, New Guinea from the US with C-47's. The 432d Fighter Squadron, 475th Fighter Group, ceases operating from Port Moresby and returns to it's base at Dobodura with P-38's.

AIRCRAFT MENTIONED IN THIS REPORT:

A-20, Douglas Havoc	A-36, North American Apache
B-17, Boeing Flying Fortress	B-24, Consolidated Liberator
B-25, North American Mitchell	B-26, Martin Marauder
Beaufighter, Bristol	C-47, Douglas Skytrain
F-4, Lockheed Lightning	F-5, Lockheed Lightning
F-6, North American	F4U, Vought Corsair (USN)
L-4, Piper Cub/Grasshopper	L-5, Stinson Sentinel
P-38 Lockheed Lightning	P-39, Bell Airacobra
P-40, Curtiss	P-47, Republic Thunderbolt
P-51, North American Mustang	P-70 Douglas
SBD, Douglas Dauntless (USN)	Spitfire, Vickers Supermarine
TBF, Grumman Avenger (USN)	Vengeance, Vaultee (RAAF)
Ventura, Lockheed	Zeke, Mitsubishi A6M, Navy Type O Fighter

SEPTEMBER 2, 1943 GAIL TO WES

My Precious Darling,

No letter again today and it has really been a lonesome day for me. Gee it helped so much when I'd get a letter at least every day or so. I know how you must have felt when they didn't come day after day.

I went out gadding with Ruth and Dottie tonight and took in the Sump and the Stone House—very dull indeed. It is now 12:30 and I'm feeling very blue and lonesome. I'll send along a kiss and hope that this X will reach you intact and bringing all my love with it. Sweetheart, if I go on with this, I'll get too darned sentimental—somehow I seem to have lost my sense of humor today (If I ever had one). I've been cleaning out the house and trying to figure out what to do about the floors, walls, etc. and where I was going to get anyone to do it after I made up my mind what should be done. Good night now, Honey, I'll finish this tomorrow.

Darling, another day. Johnny has run away twice and I had to threaten to go bye-bye without him if he didn't stick around, so now he's camped out in the car so I can't get away without him. Mother and Dad have gone to Oroville and Johnny and I have the run of the place today.

The Hoods left this morning so I guess I'll have to get busy on the house so the Smith's can move in on the 15th. Can't get the house painted. Everette is too busy. Gave up the sanding idea—no shellac, so I guess it'll be just scrubbed.

All my love

                    Gail

SEPTEMBER 2, 1943 WES TO GAIL

Dearest Darling—   #22

I see by my notes that I haven't written since Aug 26th Poor, baby, hope you haven't been missing any letters too much. I haven't been able to get letters off, Sweet, until now, nor hardly a chance to write since then. We are again, for the time, somewhere in Australia. I won't get any mail from you, or anyone, for a couple of weeks, probably, so if you are missing my letters, believe me, I'm missing hearing from you ten times more! But all will come out in the wash, and one of these days I'll catch up with my mail again! I'll bet those cigars will taste good—if I ever see them! Maybe they will be in time for Christmas.

Lover, continue to use the above APO NO. until I give you another one. Don't know nothin' about nothin' just now.

Van and I are practicing the Morse code. We spend about an hour each evening flashing our flashlights at each other, sending naughty words! It relieves the monotony.

I am getting so I enjoy shaving with a razor—think I will stick to it when I get home and give the electric to John when he grows up.

All my love,

Wes

SEPTEMBER 2, 1943—SOUTHWEST PACIFIC THEATER OF OPERATIONS (Fifth Air Force): B-25's, with P-38 escort, attack shipping at Wewak, New Guinea harbor, claiming 1 vessel sunk and 2 left aflame; 10 enemy interceptors are claimed destroyed; barrage balloons offer some protection to the enemy ships. This is first AAF observation of Japanese use of such balloons in the Southwest Pacific Area.

SEPTEMBER 4, 1943 GAIL TO WES

Sweetheart,   #6

I'm writing this at the office. I've been here all day today and it has been pretty busy. Dr. came down with a temp yesterday afternoon to celebrate his week-end off—Margarite took a slide on him and found some malaria bugs running around. I guess that he has had malaria off and on since the Spanish American War when he was in the Philippines. Margarite seems to think that he will feel much better when he finishes with his quinine. They have gone off up to the house at Cromberg. Dr. was getting homesick. When they go off I stay in the office longer so there will be someone here to watch over. Well, I've been interrupted by the head of the T. B. Assoc. a Dr. Something or other who is sitting right here in front of me. Besides all of that it is five o'clock and I have to get up to the house and water the lawn. I'm busier than ten bees and have been the last week. Am practically wracking my brain to try to think of someone who would clean those floors up at the house. Have to have it done by the 15th. Will write the rest of this at home—bye now, Honey.

It's Sat. evening and I never did get the lawn watered. Johnny ran away twice between the time I got home at 5:45 and 6 o'clock. He only goes down to the beer joint but it is awfully hard to get him home.

Tomorrow a. m. I'm going to take Floyd Shaw over to Squaw Peak to see where their hunting party is going to camp and then go over and sit down at Susanville—in the T Craft 55. By the way the airplanes have been coming in to Sky Harbor by the truckload. We now have 4 Luscombes on the field. I don't know where they are going to put any more if they come in.

Gee Sweetheart, I get so lonesome, wish I could see your smiling countenance beaming out reassurance that the world is round and the sun still shines! You have that faculty you know my Sweet, to make my sun shine or make my sky cloudy. I wish the letters would start coming again.

All my love, Darling, forever and ever.

Gail

SEPTEMBER 6, 1943 GAIL TO WES
(Labor Day)

Darling,   #7

I'm about to park my weary bones in bed. Had a hard day today. Managed to get the venetian blinds done, the spider webs swept down and some of the dirt out of most of the corners. I've been reduced to practically begging "Little Walter" to come and do the floors. Then he won't work; they all have too much money—so most of what gets done up at the house I'll do myself. Margarite came down today and she "watched over" during the day and I went up during office hours tonight. Dr. B. scooted off tonight without even looking in on the patients and Mrs. Carter was having a time with one old duck who has trouble breathing. We tried to call Dr. B. but they told us he'd gone out until 11 and couldn't be reached. Fine thing! His ideas of responsibility are slightly warped at times.

One of the CAP girls landed too high tonight and slid in on her nose, washing out the landing gear on the way—there were two girls in the Cub, but they didn't get hurt—only slightly ruffled.

Well, Sweet, my eyes are about half-mast and my bones aching, so will send you a big kiss the best way I can.

All my love
Gail

SEPTEMBER 8, 1943 GAIL TO WES

My Dearest,   #8

The news of Italy's surrender certainly was a chunk of sugar candy to take, as well as McArthur's scouring of New Guinea—I've been wondering if you chaps are getting in on any of that sort of *[unreadable]* imagined that you might be moving that way. Keep good care of yourself Sweetheart, and don't go poppin' your head up at the wrong time.

I've spent two pretty busy days at the house—cleaning from stem to stern and I'm telling you there's plenty to do. "Little Walter" didn't show up, so Bessie, the colored gal, and I did the woodwork and cleaned the floors. Tomorrow we wax them. Friday Elmer Wilsey is going to lay some linoleum on the back porch, and I hope that Bill Dixon will show up and fix the Bendix.

I spent a couple of hours in the office this evening catching up on my book work and reports. Dr. is back and seems to be feeling better—which is certainly a relief to me. Gee I hope nothing happens to him, I'd certainly be on the frying pan then! Doris is arriving on the 22nd. I am going up to Portola to meet her because they won't stop the flier here. I certainly hope she likes it here, 'cause she's going to be a big help to the Institution. Eunice Stenberg is having another baby in January, so I guess about December Mrs. Carter will take all of her shift.

Sew 'em up over there, Honey, and come on home—I don't like this widow deal at all!

All my love forever and ever

Gail

SEPTEMBER 8, 1943 KATHERINE WATSON TO WES

Dear Wes,

Congratulations on your promotion! It is probably an old story to you now but we are still thrilled about it. I think that was grand of you to write me and we all enjoyed your letter.

We were in San Francisco last week and I had a grand time. Uncle Doc had to go down on business and I couldn't stay at home! Haven't seen Gail and Johnny since we returned. They were up one evening for vegetables but I was taking my hydrotherapy (?) treatments or exercises. Think my knee is improving. It didn't cramp my style much in S. F. I couldn't get a bandage made to order but think I had one that fits better. Don't plan to do any more about it until after the war. It is awful sitting around doctor's offices these days. It is nothing urgent and muscles heal themselves, don't they?

Dr. Kupka, from the State Dept. of Health was here Saturday night. Do you know him? I liked him very much. Some of the members of the T. B. Ass'n met with him. We saw some of the films taken after our fluoroscope program and discussed work in the county for next year—chiefly patch and skin tests. I'm still Seal Sale Chairman but have Mrs. Ray Smith as my assistant. Dr. Rees of Portola is President. The secretary and publicity chairman are also there so I have gotten rid of lots of work I had last year!

We had a letter from Arthur *[Watson]* last week from Sicily. Wish we knew where he is now. Was excited this morning when I heard that Italy had surrendered. One down and two to go, as they say, but think we have two hard ones left. Young Dan Baldwin is home for four days. Has his commission and is going back to study liaison (?) flying. Cub Landreth and his family are also visiting the Baldwins. Cub is a commando. Will be glad when you and Arthur and all the men are home again and we can really hear about things. Arthur can write little either, but as he says he can't write anything but it all comes out over the radio and in the newspaper and is ever pictured in Life. (Still many thanks for our subscription to Life)!

Love from Dot and me!

Katherine

SEPTEMBER 8, 1943 ESTHER TO WES

Dear Wes,

So very glad to get your last letter and especially to know that your Captaincy came through. Congratulations!

We are having the most glorious Indian summer—we had such a miserable spring and a very short summer but these days are making up for all the bad weather we had earlier.

I can't remember now whether or not I told you about selling the house. Dad thought it would be so much easier for me if we were to be in an apartment so we sold the house thinking we had an apartment at the Camlin just to find it was only one of these wall-bed affairs. I just couldn't see Dad there especially when he is working so very hard. He deserves so much better, so after looking high and low we refused to give up the house. It cost us the commission but we are ever so happy we made the decision. Now our home looks better than ever to us.

The boys left last week and of course the work is much lighter—how much so I am amused to find. We are glad they could be with us because I think it did them a lot of good and was fitting that Marian and Cy should be alone for awhile. Guess they enjoyed the two months thoroughly.

Had a letter from Gail the other day and she seems to be keeping pretty busy and managing to fill her days, but she will be a happy person to have you back, but no happier, I am sure, than you will be to come back.

The news this morning that Italy had made an unconditional surrender is about the best we've had since the war began, because now we have a real foothold in Europe. Of course it will take a bit of time to clean up the Pacific, but our boys are capable of doing it.

David Rogers has become very close to the Meyers (Phil and Carleta) and Carleta's parents are very close friends of ours. Carleta and the baby are here visiting and we just learned that Phil is flying up to spend a week and very likely will bring David with him, so if he wants to, we will ask him to stop with us during his visit.

Dad is planning his vacation early in October and I am planning to go south. If I can possibly arrange it, I will try to spend a few days with Gail. Am hoping one of Fred's men will have some business up that way so that I won't need to make an overnight trip of it, or it may be that Gail will find some way to come down to San Francisco for a day or two. I'd like that except that I wouldn't get a chance to see Johnny and I am terribly anxious to see him since he's started talking in real human fashion.

We've been wondering what you would like for Christmas. Wish you'd send us a suggestion. We'd like to send you a really good bottle of Scotch or Bourbon but, of course, that is out and they tell us not to send cigarettes, so any suggestions would be welcome. All packages must be mailed by October 15th, I understand.

Heaps of much love to you, Wes, from us both. One of these days, Dad will settle down to writing you himself.   Esther

SEPTEMBER 9, 1943 GAIL TO WES
(Thursday night, 8:30)

Sweetheart,

Johnny and I are holding down the fort alone tonight. Mom has gone to a Forest Service party and Dad has gone out to the Stone House to a meeting of the CAA (O'Brien), the airport manager and the Executive Committee—I don't know what the pow wow is all about. The Inspector was right pleased at the new management and the improvements around the airport. Did I tell you Dad talked Harry out of a little more of his orchard? Hangars are going up right and left and Draper (the new manager) is trying to put up a good shop so he can get a permanent A & E. He is a progressive sort of a fellow and a good manager.

Bessie and I spent today waxing the floors and do they shine—including the one we laid upstairs and the bathroom. What a job! Two coats on all of them. I think the place is cleaner than it's ever been before in its existence, and gee, I wish you and I were moving back instead of the Smiths moving in. I've had fun just working around with so many swell memories popping up in every room. Wish they weren't just memories, Honey, but guess I'm lucky to have those.

I'm 'bout to fold again tonight, so guess I'll turn in—Good night Sweetheart—Hope you are still grinning like you are here in your picture—it's very comforting.

6:15 Friday. Darling, I just bolted my Friday beans so I can scoot back up to the house and direct Elmer Wilsey in his linoleum laying.

My Sweet, today has been a bright day for me—a letter arrived from you—the first in two weeks! It was written on the 22nd and postmarked September 3 American Base Forces APO 922. I noticed a new APO for you so I'll use it this time.

Hersh was a friend of Ned's, and a mining partner—he flew for United and Mother says that he and Hersh talked about Dinty down here one night. He knew Dinty. The latest dope on his death is that he was taking Jap prisoners to a concentration camp and one of the Japs had a hand grenade with which he proceeded to blow up the works. Don't know how true it is.

Jan Finnegan is coming along swell. Her newest worry is that Baby Ann has very flat feet and knock knees. I guess she's going to take her to Bost if he's still around.

Will deliver your message to the boys, Sweetheart, and prod them into writing. Ken has been intending to for some time. We'll also look into the tobacco situation. Am glad you are enjoying your pipe.

All my love, Honey, forever your

Gail

<u>SEPTEMBER 9, 1943 WES TO GAIL</u>
(Somewhere in the Southwest Pacific)

Dearest Darling—   #23

A whole week since I've written. Forgive me, Dearest, but there has been nothing I could say except that I love you—*[unreadable]*—and you know that anyway. I'll be able to write and mail letters oftener. No chance lately. Am all well and safe and getting a glorious tan. I had a haircut yesterday. I told the barber to leave it half an inch long, but I guess he wasn't feeling any too well and I came out with just about enough to get hold of all around. My but my ears really do stick out thoroughly now. You should see me. I'm living in shorts and slippers. The air is wonderfully soft and gentle in the evenings, and the sun amazingly hot in the daytime. I am thinking it will be something at the height of summer—next Christmas!

I am hoping soon to have a whole armload of letters from you, when I can do some writing in earnest.

So no more for now, my sweet. Always loving you, Dearest Sweetheart—Your Wes

<u>SEPTEMBER 11, 1943 WES TO GAIL</u>

Gail Dear—   #24

It's a long time since June 26—almost 2 ½ months—and there has been so much to talk about since then. My, but California seems far away from the S. W. Pacific. I wonder if it will take as long to retrace our steps as it takes to get to the destination—wherever that may be. One goes about with a semi-knowledge of what is to come next—it being best that all is not too well known.

Am hoping for mail—lots and lots of it soon. It will be so good to read your letters again, and know of all the little things you do and John's little pranks and signs of impending wisdom. Maybe he will actually be in school when I see him again. It's curious to think of that little life following through the same processes we passed so long ago. It's going to be interesting to watch, don't you think, Darling?

I dreamed last night that one of my patients, you know her well, Norma Goldstein, called me frantically about her little baby boy with the silly name, Billy Utter. Had a fever of 108 degrees and I started off and had another frantic call, another sick baby—I was downtown and couldn't remember where I parked my car! What a mess. Are you an interpreter of the fragments of a dream? Tell me what that one means!

I love you, Sweet, and wish I could hold you *[unreadable]* close in my arms; I'd never let you get away from me.

Always yours,
                    Wes

SEPTEMBER 12, 1943 GAIL TO WES

Darling,   #10

Just tucked Johnny into bed and he insisted in reading Mother Goose to me. Anything to take a little more time and stall off going to bed. I got your letter of August 28th today describing the moustache—a very fancy drawing I must say; however, you neglected to tell me what color that work of art is turning out to be. How's about delegating me as the one to shear it off for you. I'd like to see it first and then start to work on it.

I'll be waiting very impatiently for the ring to show up, Honey, the purses (Darn it, just went out to put the car up and put my pen in my pocket to fill it on the way back and lost it. It's too dark to look now, so will have to go out in the morning and search). Anyway—the purses haven't shown up yet.

So Giles is your buddy now—I remember your saying you had dinner with him. Too bad we didn't get to know them better in Great Falls. He had a mighty sweet wife—she had a Coke with us a time or two out in the shade of the little maple tree. Are you anywhere near Julian—I've gotten it in my head that you must at least have the same kind of soil under your feet. Maybe I'm wrong—maybe you didn't move.

Think you're smart, doing high diving now—just because you have windows in your sinus you get fancy in your old age!

Sweetheart, the Smith's are in, and did I ever sit with a long face yesterday after the last try they made and when I gave them the Key! Johnny had so much fun there that I wanted to move back.

I hope this is dark enough to show up—looks pretty light complected to me.

All my love, my Darling, and keep away from the sharks!

Gail

SEPTEMBER 14,1943 GAIL TO WES

My Darling,   #11

Received the ring this morning all intact and am thrilled to pieces. It is grand! It's just a little too big for my little finger and a bit too small for my next one, but I'm wearing it on my little finger with a little string until I can get it fixed right. It's so perfect, I don't want anyone to touch it.

Your airmail letters of the 28th beat the airmail of the 27th and the V-Mail of the 24th by two days.

Believe it or not, Sweetheart, I'm working pretty hard, and when I get time, I'm going to write Mrs. Van. I haven't even written my thank you letters for my birthday presents, and those are practically a month late.

Doris will be coming next week and I'm going to have to keep her occupied so she won't get lonesome and want to go home. I'm going to meet her in Portola on the 22nd. That darn train is always late and it isn't due until 9:30 PM. Can't you imagine Doris' reaction at being turned loose in Portola in the wee hours of the morning all by her little lonesome! Please tell Chris that I'll take good care of her.

I guess that Mother wrote you that David is marrying a Texas gal *[Maribelle Ricker]* about the 1st of November, and we are trying to figure out how we can get down to the wedding. He sent us a picture of her and she looks right cute. She is just getting out of a Texas university. Guess David wasn't really in love with Mary Fran. Wish I could get CA to fly down. I don't like to think of riding. Couldn't get that much gas anyway.

Thanks again, Darling, for the sweet ring. I'm crazy about it.

All my love, forever and ever, my Sweetheart,

your Gail

SEPTEMBER 14, 1943 WES TO GAIL

Darling—   #24

It was wonderful to get all your letters and the telegram. You've no idea how mail from home changes one's whole outlook. We hadn't had any for so long. Altogether I had 10 from you, 2 from Ruth and Del, 2 from Esther, 1 from Mother, 1 from CA, and 1 from Barney—and, of course, your wire, 2 months after the promotion! Thank you, Dearest, for the cable and congrats. I was amused at your earlier letter of July 24—hoping it would reach me by my birthday—and I just got it last night.

We were in *[censored]*, Australia. Now, still, "South West Pacific." The new APO for the present is 503, of course c/o P. M. San Fran.

Honey, it's simply beautiful over here, right on a fine sand beach with coconut bearing palms in the background. The water is so warm, more so than Honolulu, and we strip off 4 or 5 times a day and swim for awhile. Last night we swam in the tropical moon, nearly as bright as day. We climb the trees and get coconuts, drink the milk and eat the meat, and boy, is it good. The natives will get them for you for a shilling apiece, which is highway robbery, as they say before the Americans spoiled them they would get them for a cigarette, a bit of cloth, a bead, etc., or particularly an old razor blade. I am told that in the more virgin areas one can have a native wife for about a week for a pack of cigarettes! Have seen a few of the native men, only, so far, I haven't decided whether to smoke or barter! These *[censored]* are most unattractive, to say the least. They wear only a loincloth, and their feet look broad, filthy, and horny. They can go up a tree like a monkey. Their hair stands about six inches up, all a mass of kinky wool, many a dirty reddish color. For the most part, their skin is pretty dark brown, about like Bertha. I haven't seen any high yellows! They say the women wear only a grass skirt, no undies and no brassieres. I'm going to try to get hold of some pictures of some. Darling, if you can get one of those cheap plastic box cameras and some film to fit, for Pete's sake, send it to me. We will undoubtedly be overseas for quite a while and I sure would like to have some photographic souvenirs.

This is a crazy letter—I have so much I want to tell you, so many letters from you, and so many distractions. If you find a few crushed ants, etc., don't be surprised because the bugs are really thick in the tropics. I saw some ants an inch and a half long this morning—their bodies looked like blackberries! I have my pad on my knees, and keep jumping and slapping away bugs, so the writing is exceptionally horrible. I'm not going to try to answer questions this time, but probably will be writing a couple of times a day for awhile to catch up with you.

Julian is a couple of hundred miles away. I'm going to write him today. As I need some flying for this month, I will try to catch a ride to where he is and we'll have a big "Old Home Week" together.

Sweetheart, I'm so hot, sitting here on my birthday suit I'm just going to have to knock off for now and take a swim before lunch. Will write more this afternoon. Am enclosing the signature card. All my love Dearest Darling – Wes

Same day, same letter. Had a marvelous swim and wonderful lunch. I went up the road this afternoon to a spot we are to move into tomorrow, and it is twice as gorgeous as here. I'll be in a tent with Van right on the beach, 20 yards from the water at high tide! Wowee! It is lonely. Cut right out of the jungle. I wish you could see the jungle growth. It is the most luxuriant thing imaginable, thick with banyons, palms and banana trees, all interwoven and interlaced with vines, and a trailing stuff about like clothesline called "lawyer cane." Everything is green and lush, and the grass stands about six feet high. Progress through untracked jungle here is a matter of literally cutting your way. The jungle noises are really something to hear. There are thousands of different-sounding chirps, songs and chatters. Chiefly there are multi—and I mean brilliant-hued parrots by the thousand. You don't see the monkeys, but they say they are there. Malaria control—mosquito control—has become a fine art and they are not a tenth as thick as up at Gold Lake. We take atropine once daily, six days a week, as a prevention, nevertheless, and continue it for six weeks after leaving a malarious area.

By the way, I saw some native women up near our new campsite this afternoon and have definitely decided to smoke my cigarettes! Believe it or not, one little ugly, saggy-breasted female (I could hardly call her a woman) I saw suckling a pot-bellied, scrawny babe at one breast and a baby pig at the other, walking down the road! That really stopped me.

I'll have to stop now as it is getting dark, and it really gets dark in a hurry in the tropics. The sunsets are most gorgeous colors of old rose, cerise, lavender (particularly beautiful shade) I ever saw. Since I started this page it has gone from favorable light to the point that I can just barely see.

Darling, more tomorrow, and all my love, always and forever—and don't be blue as of Sept. 3, which came this afternoon!

Yours—   Wes

My Dear little brother:

I'm so proud of your being a Captain, I could bust—don't even mention it. I am all sorts of a heel to let so much time go by before writing you, but I promise it won't happen again. We were so happy to hear from you, but I don't like the idea of your being 'way over in the Southwest Pacific! I felt so safe in the fact that you were in Australia, but I suppose you are happy to be where you are, so I'll shush.

I was afraid you'd think I had taken you seriously about the work when I read my letter over, but there wasn't much I could do about it then—no more room on the paper. I was kidding you too. However, I really did work for six weeks while relieving three different girls during the time they were all on their respective vacations! Now vacations are all over, and I hope to do better by my brothers.

You really make me ashamed saying that you feel sorry for the civilians—maybe we do work hard and fight with each other to be the first to the butter counter, or to get the last ounce of hamburger, but shame on us! Think of the things all our boys are doing without home, family, etc. etc.! Of course, I'll grant that maybe some of the poor husbands left wish they could get away from wifey's lashing tongue.

What to you want for X-Mas?

The boys are home from Seattle now, and they really had a wonderful time. You are right about Mick being lazy about letter-writing—his intentions are good, but he doesn't get any further than the intentions! I'll fix him, though. He's very crazy about both of his uncles, so maybe you'll be getting a letter pretty soon. Cy has been so slow in getting the dark-room urge this time—poor little Gail is still waiting for the pictures we promised her of Johnny and you and David. Also, I haven't written her. Much correspondence to catch up on and, again, shame on me for being so pokey! Anyway, I started to tell you that they started back to school yesterday. Mick thinks now that he'd like to be a doctor, and he's signed up for Latin, English, Algebra, Gym and Life Science! Knowing his lack of interest in study, I'm wondering how he's going to make the grade! But, if he can do it, more power to him. Bob has gone back to John Burroughs—he just has one term left there, so we didn't make him change schools. He says there are so many Jews there that about four of his pals sit together in the back of their home-room, and call it Gentile Corner!

Did I tell you in my last letter about the delicious corn we had from our own garden? It was good, also we had some good string beans. Our one handful of peas was worth writing to you about also—next time we'll plant more. However, Cy seems to be getting interested in fishing, and it looks as if the garden will go to plots—tell you next time.

I just ordered two pounds of Velvet for you from Bullock's and they say it will be sent right away. Did you get your V-Mail stationery?

Your sister is a screw-ball. I'll try to <u>seem</u> a little more intelligent next time.

                Lots of love,

                   Sis

SEPTEMBER 16, 1943 KEN METZKER TO WES

Dear Unk,

Suppose by the time this reaches you, you will be a General. All of us pleased to no end when we heard of your promotion. Seems a good man cannot be kept back, even in the Army.

Would you have a chance to *[unreadable]* hear anything from Barney. No one here does, to my knowledge. Everything coming along pretty good on this end, Wes. Business awfully quiet, no young men any more, only us 4F Charlie's. No doubt you get homesick now and then but take it for me, outside your family you are not missing a thing.

Gail worries about the business at times I think, but honestly hasn't a problem to speak of outside of your being away. Dr. B. blew his wad when old Bart took him in tow and I believe things are now working out swell for all parties concerned. Of course all of us have it in for the K—, so it is difficult seeing him around, but Old Bart is plenty smart. At any rate, Wes, you have several of your old standbys with their eyes on the situation all the time unbeknownst to the several parties, so rest assured we will take care of your little girl and your interest here until you get home.

We enjoyed hearing from you very much and am awfully sorry for the long delay in replying. As you know, Addie and I are trying to build a sawmill and we have been having quite a time. We got out on a timber limb and Dave came to our rescue. Sure saved our bacon. The sawdust is almost ready to fly. We are doing our own logging, trucking, etc., and sure have a very nice little operation. It is small but should be a good outfit. Lots of headaches. Not enough dough, few materials and poor help. An excellent combination. Should be ready to go in a couple of weeks.

Haven't seen Stub lately so have little to report from a strange Nukie standpoint. Auddie and I have been to Sac. and S. F. several times lately, but they ain't what they used to be. Have to beg for a meal or a drink. Bailey looks aghast if an inquiry comes in for a pint anymore. The bars have all raised the price and then fill her up with water, so I have almost sworn off. Good excuse to quit.

We were in Lakeview last week for a couple of days. Louie and I sneaked in an afternoon of fishing. Had very good luck although nervous in regards O. P. A. and Game Warden.

Write us when you can, Wes, and I promise to budget more time for replies in the future. Don't worry any over this end. We have the situation well in hand.

Get your end cleaned up and come home.

                                        Ken

SEPTEMBER 16, 1943 GAIL TO WES

Darling,   #12

News of David's wedding is getting hot. The date is set for October 30th, Mom and Dad's anniversary (but they didn't know it). He really sounds like he means it this time. Mother and Dad are planning to go to Phoenix for it and I am sitting around thinking of it. The mother-in-law to be gave David a $2000 family ring that she said she had always wanted Maribelle (that's her name) to have—some stuff! She is 19 and finishing her junior year at college.

Sweetheart, I got your letter of the 26th today—am glad that you are enjoying sunbathing, am just wondering if you gave gained any weight over there or do you lose it *[unreadable]* in fluid.

No, Darling, John can't swim yet, in fact it is practically fall here and the water is icy. Johnny does what he is told (when there is a *[unreadable]* to emphasize the need of any action). Today he told me that if I went to work he would leave home!

This is a deep dark secret but I'm telling you anyway. The Vets of Foreign Wars of Quincy are looking into the Iron Lung situation and hope to buy one. I think that they will put Dr. L. in charge of it because they hate Dr. B.'s innerds. We are trying to figure out where it could be set up in our hospital (just in case we get it). You should have an application from this group. I hope you sign up because they are among your strongest boosters.

All my love, Darling   Gail

SEPTEMBER 16, 1943 BOB HUDSON TO WES
(Los Angeles, California)

Dear Wes—

I got your letter the other day and I couldn't write because we didn't have any V-Mail. I had a lot of time to write you during the night on my vacation and I should have written you more letters. I caddied part of the time and swam the rest of the time. You aren't too old to count birthdays—Mom still counts hers!

I have heard quite a bit of Aussie slang in Coke a Cola ads. It's strange that one has to be away from one place to really know how lucky one is. I think Mick is lazy about writing. I don't think he likes to very much either.

Boy! I sure am proud to be the nephew of a Captain—it sure is swell.

I am a Senior over at J. B. now and I'm pretty busy with homework and trying out for the A team in football.

I'm sorry I didn't put "Uncle Wes" at the top, but I'm so used to hearing Mom call you Wes that I sort of forgot.

We haven't been having such hot weather up here where we like but it's been pretty down by Nonnie's *[Mary Louise Carr]* house but probably not as hot weather as you and the boys in your outfit have experienced.

Don't catch cold! Love,   Bob

SEPTEMBER 16, 1943 WES TO GAIL
("Paradise in the Pacific")

Gail, Dearest,   #26

This little spot of ours is truly as indicated above. Our new camp is delightful. Although temporary, we have worked hard in the two days we have been here. Yesterday I was so tired that I practically fell asleep getting to bed and couldn't manage the promised letter.

We really have tent life deluxe. The flaps are all carried out horizontally on a 24 foot pole cut from the jungle in place of the standard 18 foot pole. Instead of a 12 x 12 space with room to stand only in the center 6 x 6 area, we now have a 16 x 16 foot room, with clearance to stand throughout, and lots of fresh sea air circulating. We are wired into the hospital generator and have—believe it or not—electric lights!

We built a table around our outer pole, dug a well outside and built a wash stand. I don't believe I told you about our mosquito bars—we had to use them for about three weeks now, and they are marvelous. I cut four tall bamboo sticks and have my net fixed beautifully, with a four foot space to sit up in, in bed air mattress and all. I wove some larger cane to hold split cross pieces, etc., all very frontier-style. Also, I made a rack with poles I cut to hold my two boxes (Footlocker and homemade box).

We have folding chairs from the Red Cross and are we comfortable. Tonight we started the officer's mess and for the first time in a month actually sat down to a table and were served instead of "sweating out" the mess line for half an hour, sitting on the ground among the bugs to eat, and "sweating-out" the mess-kit wash-line. Now, all I need to make life perfect is one Gail R. Moore, wife!

Now for some very special news. Today, I am really a FLIGHT SURGEON! Hot dog! The Personnel Orders came through today, and guess when they were dated—August 2—my birthday! Wasn't that a real present? Now I must fly four hours a month instead of one takeoff and landing a month, and I get half base pay extra (Base Pay is $200.00 for Capt.), instead of $60.00 per month. My full salary, with what you get, mess allowance, etc., will be in the neighborhood of $450.00 per month. As I have not much chance to spend any, I'll be sending some home when I get where I can. I didn't collect last month's flying pay, so will get it at the end of September. I broke open a bottle of old "Corio Special"—Australian rot-gut—and we all had a snort in celebration of the big event, then a wonderful dip in the ocean, and to mess.

Going to be lights out—have to quit—All my love, Dearest—

                                             Wes

SEPTEMBER 17, 1943 GAIL TO WES

Sweetheart,   #13

I got up at six fifteen this AM and climbed out through the frost and up to Nina Brown's where I had a swell ham and egg breakfast and we built a parachute out of a big red bandana and tied the papers to it. Then we went out to the airport and to a 1½ hour ride in the little T Craft. We tried to find the camp where the hunters were and located some smoke up by Squaw Peak so we shoved the papers overboard. Our parachute worked out swell but we don't know whether the hunters found the parcel or not. It was great sport but I'm 'fraid we heckled some hunters that weren't expecting us too. We skimmed along the treetops and if we didn't scare the deer into the open, we certainly must have made them run for cover. I sort of expected to look like some of these flying fortresses do when they come home with their tail feathers pretty well peppered. I wouldn't have blamed them if they had sent a shot up to scare us on home.

We went over a couple of fires—one at Mohawk, behind the Mohawk Tavern and another at Portola—it was going up the slope just north of Portola. Started in someone's backyard. When we got back home, we had a visit from a couple of P39's and did they give our little airport a buzzing! Lee Jorganson was coming in to land just as they came barging down the field—one wasn't more than 10 feet off the ground. I don't know whether Lee saw the planes or whether he saw the dust whirling around, but he cut loose over the mill and promptly got out of the way.

Guess I'd better fold this up for tonight Sweetheart and get to CAP. I missed last meeting— was laying linoleum, and they have a new ruling about missed meetings. Before I forget it, if they get the Iron Lung, I guess it goes to the County, because it is the logical place for it—I'm very disappointed—Bye now, Darling!

Bill Bailey and I are getting together a package to send you. I'm to mail it at noon. It is composed of a big package of Velvet inside of which is a little sample of Mountain Dew which "Doctor" Bill thought you might need. 'Course it displaces a little tobacco which you will find in the tobacco pouch—a present from Bill. He put in some gum, too, to fill up the spaces. If you don't want the gum, no doubt it will be an easy article to get rid of.

The Smiths seem to be well settled and enjoying the house. The furnace works and every-thing is rosy. Ray seems well pleased—he says when he gets in the doghouse, he can go hide and not be found for at least 10 minutes, instead of being stumbled over.

I gave Ken your new address to write you soon. I bought him a pint of Canadian Club (which I had to climb back in Bailey's darkest shelves to find) for helping me out with my troubles and being my business advisor. He has really been swell.

Dad has several fires caused by careless hunters and he was declaring he'd have them out fighting them pretty soon. Fred Russell has gotten in on quite a bit of scouting which pleases him no end. Stu hasn't gotten his Waco in condition to fly for the F. S. yet, and he's been dickering for a new plane.

It's almost noon, Honey, and I have to get down to the P. O. and get that package off to you so it will get there by Christmas.

All my love, forever and ever. Yours,   Gail

SEPTEMBER 19, 1943 WES TO GAIL
(American Red Cross Stationery)

Dearest Darling—   #27

I have been so busy I couldn't write. The heat has been something terrific the last four days so that every effort is accompanied by profuse sweating. I have been away from our camp by the sea, inland, where it <u>really</u> is hot and dusty.

I flew over to see Julian and stayed overnight there. We had a grand visit, and a few drinks, etc. He seems to have a wonderful job as sort of adjutant—can't tell you where or what. He is a 1st Lt., with the manner of a Colonel. You know old Julian. He's quite a smoothie. I met all sorts of Majors and Colonels—even met a Brigadier General. I was so surprised I forgot to salute him! But then, no one bothers much about saluting, anyway, I saluted belatedly.

The trip was only about ¾ hr. in a transport, and except for the takeoff and landing, I flew all the way. Coming back, it was broken clouds over some hills, and I went up through them, and was "on instruments" for about five minutes! Some thrill. Those old things are like trucks on the controls—for much of a banked turn, it requires two hands on the wheel and plenty of rudder pressure. I can't mention the type of aircraft, but it was what Dinty flew regularly before going to Army work.

Julian looks fine and has lost some weight. He said while at OCS in Florida he went down to 155—now I guess he's about 175, but good and firm.

It really felt good to get back to camp and the ocean yesterday evening. I was driving a jeep around near the airport and was just black with dust—my face looked like a native's. I certainly was glad I had my summer flying glasses.

I tried to do some washing today, and by the time I had boiled the stuff up for an hour in GI soap, I was so exhausted from feeding the fire and stirring the mess around, and so wringing wet, I gave up and just flopped into the ocean. I haven't had the heart to go back to it today, so it's just sitting there. Hope it all rots and I can throw it away! I'd sure give a thousand dollars for a washing machine right now! We wash in 50 gallon gas barrels cut in half lengthwise—so, set on a couple of green limbs on the sand with a fire beneath—haul well water in buckets to fill it. What a job in the heat!

Tojo makes a "milk run" nearly every night—we had seven red alerts three nights ago, but they never unload anything. It's chiefly a nuisance. We got quite a kick out of it all, at first, but now it's just a damn nuisance turning lights on and off.

Van and I have a whole tent to ourselves now as Al and George (the dentist) are off on Detached Service. I'm afraid we will be leaving our Paradise on the Pacific before long to hotter climates away from the welcome ocean breeze—then we really will be hot.

I received a couple of roaters [Rotary Rooters] and your letter #6 (September 4th). I'll be glad when you start getting letters from me again, Darling, so you won't sound so blue. I love you, Dearest, and wish I could be with you to cheer you up with a few smiles—and some other things—

I'm sorry you've had so much trouble about the house. If Ray doesn't like the floors, tell him ours are sand and dirt with plenty of centipedes, ants, spiders and tarantulas to relieve the monotony. Also, there isn't a Bendix in the place!

Well, Sweet, no more now. I love you heaps—for keeps

Your Wes

SEPTEMBER 19, 1943 WES TO GAIL
(Red Cross Stationery)

Sweetheart—   #28

I am lining up your letters and reading from August 18th on so thought I would write again this afternoon and answer some questions. I have a total of 28 letters from you, as follows. June 29, July 1, 6, 9, 11, 15,* 19, 22, 24, 27, 29, 31, August 2, 4, 5,* 9, 11, 13, 15, 16, 18, 20, 22,* 26, 28,* 31, September 2, and 4. I guess that there are four missing, where I marked the *—probably airmail, which is coming by boat.

I did meet Julian's Lt. Bartholomew, and a very nice young lady. I forgot to tell you about that. We went out to the hospital and visited her and another one, the gal friend of one of Julian's friends who had to work. The gal had a broken arm—Lt. Anderson—and was not awfully good looking. But it was nice to talk to a white woman for a change! We don't have any such luxuries as nurses where we are! Anyway, I presume that Julian is always talking round about ways home from the kidding they gave him about "short cuts." He must be interested because he said he doesn't phone her when he goes to see her anymore, but only when he is not going to call on her! She's short and blonde, and rather pretty. I'm afraid he would be insulted at my description, so don't broadcast it—he thinks she's about the prettiest gal around the place! Guess he must be in the stage where even the black ones (natives) begin to look white! Julian has both a jeep and a staff car at his disposal, so he really gets around. All I have is a jeep and an ambulance! (There ain't no staff cars here, anyway).

Am hoping to get the pictures soon. For Pete's sake, have Bill take one of you, Honey—for me.

I'm proud of you on doing your mission so well with CAP. Tough on CA missing his. How many hours have you? I tell everybody you have 200. Why don't you get a Commercial and Instructor's ratings, Honey? And a horsepower rating. You must have some higher horsepower ships around now, from the sound of things.

Sounds like John really is growing, requiring a size 6! Boy, I'd like to see him. Tell him to take care of all the Japs over there and I'll take care of them over here!

I'm glad Dr. is getting along well. Hope his dose of flu doesn't get him down. I read that he was getting it September 4th. Give them my best regards—and say, that, $1574.00 is marvelous. I just don't know what to say. Isn't he swell to do that for us? I am also proud that you are paying off the insurance debts. Thank you for being such a good little manager, Honey.

As far as what I want for Christmas, Dear, there's only one thing—that's you. If I can't have that, I don't know what to suggest! I have so much junk now, I'm figuring maybe I'll ship some home and throw some away. It's so hard to send candy, etc. Maybe you could send some hard candy if you pack it well; this is a request to show the postmaster—as it would get here all right. I am still looking for the cigars. I smoked one of Julian's sent by CA, and he assures me that it takes a long time for things to get here, so I'm not worried. Candy and liquor are the most sorely missed items. Oh, I know, I need another pipe—will you send me one? I have just the one, and when smoked too steadily, a pipe gets to tasting badly—ask Dave!

Thanks for starting a new number series on your letters. It helps to keep track. I keep the dates and numbers of my series written down in my writing pad, so I know. I couldn't remember them—you know me!

I started running away about the age of five. Mother put a ring on the clothesline and tied me to it and let me yell for awhile. I believe that helped—try it on John, Dear—if you can stand the noise. Tell him Daddy says he mustn't run away, but stay home and look after Mama while Daddy is away.

Well, Honey, that's all for now—and I hope the sun keeps shining for you, even if you can't see my smile, it's here all right! Like this *[drawing of a smiling sun]*.

All my love, Sweetheart—

Your own Wes

SEPTEMBER 20, 1943 Dr. MARY CARR MOORE TO WES
(Los Angeles, California)

Dearest Wesley—

It was so good to hear from you—and you have been so good about writing—which is, of course, a great comfort to me! I imagine you are being kept pretty busy and I hope you are able to stand the climate. As you see, I have changed from the typewritten to pen—as my ribbon is too faint (have to write each line over to make it clear) and I have neglected putting in a new one!

I've kept pretty busy with pupils, although no classes at Chapman—as it is still combining with Whittier.

I had a new roof put on the house, as it was badly needed. It cost $300.00, but I got an F. H. A. loan for three years, so I can handle it easily with the small payments. I may sell the house if I can find a smaller one that I like. They are hard to get, with a living room big enough for my piano! I like this place and hate to give it up—it seems like home. You remember you helped me select it?

I had a letter from Byron about a week ago—with a check for his bills. He sends me one check—I *[unreadable]* out checks for his regular bills—like *[unreadable]* Richard's *[Richard Carr Moore]* check, etc. Richard has visited me twice during the month just preceding school. He is a dear! How I wish Gail and John D. lived nearer to me!! The boys came home from Seattle looking a foot taller! Marian and Cy are well, working hard and happy. I am the same as ever; reaching seventy was not fatal!!

I will send you some clippings soon, about my birthday. Everyone, including your dear self, was very good to me!!

Love to you Darling, and all my good wishes,

Mother

SEPTEMBER 20, 1943 EDITH TO WES

Dear Wesley,

We had just about decided that we would never receive the purses when lo! On Saturday they arrived. Thanks so much. I think you are awfully thoughtful to send us something from Australia. The purse is so useful and Dave has had a fine time with his mat.

John is outside playing and Gail is working. She is going to King's for dinner. The Cofolls are there. We are trying to make plans to go to the wedding the 30th of Oct. Don't know what we will do with John if Gail goes.

Best of luck and happy landings. Can't get much news on this.

Affectionately,

Edith

SEPTEMBER 21,1943 ESTHER TO WES
(Seattle, Washington)

Dear Wes—

Your August 22nd letter arrived on Saturday. To be sure you wouldn't think Dad appreciated them very much, but he truly does. This letter was to be his but he has been terribly rushed today so maybe tomorrow there will be a lull so he can take time out to write his baby.

He went off Saturday with Bob Earnest to run his two dogs and came home with a sting on his ear which is a beaut—his ear stands out like the Yaller Kid's and added to that, he got three lengthwise scratches on his nose from some bramble bushes. I felt sorry for him but couldn't help laughing—he looked so funny. Added to that he had to dress and take me to a cocktail party, so picture it for yourself.

This cocktail party was given for the Meyers who are very close friends of young David's. Major Meyers is David's superior officer—his wife is the daughter of our very close friends, the Williams. Phil Meyer told me that David was to be married to some Texas girl early in November. He said the girl's mother had sent David a whopper of a diamond to give the girl, so guess it's all settled. Am wondering if Gail will go down to the wedding.

Am leaving here on the 4th for San Francisco and will spend some time in Los Angeles. Have written Gail trying to figure out how I might work it so I needn't spend two extra nights on the sleeper to get to Quincy. We know how you must miss her and J. D., but I bet you don't miss her any more than she does you.

We sent you two cans of tobacco today—thought it better to send two smaller cans than one large one because it will keep better. Hope they reach you in good time. We'll figure out some way of getting those ice-cubes to you. As far as the liquor is concerned, we are almost in the same boat you are. We are now permitted to buy only one pint a week and that wasn't so bad, but for the past three weeks we haven't been able to get a decent bit of Scotch or Bourbon.

Should you run across Capt. Orrie Richardson, Company K-15th Replacement Battalion— say "hello" for us. His wife is Mrs. Williams' sister and also a patient of Dad's. She is a little Honey. Capt. Richardson has been over there for way past a year.

We haven't heard from Byron for quite some time. He had been writing off and on and the last letter we had from New York said he had just gotten in from Africa and there was a possibility of his being stationed in San Francisco—he seemed to want that. He too asked for ice cubes but also some modern plumbing.

Are you playing any poker? I won a goodly sum the other night at that two card game— high low.

News from the Pacific seems fairly good. Hope it gets better and that it won't be long ere you are heading eastward.

Much love to you from us both.

Esther

P. S. I assume you got my letter telling you that we didn't sell the house after all and we are more than happy about it. Incidentally we miss your typewritten letters.

SEPTEMBER 22, 1943 GAIL TO WES

Darling—   #14

Received your letter of Sept. 2, Monday and was glad to know that you were again in Australia. Guess you are on your way again by now. Wish I could figure out where all you are going. Alene had you in New Guinea several times by our figuring.

Sweetheart, I've been buzzing around 90 to nothing the last few days. Sunday I went on a picnic with the Metzkers and Monday had dinner with CA and the Campbells out at CA's. Yesterday Irene and I flew the Luscombe to Susanville—my physical is due. After we got over there, we found that Dr. Packwood was in Westwood and would be back about 6. So we stuck around. Dr. Burnett saw me at 2:30 and said I was OK. I got my eyes done at 6 and then we had to get a taxi to the airport ($2.50)—find someone to crank us up and scat for home so we'd get there before dark. (We did). Then we had dinner with CA and the Campbells again. The office and hospital have been awfully busy the past week—so I'll be more than happy to go up and collect Doris tonight at Portola. Irene is going up with me so I won't have to sit around the station alone.

An AT-6 just went over—it made a few passes at the field but I don't know whether it sat down or not.

Love, Gail

SEPTEMBER 23, 1943 WES TO GAIL
(APO # 713)

Dearest Little Darling—   #29

I'm going to write you a short note tonight so you won't be worried about me. Truth is I am so tired—as are most of us—I can hardly stand. Have swamped out jungle trails for 3 days, set up an aid station and a hospital (separate units) and helped dig two latrines and a good deep underground shelter near our tent. I haven't done so much manual labor in my life, and I ache so in the mornings I can hardly get up. However, rising frequently during the night, one doesn't even notice an ache.

We were kind of short of facilities on first getting set up here and more or less surprised by a few little matters during the first night, but are very happy and well taken care of now. There is no need for apprehension as far as mosquitoes, spiders, bugs, and other things are concerned. You should see the spiders—they run from one to _four_ inches in diameter, and scorpions about two to three inches long. Of course, we have just cut areas out of the thick jungle for tents, etc, and good old mother earth for a floor, so the bugs really visit us. Oh, and there are some sort of black ants about an inch long, which, when you are swamping out a trail, land on you and really bite—boy do they hurt! I'm scratched and bitten all over my hands, arms and chest—you can't bear to work with a shirt on, and even stripped, you sweat like being under a shower. (English pretty poor—too tired to care!) This is really roughing it, and if I don't develop a little muscle, I'll really be surprised.

Well, Honey forgive me for such a delay and so short a letter. I love you with all of me, and will try to do better by you.

Goodnight, Sweet—

Wes

SEPTEMBER 24, 1943 GAIL TO WES

zZ Dearest Wes,   #15

John started this letter with the zZ's, but he is in bed now so I can go ahead as planned. I got your letter of Sept. 9th and was glad to see it in the box! I hadn't gotten one for several days and I've just been haunting that post office.

Sounds as if your are absorbing quite a bit of sunshine. I can just imaging what the haircut looks like. Maybe you'd better borrow some of that on your upper lip to protect the modesty of your pate!

Doris' train was 18 hours late yesterday but she wired me from Salt Lake that it was 8 hours late, so I didn't even get up there until 5 AM—I only had 5 hours to wait so that wasn't quite as bad as waiting the full 12 hours. I took her up to the hospital and she met everyone and looked around. She stayed with me last night and tonight we are going up to tuck her away in the big room in the back. She hasn't kicked about anything yet, so maybe she will stay awhile, I hope. She really came at the right time. Our nine-bed hospital has 11 patients and a baby with another maternity ready to bounce in at any time. There is one old Swede upstairs in the little room right next to Doris. He's quite a fellow. Dr. enjoyed working on him—he cut his knee with a saw and had to have a barrel of stitches in it. Dr. says he is one of the real lumberjacks. I watched his face while Dr. took the stitches and he didn't even make a face, just sat there and told us about the one that he had taken three stitches in himself. He said that he had borrowed the thread from the cook and sewed it up himself. When I asked him why he only took three stitches in it (the scar was two inches long), he said that was all of the thread that the cook had around. I think that he must have come in to you—he said that the next day they brought him in to the Doctor and that the Doctor said that he couldn't improve on the job. It seems to me that I heard you tell that story.

The loggers have really been taking a beating this last week. We have a little four year old in with a fractured skull. He was sticking his head through one of those big logging truck tires and the thing fell over and banged his head against the pavement. The poor little thing is a sight, however, he hadn't had any temp and has been conscious all of the time and seems to be getting along pretty well. They sent us a broken hip from Portola. Dr. X-rayed it and sent it back to McKnight (their Xray equipment seemed to be haywire). He tried to get Haig to take it to Sacramento, but he couldn't get a bed in the hospital. The patient is Mrs. Palmer's sister and she is pretty old, a little balmy and has a nasty break, just below the acetabulum and the femur is practically straight up and down. Well, I guess she is Mac's worry now. By the way, Mac is going to be the only one left in Portola about next week. The woman, Dr. Wright, is going into the Army and so is Lohenberg. Mac hasn't been well either—overworked.

Tomorrow night the gang is putting on a housewarming for the Ray Smith's. Ken called me up and wanted me to go with them to take them out to dinner and while we are out the house will be overrun by the crowd. The purpose, I believe, is to pull Laura out of her shell and get into the swing of things. They seem to think that Ray would enjoy life better if his wife would get out and go with the rest of the folks.

You couldn't guess who dropped in on us last evening. No other than James Keller. He right away fast hounded Dr. for a prescription and Dr. is definitely suspicious of him. He's had a couple of crackups—A 20 and P40. He seems to be a bit more balmy than in the good old days. He's getting a few days leave and expects to come out in your territory some of these days. Mother invited him to dinner and he certainly stowed the roast lamb away. I hate to think that Dr. is right, and if he is, I don't see how the Army missed that in a 64. He says that he has about 2800 hours now.

Well, Darling, I'll let you mull this choice little bit of news over and the next time I write I'll probably have more to tell you. I certainly miss you, my love, and do my bit of praying every night for you.

Love Gail

SEPTEMBER 25, 1943 WESTERN UNION WES TO GAIL

DEAREST ALL SAFE WELL RECEIVED LETTERS AND CABLE CHRIS HERE JULIAN NEAR PAY DORIS FARE LOVE==JOHN W. MOORE

SEPTEMBER 25, 1943 WES TO GAIL
(APO 3713 VIA 3503)

Darling—   #30

Everything got wet yesterday. We had a torrential tropical rain which just about inundated us. Some of your letters got wet and a lot of my brand new clean clothes, bed, etc. Fortunately my B-4 bag was in a dry place. I don't know what all I told you in my last letter about this jungle. It's wonderful. Van and I took a walk today and just about ate ourselves sick on fresh coconuts, coconut milk, and fresh bananas right off the tree, with a little paw-paw to fill in. I'm about worn out cutting out brush with a machete, setting up the hospital, etc. Guess I mentioned all that, now I recall.

I bought a Jap rifle for five pounds, in pretty fair shape. It has some rust spots on the outside of the barrel which I have been cleaning up in the evenings. The bore is in quite good shape. It is a long thing—about 4 feet long, a 25 caliber. I got 14 rounds for it but think it may accommodate some of our own shells. When I get some place where I can mail it, I'll try to send it on home for a souvenir.

You'll note the APO is 713 via 503—Don't know exactly, yet, which will reach. Mail has been plenty scarce, although I did get a Rotary Rooter today. Have your Aug. 30 airmail, Sept. 6 and 8 V-Mail which came since we have been here. The hospital and home town news is all very interesting—Blank doesn't sound so hot as a surgeon—or obstetrician! Am glad you are keeping watch over D. F. However, I don't want you tied down to that hospital, Honey. There's no good reason for you to work yourself so hard there.

Give my regards to Doris, and tell her I'm glad she is there. Chris came in today, although I haven't seen him. We are scattered throughout the jungle so that we don't see other units very often.

I haven't had a bath of any sort in a week—different from 503—and am getting so I can hardly stand my own stench—if you can believe that! I heard there was a creek a few miles away. Someday I'll take time off and go hunt for it. I used to change my socks every day, but am afraid I'll run out if I keep it up. I have a bundle of laundry that would take 3 ½ trips in the Bendix to get clean! However, one of these days there's going to be a real washing done!

I'm getting a large kick out of all this, as are 99% of the boys. And, say, your picture is sure seeing some strange sights! Wish I had the real gal, Honey. I'm afraid, though, I'd have to sleep through the first night of my vacation, these days! (No oysters up here!)

Sweetheart, in regard to possibilities of Dr. B. going out of the picture, try to get some other Dr. there. Dr. Fletcher—and keep Dr. B. on salary, or else sell him the whole shootin' match for $50,000.00 (Fifty thousand dollars)—no less. Then let him Jew you down to $40,000.00 but no lower. It will be worth all of that the first few years after the war, before the depression hits, and I think he's smart enough to know it. Then, if you or any of the family get sick, go to Dr. McKnight! Awful way to talk, but I feel just as you do about him. Don't get the idea I want to sell out after the war. I don't, but if something happens to Dr. L., I don't know what sort of practice I'll have left. Talk this matter over with Dr. L. and also Ken and Del.

I'm quite interested in Dr's *[Dr. B.]* method of handling Louise Arthur's enterostomy. Let me know how she comes along. She's a sweet old cookie, ain't she, Honey, and you're pretty good at acting as a surgical nurse by now, by the sound of your experiences. Do you like it? I do. And I love you, more'n anything in the world.

Don't worry about me—or any of us—as, although the life is rugged, we are all perfectly safe and having a swell time. Only thing is, it's too hot to feel like drinking much. Only about one shot of rum before supper is all I can stand. I don't know how people can drink in the tropics-and we sure are in 'em.

Enough for tonight, Sweet. All my love, always—

Wes

SEPTEMBER 27, 1943 GAIL TO WES

My Darling   #16

Received your wire Sat and can't tell you how swell it was to have it. Doris was almost as thrilled is if it were a wire from Chris. We've had you in all kinds of scrapes. Wish you could tell us what you've been doing!

The party for the Smiths Saturday was dinger. We didn't get to dinner until 9 o'clock 'cause the war bond parade and auction held us up. They were auctioning hams, bottles of whiskey, etc. CA paid $65.00 for a ham. Tom Beale paid $7,000.00 for 2 boxes of Julian's shot gun shells (CA brought them down—Julian knew nothing about that) 'course all that money was put into war bonds and would have gone into them anyway, but it made the drive more spectacular and interesting. They raised $26,000.00 and they still have 4 days to raise $55,000.00, which is lacking at the moment.

Last night Doris and Johnny and I were riding around and happened by the airport. We got there in time to see Draper's new hangar burning down and the Cub trainer with it. 'Course no part of it was insured. Luckily it didn't spread to any of the other hangars. Our new mechanic was welding a landing gear (inside the hangar) and poof it went!

Well, Darling, have to get ready to go to the office. We have 18 patients in your 9 bed hospital.

All my love,

Gail

SEPTEMBER 28, 1943 WES TO GAIL

Honey—   #31

I'm sorry, I have skipped you for 3 days. We've been terribly busy. I guess I mentioned that we had to move camp a short distance. On top of our confusion we've had a couple of inspectors on our necks— 'nough said—anyway, when we get set up, we are really going to have the show place. I've got a pretty free hand in setting up my hospital and aid station and am working in all the good ideas I've picked up around the country. I wish you could be able to see what it looks like. I can't even tell you how big it will be—but we are really going to be something. I'm very pleased—so long as I get to run things my own way for awhile.

I'm not feeling like writing much, I'm so tired from swinging a machete and brush hook all day. I find that I get more work out of my boys than anyone else in the outfit by getting in and working right with them, and it's good for me, too.

Sweetheart, we haven't had any mail for nearly a week, so that it's doubly hard to think of what to say. So much to tell of great interest, if I only could.

All my love, Sweet—Be good and don't work too hard—   Your own Wes

SEPTEMBER 29, 1943 V-MAIL GAIL TO WES

My Darling—

Congratulations upon beginning your career as a Flight Surgeon! Was thrilled with the news and I know that you were too. That certainly was a grand birthday gift. I received your letter of the 18th today and I'm glad your new home seems so comfortable. At least for awhile you have been busy getting organized, I was amazed that you had nothing to say about the card from the bank and the amount upon it—weren't you interested?

Dad has had his maintainer out on the airport grading the orchard and he's put up a Blondie and a Dagwood—those beautiful forest brown numbers, which are quite an addition.

Yesterday a couple of P39's let down their wheels and touched the ground but didn't slow down very much. David said he could set one down out there so I guess he'll have to do the pioneering.

Doris seems to be getting along OK and as far as I know, she likes it. She hasn't said much one way or another. Maybe when Chris' letters start coming here, she will like it better.

Am at the office now, and things are rolling along pretty smoothly. We've cleaned house and only have 5 patients now so things aren't so tough. Everyone says hello and good luck to you.

Am going to fold up now and do some ironing, so bye my Sweet,

with all my love,   Gail

OCTOBER 1, 1943 GAIL TO WES

Sweetheart—   #17

I've been busier than any ten people in town today—Started the day at 6 o'clock, when Floyd Shaw and I went out and wrang the T Craft out. I was giving Floyd some dual—1hr and 45 minutes—dueling all the time. This afternoon I had a busy day with the books at the office and about 5 o'clock had to go up to the house and hoe the water heater out—some fun. Got home at 7, had a snack and now have to get ready to go to CAP. Bill's druggist walked out, so he won't be there tonight. George is taking over.

I got the pictures of you taken in Australia, and Honey! They are swell! I'm going to try to get one enlarged. You look like you have gained more weight. I certainly hope so!

Margarite and Dr. are moving back to Cromberg tomorrow and are going to commute. When the weather gets too bad they will stay here in the hospital. I am taking the night office hours with Dr. B. Some fun!

Doris is having a fit 'cause she hasn't heard from Chris and she wants to know if he is all right. For heaven's sake, tell him to write often. I think she will be satisfied then.

Yesterday Ruth took Doris and Johnny and me to see the mill and she enjoyed that. She is writing to Chris at APO #503—Hope that is right.

We are not going to be able to go to David's wedding because they are going to be married in Texas. Hope everything works out all right. He seems to be real happy about the whole affair and I think, at last, he is really in love.

All my love, my Darling —

your Gail

OCTOBER 3, 1943 GAIL TO WES

My Darling,   #18

I haven't had a letter for eight days now. Haunting the Post Office doesn't seem to do any good. I guess you have been on the move again. We have all been wondering whether the sea breeze hit you from the North or South. The swimming sounds elegant. Wish that I could partake of a little of it. Would like to take a squint at the jungle too, 'cause never having seen one, it would be quite a revelation to me.

When the pictures of you came, Honey, Johnny wanted to know if you were going to bring that bear home for him to hold. He spends most of his time out in the Golden Glow beating bears out. He thinks that is wonderful fun. He is growing so fast now, Sweetheart, and he is really quite a bit easier to manage—I guess because I manage to bribe him. He'll do anything if he thinks that he can go riding.

Today I can put 5 hours and a half down in my logbook. I got up at 6 this morning and Floyd and I went out and shot landings and then went up and heckled some hunters, then swooped down on Dr. and Margarite, dodging the cottonwoods around Ruth's ranch. We had the cows and sheep running so we thought that we had better get out of there before the farmers came out and took a shot at us for running the stock. It was loads of fun though. When we got back, CA and Irene were going to Susanville so we tagged along, went into town and had lunch and came on back home. Pretty cheap time, if you ask me. Hope that Floyd doesn't have to relearn all the things that I have told him—'course I could be wrong! And how!

Later: to be exact, 9:45 PM and Doris, John D. and I just came home from the show—"My Friend Flikka." John did pretty well for awhile, but when he got tired it was horrible. He couldn't get comfortable, so he squirmed and crawled and fell until I thought that I would go crazy. When I shushed him for talking out loud and told him that people didn't talk out loud in the show, he came back with, "But I do!" Well, anyway, that's over and I won't take him again very soon. I thought that he would like the horse picture, but I guess I didn't explain it enough.

Everyone has gone to bed, so I guess that I'd better quit pounding this thing until tomorrow morning. Good night my Sweetheart, I hope that your canopy keeps the bugs out.

Monday morning—Ned Bedell has been here already this morning and I guess the story that I gave you about Hersh was all wet. Ned says that one or two of the four motors went out and that before they could get the thing righted (they were taking off at night) they had hit the ground. Three out of the five crew members were killed and six or seven of the Japs.

Esther is taking her annual trip South starting today, and I guess that she will be in S. F. this weekend. Ruth has been trying to get me to go down with her Friday—she wanted company so badly that she even said she would pay all of my expenses. She is going to see Bob who is at San Raphael Military Academy. Being as it is Dr. and Margarite's weekend on, maybe I'll go on down and see Esther. I can pay my way, Darling. I wouldn't think of letting Ruth do it!

By the way—the loans on the insurance policies are all paid up. Isn't that something? Pretty soon I'll be able to save something when I get some of the debts paid up. I will feel a lot better when people stop sending little notes that there is so much interest due on this and that. Don't you think that is a good idea? Seems to me that when that income tax is made out that the Moores aren't going to have anything left. I don't know whether I'd better worry about that or leave that up to you. I have been waiting for a letter from the "U. S. something or other" to come in any day!

Gee, Honey, I'm certainly glad that you decided to smoke your cigarettes. I'd hate to have any colored stepchildren way over there on the other side of the world. Just think, I might not ever get to see them!

I hope there is a letter in the P. O. All my love, Honey,

Gail

OCTOBER 4, 1943 WES TO GAIL

Darling—   #32

When I said there might be a three or four week break in the mail, I believe I got twice as many letters off to you as I have during the past 2 or 3 weeks. Tonight is the first opportunity I've had to sit comfortably at a table with a decent (electric) light in a long, long time. We have worked hard fixing our tent. It is all framed with palm logs and latticed with bamboo, and we have a swell clothes rack and trunk rack rigged up with bamboo, freshly cut from the forest. All this is done in spare time—oh, also, a wash rack and shower arrangement. Mainly, I have been working very hard on my hospital setup. It's been a "from the ground up" job. We've made patient's charts and I've tried to drum into the boys' heads a few simple nursing procedures—and that really is a job. We have our Xray set up and operating, and I just finished putting on a cast this evening.

The first week we were doing the hard work, we were just worn out, but now, I can swing an axe or a machete all day and not feel too tired. It's a matter of learning not to work too fast, and of taking salt tablets in proportion to the amount of sweating. Bathing has been a problem and I went for four or five days at a time without washing more than my hands, and no clothing change for a week. The stuff really began to stink. I collected 26 pairs of dirty sox, 5 shirts, 3 khakis, 6 underwear, 1 PJ's, 6 towels—all so filthy they'll never be clean again. I've hired one of the boys to wash the stuff because I absolutely haven't enough time.

I got your No. 10 letter yesterday. First letter in quite awhile. We hope to get a bunch of mail in a day or so, and will be happy.

Speaking of my moustache, I had to get busy and trim it to keep it out of my teeth, it got so long. It's neat again, now, for awhile.

We are having a bad time on packages, aren't we, Dearest? You don't get mine and I don't get yours! I heard of one fellow up here who received a package. Xmas which had been mailed the preceding February. So I'm still hoping to see the cigars some day. The mail service is really being improved, though, and I understand that they are going to fly all soldier's mail, whether airmail, V-Mail, or otherwise—so if that goes through, you can start writing airmail again.

You will know by now that I am about 400 miles from Julian. I expect to go to where he is in the next few days on business, and also to get in some flying time. I'm still short 4 ½ hours. All travel in this area is by air, and there is uncertainty about mail, etc. because of weather and the amount of freight and passengers that must be hauled.

Well, Dearest, say hello to Johnny. I'm glad to know he is reading to his mamma instead of vice versa. Give him a big kiss from Daddy—my love to the family. Tell Katherine I'll write her soon in answer to her second letter.

All my love, Darling—

Wes

OCTOBER 5, 1943 GAIL TO WES

Hi Sweetheart,   # 18

I got a letter today and I'm living again. Please, Honey don't pay any attention to my moanings and groanings—you know they don't last so long. I really didn't mean to get them into a letter, but somehow they just seem to crop up.

The letter that I got today was #27, written on Sept. 19. It said that you might be going to hotter climes, but from the description of the heat there, I couldn't even guess where it might be hotter unless you are going into the middle of New Guinea.

CA was awfully glad to hear that you had seen Julian and that he was OK because he said that he hadn't heard from him for about six weeks.

Your letter tickled me—I wondered if your mouth flew open when you saw all the stars on the General's shoulder. So they have the old DC-3's running loose over the jungle. I never will forget the day that Dinty tried to take the chimney with him back to Los Angeles, when we were down at Balboa. If those things are like trucks on the controls, they must be something like Dicky's Porterfield. That thing really is like a truck!

Doris is really eating up your letters, Sweetheart. It gives her a little inkling of what is going on over there, but if she doesn't get a letter from Chris pretty soon I'm afraid that she will go on home. She is slowly getting acquainted and tonight she is going out to the show with Doris Carter Ward and Thursday morning I am going to take her and Margarite for a ride in the Luscombe. What Doris wants more than anything else though, is a letter from her old man. She seems to have made her room real comfortable and is more or less happy about her surroundings—'course that may not be the way Chris hears it. She is writing to APO 503 despite the fact that she has not heard that that is his #. When you said in your wire that he was there, we decided that the APO #'s would be the same.

Yesterday, we had a visitor—a four-motored baby that came right down over the tops to say hello. It was a beautiful sight. It was the first 4 motor deal that we have ever had come right down to the front door. I wouldn't have been a bit surprised to see it land if the Forest Service hadn't had the whole lower end of the field plowed up. It was a split tail deal— either a 24 or 25, I can't tell them apart. I'd certainly like to know just what the dickens they were doing down here and if anyone from Quincy was aboard. The 39's have left me alone lately and I haven't had to quit work and run out in the street to see just what they were doing. That is agony to have them zooming overhead and here I sit in here pounding away at this darn noiseless or trying to get more files into that darn crowded filing case and sawing my fingers with every new one I try to get in.

By the way—I'm going to clean it out one of these days. Right now I am up at the office assisting Dr. B.! I have spent the day up here and now I know how you used to feel when you would gobble your dinner and have to rush back down here at 7. Gee, I'd sure like to get back into my slacks at 5 o'clock and call it a day. I guess that it will be every evening for the duration so, Honey, hurry up and clean things up over there and come home, will you? Really, Sweet, I'm not griping. I don't mind it so much, but golly, I sure do miss you!

Ruth is going to the city Friday and I guess that I will go with her over the weekend. Esther will be there, I think, and maybe I can take her to lunch, or something. I'll catch up on what has been going on up in Seattle and how everyone is. Ruth is going down to see Bobby. I guess that he is getting pretty homesick about now. Ruth got a letter from you today and I let her read the one from you. Everyone is getting quite a kick out of your letters and think that they are very interesting. I can't wait to read that part about your floors to Ray Smith. I think that they are really going to be pretty good tenants, and they seem to like the house lots. Ray says that when you come home he is just going to buy the house instead of moving again.

Well, the lights are due to go out and Dr. B. is going down to do an autopsy and then to the show—he can always make the show.

Love,

Gail

OCTOBER 6, 1943 CA KING TO WES

Dear Wes,

Things are moving along toward the close of the season and it has been a struggle this year. Glad to report that the hospital seems to be running pretty smoothly and Gail is devoting quite a lot of her time to it.

The airport is showing improvement. Dave is Chairman of the Committee and getting results. We even have two Chick Sales out there now.

I envy you sitting at the controls of a DC-3. Guess I will have to stay with the Silvaire for awhile. I still think it will snap roll better than a DC-3.

Regards,

CA

OCTOBER 7, 1943 J. C. MOORE, M. D. TO WES
(Seattle, Washington)

Dear Wes,

I suppose you are by this time in the thick of things and are becoming accustomed to the climate and the liquor.

At present I am a bachelor as Esther left for California on the 4th of October. I expect to go to Eastern Oregon for some pheasant shooting about the 16th of the month.

Under separate cover we have sent you some smoking tobacco which I hope you will receive in time for Christmas.

We enjoyed getting your letters and hope you will write often, as I am interested in what your duties are, etc. We hear from Gail occasionally. She seems to be a pretty busy girl, what with her civic duties and looking after the hospital. We doctors here are pretty busy owing to the number who have gone into service and the influx of new people.

Hope you are enjoying good health and have comfortable living quarters, etc.

Affectionately yours,   Dad.

P. S. Thil says to tell you she is still on the job and wants to be remembered to you.

OCTOBER 7, 1943 GAIL TO WES

My Darling—   #18

We are at the office again—Dr. B. and I. It's pretty slow tonight so he's been giving me a lecture on Syphilis. He's busy with a contract now.

I took Doris and Margarite up today and was it windy. We bounced all over the sky. Marg got a little sick but Doris really enjoyed it. We went up over the burn—Mt. Hough is burning off again. It started at Oakland Camp again, on the railroad, and is now having a swell time in the timber that was left there. CA was worried to death that it would get into his logging area, but so far it has missed.

I guess I forgot to tell you that Katherine gave the "flying Moores" a book, "Take Her Up Alone Mister" which is just about like following David through Primary, Basic, Advanced and it is really very interesting. I'm saving it for our library because it will be a swell book to keep.

I guess Ruth and I will take off for S. F. about 8 in the morning. She can hardly wait to see Bob. Wish you were going to be there Sweetheart. It will be very dreary there without you.

All my love forever
                                        Gail

OCTOBER 8, 1943 WES TO GAIL

Dearest Darling—   #33

Another four days before I get to you. Sweetheart, I hope my mail is getting through to you better than yours to me. I haven't had a letter for nearly a week, and I know there must be plenty on the way. It's hard not to hear from you, but so good when the letters do come.

The hospital has been lots of work but some very favorable comments from a Lt. Col. Flight Surgeon yesterday. My boys have been very faithful to me and really have done wonders with a few tents. They are keeping the records in apple pie order, and everything else accordingly. In addition to this very absorbing and time consuming duty, I have been busy chasing down aircraft accident data for my reports, as I have several units under my wing. Then, too, I've had to get in a lot of flying, and that always involves considerable sitting at the strip waiting for the flights. I need to have 12 hours for August, September and October, and have only 6 hours. Yesterday I had the swellest ride ever, in one like Dinty's (before)—we flew 2 feet above the ground, 185 mph, mile after mile, and I'm here to tell you that's a thrill. I had a front seat (copilot) for the whole show!

We have a new CO who is a peach, and I get along swell with him, except that he is too fond of poker, and the hours are sometimes a little late for me. I like to hit the hay about 8, and 1 or 2 AM is rugged for me! However, I've held my own pretty well, only about 3 pounds (L3) down in a couple of weeks.

I sent $150.00 to you today. It will be several days before it gets on the wire, but you probably will receive it before this letter at that. Next month should be better, as I only collected September pay and August flying pay this month and should have Oct. pay + Sept & Oct. pay next month $100.00 per mo. flying pay). We spend surprisingly little, chiefly owing to the fact that there is absolutely nothing to purchase, except, perhaps an occasional trophy from the Aussies—and poker.

There are wild boars, kangaroo rats, snakes and myriad insects hereabouts; the boars and snakes occasionally parade through the tent and the insects are thick. It's a great life, but all in all, we are fairly comfortable.

I haven't gotten down to see Julian again as yet, but hope to in another week. Have been too tied up to get away for more than an occasional afternoon.

I miss you lots, Darling and am so interested in Johnny's growing up. I had a lovely letter from Mom several days ago with a picture of Johnny on Lee's lawn, and he looks so different. Also, the picture of you and me in front of Bailey's came—it's awfully cute. Darling, please send me pictures of you and John whenever you can. They help a lot. I love you so, and it's so wonderful to see a picture of you now and then.

I hope a regular mail will be in force soon, so letters will come more regularly.

Be good my sweet—all my love, and loads of it—your own—always,

Wes

OCTOBER 11, 1943 GAIL TO WES

Sweetheart—   #21

It is now 9 o'clock and I am up at the office. Dr. B. and I just finished opening up a couple of infections. This gal tonight was a bigger baby than I was up at Great Falls with that little number on my leg. She wasn't going to let us do it.

I got your #28 and 29 Friday morning before Ruth and I got started for S. F. Gee Honey, I thought that you weren't going to be right in the middle of it, but I guess that I certainly thought in the wrong direction. From the sound of things, you are sitting in the kettle. Everyone has been very interested in your letters and Esther asked me to make carbon copies of them and send them to the relatives.

Now, I'll tell you about our trip. We started out from here in a rainstorm about 9 o'clock. When we got to San Raphael about 3:30 PM we found that Bobbie was on restrictions and couldn't come out of the dorm because some boys had messed up another boy's room and they wouldn't confess. So, to make a long story short, Bobbie stayed in the whole weekend and Ruth stayed over there with him most of the time.

Saturday morning I went up to Esther's hotel and we went out to breakfast. Then did some mighty fast shopping. Dr. B. and Aunt Dora met us and we went over to the Persian room for lunch, then we raced for the train so that we could get Esther on it and headed for Los Angeles. On the way back Aunt Dora and Dr. B. and I had a flat tire (at 3rd and Market. What fun!) We passed about an hour and a half sitting there by the curb having people honking, swearing and hitting us. Also picked up a couple of drunken sailors that had just gotten to town and they insisted that they were going to fix the tire. Poor Aunt Dora didn't want to hurt their feelings but at the same time, she didn't figure that they were competent enough to do the tire any good either.

Aunt Dora dropped us at the *[unreadable]* and then Betty and I went out to dinner and to a show. Sunday, Ruth and I spent at San Raphael with Bobbie—on the front lawn. While we were sitting there who do you think sat down across from us? Dorothy Brown. Howard and Dorothy's oldest son is going there too. We had quite a chat and finally we all went down to the parade grounds to watch the boys doing their stuff and it was really thrilling.

Bob is going quite well and he likes it. He was a little upset, however, when he couldn't get off this weekend.

Oh I forgot, Dorothy said that from all indications, Fred Foote would be here at Christmas time. That was good news.

My Darling, I hope that you can make head and tails to this letter. I am so tired that I can't seem to hit the right keys. Wish I could stay in bed for a whole day and catch up on a little sleep.

I brought Johnny a little red wheelbarrow home from the city and does he love it. He has been playing with it all day and thinks that it is wonderful. This evening, he helped Dad haul blocks down into the basement and did he love that. His little playmate that was next door has moved and so now he is a lone goose again. He really misses Susi and I certainly hated to see Sue leave. They moved up into the house that the Bordwell's used to live in.

The latest little deal that I have to worry about is that the roots have gotten into that tile drain up at the house and plugged it up making the water back up into the basement. More fun. They were awfully good about it, though, and Ray called up Clarence to "See what the Hell this is all about" and when he found out where the tiles ran, he dug them up and pulled out the weeds. Ray is really quite a handy man around the house and I think enjoys doing those things so he doesn't crab about that. However, Darling, I think that they are about as good a renters as we could have gotten in the house.

By the way, I got one of the loans on the hospital back through the mail today. Now I guess we are only paying on the one. Isn't that wonderful?

I haven't written you since last Thursday, Sweetheart, so there is going to be a great big gap. I hope that you aren't too disappointed.

All my love my Sweet—

Gail

OCTOBER 15, 1943 GAIL TO WES

Hello my Darling   #27

I got your Oct 8th letter when I got home about 1 AM from San Francisco, California. Was I glad to see it, too. It has been over a week since I had the last one and there has been a lot of activity where I thought you were. Your account of flying 2 feet off the ground raises the hair on the back of my neck. I'd love to get in on something like that, but I'd be so darned scared that I don't think that I'd appreciate it.

I'm glad that your hospital has turned out so swell, Sweetheart. I'm glad that you seem to be enjoying it.

We had a very nice trip to the city—Ruth and Del and Dottie and I. I spent lots of money, Honey. I bought a Christmas present from you to me—a whole outfit. Brown suit, lizard shoes and bag, and a new hat. You would like it, I know. I certainly wish that you could see it. In case you were worried about a Christmas present for me, you can rest at ease my love, because I have it all tended to. In case you are worrying about any of the family—as far as Christmas presents are concerned—I've gotten most of them taken care of, too. Dinty is the only one who stumps me and I just haven't any idea what to send him or where to send it.

I'm glad that you enjoyed the pictures, Honey, and only wish that I could send you some more. So far, Bill hasn't gotten anything that would fit my camera—I haven't given up hope, however.

John is really a big boy now—at least so he says. Today he was out helping Mr. Flournoy edge the lawn and haul the extra sod away. He would keep trying to hitch a ride out of Papa Noy and climb up in the wheelbarrow when Papa wasn't looking. Finally Mr. Noy said for him to keep out of the wheel borrow. Johnny retorted, "If you don't give me a ride, I won't help you anymore." He really even acts intelligent once in a while now and then—Honey, it's right encouraging. Everyone thinks that he is a mighty good looking boy, too—he looks like you, Pop! He keeps Grandpa pretty busy from 5 o'clock until 8, but Grandpa is very patient and seems to enjoy crawling around on the floor and building things out of nothing.

I came home with a dinger of a cold and do I feel run down. I don't know how I caught the thing, but it doesn't help my typing out a bit. I'll be surprised if you can read this letter. You should see Del—he's so puffed up about Bobby that he'd blow up if you stuck a pin in him. Bob has almost a B average—something that he hasn't had before in his life, and has 100% in conduct, which is something his father believed an impossibility, I think. We picked Bob up Friday and took him and Buddy Bedell to S. F. That night we had dinner at Monaco's and the next night at John's Rendezvous, rare roast beef. Del had quite a job taking care of five of us females. Sunday, we went back to San Raphael and watched the parade and then came on home.

Dr. B. and I are having run-in's over the bookkeeping (I am writing this up at the office). He manages to forget to put down some of the cash intake, and every once in awhile I catch up with him. We have quite a session. He sits and sweats like the devil while I pour it on and then his feeble little argument of "I must have forgotten" comes out. He reaches in his pocket, drags out $2.50 and then promptly forgets the episode.

The Metzker-Dellinger mill is supposed to cut their first log today, but I guess they weren't able to make the grade. Del was going to open a bottle of Canadian Club if the big event occurred. Don't be surprised if you get a box of sawdust one of these days, though, 'cause they are going to be so proud of that place that they might just send you some.

Guess I'd better quit and go home, Sweetheart. My working day is over.

All my love forever and ever,

                         Gail

OCTOBER 15, 1943 ESTHER TO WES
(San Francisco, California)

Dear Wes

Am in Santa Barbara right now at the Biltmore with my sister who lost her husband recently and can't seem to find herself.

Had such a nice day with Gail in San Francisco before coming south—she brought down most of your letters—they were intensely interesting. She has promised to make some copies for Dad. Dad was to go to Oregon for his hunting but our gas has been cut so he went over to South Dakota. He is working so very hard that he couldn't go on without a vacation of some sort.

I spent some time with Marian—she has such a cute house and so artistic. Am so happy she has Cy. He is really a fine chap and they get along so beautifully.

News from both oceans are encouraging. Wouldn't it be grand if we could celebrate a peaceful Christmas.

Gail is such a Dear. I adore her; she's about the realist person I know.

Hope you get the camera so we may see what you are seeing now.

Much love and good luck to you and our buddies

Esther

OCTOBER 14, 1943 JACK? TO GAIL
[Three notes written on the same sheet of paper]

JACK ? TO GAIL

Dear Gail,

Just a very short note to say hello to you and Johnny D. Wes dropped in on us for a very pleasant and unexpected visit this afternoon and we thought it might be a good idea to drop you a "round-robin" letter. It's sure good to see Wes; he looks like a dude with his moustache and close cropped hair—not a darn bit taller, but still good to see.

Everything is going very well. We're well settled, doing the job we're supposed to do, and morale is high. Margaret writes that she and the children are fine, though she herself is getting to be a big girl now. Sure wish I could see her now.

Give my best to Johnny David, and Doris too when you see her. Best of luck to all of you—

Jack

WES TO GAIL

Dearest — Caught three fine friends together and am having them (the other two) announce their presence in their own inimitable way. This little get-together is associated with some remarkable experiences which, I am afraid, will have to wait until one of us gets home on leave—the first one will get the best chance to stretch everything the next ones might say. Will leave room below for the next—

Love Wes

JULIAN TO GAIL

Dear Gail —   Adding my bit to this is all that's needed to make this coincidence a matter of record, and it affords a chance to say hello and things. We may not be named in any headlines, but this week has made history for us and will furnish material for endless hours of conversation in years to come. Hope we don't tire you when that time comes. This could have been mailed from *[censored]* APO's. Best regards to Dave and Edith, CA, the Baldwins, all the Watsons, and if you see any of our friends — say hello.

Sincerely,   Julian

OCTOBER 15, 1943 FRIDAY GAIL TO WES

My Darling—   #23

Mom and I have been hoeing out. I have mine and Johnny's room about under control, so will take time out to tell you that I love you and also let you in on a little of the local gossip.

I got two letters from you yesterday (#'s 30 and 31), the first in a week and what a relief! By the way I just heard that the most exciting member of my husband's family is in the vicinity of Lae. If you should get around there be sure to look him up and give him a big hug for me—huh? Hope the Japs leave that portion alone from now on out. Haven't any idea how long he'll be there, but it sounded as though he might be on a permanent basis.

I'm tickled to death, Sweetheart, that you are getting to run the hospital along your own lines. That should make you feel right at home. Your letters were so cheerful that they gave me a new lease on life. Your letters are so interesting, Honey—keep up the good work. I spent last night taking excerpts from them to mail to your mother and father. (Only the parts that they should see!) You probably have written them but not in such detail and they are too good for me to be selfish enough to keep to myself.

The Jap rifle sounds very interesting—be sure the thing will shoot before you send it home 'cause I might take it out to try it and have it blow up!

Doris has gotten several letters from Chris that were sent home to Osco—and she is much more cheerful. I think she even likes it now. She has been writing to the APO's that you have given me, so I hope her letters are getting to him.

I can't imagine you not having a bath for a week or not changing socks daily come hell or high water. I bet the washing has you stopped.

Things are rolling along fairly smoothly at the hospital and I think that Dr. can hold out for some time to come. As for selling out to Dr. B., I think more of the people of Quincy than that to let such a calamity befall them. Darling, the hospital will be here waiting for you if I have to run it myself. As far as Dr. B. getting the practice—time will take care of that, and I think he will cook his own goose!

A few nights ago Floyd Shaw had several Berkeley celebrities here deer hunting. Among them were Comptroller of U. of Calif., Head of P. G. & E., a druggist, and the president of the Chamber of Commerce. Four of us War widows—Leda, Nina, Dorothy Parker and myself undertook to entertain them at dancing at the Stone House. (We gals were having a night out by ourselves but along came some swell dancers, old enough to be our Papas so we took the job.) We really had a lot of fun—good innocent fun! Tonight, Barbara and Irene and I are taking CA out to dinner for his birthday. The gals have gotten in the airport crowd to welcome him at home after dinner. We're not having dinner 'till 8 or after, so I can keep my eye on Dr. B. at the hospital.

I'm sending along in this letter a clipping from a paper that your mother sent me, a few funnies and a picture of John taken last summer at Oakland Camp. The apparently nude figure on the logs is yours truly, but it isn't as bad as it looks. I have on that yellow striped suit but it doesn't show up in the picture. Dad says I should cut that part out. It is a queer looking mess, I agree, but I thought you might get a kick out of it. Am also mailing a package of funnies today that Mother wrapped up. Hope they get to you on Sunday, if they get there at all.

All my love, my Darling   Gail

OCTOBER 17, 1943 WES TO GAIL

Dearest—

I'll leave this letter unnumbered, as I am not "at home" and don't have my number series available. I am sitting in Julian's office and it is a day after completion of a wonderful trip with Julian and his superior, during which time we saw Jack (can't mention his last name} and together wrote you a "Round Robin" letter, which is now in the mails.

Jack is well and working hard. His is at a beautiful spot of coral and palms, native villages and a mission. He says Margaret is doing well and expecting early in December—the two children are fine. We visited other beauty spots of the Southwest Pacific in a 1500-mile sweep around the area. It was an experience I shall never forget. We were treated royally everywhere, swam on coral beaches far more beautiful than Waikiki ever could be, toured native villages by jeep and came home loaded with souvenirs of native art, such as grass skirts, carved wooden objects of various sorts and woven bands worn as jewelry.

Now I am "sweating out" a ride "home," a process sometimes lengthened by weather or priorities. I am particularly anxious to get back, in the hope that there may be some mail there from you. I have been gone a week and it was about 12 days prior to that since I had any word. I am going to try to send you an E. F. M. message from time to time as I expect you are not hearing very regularly from me and might worry. I want to assure you, Darling, that there is no need for any worry on your part, as I am not in danger. Tojo's occasional milk run is of no consequence, truly.

Julian handed me the Sept. 13th and 20th Rooters which he just received in the mail and it was most enjoyable to read, in your father's Sept. 13th issue, excerpts of letters from Julian and myself as well as Cy. Most gratifying, too, is the wonderful showing Quincy has made in the 3rd War Bond Drive—particularly Tom Beale's and CA's marvelous purchases.

It's so hard for me to set down to a regular letter to the Rotary Club; tell Dave to use whatever he thinks might interest them from my letters to you.

We are in the middle of an extremely interesting phase of the War in the S. W. P. area. Undoubtedly you are hearing lots about it back home. As a matter of fact, the occasional news-cast we hear and paper we see seems to be better advised on most things than are we in the thick of it. I'll have many interesting things to tell when I see you again, Sweetheart—how wonderful it will be, to see you and John once more. I love you both so, Dearest and wish I need not be away from you.

How goes the flying? Are you managing to keep at it? Don't get tied down too much, Dear. I want you to have plenty of relaxation and not be worn out with cares of the hospital, etc.

Send me more pictures of you and John, Dear—they are wonderful. I keep the one of you and me in front of Bill B's establishment, with the reflection of your profile in the window. It's real sweet of you.

No more now. When I get back, I'll probably have lots of questions to answer in all those letters that will be waiting for me.

All my love, Darling—

Wes

OCTOBER 17, 1943 GAIL TO WES

Sweetheart,   #24

Johnny and I had dinner (duck and wild rice) with the Dellinger's and Dottie. You would have been proud of John, Darling; he was a little gentleman. After dinner we went down and picked Doris up, and we all went to the show. Johnny went to sleep, and so did my arms, but the show was good.

I forgot to tell you that we dispensed with John's nap and most of our discipline problems disappeared. We've put away the switch and get along royally. As long as there is something going on, he is a model boy. He does anything I want if I'll just let him go with me. It doesn't matter where if he can just go. He's even staying home now. We had a load of blocks that has kept him and Grandpa busy all week. I brought a little red wheelbarrow home from the city and he has made trip after trip with loads of blocks to toss in the basement—to say nothing of the leaves and other stuff he's hauled in it. You'd better plan to take him fishing when you come home 'cause he's certainly looking forward to it!

Del said that he wishes you'd been here to go duck hunting with him 'cause it was good hunting in Indian Valley—bet your mouth waters at that!!

All my love my Darling

Gail

OCTOBER 18, 1943 WES TO GAIL
[Written on stationary from Randolph Field, Texas — crossed out]

Darling—   #34

Just got back to APO 713-UNIT ONE, and was delighted to find a whole smear of letters from my Sweetheart—No's 11, 12, 14, 16, 17, 18 (on Oct. 3) and another 18, Oct. 5. What a pleasant time I had reading them. You've no idea how close it brings you to me, Darling.

I'm awfully tired from my travels, and won't write but a note now to include with the letter I wrote at Julian's place of business and didn't get mailed. "Sweating out" these unplanned trips is rough work—oli—oli—have to stop for awhile. Later—

Well, lost my train of thought! Anyhow, I'll answer your questions tomorrow, Dear. I'll check Chris about writing Doris. So glad to know she's there—and I did expostulate about the huge bank balance in my next letter. It's wonderful, Dearest.

Can't get the old brain to going much now, so more tomorrow. By the way, you haven't answered my question about "Lady Astor." Did that interest you any?

All my love, Dearest Darling—

Wes

OCTOBER 19, 1943 GAIL TO WES

Hi Darling—   #25

I'm glad we aren't starting out on the trips we did a year ago tomorrow! It's raining pitch-forks now and it has been snowing at Bucks. Swell weather for ducks! Pendleton would have seemed a "fur piece" today. Some of my crazy pilot friends are out here buzzing over the treetops in the rain. It's six o'clock and getting dark fast—hope they make it to the field!

I spent the afternoon taking old folders out of the files at the office so I could get new ones in without slicing my fingers. When I get through, there probably won't be much left. However, there are still a few old fogies around and they still get hurt.

I forgot to tell you about CA's birthday party—Irene, Barbara and I took him out to din-ner—the Devil's Elbow in the Sump—Irene provided nickels for him to play the slot ma-chine and Barbara bought his drinks and I got the dinner. He had the time of his life. Everyone was wondering what in the world went on when CA would come back from a slot machine and say, "Baby, I'm all out of nickels, please give me some more." After dinner, we went to his house and the airport crowd gathered to welcome him home and shout, "Happy Birthday." We had a lot of fun—Wish you'd been there, Sweetheart.

Guess I'd better see to dinner. All my love, Honey   Gail

OCTOBER 20, 1943 WES TO MARIAN AND CY

Dear Marian and Cy—

How are the turtle doves making out in the little love nest! Your letter of Sept. 14 came a couple of days ago, and Bob's, too. I got a letter off to him, and won't repeat what I said therein. He's a real guy to write me so well and often. I'll bet I hear from Mick soon.

So you are worried about me—well, my love, I'll tell you I'm lots safer than when I drove taxis in L. A.! Anyway, what do you think I got into this fracas for? To sit on my fat butt in some office so far from the front that it would take a week to get a letter? This is more damned fun than I've had in my life, and here you go moaning about it!

Do get some pictures of all of you off to me, and a shot of your new house. Pictures are second only to letters for pure enjoyment to us GI's.

I'm going to get an eye-lane (dark eye room) for myself at a nearby hospital, and will do all the refractions (fitting of glasses) and other eye work for a large area. I happen to be the only one capable of this work at the present, which tickles me no end, as I enjoy it immensely.

I'm proud of Mick's ambitions, and I know that, though he has bitten off a big chunk of study, he is just the man that will go through with it.

How is Butch? Please give him my love. If he will write me, I'll surely reciprocate. What do you hear from Dinty? I must write him soon. Somewhere, I have his address.

Hope you don't get poisoned on your garden products. Just imagine my little sister digging in the dirt—sounds like these movie stars who are photographed at labor on the good earth—but only for publicity! But all kidding aside, it's a grand job you are doing at home and at work. I'm proud of all my family, doing their part to help us win this war.

Thanks for ordering the Velvet for me. I'll really enjoy it and will let you know when it comes, which won't be 'til Christmas or New Year's, likely.

The V-Mail stationery hasn't come yet. Don't send more, as we are getting a ration on it and only use it for short notes when I can't afford time for real letters—airmail is faster from this side, but not from yours.

Lots of love to you all, and write again soon—

                                            Wes

Cy, get hot on that dark room, tried *[unreadable]* It's so damn damp the envelope flaps stick down and clothing is all moldy. My uniforms won't be worth much when I get back!

OCTOBER 20, 1943 WES TO BOB HUDSON

Dear Bob—

Your swell letter of Sept. 16 came a couple of days ago, and I hasten to answer it. I'm sure your penmanship is far and above mine at your age, because it certainly beats mine right now!

I can hardly realize you are a J. B. Senior. I'm proud you are going out for football— whether you make the team or not. The experience and physical discipline will always stand you in good stead. Don't call me "Uncle Wes"— I don't call you "Nephew Bob"— men can write to each other without all that red tape—so keep up the Wes stuff—I prefer it.

I had a wonderful trip last week. It was in the kind of a plane Dinty used to wish he could fly—now he can and does. I was gone for several days—6 to be exact—and was allowed to do some of the flying myself. Talk about your thrills—that was really tops! We covered a big sweep of over 1500 miles, stopping many places overnight, and I saw country more beautiful than I ever imagined existed. Coral islands are the most wonderful spots imaginable—and the natives—the gals only wear a short grass skirt, you know, and I'll have to admit, some of them are not such bad lookers!

I bought a grass skirt, a carved wooden pig, a carved sword and some woven armbands. Unfortunately, I'm not allowed to send any of these home now for military reasons, but may be able to do so later. I also have a Jap gun, and may get another—whether I can send these home is debatable, so that will have to wait until I return in person.

I wish I could tell you where I am and what interesting and exciting things happen every now and then. Maybe I can tell you that I am really right up there where the show goes on—if I can't say that, the censor will cut a large hole out of this!

Well, Bob, thanks again for your letter. Give Mickey my love and tell him I'd sure like to hear from him—

Love, from

                                                    Wes

OCTOBER 20, 1943 WES TO GAIL

Dearest Beloved Gail—   #35

Darling—two more letters from my Sweetheart yesterday and some wonderful funnies! Boy, I settled down to a pleasant hour with Jiggs, Tracy and Co. Did I say 2—I mean 2 V-Mail, #15 and 16, and airmail #13. So at long last I am really catching up.

You know, I've had bad luck since leaving Australia—I fell in the bay one day and dunked my wrist watch—now it's shot 'till I can get home. (Don't dare trust it to the mails.) I hung my dog tags on a tree while bathing and forgot 'em, and just the other day on the tour, I lost my fountain pen—dammit—now I'm borrowing Van's.

Honey, I think it is perfectly marvelous the way you are running the finances and paying off our debts, life insurance, house, etc. I'm so proud of my Darling I could just bust. And on top of that, the wonderful way you are pitching in at the hospital—I hate to have you have to work, but I am proud that you are willing to sacrifice yourself to help out with your BIG share of this War Effort. Really Darling, it is those things done by yourself, Dr. and Margarite, and Doris, that makes it possible for America to go on with home production while still releasing essential personnel to the Armed Forces. People like you make our country what it is—the finest place in this whole world. It really is, too—we can say that without kidding ourselves one bit when we just look around. If people only knew how desperately medical men are needed in places like this, and that even if they are limited service (e. g. poor eyesight) they are capable of releasing able men to the field by filling their places in Base Hospitals.

I am proud that I'm able to be out here, doing something real and active, actually knowing that my service is definitely helping in its own small way to help us win this war. I am so thankful to Dr. Lasswell for his unselfish sacrifice that I just cannot express myself. His service is every bit as useful and important, if not more so, than those of us out here.

Forgive me Darling, if I seem to run on. These are things I can talk to no one but you, my Dearest—thoughts which when expressed release a pressure inside.

Will you tell me some things, please, in your very next letter, as I am terribly interested in knowing:

1. How much do we owe A. On the hospital. B. On the house. C. Other debts, if any.
2. Are you receiving your allotment and how much.
3. How much money other than allotment have you received from me. (I sent $100.00
   4 or 5 days ago and expect to send $350.00 in about 2 weeks.)
4. When will I get more pictures of you and John!

Now—about the swell trip Julian and I made, and during which I got nearly an hour up there where I love to be, in the driver's seat—it was one like we went through at Great Falls when we weren't supposed to—remember? Talk about a thrilled GI Doctor!

I've been up since 3 AM—Someone got an insect—probably scorpion—bite and required M. S. and hospital care. When I got finished (4 AM) the cooks were at it and I had 4 (four!) beautiful fried eggs, bacon, toast and coffee! I felt so good that I couldn't go to bed, so took a jeep ride in the rain and called on a major about 5:30 who is a particularly good friend of mine. He is going to help me get set up with a nice eye lane and send me all his eye work and refractions, and am I going to have fun. There are lots of broken glasses, etc. and a fine field for me, and I'm the only one in quite a large area who is capable of doing refractions! I've been beating the old books on it some more and just having a hell of a time! If I write more now, I won't be able to stuff it all into one envelope—so, darling Gail, I love you so much and am so proud to have such a beautiful, sweet, modest, and capable little wife.

I'm liable to sail through the clouds and not come down for a week!

Always your own, Dearest

Wes

OCTOBER 21, 1943 WES TO GAIL

Hello, Sweetheart—

Do you know, after writing yesterday, I went through all your letters and put them in order, punched them and clipped with an *[unreadable]* binder. I have all your letters now, up to Oct. 5, including two number 16's and two number 18's! Have I doubled up on my numbers occasionally?

I was very industrious today. Got all my clothing out and packed the woolen stuff in a box with naphtha flakes well scattered. Lord, but the mildew is terrible. I hate to think what the stuff will look like after the rainy season. It's plenty thick now and has that musty stink. I brushed off all I could, then I re-packed neatly the rest of my clothing, threw out a load of junk, and arranged it so I can get at the often-used things easily.

My envelopes are all stuck and I have to cut the ends off and put scotch tape on them! I am now using the desk to write this letter on, with you perched on top smiling at me!

I collected a mess of cigarettes at Brisbane, thinking we might be short on them up here—I have 19 cartons, and we get a free issue of a pack a day! I'm not drawing mine, consequently, until I use up some of these. I'm afraid they will get musty. Gee, I hope those cigars get here soon—I sure enjoy the occasional one I've had. Guess I told you I got a chance to buy half a box 3 weeks ago—am down to three!

Just met one of my classmates from Randolph at supper—he's eating here for a few days until their own camp is set up. He's going to drop by in a while and we will celebrate with some beer—have three bottles left from the Brisbane stock we brought. Lord knows when we'll get more. Well, it's a good cause!

One nice thing about this place, It may be hotter than hell in the day, but it cools off and a nice breeze springs up in the evening, blowing up from the coast. If it weren't for things being eternally damp and moldy, it would be a delightful spot.

It's about time for Mac to show up, so I'll sign off. I was real ambitious yesterday and wrote twelve letters. Can you imagine that! Had lots of time, though, after getting up for a patient at three am, eating at four, and not going back to sleep because I was too wide awake!

All my love, Dearest—   Wes

P. S. Tell John I saw a little bear the other day that looked like the Koala in the picture, only it had a beautiful light tan, thick fur, was bigger, and had a baby looking out of the pouch! Right in camp.

OCTOBER 21, 1943 GAIL TO WES

Sweetheart,   #26

A B-17 made a forced landing at Beckwourth without any mishaps.

No letters for a week, but I guess it's hard to get them out now from the sound of things—I guess it's plenty hot, Honey, and not from the rising sun but the setting sun!

Due to your howl about bathing facilities, I almost went up to the house and got that hose and shower attachment to send you for Christmas! By now you probably have that problem solved.

Barbara Wood called me from the city yesterday and she was taking off for New Orleans, which is Jack's new post for a short time. She wanted Katherine Theus' address but Katherine is in Georgia.

Winter has started taking its toll of Quincy old people. Mrs. W. J. Miller passed away and also Mr. Buisiendorfer. Dan Robertson is in the hospital—obviously mental along with the heart condition. Ernie Leonhardt is in now—heart—and Jimmy Cloman had a heart attack of some kind. The OPA is wearing down our grocers. Right now there is a milk shortage that is driving them crazy.

Old Dody quit at Bill Bailey's and poor old Bill is wearing down swinging the shifts alone.

David is having a little grief because the priest won't let them have the wedding in a private home. I don't know how that will end up.

Del and Ruth and Dottie are going to the city again this weekend. Guess I'll tag along and spend a little of your hard-earned money on some winter clothes Sweetheart. Hope you don't mind. Wish you could help me pick them out.

All my love   Gail

OCTOBER 23, 1943 WES TO GAIL

Dearest Darling Sweetheart—   #37

Your hubby has been trail building again. This time to a creek where we want to build a swimming hole. We took a jeep and rammed our way through the brambles in low-low gear, four wheel drive—stopping to chop trees and trim out the stickers and miserable streaming vines with sharp stickers which abound through the jungle. We made about 250 yards in three hours, and were we tired (Van and I). Tomorrow, we will start at dawn and clean out the creek bottom of mud. It's just a little fellow about 3 feet wide, but has a good flow. The water is lukewarm! (This damned pen—wish I had my own). Now we are thoroughly pooped and filthy dirty—have to bathe out of the wash basin tonight as usual. Maybe tomorrow night we'll have our outdoor heated bath—I hope.

I'm helping out another Flight Surgeon half days for a short time until the rest of the gang arrives. Nothing I can't tell you about that job without violating censorship—but it's fun. I think I'll be able to get a little Cub time tomorrow.

I'm really too tired to write much, but I've been neglecting my Darling so that I want to make up for it. Yesterday I received letter #18, Oct. 7—which makes three no. 18's. Honey, I'm afraid my baby is working too hard. Won't you please try to get out of that damn office 3 or 4 nights per week? Can't you pay someone, perhaps Nan—even if it's a lot of money, to take over in the evenings? Your health is far more important than money, Dear, and I want you to keep yours. I'm watching mine very carefully. It won't be a happy situation for you or for me if I come home at the end of this war and find you worn down and a nervous wreck. I'm in here pitching so my home will be the happy place I left it, and it's just as much your duty to look after your health as it is mine to be over here. I'd rather see the hospital close, or give it to Dr. B. than to have you hurt your health and nervous system, and I am very serious, my sweet—Please show this portion to Dr. Lasswell, Honey, and see if he doesn't agree with me.

Now, the lecture is over! I love you so very deeply, and want to see you so badly. Due time, that happy situation will occur. We'll lick hell out of these bastards before too long.

Goodnight Darling—All my love—and forever, too—

                          your Wes

OCTOBER 27, 1943 GAIL TO WES

Darling—   #28

Johnny and I are going to ride down to the sawmill with Ruth—with the hope that they'll saw their first board. Everyone is watching but nothing happens. It has been raining for the last few days, so I guess the market has slowed up some.

Now that Polio has subsided, we are having an epidemic of Scarlet Fever, 8 cases to date. If it isn't one thing it's ten others.

David is having an awful time trying to get married by a Priest. The latter won't perform it in the home and the mother-in-law has the home wedding all planned. I don't know how it will end up but the 30th is pretty close. Marg Young might be the only Quincyite to be there. She and Lenn are in Texas somewhere.

Guess what, Sis is going to have a baby in March!

The flying fortress that landed at Beckwourth turned out to be a B-24 that was going from March Field to Fresno. They apparently couldn't get down anywhere else. They had 50 feet left when they landed, and managed to take off without any mishaps.

You certainly have Doris and me going—we can't figure where you'd find enough room to fly 185 mph two feet off the ground mile after mile. Well, I guess we'll find out when the war's all over.

All my love Sweet—   Gail

OCTOBER 28, 1943 HON. J. O. (JUDGE) MONCUR

Dear Captain Wes:

Thanks very much for your congratulations on my election as president of Rotary. I hesitated about taking the job, but am finding it interesting and I derive some pleasure from it. I appreciate very much hearing from you and I am glad to know that at the time of writing you were comfortably and pleasantly located, even if only perhaps temporarily. All of your folks here are well except Joe *[Arthur J. Watson]*, who I hear has a cold but not a severe one. I haven't seen Gail just lately as our paths do not seem to cross. I saw little John several days ago on the street with his grandmother. He is getting to be quite a boy and it is thought that he is going to be like you—alert minded, quick-thinking, and energetic. Not bad. Tiny *[H. S. Watson]* is still actively functioning on the Selective Service Board and Anne *[Anne Blench Lepley]* is quite busy with her probation work. Mr. Watson *[William Watson]* is holding up very well.

Tomorrow evening, Friday, Rotary is having a reception for the teachers and we are curious to know what the Committee will spring on us. We have had a fine fall thus far and the mills are making an excellent cut. We are fortunate in having three doctors here, so our health is being adequately safeguarded, I hope. I thought of you when I had an attack of Flu in the spring.

We do not hear much about Barney. Business is holding up well and the stores seem to be doing an excellent volume. Garages, of course, are more or less restricted in their operations. It is rather quiet in court circles and if it were not for the upsurges in juvenile delinquencies, there would not be a great deal to do except in the larger cities and in sections where war activities are found. Court work generally has slackened up, and except where necessity requires, litigants and attorneys do not seem inclined to try cases. I found the same situation existed during World War One. It is probably part of the psychology of conflict. Criminal business seems to have fallen off at least sixty-five percent. Perhaps those who are prone to commit infractions of the law are too busily otherwise employed and are earning enough money to remove any criminal incentive.

When the war is over the experience gained in your profession and the allied sciences will be productive of many valuable aids to the preservation of health and life. Your profession is taking a wonderful part in this conflict. We are planning and organizing for the creation of a work pile, both in public improvements and in industry, so as to be of assistance to those who may return here when peace is restored.

Trusting that this finds you well and still comfortably and pleasantly situated, and with the kindest regards and best wishes, in which Mrs. Moncur and Mrs. Butcher, to whom I am dictating this letter, join me,

Sincerely,   J. C. Moncur

OCTOBER 29, 1943 GAIL TO WES
[Plumas Industrial Hospital]

Sweetheart—   #29—I think—

I got your letter of Oct 4 yesterday—about a week after receiving one written the 8th. You never can tell when they'll arrive, but gee! I hate for them to be so long in between times. I think there must be lots of letters on the way because, gee! I haven't gotten many lately, Honey!

We've had quite an interesting day here at the hospital. A fellow came in when a piece of steel from a wedge (looked like shrapnel) flew in his shinbone. It was really quite a hunk and a mean looking business. Dr. L. worked on it—thank goodness! Then about quitting time an auto accident came in and one fellow came in cut all over the head. Gosh, if he wasn't a gory mess—Dr. L. stitched and stitched—'course I had my nose right in the middle of things a la Dr. B.! If you don't hurry home, my Sweet, I'm liable to be a pretty good stitcher-upper.

Johnny is really getting to be a character. He's picked up "OK Keed" from somewhere, and instead of saying "no" to everything he's asked to do, he startles us all with "OK, Keed." At meal times, he climbs up on the stool and in a very demanding tone says, "I want my dinner." Sometimes, he goes in and drags poor Grandpa out of his chair and hauls him in to dinner. Mother gets quite upset because Johnny has us all arranged and eating even before she gets everything on the table.

Ration Board: I came down here after office hours and ran into a lecture—someone is here from the Scat. Office, so I'm over here in the corner continuing my own sweet way. "Course I get a few interruptions now and then.

Nina Brown just tells me that Roy is officially in the Sea Bees—Chief Petty Officer, and is he tickled! 'Course Nina isn't so thrilled. Roy wrote to her from Salt Lake and for his address?

Ken is having a marvelous time with the sawmill, he says that he just can't get interested in the oil business—there isn't enough excitement in it.

By the way, we've been cut to 3 gallons per stamp. It is plenty for my needs especially during the winter. I'm waiting to get the tires recapped until they can take them in Reno, they have certain days for it. I guess I'll send all four at once.

To go on about the sawmill: Del is having a big time too. They had a poker game to celebrate the first log going through. First poker game in ages. Dad says that their mill is a good one and thinks they'll get along OK. However, he says that there are a lot of kinks that need ironing out.

Honey, you sound as though you've gotten things whittled down to where they are comfortable—guess I'll forget about the shower deal I had cooked up for you. The description of your laundry appalled me. Why only one pair of pajamas? I'm glad that you got one of the boys to wash them for you—seems to me you should have more important things to do.

How about the flight surgeon work—are you getting any? I guess maybe that is something you can't answer, but it sure would be fun to know.

Tennye and Willis are having troubles. He seems to be spending his time in the bars with Ruby Williams. Tennye is all upset over that, and Gloria is having some severe attacks. It sounds as though there might be a split.

Dr. B. postponed the annual Rotary teacher's party because of the Scarlet Fever, but he hasn't closed the schools.

I am enclosing a board from the new mill; I hope it reaches you before it becomes sawdust.

Goodnight, my love, keep those *[unreadable]* screened out of your four poster *[bed]*.

All my love, forever and ever,

your Gail

OCTOBER 29, 1943 —SOUTHWEST PACIFIC THEATER OF OPERATIONS (Fifth Air Force): 37 B-24's, escorted by 53 P-38's, pound Rabaul area on New Britain Island, claiming 45 airplanes destroyed on the ground and in the air. 17 B-25's hit the Madang, New Guinea area. P-47's attack shipping in Hansa Bay, New Guinea area and strafe the Cape Gloucester area on New Britain Island. B-25's sink a vessel off Tanimbar Island in the Moluccas Islands while B-24's bomb Selaroe airstrip on Tanimbar and attack the Waroe Bay area of New Guinea. The 8th Fighter Squadron, 49th Fighter Group, transfers from Tsili Tsili to Gusap, New Guinea with P-47's. The 63d Bombardment Squadron (Heavy), 43d Bombardment Group (Heavy) transfers from Port Moresby to Dobodura, New Guinea with B-24's.

OCTOBER 30, 1943 GAIL TO WES

Darling—   #30

Mom and Dad's wedding anniversary and David's wedding night! Saturday night and at the office again. I have to get here right at seven so the patients can come in 'cause Dr. B. doesn't get here until 7:15or so. We really are making out fairly well, though, under the circumstances.

I got your round-robin letter today and we've all had a great time trying to read between the lines. Part of Julian's note was cut out—the part that read, "This could have been sent from *[censored]* APO's." We've made it to be Japan and that the Japs had been right close in and that you all might have seen the whites of their eyes.

Did you have a lot of medical work to do? Gosh Honey—you should import me to help you. I'd really get goggle-eyed then.

I got the $100.00 check yesterday and wondered if you had run into a poker game on the way to the P. O., or if you made a mistake in writing it $150 or if it cost $50 to wire $100. Thought I'd better check up with you. Thanks a million, anyway—whatever it is supposed to be. Would you like me to make a down payment on the house, save it to pay the income tax with when you get out, or save it to buy an airplane with after the war?

I wrote you an airmail letter yesterday and I think it's a good thing I won't be around when you get it. I'm starting to send you dirty jokes. I've got a rip snorter to send on one of these days.

All my love
                    Gail

NOVEMBER 1, 1943 WES TO MARIAN

Dear Sis—

Thanks for another nice letter—of October 19th. You're sure improving on your correspondence rate. I think you're growing up more, too—you sound more like a staid married gal. Tell the old man I think he is good for you.

As I just wrote Mother, don't worry about the addresses. If you used an old one, it will catch up to me. It takes packages two to four months to get here, and a few more days won't make much difference over here. Although the V-Mail you sent did come through quickly—I got it up here at this address, and you had sent it to one of the older ones.

Esther must have been highly impressed with the roast beef. That must be quite an accomplishment these days. I sure feel sorry for you folks. We got plenty of meat, and some damn good steaks, too. We had steak three times last week, roast beef twice, and again today (Monday). The only chow I don't like is Friday when we get goldfish (tinned Salmon). Plenty of coffee, too, but Honey, it ain't Hills Bros. I'll sure be glad to get home to a real old fashioned cup of H. B. coffee—after I down that, I'll be ready to go to work on the old lady (Quoting rates, $50.00). I'm also getting a little of the pre-war bonded bourbon, now that the medical supply is on the ball. Of course, I only write myself a prescription when I'm ready to faint from weakness or something.

Did I tell you I had a swell letter from Dinty? Sounds like he's "really living." Got a house and servants galore. What a life! It's a good thing I'm far from temptation.

I don't know—or remember—all the fancy joints you took Esther to. What and where, is the "Strip?"

Guess you're about ready to choke with all this line of bull. Besides, I've got to examine a couple of hundred GI's yet this evening.

Write again soon, your letters are swell, Honey. Love to Cy and the boys.

Love,   Wes

NOVEMBER 2, 1943 DORIS AND GAIL TO WES

Dear Wes   #?

You have quite a hospital here, Wes. It surely has been an experience, and some very different from any nursing I have done. The strangeness of it all has been something of a problem, but then, Gail does right well and here in the office you'd be very proud of her. We are headed for the Sump for a bit of refreshment. Care to join us? She will take over from here if I leave any space for her.

Understand your jungle hospital is something for the records. Native nurses?

I'll sign off—she is pestering me. Cherio, Wes—   Doris

Honey—

That woman used up all of my good space. This is being written in Bunker Hill over a couple of tall Cokes. Doris is giggling over some of the fine literature that I collected at the ration board.

I went flying today all afternoon—first time in a month. The CAP sent 3 cadets up that have never been up, but are scheduled to go into the Air Corp (17 year olds). Bill and CA and I took them up and then I took Floyd Shaw and Nina Brown—quite a day! Got your letter of the 21st today. Still haven't had a very good account of your visit to see Julian. CA said that Julian was making a tour of some kind. They cut out part of his message. Guess I told you that!

Haven't written since Sat., Sweet. I'll have to make up for lost time.

Love

Gail

NOVEMBER 4, 1943 GAIL TO WES
(9 PM, Office)

Sweetheart,   #32

I've been trying to make the books balance, but have given it up as a bad job tonight—don't feel in the mood.

I received two more letters from you—very interesting ones too, I might add! You don't seem to have any lack of things to do. You must have had an elegant time with Julian and the Flying Fortress! Oh boy! Weren't you confused by the instrument panel?

I'm glad that you finally got the funnies—I'll make some more stabs at getting some to you. They certainly tried to discourage us from sending them.

Gosh, Honey, you must be getting absent minded leaving your dog tags around and losing your pen. For shame. I'm wondering what in the world you do without a watch? Isn't that almost essential?

Please let me clear something up here and now. Darling, I'm not working very hard—you make me ashamed with all your praise. It's just like Mom says—"Try as they might, no one can work me too hard." She says if it's play, I don't even need urging, but when it comes to work, I make myself scarce. I'm sure that Dr. and Margarite would both verify that fact. As far as paying the debts, my sweet, you are making the money and I'm just sort of tossing it around to decrease the interest in various spots.

I've read parts of your letters to Dr. and M. and it really does them a lot of good. I think they were especially pleased with the last one where you commented on how much you appreciated what they were doing.

By the way—you would probably be interested in knowing that after Dr. L. took home his $300.00 out to balance Dr. B.'s $300.00 from the county—they split $63.00—was Dr. B. ever griped. However, he's still making enough on the side (that never goes through this office) to buy a form for himself—not that he has [unreadable].

I'm glad that you feel the way you do about being there—It makes me proud all over. You sound so cheerful and are making the best of it, Darling, and it certainly helps me along.

Chris is doing right well by Doris in the letter writing and I think she is much happier than when she arrived. She's met lots of people—has lot's of friends. Everyone likes her.

Now to answer some of your questions as best as I can: We have—Hospital, about $3000, House (plenty) $4300, and thank heavens no more debts that I am aware of. I am receiving $217 each month. Got your last $100, and thanks, Sweetheart!

You'll get some pictures of me and John pretty soon, I hope. Bill has promised to take some.

David seems to be happily married. They started out and went to El Paso from San Angelo. Who should they run into in Juarez at the Tivaloi than Margaret and Linn. Sis was tickled pink and wrote a very descriptive letter about the bride—she says she's wonderful and she really sounds all of that. When mother gets through showing the description around, I'll send it along.

I'm going up to Ruth's, so I'll leave her a little space to say hello.

All my love, Sweetheart, forever and ever   Gail

Hello Wes—Gail left me a small spot to give you my regards. We are, of course, very involved in the sawmill; sawed 30,000 *[board feet]* the other day, and Del comes home every night with sawdust on his hat.

Proud as can be of Bob at school. Grades are grand and got merit badge for conduct.

Had a short letter from Barney. Didn't give much news but imagine is close to you somewhere. Need to write a more lengthy letter later.

So long   Ruth D.

NOVEMBER 6, 1943 GAIL TO WES

Hello Honey—   #32

It's Saturday afternoon—my afternoon off. We had been having a pow wow at the office this morning about whether to put that $1500 on the Bank Loan on the hospital, thus saving 4% interest, or to leave it in the bank to collect 2%. The winter is beginning to pinch already. I think it would be best to cut down the loan.

Dr. B. really blew about the check he got this month. He's trying to make different arrangements. Don't know what they will be, but I hope he complains to Fletcher. I think he knows better than that, however.

Doris and I have been invited out this evening by some of the gang from the Forest Service school—it seems they want dancing partners. Most of them are Supervisors and Rangers, some from the R. O. Kelly Traugh is among the outfit. Do you disapprove? I think the party is to be at the Stone House, which no doubt will be something on a Sat. nite.

Tomorrow I'm going up to Janet's and have dinner with them. Haven't seen Jan in ages. She's due next month. We have 3 nurses due in December: Jan, Smitty and Eunice Stenberg. The maternity cases seem to be coming right along.

Wish I could go out and fly this afternoon, but can't take Johnny, so guess I won't get there.

All my love, my precious,

                        Gail.

NOVEMBER 7, 1943 Dr. MARY CARR MOORE TO WES
[Los Angles, California]

Dearest Wesley—

I have been thinking of you so much today—Sunday. I have been over to have dinner with a dear friend of mine, and a PEO sister of Seattle days. When I knew her, she had three little boys and a baby girl—that was just about the time you were born, and before—when we lived on Denny Way. Sometimes the Chapter met at my home, and once we met at hers. Later, she moved away, and also had two more little girls; six in all. About three years ago, she lost the youngest daughter. Neither of the girls have married, although they are very beautiful girls, both of them. The younger son, Harold, was at home today, and the two daughters. The older boys are married. It took me back to the old times, when my children were little.

So, thinking of you today, I see you again as a little boy, very active and very smart. I remember when you used to recite all of the "Hole Book," page by page, with the pictures, as if you were reading it. Also, when Byron showed you a magazine cover of two blue-birds, one in the nest and the other on the branch beside her; and Byron said, "See Wesley— this is the Mother bird, and this is the male bird," and you said, "But where are the letters?" You were a cute little tyke. Johnny makes me think so much of you—except that you had been very sick and Johnny has always been pretty strong. You became very sturdy, once you began to *[unreadable]*, but I always felt like handling you as if you would break— until later on; when I handled you occasionally with a switch, but not very often. You were pretty good, in general.

I think I told you in my last what a nice thing Gail did in typing some excerpts from your letters for me. We have all enjoyed them so much. I have been working many extra hours this last two or three weeks; was engaged (incognito) to remodel a score of an Indian Pageant; maybe I have written you about it—it was an almost all-night job, and part of the day for about twelve days. I finished in time, and heard the performance, and the pageant was very interesting; authentic Indian Dances, and good melodies; only the continuity, and some supporting accompaniments were what were needed. I was glad to be able to help with it. Haven't got my check yet, but it will come all right. The performance was only about a week ago. Since then, being rather tired, I haven't done much except catch up on my own neglected work.

Also, with Mrs. York and her little son here, there has not been the same freedom from conversation that I have alone; but never-the-less, I am glad they were here, as she is a dear, and little Dick is rather a marvelous little fellow; very unusual—sweet, and somewhat sensitive. He misses his Daddy, of course; Major Thomas York, HQ. J. or I. Corps., APO 301. If you run across him, tell him I am quite "sold" on his wife and little son. I am taking this from the address on a letter to Dick that Ann (Mrs. York) showed me, and left in my room to read—all about coral reefs and star-fish, etc. Very interesting to a small boy. Dick really misses his Daddy. But his mother is a dear and devoted to him.

Oh Dear—this is all! Ever so much love to you Darling

Mother

NOVEMBER 8, 1943 GAIL TO WES

Sweetheart,   #33

Two letters today; #37 and 38. It has been several days since I got the last. Was very thrilled. I'm envious of your swimming pool—but not your bugs!! We are wrapping up like Eskimos—it's been pretty cold.

Our party Saturday night ended in a tragedy. Our Forest Service gang decided to go to Paxton to dance the wee hours away and four cars of airport gang were coming too. We got there, but the airport crowd never did show up. On the way home we found out why. One of the boys—and he was just a kid—ran into a hitch hiker and killed him. The worst part of it was that Bob Commons knew and worked with the boy he killed (they are both about 21). Bob is not being held because from all appearances the boy hitch hiking was at fault—out on the pavement and in dark clothes. The boy killed worked for the Forest Service. I tell you the starch was taken out of that party in a hurry.

Darling, your son is really growing up. Today he wiped all the dishes for Grandma! Not taking after his Pop! This morning he told Grandma to take care of his Mommie 'cause he was going down to Grandpa's office to work. He disappeared shortly thereafter and I guess he went down there all right.

Please don't worry about my health, Honey. I've gained weight and am fat as a butterball. As I've said before, no one can make me work too hard!

As always and forever

your Gail

NOVEMBER 10, 1943 GAIL TO WES

My Darling,   #34

So you don't like my number sequences! I thought I had done pretty well. However, that's the way I do everything.

We have a new arrangement at the hospital. Dr. B. is there from 3-5 and 7-8 every day except every other weekend for $100.00 a month. He certainly hit the ceiling about his cut last month. However, he's still making enough on the side. As long as the bills are paid every month and the place keeps open, let him play! It's a little tough on Dr. and M., however.

Tonight I'm going up to the Smith's to Ray's birthday dinner; the Metzker's are invited too. Ray has a case of champagne that he said he was going to open. If we have many customers at the Plumas Ind. tonight, I'm liable to miss the champagne—tonight I'm hoping for no business.

Dear Daddy—I just had my pistol out to shoot some Japs—couldn't see the whites of their eyes, so I missed. Please send me a skull (Jap) to practice on. I am being a good boy and taking care of Mamma & —.

You had a card from Brother [David]—it reads: "Just a card to let you know I'm well and kicking. Am just about through my course at O. C. S. Will write later, haven't much time, keep pretty busy. Bobby is in the Navy Air Corps at San Luis Obispo. He's got about 10 months training to go." His address is kind of hard to read but I'll try and get it all: Candidate F. S. Eckel, Jr. 39045896, 12th Co. 3rd Student Trg. Reg., Fort Benning, Georgia. I guess that we didn't ever let him know that you were going into the Army. I'll try to get a note off to him pretty soon.

All our love, Sweetheart—we miss you terribly   Gail & Johnny

NOVEMBER 12, 1943 ESTHER TO WES
[Seattle, Washington]

Dear Wes—

When I arrived home, Dad had your two letters dated October 4th and October 20th; this morning your last one arrived. You haven't any idea how much it adds to Dad's peace of mind to hear from you so often even though he is negligent in writing. He is so frightfully busy that it means writing at home and that is a bit difficult. However, you are in his mind all the time.

I came home to find him tired even after his hunting trip, but the week I was home made such a difference in him and he was looking like a million until last Tuesday when he got a very bad attack, and even he was disturbed. X-rays showed it to be a very small stone in the kidney, so you know what excruciating pain he suffered. He is all right again and I do hope the stone stays where it is, or if it must pass, that it won't bring on another attack.

I am determined that he is not going to work so hard and it will be my own aim to see he gets as much relaxation as possible. He has such wonderful recuperative powers that it will be difficult to keep him down. He was so very proud of himself because he found a maid who is to come to work for us on Tuesday. I'm particularly grateful because it will relieve me for more work at the office, and the more I can do, the more it relieves Thil so she can do more of the intravenous and check-ups.

News of the Southwest Pacific seems particularly favorable right now. We are happy that you have such an active part in keeping our boys fit. Your letters are so intensely interesting—we've passed copies on to so many of our friends who are interested in you. I mean your letters to Gail—fear not—she has deleted the personalities but included all the impersonal references.

I was quite disappointed to find when I got back from Fresno that Gail had been down to San Francisco again. Had she wired me, I would not have gone to Fresno but it never occurred to her that I would be high-tailing it off again. She is such a honey that I disliked missing out on another visit with her.

You being down in the tropics now makes it difficult to visualize us wearing sweaters around the house in order to conserve on oil—our oil has been severely out and so are depending largely on the fireplace whenever possible. Seattle is particularly beautiful right now in her autumn outfit. The coloring is more intense than usual because of our early frosts. We hope you have some sort of a Christmas and my one hope is that we may all celebrate next Christmas together either in Quincy or up here. It's an ambitious hope, but let's look forward to it.

Did you hear of the pregnant moron who was so thrilled when she found she had a little inside dope? Could send you a few more but I'm afraid the censor might blush for me.

Much love to you, Wes Dear, from us *[unreadable]* and we will be thinking of you during the holidays—wishing you were here with your family and—possibly up here with us.

Esther

NOVEMBER 12, 1943 GAIL TO WES
[At the Office—after hours]

Darling,

Received your typewritten letter today and was awfully upset about your swimming pool. Can't you do anything about it? Seems to me that if you are ingenious enough to construct the pool and dig out the jungle, that you could do something about the interference. Maybe you had better insert a strainer just above the pool to correct the difficulty.

I'm afraid that the censors didn't care for your remarks about them—at any rate, I think that is what was cut out of your letter. When they got through with it, it read like this: "I'm afraid the temptation must have been too great for the censors in the matter of the cigars." Am I right?

I hope that Van got along OK with his GI's. I still haven't written to his wife, for which you should whip me soundly, Darling, 'cause it isn't that I haven't time, but that I just can't seem to get around to writing to anyone but you.

How did you like your job as Acting Group Surgeon?

Just wanted to tell you that Corny Gallup sent a grass skirt home from somewhere down there—Celebes, I think. Stella has all kinds of gadgets that he sent home to her and she has them all on display up at the Treasurer's Office. Am looking forward to seeing the souvenirs you have collected; hope they get through all right.

Bill Bailey just howled over the Pom-pom deal today. I had a milk shake at the drug store with him today and he certainly seemed dissatisfied—he said he'd certainly like to be in there pitching with you. He's a bit upset at the moment, because Helen *[Bailey]* fell down Schott's basement stairs and broke her wrist. To go back to the beginning of the story, though, it all starts with Ole getting sick and having to go to the hospital. As near as they have it figured out, there was a bit of afterbirth left and she got some kind of infection (she is much better, though, tonight). So, Helen was taking over care of Mike *[Schott]* and she started into the bedroom, got the wrong door and plunged down into the basement (personally, I can't see why she didn't kill herself!) She figures she was just lucky because she didn't have Mike in her arms. Clarence called the office just as I was leaving to go up to Smith's to Ray's birthday party, so I stuck around and held Helen's hand while Dr. B. X-rayed the other arm. We couldn't find any Aromatic Spirits of Ammonia. Dr. B. had used it up on a drunk, and nothing seemed to go right—then to top it all, he told Helen that he didn't think that the thing was broken. That made Helen mad. Finally, the X-ray showed a Collies (?) fracture, so Dr. B. went to work and put a cast on it, and then took another picture. The next day I got busy and put the bee in Bill's bonnet to send her down to Haig. So Bill came up and had Dr. L. go over the X-rays and asked him what he thought of the idea of sending her down. Dr. said that he would, and made all the necessary arrangements for Bill. Is Bill ever a grateful person tonight. He had word from Helen that Haig gave her an anesthetic and took half an hour to set the arm. When it set in, it just sort of popped.

I suppose that I should keep my nose out of things like that, but even I could see that bone sitting out there where it shouldn't be. I've lined up enough bones in my anatomy courses to know a little bit; however, "a little learning is a dangerous thing." I got to the birthday party a little late but got 4 glasses of Champagne out of the deal and a swell turkey dinner, so didn't do so badly.

Ken and Helen were there too. I had quite a few of your letters typed up and took them along. Ken read them and I'm afraid that you would never have recognized them. I had omitted all of the real personal touches, and when he read them aloud he added his own version. It was really rich. I knew them by heart and when he got out of line, I managed to stop him before he got too wound up. Despite his horseplay, the crowd enjoyed your letters immensely, Sweetheart, and they certainly prompted plenty of conversation.

If you haven't written your letter to Nan yet, my Sweet, I'm afraid that you are too late. She is taking off tomorrow to go down to Texas and take a stab at the WAAF's. Anyhow she has been trotting around all week with a diamond ring that Bob Peckinpah gave her, so I don't know whether you could make any impression right at the moment.

I paid off a debt to the Schott's today—a matter of $63.17—which seems to have been credited on any bill they might have here at the office. I think that under the circumstances that it shouldn't be up to Dr. L. to absorb that debt. I Hope you don't mind my business methods. I'm learning slowly, my Sweet; maybe pretty soon I'll know what it is all about.

I'm sending you some more of the ration board literature. I'm glad that I'm not delivering these in person—well, you probably never would see them if I had to do it, but being as I don't have to show my face, it isn't so bad.

I guess I'd better close up show and go up and compare notes with Doris. She has been getting letters dated later than I have. Can't understand it. Mine today was dated the 28th of Oct. and hers was the 29th. By the way, the E. F. M. message that you mentioned in your letter today hasn't arrived yet—maybe you had just better write another letter instead!

All my love, Honey

Gail

NOVEMBER 14, 1943 GAIL TO WES

Hello my Sweetie Pie—   #36

I sent you an unnumbered letter straight mail—with funny papers aboard on Nov. 12—it should be #35. It doesn't seem to make much difference whether the letters are airmail, V-Mail or what; so long as they are in the form of letters, and not packages, they eventually get there.

Well, Sunday rolled around today and I was going to take Doris to look at the Sunrise in the T Craft. However, she was busy delivering Eunice's baby girl (or I should say helping to deliver) so she begged off and went to bed instead. So later in the morning I took Red Larison over to Susanville and put in 2 hrs. & 15 min. in T Craft 20429. We had a big time. CA and Irene went in the Luscombe.

Last night Doris and I went to the show and saw Alaskan Highway, part of which was filmed up on Dad's Chilcoot Road. Bob Cotter *[Robert J. Cotter]* happened to come in and sit by us so we got first-hand information about what went on the set.

Johnny is here beside me and he insists on telling you that the Gremlins are chewing his bicycle tires of—especially that Gremlin Gus. He wishes they'd leave them alone 'cause he needs his tires in his business—speaking of tires, I had 4 tires recapped—a mistake was made and they are Grade A rubber instead of Grade C. Floyd sent them in for me—quite a deal, don't you think?

Have to tuck John D. away, so 'nite Sweetheart. All my love

Gail

NOVEMBER 17, 1943 GAIL TO WES

Hello Sweetheart—   #37

Things are settling back to normal. Ole can go home tomorrow and Helen Bailey came back from Dr. Haig with her arm in place, or I should say, her bones. It took Haig half an hour to get it back, though.

Just wanted to tell you, Darling, that the files are being carefully put away and saved. However, I'm not cutting my fingers any more. Another thing I wanted to tell you, a boy who came home for flight training wrote to a friend of Doris' and told her Chris was near a little town "Nedzab." We've searched the map over but imagine it would be looking like Quincy on a world map. Anyway, we know just about where the spot is 'cause we added about 29 miles onto Lucille Arthur's enterostomy and put a dot on our maps.

Last night the radio told of the Japs strafing the Aussies in Southern N. G. Guess none of that got in to you. I mean the repair jobs.

It is raining this morning—visibility is bad but our little jeeps are up braving the storm—crazy people.

I'm having Wednesday Club tonight—John is down licking the frosting pan and I have to get busy and do some cleaning.

We had to take a picture of Del's leg yesterday—he's a real logger—gets hurt just like the rest of them. However, the film turned out negative, to the relief of all concerned. Won't you take a vacation, my Sweet, and go to supper Club up at Dellinger's on Sunday? Surely wish it were possible.

All my love, Gail

NOVEMBER 18, 1943 BOB HUDSON TO WES
(Los Angeles, California)

Dear Wes,

I got your letter the other day but I haven't had a chance to answer it because of my homework.
Last week we had a swell A's and B's football game which came out to 0 to 0, and that night (Friday) the scouts had a swim meet which we didn't do so good.

I sure wish I was in your boots when you took that trip. I think I'd come down to the Coral Islands and see some of those native gals—I sure wish I could hear about some of your experiences, but I guess I will have to wait until you come back—which I hope will not be very long.

Mom let me read your letter of November and I'll bet you feel weak an awful lot—of course Cy sure wishes that all he had to do to get some liquor would be to fill out a prescription.

Incidentally, I learned Morse code the other day and just in case you do I'll write you a message: *-/.-/-.-/.//-.-./.-/.-/.//—-/..-./-.—/—-/..-/.-./...//.-..*

As ever,

Bob

NOVEMBER 20, 1943 GAIL TO WES

My Darling—   #39

Still no letters from you—I guess that boat hasn't come in or they are too busy doing other things with planes and boats and transportation facilities in your vicinity. At any rate, the S. W. P. A. seems to be a hot spot, so I really shouldn't expect anything until it cools down a little. On the map it looks as though Bouganville and Buka are pretty close at hand and that you might get a little business from those spots—to say nothing of your own region.

Tonight the war widows—Dottie, Leda and Nina and Doris, if I can get a'hold of her—are coming down to help me eat a chicken. I'm glad that I don't have to live by myself, Sweetheart; it would be awfully lonesome. Had to invite the girls in for Saturday night to keep from talking to myself.

Guess it will probably rain on Mother and Dad in S. F., but they will enjoy just getting away. Last night I went up to the Metzker's—they had buffet dinner for 18. Was awful lonesome for my Honey!

Supper Club has been changed to Sunday and Leila *[Bedell]* is having it at the Hotel. I guess that is about where I will have it when my turn comes along.

Del said to tell you that the farthest he got for duck hunting was Indian Valley, and that you didn't miss anything, and besides, the Thule Lake Japs have been giving lots of trouble.

All my love and forever, your

Gail

NOVEMBER 28, 1943 GAIL TO WES

Sweetheart—   #43

I got your letter # 43 today, and after a week of silence, can tell you I was very happy to have it. I didn't like the sound of the vapor trails. Why are they—the planes—going so darned fast, and whose were they? ('Course I know you probably can't answer that, but I can wonder, can't I?) I'm relieved that it wasn't the vapor trail from a bomb! Or was it? The news sounds red hot around your neck of the woods. We found Woodlark Islands and Milene Bay on the map but couldn't locate the other two islands. Guess they didn't know I'd be looking for them, Honey, or they would have put them on for me.

Spent yesterday afternoon dog fighting in the Silvaire with Draper in his Luscombe. We were faster and he couldn't stay on our tail, but we would have been cooked geese a couple of times if he'd had guns. CA has a Fablin prop now because the Freedman Burnhams have been condemned. Today Clarence *[Schott]* checked me out in the Cub Coupe, and Ivy *[Grover]* and I took a tour to Susanville and Beckwith. Spent 2 hours flitting around, so I got in about 5 hours this weekend. Had a great time.

Dr. B. went to L. A. over Thanksgiving, so I took some days off too. Guess I'll have to go back to work tomorrow. Things seem to be running pretty smoothly now.

I'm going to crawl into bed now Darling—so good night my Sweet and take care of my heart—

It's all yours—   Gail

NOVEMBER 29, 1943 GAIL TO WES

Hello my Sweet—   #44

Dr. B. didn't get back today. I don't take the office tonight, so here I am going to tell you how much I love you without having to rush off somewhere. 'Course you don't know that I love you, and I should find some subtle way of revealing to you my true feelings, but Sweetheart, somehow I've always been blunt and to the point and perhaps I should add that I haven't changed since you turned me loose in this cold cruel world.

I've been transacting business today—received a check for $400.00 today, deposited it and immediately plunked $500.00 down on the house. Thank you, my Precious, hope you approve! Then I drew out $1000.00 and tossed it on the Hospital loan, bringing it down to $1750.00. Gosh, if we're not careful Honey, we'll own the place. Paid $5.00 to the TB Association and now the Salvation Army is attacking me. Haven't fixed up your dues to for Vets of Foreign Wars, but will do that tomorrow.

Maggie Morris asked me to join the Soroptomists today and in the capacity of Hospital Management (what a laugh—me manage anything!) Anyway I was greatly honored but have been trying to formulate a reply in the negative without causing too much disturbance. I feel that if I have spare time, it belongs to Johnny right now.

My love forever, Sweet   Your Gail

NOVEMBER 30, 1943 WES TO GAIL

Dearest—   #49

Two more nice V-Mails today from my Honey. I was delighted to know that Chris' friend told you where he was—and quite true. Now, another spot about 75 miles further is still another interesting place—one of the boys may some day tell you about that. Don't worry about all you read in papers, it's most interesting but quite harmless to us here. I wouldn't miss any of this for the world!

So John's having Gremlin trouble! What sort of Gremlin eats tricycle tires? Tell him he'd better keep that bad Gremlin away 'till Daddy wins the war, because Uncle Sam probably won't let him have any new tires before then. I'd love to see our little man.

Honey, I know it's hard to get pictures, but I do appreciate them, oh, so much—I want a picture or two of you by and in an airplane. You see, I'm always bragging on your prowess. Maybe there are some old pictures you can find, and please send some of the house too, Dear. I'd like to have them so much.

I didn't hear about Helen Bailey's arm. Maybe it's in another letter—give her my condolences and tell Del to keep out from under those logs!

Do you know, I must be getting old. I can hardly read some of the V-Mail without my glasses. I hate to wear them but guess I'd better start carrying them for close work.

We had a pretty good movie last night—Bob Hope in "They Got Me Covered." No interruptions for a change. Movies are really swell entertainment out here in the Jungles—allows one to "live" again in civilization while watching them. Hot and cold water, sheets, iced cocktails, table clothes, civilian clothes—all will seem quite wonderful, I expect. There's no worry of choice of wardrobe here! Just the old khakis and GI shoes. Sometimes the insignia, and often not! I haven't worn my summer flying suit much as I'm saving it for use at home. Remember how we "sweat it out" at Hamilton Field, seeing so many people? The brown zippered outfit. The visored cap I wear every day, and the flying glasses, are really indispensable here.

Which is T Craft 20429? Nan's? She isn't writing me any notes on the Rooter, and I wrote to her too. Build a fire under her, will you?

Nice deal on the recaps. How do they seem to be holding up? And how is the old bucket of bolts running these days? Make old Del take good care of it.

I got my ears set out today. We have a barber out at the line. He put me back to my half-inch status.

(This letter looks like the devil, but the wind is blowing through the mess hall tonight so we hardly can hold our paper on the table). It gets quite pleasantly cool in the evening here.

Bob Hudson and Mother and Esther wrote me so I must answer them. Esther says Dad isn't too well and has had a kidney stone. Not so hot at his age. I hope he doesn't have any trouble. I feel quite worried about him, as he isn't so young any more. He has worked terribly hard and played equally hard all his life. I appreciate your writing them and sending excerpts of my letters, Darling. Write them when you can. Think I'll sign off and write the "family."

All my love Dearest, to you and John—be good—and careful Sweetheart.

Always, Wes

Downtown Quincy

Courthouse, Lift, and Quincy Hotel

DECEMBER 1, 1943 GAIL TO WES

Sweetheart—   #44

Received a letter today from Wally's wife in Dallas, Texas—presume he must be a flier. She gave me the location where you must have been, (right close to the Jap lines, if you ask me). I guess the longitude and latitude hat she has is old news now. Why don't you tell your friends goodbye; Chris said he didn't know where you went. I'm going to get busy and write to Wally's wife and tell her what I know—which isn't very enlightening. It was awfully swell of her to write me and I appreciate it. Thank you too Honey.

Mother just told me tonight that the Western Pacific Railroad was given orders to get their roundhouses ready for more concentrated movement on their lines—sounds encouraging. Guess they will take over equipment from other lines so they can pack troops and equipment after they get through mutilating Hitler—the boys are certainly sending out the bombs en masse.

Darling, I'm so sorry you're missing Johnny's development at this stage. He is most interesting and seems to be learning fast—probably not the things he is supposed to be learning—his vocabulary is amazing. He has his nose in just about everything that goes on—can't miss a thing. I think he's built of curiosity. Gee, Honey, you'd enjoy him so much! Please, please take care of yourself and be careful. Silly warnings, I know, but Honey, please do!!

All of my love

                    Gail

DECEMBER 1, 1943 WES TO MARIAN AND CY
(7th Fighter Squadron, 49th Fighter Group, APO 713-Unit Three)

Dear Marion and Cy:

I am afraid I am quite overdue in writing you. As you see, I have had a change of Unit and address, which is much to my liking. However, it somewhat upset my writing schedule.

I received two pounds of Velvet, which I think you sent. Thank you very much—it fits the pipe just right. You spoke of some other package (I haven't your letter with me now, being out at the line) but I haven't seen it as yet. Packages are extremely slow in this part of the world.

I just wrote Mother, describing the area as well as I could, so won't repeat. There is something that I wish you could try, and that is a nice ripe pawpaw, fresh off the tree. You have never tasted anything so delicious; better than the best honeydew, or casaba, or what have you. Wish I could send some home.

Bob's nice letter came yesterday, and if I have time, will write him after this. I enjoyed his Morse code, and read it easily. I guess Mick is too busy in the business world to have time to write. I don't blame him at all. Remember how you used to force me to write letters when we were visiting Seattle?

I had a wonderful ride the other day with—but I'll save it for Bob. This is a swell life here, and I'm in the kind of job I've been looking for, ever since I joined the Army. You will be jealous to know, I'm sure, that we are all well provided with, but good, bonded, bourbon whiskey. I always have a quart for personal use. There are some advantages to fighting a war! As I told Mother, we had a swell turkey dinner Thanksgiving, with all the trimmings. I neglected to mention, that being away from my unit on a trip, I ate elsewhere at noon, and got in on another turkey feed, so fared pretty well. I don't know what we will have for Christmas, but it couldn't be better than Thanksgiving, unless there was ice cream. Boy, what I wouldn't give for a big dish of chocolate or strawberry, or even vanilla—so help me.

There seems so little of all the interesting things I can tell you. It is most annoying and makes letter writing difficult. Have you heard any more from Dinty? Hope he comes down to this part of the world, and we can get together—it will be rough.

Lots of love, keep writing, and don't work too hard,   Wes

DECEMBER 1, 1943 WES TO BOB HUDSON

Dear Bob:

Received your swell letter yesterday. It's fine to hear from you so often. Sounds like you are getting to be quite a football player. Wish I were your age all over again. I'd like to play some football and train to be a fighter pilot. I really envy these youngsters, not so very much older than you—eighteen years and up. They really have a time in the air. Which reminds me—I had the thrill of my lifetime the other day. I talked one of the fellows into taking me up. Of course, there isn't much room, and he had to sit on my lap, but we managed all right. He certainly gave me a ride, with loops, rolls of all kinds, Immelman turns, hammerhead and whip stalls—I mean, it was more fun than I have ever had in my life. He disappointed me a little by being too cautious, and only got up to 350—I would have gone for more. Once I almost blacked out, but taking a deep breath and holding it real hard, came out OK.

There's lots of excitement over here, and I'm really enjoying it. Of course, I miss Gail and John, and all of you, and the good old U. S. is going to look mighty fine to me when I get home.

John has some vicious ideas. He told Gail he wanted me to bring him a Jap skull so he could improve his aim with his pistol. He's really looking after things.

There are plenty of jungles around here, and also beautiful open valleys. If a fellow ever got lost, he could certainly find plenty to eat, like wild bananas, pawpaws, and boy, they really are good.

I spent lots of time out at the line keeping an eye on the pilots and enjoying lots of airplane talk. They sure are great guys, and full of fun. I have a jeep of my own and more or less go and come as I please. Of course, I hold a regular sick call, and am learning a lot about tropical diseases that I never saw at home. I studied about these diseases at Randolph Field, and it certainly is coming in handy these days.

I guess there's not much more I can tell you. Oh, by the way, thanks for the practice in Morse code —TAKE CARE OF YOURSELF—

-...-/./.../-///.-./././—./.-/.-./-../...////

Wes

(I hope the censor understands Morse Code—he may cut this out)

DECEMBER 3, 1943 GAIL TO WES

My Darling,

I'm just as thrilled as you are over your new assignment. It took a long time but somehow Darling, Wes Moore always comes through with what he sets out to do. Hurrah for my Honey!

I waited most anxiously for those two letters that I got today, and I can tell you I was so thrilled that I could hardly work all day. Dr. and I spent about an hour trying to find Gussie but there wasn't anything even approximately like Gu—. It must be something established since our National Geographic maps came out. We've been wondering if you are 75 miles S-N-E-or W of where you were, and have come to the conclusion that it must be N. However, what in the devil were you doing way over in Julian's bed, because we thought that we had Julian pretty well situated at Moresby. That little item threw our calculations all off. Nevertheless, we've put a dot on our maps somewhere between Finchaffen (?) and Madang and said, that's where Wes is. I 'spose we are all wrong—Huh?

Glad you like your C. O., a Flight Surgeon, or are you the only F. S. that was with the 7th Ftr. Sqdn? I expect that is military information, but I hope it is not the kind I have in the back of my head.

I guess you won't have as much time to write as you did, Honey, but gee, I hope you can find time to keep me in letters 'cause they certainly keep me going. By the way, why don't you write on both sides of the sheets and then I won't have to put six cents out to get every letter out of hock. Not that I mind the 6 cents, Sweetie—I'd be more than happy to put out a dollar if it would bring me a letter from you every day. They never cut anything from your letters, it adds more weight for them to ship overseas and it takes 6 extra cents that I could put on our Honeymoon House. They are all good arguments, Honey, but you go ahead and do as you pretty please, if you just continue writing.

It is 9:20 PM and I'm writing this at the hospital. Just finished helping Blank pump out a stomach. Nothing serious, but if anyone has eaten too much or has been vomiting, she pumps 'em out. We sent a little boy home the other day that she had been working over. As nearly as anyone knows, he had some kind of encephalitis. He seems to have come out of it with a little bit of paralysis. However, no one ever did diagnose his case.

The lean days are on, so I've spent the evening gathering together all the bills 'n sending them out. Even got Keith McDonald's out and itemized it from 1941-on, adding "any small payment that you could make on this bill would be greatly appreciated—G.R.M." Keith probably won't even look in my direction tomorrow. I'm saving Everett Wilsey's $480 until Spring and then will camp on his trail until I get the Hospital roof done and the house painted. I'm certainly getting mercenary, Honey.

Doris got a letter from Margaret Claire today and the 3rd little Claire is still in the dark. She said the event was "called off for lack of labor" until about December 10.

Guess I'd better scoot on home now 'cause Mom will be sure something has gotten me. Please, please, be careful Honey, and don't go on any unnecessary jaunts unless you just can't stand it! Wish I could be there to help you!!

Goodnight, Sweetheart.   Yours,
                                        Gail

DECEMBER 5, 1943 GAIL TO WES

Dearest Wes,   #45

From the looks of my number series, it looks as though I might have omitted numbering a few letters. I guess I got so excited over your new assignment that I wasn't very responsible. I don't think you need to worry about being a good Flight Surgeon, Darling—anything you set your heart and head to do you come through on top! We're all so proud of you!

I sent you a piece of our Christmas tree in the airmail letter that I sent off to you Friday. It might not even get to you, Honey, but I thought it might, and you'd have something concrete to look at on Christmas Day to remind you that there still are real Christmas Trees. With that little bit of green foliage comes all our love and a wish for a peaceful Christmas. We hope with all our hearts that this will be the last Christmas you will ever be away from us. By the way, thought you might be interested in knowing that you are giving John a machine gun for Christmas. He has seen a few and seems vitally interested in obtaining one so he can go help his daddy clean up the Japs!

We took a ride up to Dr. L's today and rode partway through the snow. The wind is whipping around the house right now in true winter style. Guess we'll end up with a "white Christmas."

God Bless you, Pop, and praying He keeps you safe for us.
                              Your Johnny and Gail

DECEMBER 5, 1943 WES TO GAIL
(Somewhere in New Guinea)

My Darling   #50·

I have been very neglectful of you, Dearest—five whole days. Please 'scuse—I've been getting a new dispensary built, had to take two days at the hospital in a row because my Group Surgeon has Dengue, and yesterday went to visit Nan! By golly, Nan finally got his majority, and so of course, there being beer on ice, I had to stay overnight! Saw Chris, and he was looking very well. He had a trip to where Julian is, in the two-seater, and managed to run into a little excitement while there. Guess it was close enough to him to require a little extra laundry for the week—use your own discretion about telling Doris!

Your letter of Oct, 15 (#23) with funnies and John's picture and clippings arrived—and a V- from CA, and a nice letter from Nan telling of the ring from Bob. Should be a nice couple.

You were speaking of the *[unreadable]* when I was unable to bathe for days at a time, or have a clean change. That's the worst hardship I've had from this war so far, so you can see the going hasn't been too tough. I did last that part of it through. I'm able to shower and change every day now, and it really makes life worthwhile in the tropics. I took my laundry to that "little town" this trip again, but for the last time. They are putting in a *[unreadable]* laundry. We also are going to have one here, so there should be no necessity. I understand we are to have an ice cream machine too. That will really be a luxury here. Hope they make some strawberry!

The Jap rifle is still at Van's, as it's too much bother at present. My wooden pit and grass skirt from Kirivina are also there. One of these days I'll get real ambitious and send them home. I can't send any shells for the rifle—that's not allowed, so it will have to be re-chambered to fit an American-type shell, 20-20 or 25-20, or something. George Cotter would know when he sees it.

I'm weary from my travels, Dearest, so, all my love—always. Good night, Sweetheart— Goodnight, John—   Wes

DECEMBER 6, 1943 SOUTHWEST PACIFIC AREA (SWPA, Fifth Air Force): In New Guinea, B-24's and B-25's bomb the Alexishafen and Bogadjim areas; A-20's attack targets along the road from Bogadjim to Yaula; B-25's attack targets of opportunity on the Huon Peninsula and others hit the Borgen Bay area and P-39's strafe barges at Borgen and Rein Bays.

DECEMBER 6, 1943 GAIL TO WES
(Plumas Industrial Hospital 8:30 PM)

Honey,

I'm sitting up here at the hospital waiting for Bill and Helen Bailey. I asked Bill if he wanted to see the X-rays on Helen's arm before I sent them back to Dr. Haig, and he said that he did so I have them up on the screen—both Haig's and Dr. B.'s—so that he can see why Helen's arm kept on hurting after Dr. B. "set" it. I guess that I'm not very ethical, but I was never trained to be, so I guess that it is all right. Helen is feeling swell and even played bridge with the Wednesday Club over at Betty's last Wednesday night. She manages to do quite a lot, broken arm and all.—Well, they just came in and Helen moaned, "Oh I'm so glad that I went to Dr. Haig." She said that when that arm popped into place that she didn't feel any pain any longer. I told them that in all fairness to Dr. B. that I would show them the pictures of another Collies (is that the way you spell it?) fracture that he set today. Not having looked at the pictures before, I was kind of anxious to see what they looked like too. When we put them on the screen Bill exclaimed, "My God, I'll bet that poor devil's arm hurts."

While the fracture wasn't as bad as Helen's, he did just about the same kind of a job on it. The piece that is broken sits way away from the line of the rest of the bone and it looks as though there might be a little jagged piece that it sits on holding it up there. I'll bet that you are just thanking your lucky stars that you didn't have a snoopy nose like me around when you were starting out. However, my Darling, at your worst you couldn't have pulled some of the deals that he comes through with.

Mother and Dad are planning to go down to Phoenix to visit with the newly weds sometime in the Spring and I have been toying with the idea of taking John up to see his Grandpa Moore. Esther would probably throw us out after the first couple of days, but maybe if I work with John and teach him some cute things and not to put dirty hands on her walls and be destructive in general, well, maybe she'll let us stay a week. The thought is only in it's infancy and I haven't really made my mind to it, but they were so disappointed when we didn't get up there before we left that I feel it really is my duty to get up there if it is possible. I wouldn't be able to get to the office much if Mother is gone, and by that time, I think that Dr. B. will be one of the khaki clad thousands—that thought, too, is only in it's infancy, but come January, we'll see.

It has been rumored that we are going to be without gas coupons about the 1st of January, so Mother and I have planned a trip to Reno to see what we can buy and if there are any bright lights over there. Doris is going with us. Guess that we'll take off about Wednesday. Poor Johnny is going to be desolate when Lena [Redstreake] comes to the house to take him over for the day. I really don't know why he feels so bad when he gets left with her because she lets him do anything he wants. She takes him downtown and buys him ice cream and gives him jellybeans and generally spoils him. However, it's good to have someone that you can rely upon to take over.

Saturday night I went up to the Dellinger's to help them eat up some crab and prawns that Ruth brought back from the city. Baby Stokes was also there. After dinner Del escorted the three War Widows and Ruth down to the Sump. He tried his damnedest to get out of it, but he really didn't mind so very much.

Dottie tells me that Bunky has been in the hospital about two months. The last report was that they had found a diphtheria germ in his throat. He had that disease when he was a child—are there such things as carriers of diphtheria? She was hoping that he might be sent home.

Everyone that I meet says to tell you Hello for them, so just go down the list of your friends, Honey, and some that you didn't know were your friends, and say hello to yourself so I won't have to go back over the weeks' wandering and think them all up. Guess that it's time to go home now.

All my love   Gail

DECEMBER 7, 1943 GAIL TO WES
[Pearl Harbor Day, 2 years after the attack]

Hi Sweetie—   #47

Got your letter of November 21ˢᵗ today and was glad to hear you seem to be fairly well settled. How much did you have to pay for your 6 quarts? $40.00 apiece? You have to know the right people to get a quart over here! I guess I should say pint 'cause if people have quarts, they certainly are hoarding them. I've been wondering what kind of steaks you have—alligator steaks? Don't tell me that it's good old steer? I certainly hope that it is, though, Honey, 'cause that should be good for your morale.

Well, we have a load going to Reno tomorrow—Mom, Doris, Marg Morris, and Ruth Dellinger. I'm going to try to get a hat and coat for Johnny. He's stretching out of his coat—looks more like a jacket. As he says, "I'm a big boy, Mommie." He's "right insulted" if you call him a little boy. It is really amazing the things that he will do if a big boy does them too.

We are starting out now with real cold days and nights. I was hoping to get in a little skating, but I guess if I did it, it would be with your skates.

Darn, I'm running out of time and this is the only dark ink around the place, so if I run out, you will know what happened.

All my love Darling,   Gail

DECEMBER 8, 1943 WES TO GAIL

Gail Darling,

Two—I mean three—sweet letters from my baby in the last two days. It is pretty swell to have the letters catching up with me so well. And, believe it or not, the two boxes of cigars arrived, and in excellent shape. I have really been having a spree. They are the swellest thing yet, except for your letters. Just think, having Corina Cerinas and bourbon highballs in the jungle—I'm afraid they are going to ruin us soldiers.

I'm glad to note that you are not going to be tied down to the hospital so constantly. That had me a bit worried, Darling, having you grinding away up there every day.

No objections to plunking $500.00 on the house—as I said before, you are the best judge of what to do with the money. Speaking of that, have you received the $400.00 I sent you last month? Since I've been away, I have sent the following: $50.00, $100.00, and $400.00. I knew you received the first two, but haven't heard about the last. Don't let yourself get short for the lean winter—it's no fun if you pay out too much and then feel pinched for three or four months. (Boy, I'll bet you'd fire me in a hurry as a typist. Really, I can do neat work if I take my time; and have to on reports, as there can be no typographical or grammatical errors and no erasures or strikeovers in official correspondences. My Clerk is not very good, so I had to do my own "Care of Flyer" report the other day—I did the D——d thing over four times before I got it out).

I have received a few sporadic issues of the "Bull" *[Feather River Bulletin].* I'm sure it isn't Pop's fault, as that type of mail is always slow and irregular. Everybody is starting to get Christmas packages now, so mine should be along soon. They will be a little delayed because of the address change. By the way, the P. O. is established here now and the final designation is unit 2, APO 713. (Not Unit 3). Same place, same time, same war…

I get a big kick out of your map-reading—very good, too. I am collecting some fairly decent maps to bring home for souvenirs. I know you will enjoy seeing them.

I am surprised that the Christmas card came through so quickly. It must have gone airmail. The artist was our Master Sergeant in the old outfit, a boy named Roberts. You didn't know him, I believe.

I'll certainly be delighted to get the old fountain pen. Believe me, I'll sure hang on to it this time. It's awful to be without one. If you need a request on that, this is it. Now, I will request one, two, or three pair of pajamas—need them badly, as the two I have now are getting worn out rapidly. I'll request the other things in subsequent letters, Dearest.

How was the family Thanksgiving dinner? You will probably answer this question soon, so don't bother with a second answer! Wish I could have been there—maybe next time, I hope.

There is no news to report. I am getting well acquainted with the pilots and enjoying my job no end. I am now established in a nice building, 18 X 20 feet, with metal roof and screening. So far, the floor is dirt, but have been promised tongue and groove flooring. I fixed a little office for myself, 8 X 10 feet, partitioned off with beaver board, so I can have privacy for consultations that warrant it. Also, I am going to keep my personal correspondence file in here—I'm in here now, as a matter of fact, or did you guess it?

Darling, I love you with all my heart and soul; dear John, too. Behave—

> Always yours,
> Wes

DECEMBER 9, 1943 GAIL TO WES

Hello Darling,   #48

We got back from Reno all intact—and it is certainly a wonder too. On the way home we ran into a little bit of snowstorm and a whopper of a wind. It has been blowing ever since too. First I'll tell you about our trip to Reno. We got over there about 10:30 and found that the stores wouldn't be open until about 1 o'clock. It seems that they do that every Wednesday and stay open until about nine so that the Lemon Valley airbase can do some shopping. We nearly froze to death waiting for the doors to open. We had lunch at the Trocodero and then did what shopping we could—there really isn't very much to buy. We met at the Troc, had a drink and then took Doris over to the Town House; had another and then went down to the Fortune Club for dinner. Very nice dinner and a pretty good floor show. We started home about 10 and got here about 12. Last night I thought the house was going to blow apart, the wind was so strong.

Today we had a fire out on the flat. At first I thought it was the Quincy Mill, but I guess that was the wrong impression. Anyhow, it was a terrible day for a fire. Mother just called me a little bit ago and told me that this blow was coast wide and that there were some pretty big fires in Oakland, S. F. and Vallejo as a result of it. She was going to listen to the radio and see if she couldn't get some more details on it. She also said that I had a big fat letter from you there and I can't wait to get home to see what is in it. I thought that it was a package notice, but apparently it was a notice that I had a letter that had a 6 cent due business on it. I'll save the rest of this space and answer any questions that you may have asked in your letter.

7:15 PM. You certainly get around, Honey. Your letter was written the 24th of Nov. #47 and it sounds as though you keep busy running from one spot to another. I should think that would be a great help in breaking the monotony of jungle life. Hope you got your trip in the Stinson! Wouldn't mind one like that myself.

Guess you aren't suffering from lack of turkey over there. I'm certainly glad to hear that Darling—at least you have something to remind you that it is Thanksgiving.

I haven't enough room left to tell you of the Dr. B. deal at the time of your letter. Anyhow, I think the whole thing is going to change. Will let you in on it when it does change.

All my love,

                    Gail

DECEMBER 11, 1943 GAIL TO WES

Wes Darling—   #49

It's Saturday again and a workday at home. Last night the gang—Metzkers, Bedells, Baileys and Ruth and I gathered at the Cotters for a pheasant feed, and it certainly was good. Ken was holding forth on his latest experiences—seems the draft board requested that he write a letter to the effect that 2 former employees, Hugh Hulsman and Frank Weiland, were available for induction. Ken proceeded to do so, embellishing the statement with the fact that they were certainly no loss to the lumber industry. It seems that the draft board showed this letter to the boys and they proceeded to jump him as he came out of the Post Office— the boys being backed by the Benner tribe. Even Ken couldn't talk his way out of that one. He said he thought he was going to have a fight on his hands.

Chuck Grace and wife arrived here yesterday. Chuck is a 2nd Lt. and is flying B-24's. He's stationed at Wendover. The B-24 that I mentioned cruising over our rooftops a couple of months ago was Chuck showing his crew the "real west," and he sure brought them down to take a good look.

Darling, I hope some of your Christmas packages catch up with you by the 25th, and that you get a letter or two.

All my love, my precious,

                    Gail

DECEMBER 12, 1943 WES TO GAIL

Darling—   #52

We have been, oh, so busy the last few days. The old P-40's are really doing a beautiful job of work, and yours truly's not too far behind. It's fun—glorious—I love action such as we have had from time to time. Honey, I'm so glad I came out here. We are really of value to the AAF.

Your #33 of Nov. 8 came through a little out of line, but tremendously enjoyable. I have a complete series up to #40 except #35!

You know, I believe I forgot to mention the fishing tackle when I thanked you for the cigars. I've been far too busy to think of fishing just yet, but sure will wet a line when a lull comes. I'm going to take a couple of days off and go up into the hills when I can. The old Jeep takes me almost anywhere—even drive it out to the latrine, I'm getting that lazy! There are fish in these streams and plenty of angleworms for the digging, so I'll be off soon.

Honey, I love you so—I miss you and dear John. It will be wonderful to see you again— you know that, and don't ever fear about me going off without you until you get damned good and tired of seeing me!

Please send another <u>nail clipper</u>—this takes priority over the funnies! You know the kind I use. I'll ask for funnies next. And Dear, don't forget pictures of <u>you, John, and close friends</u>.

I was sorry to hear of the auto accident wherein the hitch hiker was killed. Guess it's all blown over by now.

No more now, Dearest—but will hope I can keep up the schedule better for awhile. I'm well and <u>not in any danger</u>—so don't worry about me!

All my love, always Dearest Sweetheart—

Your Wes

P. S. Am sending clipping from the "Bull" to Chris—about Doris.

UNDATED. GAIL TO WES

My Darling,

Just mailed your Christmas package. I sent along a present from Esther and Dad Moore. Esther wanted it to be a separate package, but I mailed it in mine. I'm 'fraid you won't like the pajamas, but it was all I could buy. I just got a pair from Ruth that are like your old ones and will send them along in a week or so.

Del just came home from a hunting trip (5 days' duration) with the biggest buck that he had ever seen—said it took 2 Indians to haul it out. He went over to Nevada to get it.

I went on up to the house and dug out some of John's toys, including the rocking horse, and he is having a wonderful time with it—I guess you got it when he was a little too young to appreciate it Honey. When we were up there, he wanted to know if we couldn't live there again. Gee, Sweetheart, I wish we were—all three of us!

The CAP finally fixed Charlie Beattie's plane up—some 500 hour Bay pilot landed it down in the lower end where it was all plowed up. The occupants didn't get hurt much, but I guess the ship is a mess. I thought it would get wrecked long before this!

All my love, my precious

Gail

DECEMBER 13, 1943 TELEGRAM WES TO GAIL

LOVING WISHES FOR CHRISTMAS AND NEW YEAR. ALL WELL AND SAFE. ALL MY LOVE=DEAREST==JOHN W MOORE

DECEMBER 13, 1943 GAIL TO WES

My Darling,   #50

Got a couple of letters from you today, #'s 48 and 49. Number 49 was written on Nov. 30th and got here in 13 days, which is darn good time if you should ask me.

Gosh, I just get started on this and a big old hurricane blows Dr. B. in the door. Dr. and Margarite are just on their way home. Dr. did a hernia on Ralph Gill this morning. It only took him 45 minutes, so I guess that he is still doing all right. Dr. Blank would have been in there three hours if she could figure out which end to work on.

I certainly am jealous of your ride piggyback. Darn, I wish that I would get that chance just once. However, it would just about be my luck to black out at 200 mph and I'd probably miss the rest of the ride. I don't seem to have that trouble with my P-40 (the Taylorcraft L55, belonging to Shaw, Brown and Grover). If I can get her up to 100 I consider it pretty good. Yesterday I had quite the flying day. I put out 2 hours of instruction. I took Otto up for an hour and learned quite a bit about flying while I gave him a lesson. He's had 4 hours and is doing right well. 'Course he did tell me all of the things that I did that Draper wouldn't let him do, but it's about time someone was tripping me up because I haven't had any dual for more than a year, and I'm telling you that I am plenty rusty.

I had Floyd Shaw up for my second hour dual, and he insisted that I sit on the right hand side. Found out that it is quite different switching around like that—made an awful sloppy takeoff, and when I got off the ground, couldn't seem to make a decent turn; however, we managed to get up and down a couple of times without ground looping, or running into anything. Floyd made the second landing, which was pretty good, except that we would have buried our nose in the turf if I hadn't hauled back on the stick.

He can't seem to get onto the trick of taking up the slack and easing her into a three-pointer. Maybe it's because I come in about 85 like I do in the Luscombe and he thinks that if it is going that fast that we should have the nose down. The last half hour I took Margie Moore up in the Luscombe.

Bud was to report to his draft board today. I don't know where he is going to end up. He can't get into Kings City or Dos Palos, or any of the rest of them because they are requiring graduation from Randolph now. So I guess that Bud is going to have to get into some airplane factory or something if he doesn't want to go in as a buck Private.

I was going to write this in ink, but after reading your letter that you couldn't make out the V-Mail, I decided that it would be more legible if I typed it. I don't wonder that you can't read my writing, it's super, super horrible sometimes.

The "bucket of bolts" is running beautifully. We aren't getting enough gas to get very far away from home—I have half a tank to do me until January 21st. Guess I won't be going very far. I've heard that they might take a book away from us on the 1st of January, so maybe I'm ahead at that.

Guess that Esther has written you by now that they found the "stones" was something else and that your Dad has a kidney infection. They seemed right relieved about it. Hope that everything turns out OK.

CA is leaving tonight about 8:30 AM and the airport gang is cooking supper out at his house and taking him to the train. They will probably have to pour him on by that time in the morning. However, he may behave himself because if the Flyer doesn't stop out here, someone is going to have to drive him up to Portola to catch it.

It is getting along toward 5 o'clock, so I think I'll sign off before I get to the end of the paper.

Did any packages get to you by Christmas?

All my love, Sweet—

Gail

DECEMBER 15, 1943 WES TO GAIL

Gail Dearest—   #53

No letters from you for a few days, Honey—oh, but one! I forgot! #42 came day before yesterday. I wish I could be with Johnny, myself, Dear. These formative years are wonderful to watch. I do enjoy all you tell me about him. He's always been plenty smart, and plenty on the ball.

Thanks for sending the trees to Mother and Dad. She always gets such a big kick out of it. I imagine they will be scarce in the cities this year. I hate to miss that tree collecting party—two Christmases I've missed, now!

Say, Honey, those cigars are wonderful, and in excellent condition. I was surprised—they are so nice and fresh, after that long journey in hot weather. I'm really enjoying them. I'll quit when I get home—for you, Dear. By the way, it was so much trouble keeping my moustache trimmed, I cut it off the other day. If you want me to grow another for you to make me cut off, I will—later!

I went down to see Major V. today and get my laundry. He thinks he can visit me next week. I'll really get him stiff if he does! One of these days I'm going to see Julian. I would have gone there today, but couldn't catch a ride. I'd like to have the dough it would cost at home to travel so much, the way we do, here. Things are not dull lately—lots of fun had by all. Am enjoying it plenty. I picked up my Jap rifle today and will try to mail it soon. You won't be able to shoot it, so I can't send any ammunition—just look at it, if it ever gets there!

While at Unit One, APO 713, today, I sent you $200.00 (L61/19/2). Hope it gets there OK.

My dispensary is coming along swell. We are going to have a concrete floor poured in a few days. I'm very busy with the usual assortment of mosquito-borne diseases, etc.

Auntie Katherine wrote me a nice letter. Tell her I will answer in a few days.

My love to the family, and always you and John—

Forever yours,   Wes

DECEMBER 15, 1943 GAIL TO WES

Hello Sweetheart,   #50 (?)

Received your Christmas greeting today—a little early, but certainly welcome.

Guess what! I'm going to ferry a Luscombe 65 to Phoenix tomorrow. 'Course he *(Stu)* is going to fly alongside in a Culver Cadet, but nevertheless, I'm flying alone to Phoenix. The bride and bridegroom have promised to put me up and I'm carting along a couple of young steers cut New York style, so I guess they will be glad to see me. We plan to start out at daybreak and get there by sundown. We are going the same way that you and I flew, except we are skipping Parker and taking in Quartzite. Mother and Dad looked into it from every angle to be sure that there wouldn't be reason for anyone to talk about me.

Dr. got a letter from an M. D. in San Jose today. He said the P. & A. Board had told him of the situation here and did we still need someone. He's served a couple of years in the Army and has a discharge. He is 34, has a wife and graduated from Vanderbilt in 1935. He didn't say why he was discharged. From his writing, I should say that it might be chronic drunkenness. He writes a worse letter than I do.

Wish I were taking off in one of your fighters, Sweetie.

All my love forever,

Gail

DECEMBER 17, 1943 GAIL TO WES
(Phoenix, Arizona)

Hi Wes—   #51

Too bad you can't be here tonight and join our gay party—big steak with all the trimmings a la Moon! Anyway—we are thinking of you and wishing the best for you.

From a new sister-in-law —

Kookie *[Maribelle Ricker]*

Darling—

No foolin'— sure wish you were here. I'm lonesome with these lovesick folks. We—Stu and I got as far as Luke Auxiliary Field #6 before <u>dark</u> (and I mean dark) caught up with us. David and Kookie came 35 miles to collect us. It was a swell trip—didn't get lost once. 'Course Stu flew right on my wing tip to see that I didn't wind up in Parker, Arizona.

The Honeymooners are doing swell, and David really has something to be proud of—wish you knew her.

All my love

Gail

P. S. This is all the space they would allow me. Sure wish you were here to help me take care of these two. Here you are right among them. If you see any of my boys, tell them hello, but please don't let them pack me back. Get a couple of those so & sos for me as it looks like they don't think an old man like me can take care of himself in those wild old spots without a good traffic pattern. I can still get into Quincy Sky Harbor, though!!

Dave

DECEMBER 18, 1943 WES TO GAIL

Sweetheart: #54

Your letters are coming along with pleasing frequency. You're catching up with me, now. I just can't seem to keep up with my every other day schedule. I have #43, two #44's and #45—the last one was the first to be addressed to my new address. Although it said Unit one, it came right on through.

Dr. Bailey's medicine came through in good shape, and lasted about one minute. My old favorite C. C., I believe, and sure good. We are getting Old Schenley mostly now, 6 years old, and very good. Thank you, Darling, for that, the tobacco and pouch—I needed one of those. Also the bunch of funnies was very welcome. (Please send me some more funny papers). Also received Katherine and Dot's chess set, and the cards and cribbage and checkers games from the H. S. Watsons *[Tiny and Anne]*. It was sweet of them to do that for me, and I will get a lot of enjoyment out of them, especially on the days I have to spend out at the line with nothing to do but watch the P-40's take off and land. I will write them right away.

I'll be looking forward to that bit of Christmas tree—I love the smell. Dearest, I certainly echo your sentiments about being home for next Christmas. I miss you and John so much. Honey, you are a wonderful wife—no man ever had one half as sweet. I'm so happy having you for mine.

I hope John enjoys his machine gun. I know he will have a big time this Christmas—he will be able to appreciate things more than last year. Wish him a Merry Christmas from Daddy, and to you, Dear, and the family, my love and best wishes. I'll miss the white part of it this year. It will be pretty swell to see snow again one of these days.

I'm glad to know Wally's wife wrote to you. I asked him to have her write again of recent changes. You've been pretty good at your guesses. However, don't let proximity worry you, as things are far different from anything I ever pictured. It really is lots of fun at times. I'm glad to hear you received the $400.00, and hope the $200.00 will get there OK. Sounds like your use of it is sound. You are a good little business lady.

I think Van will be up to see me tomorrow or the next day. We will probably do a little exploring. I don't doubt that we will see more of the country in one day than I have since I've been here.

About your questions on vapor trails: Aircraft flying high always leave vapor trails, more or less, depending on the atmospheric conditions. Also, on fast pullouts at any altitude, they are apt to "pull" streamers, or short-lived vapor trails. The high ones last quite a while, and you can tell where the planes are even if you can't see them. It makes the action far more interesting. Like Tex Rankin at the Oroville Airport opening.

Take it easy on that dog fighting in light planes, Honey—don't pull a wing off the old Silvaire. I know you are a good girl, though, and wouldn't do half the foolish things I do in an airplane.

Goodnight, now, Dearest. All my love, always, your

                                                                        Wes

— AND A HAPPY NEW YEAR FOR ALL OF US —

DECEMBER 21, 1943 GAIL TO WES

Darling—

Guess you've been wondering why no mail. Stu and I started off from Phoenix Sunday morning. David had gotten weather reports that said we could make it to Reno—what those weather reports meant was that <u>he</u> could make it to Reno. Coming out of Silver Lake, it began to close in on us, so we went up to Death Valley to try to get around it. We got as far as the Furnace Creek Inn airport, so we decided it would be best to sit down. The Park Ranger and his wife took us in and we've been here ever since.

Honey, it's like that Parker deal—"it never rains in Death Valley," but it is certainly pouring down now. It seems every time I fly anywhere, I run into phenomenal weather.

Yesterday, Mrs. Oaks, the Ranger's wife, took us through Furnace Creek Inn. It's nice, but it can't hold a candle to Timberline Lodge. We were going to go to Scotty's Castle today, but Mrs. Oaks said we'd probably get in a cloud burst and she wouldn't take us. I can't even get a bus out of this place, and golly, I should be getting home. Guess the hospital can run without me, and when I called Mom, she said Johnny was well, so guess I'll sit tight.

All my love, Sweet, forever and ever—

                                        Gail

DECEMBER 23, 1943 WES TO GAIL

Dearest Gail: #56

Two more nice letters today, Darling, and a great big package from Rogers, Moore and Co. Thank you all for such swell gifts. John, I see you are getting to be a big boy; Daddy was proud to see that you could write on a card for him. Thank you for the soap—Daddy needed it, and it will help him to keep nice and clean, like big boys do. The books were really wonderful, Dave and Mom-thanks a lot. What did you mean about putting off the laundry three days? Wish I could send my laundry home. I haven't had anything really clean for so long I've just about forgotten how it feels! Also received a package from the Foleys, a picture of Robert and the girl, and two packages of Camels. Honey, the funny papers are really swell. They certainly are a popular item over here. I have to hide them until I can read them, or I would never see them—they sure go like hotcakes. Please send some more funny papers.

Did you think I was buying the whiskey? It's Government issue. I draw six or eight quarts every week for the pilots—and in quart bottles. That why you poor civilians have to stick to pint size. And as for the meat, I hope to tell you we get good steer meat. Steak two or three times a week. Fresh eggs are rather short, but we get them two or three mornings a week. Everyone really gets up on time for breakfast when we have eggs. In fact, the first man up usually goes around and wakes everyone to tell them there are fresh eggs! Breakfast is over—period—by 7:30, and of course, yours truly is ALWAYS up by then—well, almost always! I do hate to miss breakfast, though. Never seem to get filled up lately. I hold sick call from 7:00 to 8:00 and 6:00 to 7:00 PM. I usually get there about half an hour after sick call starts so the boys can have all the record cards out and ready, and have the routine stuff out of the way. Then I go to work on the ones that really need a doctor. I'm using a card system that works pretty well. A piece of typewriter paper folded in the middle, and turned to open like a book. I have the necessary spaces mimeographed on the front, and use the card permanently for each case.

I'm going to miss the white Christmas it sounds like you are going to have. A little cold weather would be welcome. Day before yesterday was the longest day of the year, for us "down under," in case you didn't remember, and plenty of heat to go with it.

I enjoy riding around in the transports, and it does, as you say, help to break the monotony. The only trouble is when you get someplace, it's always so darned hard to find transportation—just like when we used to flit around the country in the Aeronca. It's OK at this end, as I have my own jeep, and can take myself to the landing field, but at the other end, it's hard to contact the right person to come and get you. The field phone service isn't all it should be at times.

I'm using the paper Annie and Tiny sent me. I should have written to them on it, but it was clear over in my tent at the time I wrote them, and I was too lazy to walk over there and get it, so tell them I am using it, Dear, and that I like it very much.

Christmas Eve tomorrow night. We are to have one pound of turkey per man for Christmas—twice what we had for Thanksgiving. I am wondering how many will be able to eat their share after what is planned for the night before. I'll bet there will be several Sad Sacks around Christmas Day. I have issued an edict that there will be no hangovers treated Christmas morning, because I expect to have one myself! Goodnight now, my Sweetheart, and a Merry Christmas to you all.

All my love, Dearest, always your

Wes

DECEMBER 23, 1943 GAIL TO WES

Hello Sweetheart,

I'm back in God's Country again trying to catch up with my work. We finally got out of Death Valley—landed at Independence, and then pushed the fog out of our way to land at Minden. A couple of Army DC-3's that were fogged out of Reno and Lemon Valley came in on our tail, and while trying to get out of their way, we got stuck in the mud. Those devils aboard the big ships just laughed at us as they plowed right through the mud. We couldn't land at Quincy, so we ended up leaving the little peewees at Beckwith and Dad packed us up and brought us to Quincy.

Tom Ayoob, Sr. had a stroke and passed away. His funeral was today. Doris had a note from Teddy Myers saying they are closing Pendleton Field and they are moving to Spokane.

The Flu epidemic is going full blast. Even Margarite is down with it. Came home to find everyone in the hospital vaccinated for Small Pox. Blank had put a small pox patient in, although neither she nor Dr. B. thinks it's more than Chicken Pox.

Had two letters waiting for me, Darling, and was certainly glad to get them. Seems like a long time between letters. It just doesn't seem like Christmas without you, Honey—Can't seem to get into the swing of it. Hope Johnny doesn't sense the way I feel.

All my love forever and ever, my Darling.

Your Gail

DECEMBER 24, 1943. A COMPOSITE CHRISTMAS LETTER TO WES
[Quincy, California]

Hi Wes, We at the Schott house wish you were here to celebrate Christmas. This is a very, very special one here, as well you know. We extend you a rain check on the refreshments. Oh, by the way, our "Mike" has a tooth! Best wishes from our house: Ole, Clarence, Mary, Mike.

Hello Wes — Wish you were here to have Tom and Gravy with us. We sure miss all of you boys that are away. Hope next X-mas you all are back. Everything in Quincy just the same. I had a nice duck shoot with Jake at the Colusa Gun Club. Didn't make the Thule Lake on account of gas rationing, but we will give the fish and ducks a good working over when you come back.   Del

Merry Christmas, Uncle. We all wish we were with you in the Great Pacific. We hear so many interesting tales from there. No doubt you are very happy and contented, while we must while away another dull winter in Quincy. Sure wish we could be together this X-mas.

Nothing of interest to report in a letter like this with everybody reading it, including the "little misses," but will give you all the low-down in the near future on some of your low friends.   Ken

Dear Wes: I'm honored by being invited to add a line or two to this. When I heard the "round the world broadcast" last night, including your island (or continent), I listened carefully for your voice. However, it did not come. So, we are doing as well as we can to celebrate Christmas as we Americans should celebrate it—but it is a hard job, too many absentees. But I join the others in greeting you and extend best wishes for my family. Dan

Dear Wes — Hope you have a Merry Christmas and a Happy New Year. Hope you will be in Quincy next Christmas —   Dottie

"Doc"   Christmas '43 is rather empty without those of you who would rather be with your families, but "fella" sometime soon we hope it'll be as before and with it all the good in mankind that has been dormant can be put to more useful purpose. Knowing me, you can believe with me that I wish I were with you. Through it all, those of us that remain will do a very little to compensate for those like you doing tremendous jobs. Merry Christmas, fella—I know you'll make the best of it. See you soon.   Bill Dieleson

Hi Wes — I haven't my glasses, they're home, so this may not track straight—but anyway, here's Greetings and all Good Wishes to you, and we hope you'll be home to celebrate next Christmas and New Years. Young Dan was home for a week—a grand surprise, but he had to report at Fort Sill on Christmas to complete his Liaison Pilot training. Very best wishes from us all.
                    Barbara Sr.

Hello Wes — Hope you are having a Merry Christmas, but of course, we wish you were having it here. I could use a little expert flying instruction—Gail does her best with me, though, and it's good. Best wishes for 1944.   Barbara, Jr.

Dear Wes, The Baldwins (3) helped us eat our Christmas turkey tonight as we are suppose to have Xmas dinner at Katherine's tomorrow when Ernest will be here. Gail thought it would be terrible to have no Xmas dinner, so we called in the Baldwins. John had a very fine time last night. He had an awful time trying to stay awake until Santa (Roby) arrived at 8:30, but he had most of his toys to play with, so that helped. He really got a thrill out of everything. Opening packages is right in his line. His Pa couldn't have thrown the papers around any better. The main toy, a scooter, has wooden wheels and it really needs an elephant to push it, but he seems pleased. There were no electric trains for the Papa's to play with this Christmas.

We miss you a lot and wish this war would end. We are glad you are getting a kick out of being there. John has a wooden machine gun that he shoots Japs with. David sent him boxing gloves. Looks as if he is going to start promoting John now that he wants Gail to be a lady. Did she tell you that David was scheduled to go across, but his Colonel asked for him to remain at Luke. That was our best Xmas present. The gambling game, 3 Baldwins and Gail, is going on. Gail just remarked that it was the first time she ever overbid, so I guess she got set. We were glad to get her back out of Death Valley, but glad they had a nice place to come down out of the clouds. Harley and Mabel are billing and cooing next door. They were married Tuesday. Too bad he isn't taken in the draft—a young man with his young ideas ought to help the war effort. It's time to go to sleep, but I guess I'll play a little more bridge, so good night and good luck for the New Year.

Edith

DECEMBER 24, 1943 GAIL TO WES
(Christmas Eve)

Darling,

It's a lonesome old season without you as are the rest of the days of the year. It is 10 PM. The Baldwins—Barbara Jr. & Sr. and Dan and Mother are all playing bridge—Dad and John have hit the hay. John was certainly cute last night. He had a great time with the "toys" Santa brought him. Roby Bishop was dolled up in the Santa suit and John wasn't quite sure whether to accept Santa as a person or not. He had the most quizzical expression on his face all the while Santa was here.

By the way, be sure to write to the Foleys—Patsy and Robert—because they ask about you every time they see me.

John got a scooter, building blocks, boxing gloves, Tommy gun, suits, books and lots of other things—none of them will last very long; they all seem so frail. John is very interested in the alphabet and really does quite well.

Got two letters from you today, Sweet, and that was a swell Christmas present. #'s 52 and 53—December 12 and 15. Good time! I'll try to get your pajamas and nail clipper off to you. The nail clipper won't be very sharp. It's Johnny's. You can't buy them, you know.

Tell the gang (that I know) hello for me—and Merry Christmas. I didn't get any cards off this year, Honey, too busy gadding about the country—however, a lot of people didn't send out cards.

Don't let those mosquitoes bite you, Darling—I was reading in the Medical Dictionary about that Dengue stuff.

All my love forever—Hope you come home to us soon—

Gail

DECEMBER 27, 1943 GAIL TO WES

Hello Sweetheart,

The holidays are over and everyone is working again. I'm at the office now. It's 8:15. Dr. B. and I just put a stitch in W. P. R. R. Fisher's jaw and that was all the business for today—or should I say, tonight. The hospital is full of flu patients—most of them contract. Some fun! Everyone seems to have the flu except a few who have Scarlet Fever. No one seems to be dying, so I guess it can't be as bad as last year. I guess you know that the whole Metzker family had it. Guess Helen was pretty sick. She has a *[unreadable]*—like figure now.

Gee, New Years is coming up, Sweet, and then our anniversary. Five years and such swell ones too. If I could only be out there on that flight line with you. Gee! It must be interesting. Maybe if I had a little of that, David wouldn't have to bawl me out about taxiing out in Stu's prop wash.

Guess I'm getting sleepy—can't even seem to write things straight. I'm waiting for the sun to come out from behind our high overcast so I can take a couple of more snaps and send them to you. Don't give up, Darling. I'll get them to you.

All my love, Honey, forever and ever

Gail

DECEMBER 29, 1943 WES TO GAIL

Dearest—   #57

No news since I last wrote. Hope tomorrow will be an improvement. We had a wonderful party last night. There were 10 cases of beer and plenty of whiskey to go around. Didn't get to bed 'till 2:30 this morning. Believe me, things were plenty quiet around here today. Yours truly behaved himself well and sang loudly with the rest of the boys—all the filthy songs in the repertoire, plus a few like "Noel," etc. Can't say that I felt much like getting up this morning.

The holidays were entirely *[unreadable]* by any excitement. A completely peaceful Christmas.

Dear, excuse such a short letter. I'm heading for bed right now, though it is only eight bells (2000 hours).

Always your

Wes

DECEMBER 29, 1943 GAIL TO WES
(12 Midnight)

Honey—   #51

Just came home from Baldwin's where we all had a turkey dinner and then played bridge. John went to sleep on Dan's bed—just like old times at Santa Anna—we take him with us 'cause all his regular nursemaids have the flu. He was an awfully good boy during dinner—you would have been proud of him.

Got a letter today and was happy to hear that the tobacco and C. C. reached you OK. Sorry there couldn't have been more of the latter, but kind of wondered if that would get there. The pouch and C. C. were a present from B. Bailey. Haven't seen anything of the $200.00, but will write you immediately upon receipt of same.

By the way, Dad Watson gave us a $75.00 bond for Christmas. I know that he would more than appreciate a letter from you. I guess he wants to give away and enjoy what little he has while body and spirit are together.

Your old friend Louis Martinelli (Quincy Railroad contract) came up to the hospital yesterday—the lower part of his face blue as could be and his feet and hands and neck swollen twice their normal size. While Dr. was home, Dr. B. used up all our oxygen on him and was Dr. burned up today. He had seen Louis before he left for Sloat and had left orders. Dr. B. immediately makes his own orders and messes up the works. He proceeds to tell the hospital Louis won't last long, so it's all over town today Louis's dead. Some fun. Ah well, the Army will take all that out of him if they will allow him in their ranks!

All my love, Precious. Yours-   Gail

DECEMBER 29, 1943 WES TO GAIL

Dearest Gail: #58

I had a wonderful bunch of mail yesterday. Two V-mails and an Airmail from my best girl. (I sure enjoy the Airmails). A letter (V) from Esther telling me about Dad. A V from Bob Hudson (with some more Morse code), a very sweet letter from Aunt Harriet with one from Uncle Leslie, with a card, a Christmas card from Barney (no letter, the rat), a card and letter from George and Elda, and not the least, by far, a nice letter from Dave and Edith. Then today, an announcement of Dave and Maribelle's wedding—some crop. Oh, yesterday, also, two Rooters with notes from Link [C. Lincoln Peckinpah] and a newsletter from the V. F. W.

I think it is wonderful the instructions you are giving. Don't let those birds put you in the right hand seat until you are absolutely sure of their ability. I'll never forget the close one I had with Julian one day in the Silvaire when he did his damnedest to stick the left wing tip into the ground on the South side of the fence. I had to yank hard to get the thing out of his hands, because he didn't even realize that he was in trouble. I'm afraid you might not have the strength to overcome some dummy's mistake, so be careful, Dearest. I have the utmost faith in you, but not these dumb students!

I'm thrilled about your ferry job to Phoenix, and wish I could be along with you. We had such a swell trip together over there in the little old Air knocker. In fact, we've had some mighty wonderful trips all around the good old U. S.

Sounds like the old Olds isn't going to be overworked in 1944. That's one trouble we don't have. My little old Jeep is picked up every evening and gassed up for me, greased every week and tires, etc. checked. All I do is get in and go where and when I want to. They sure are wonderful in compound low with the four wheel drive engaged—you can go through any kind of mud, and over almost any obstacle. I sure hope I can get one after the war—they would be the real ticket for getting into Gold Valley. That old hill behind Opie Payne's would be duck soup for one. You can haul a trailer behind one with a one ton load on it.

By the way, I got quite a kick out of your efforts. Try ap instead of ie, and otherwise you are OK. That's a tough navigation problem with the kind of maps you are working from. I should try to get a better one before making that cross country with Gus. He's not any too sure of his navigation, I've found! North is the best route this time of year. Seventy five miles is right for the last lap. *[Wes just described his route in the transport via his and Gail's secret code.]*

Our C. O. lived up to the expectations I first had. He's really a prince of a fellow. Unfortunately, all good things must end, and as he has had a good two years overseas, he is going home shortly. But I'm glad for him, he deserves it.

In regard to visits to Julian—don't get the idea we were just next door before he moved. You can go quite a ways in three hours these days, you know. So don't let that upset you. Hope that I can get the chance to visit him in his new place of business next time I go flying. You mentioned his whereabouts once in your airmail letter, inadvertently, when you said between _____ and _____. I guess that will keep you guessing. *[More secret code.]*

The Flight Surgeon I replaced was moved up to Group Surgeon for the 49th Group, of which the 7th Fighter is just a squadron—as you can tell from the address. There are other squadrons, too of the group, each with a Flight Surgeon. If I stick around a year or two, my turn will come to be a Group F. S., when I will be eligible for a majority. Hope the war doesn't *[unreadable]* when I will be eligible for a majority. Hope the war doesn't last that long. I'd just as soon come home a Captain, if it is going to take a couple of years to be a Major. As it is, I don't see any possibility of getting home under a year from now. Of course, that is just a guess. Hope I am all wrong.

I'm sorry you have to pay 6 cents on my letters. I have no airmail stamps other than what are on the envelopes. We are only supposed to write on one side of the sheet, so that if anything must be censored, they can cut a piece right out without destroying anything on the other side. I'm surprised that my letters are running over one ounce. Well, Darlin', am about out of paper and must get busy on some other letters to catch up with that flood that came in. If I keep up all night on this typewriter, I'll have the skin all worn off my fingers.

All my love, Dearest, and tell John Daddy is thinking of him and loves him.

Goodnight.

Wes

DECEMBER 29, 1943—SOUTHWEST PACIFIC THEATER OF OPERATIONS (Fifth Air Force): On New Britain Island in the Bismarck Archipelago, 120+ B-24's, B-25's, and B-26's pound positions at Cape Gloucester as the US Marines take the major objective, the airfield. In New Guinea, B-25's hit Madang; B-24's bomb bivouac and communications targets near Sio, and other B-24's fly a light attack against Manokwari, hitting the town and shipping.

DECEMBER 30, 1943 WES TO BOB HUDSON

Dear Bob—

Another swell letter from you yesterday. I'll say you are a good correspondent, and keep me busy keeping up with you. I'm sorry to hear you got sick during your vacation and couldn't make a little extra dough.

A "stall" means that an airplane has lost flying speed, so that it starts to fall, usually nose first, or it may start turning at the same time, when it is said to be in a "spin." A "hammerhead stall" is accomplished by zooming and holding the nose straight up as long as possible. The airplane slides back a little like a ball that has been thrown in the air—then the nose suddenly drops, causing a violent snap, and you think someone hit you in the back of the head with a hammer—*[drawing of the maneuver]* Get the idea? .-/-/ // ./.-/.../.

There is plenty doing around here these days, and I may say, a lot of excitement. We had a swell Christmas dinner with plenty of turkey to go around—hope the next Christmas I'm home. I'd be willing to eat corned beef hash to be there, and boy, I don't like hash. We get plenty of it too!

Love to you and Mick and Marian and Cy—

Your Uncle Wes

DECEMBER 31, 1943 GAIL TO WES

Hi Sweetie Pie,

Here I am up at the office again without my numbers (letter #'s). Guess I'll have to wait until I get home to put the number on this. I got your number 55 today written on December 20th. It made pretty good time. So you are "sweating" out a Liaison Pilot's license! I don't know what good it would do you to get one, Honey; they certainly wouldn't release you from your medical duties so that you could fly liaison, would they? I'll try to find your logbooks. I think that they are in your footlocker. Just what does a liaison pilot have to do—any chance of my applying? My off jobs as instructor, barnstormer and ferry pilot are running out on me, and besides, we are going to have a good snow in a few days (Stouky predicts it), so maybe I could learn to be a liaison pilot too.

Darling, if you think that you are the only one who gets lonesome, you are just plain balmy, and if you think that I wouldn't like to be out there riding in that jeep with you, you are even balmier, but that tent, oh boy does it sound inviting! Think I'll pack my duds and stow away in some transport headed for the S. W. P. A. and come on down. Bet I'd look cute out there in the jungle stripped to the waist, now wouldn't I? Fine question it is that you ask me—do I love you? You really don't know, do you, Honey, that I love you with all I have and miss you like the very devil. Somehow, darn it all, I can't give expression to all the things I'd like to say—I told you once, Honey, that my power of expression was very limited, at least when it comes to saying it. Anyhow you know how I feel without having to put it into pretty words.

I don't have the slightest notion who the nuts were from. I'll inquire around and see what I can find out. I still haven't sent you any pictures, my love, but will get right at it when the sun comes out and I can finish up the roll that I have in the camera.

Golly, it is 5:45 and everyone has gone home. Dr. and I were just fighting the war. Now he has gone up to take his New Years nip, so I guess that I had better fold this up and get home to dinner. The prospect for this New Years eve looks bleak and uninviting. Wish you were here, Darling, so I could put my arms around you and give you a big New Years kiss—just to start the year right.

1-1-44. New Years Eve is over—Dottie and Leda and I did a pretty good job of crashing parties. We walked in on Marg. and Owen—they had a whole mess of people there and we crashed the Fireman's Ball about 2:30. Del loaded us all in the car and we went up and pulled Ray Smith out of bed—I got so darn lonesome and homesick that I sneaked out on them and came on home. Today is a gloomy, rainy day—can't even fly.

Take good care of yourself, Sweetheart, and all my love

Gail

CHAPTER 8
1944

Darling—   #59

I love you in 1944 just as much as before, maybe more!

Have a slight bit of a head today, but not bad. We had a pleasant New Year's Eve party, with the usual assortment of liquor and wit. No beer this time.

I wrote eight letters on the 30th, to catch up with the flood of correspondence which came in. Since then, I received the cute note from you and Dave and Kookie.

As I had written them just before, I haven't written again, but will when well suited. Now I am "sweating out" your return trip, which I know will be without incident—but nevertheless, as your fond husband, I feel a certain suspense, waiting for word from you on your return! I'm a silly fellow, I suppose you think—

The package of funnies arrived, with your letter about Helen's arm. I'm certainly glad you took measures, Dearest—you showed extremely good judgement.

The letter from the P. O. department in regard to female letter carriers was plenty good. The boys got quite a kick out of it. I put it on the bulletin board.

I wonder if you are still planning on visiting the folks in Seattle as you said in your Dec. 6 letter. It would be nice if you could. I know they would really enjoy it. How would you go—on the train?

I'm interested in this question of Dr. B. going into the Service, which seems to keep popping up in your letters—what's the low-down?

Could you send me a box of chocolates? Those manufactured chocolate creams seem to come through pretty well if well wrapped in heavy cardboard.

I'm glad to hear that a grass skirt went through the mail—I'll pick up mine at Van's and send it along. Still haven't gotten a box made for the gun.

Yes, there are diphtheria carriers, apparently perfectly healthy people. Sorry to hear about Bunky.

I'm going to desist now—all my love, Sweetheart—

Your Wes

JANUARY 2, 1944 GAIL TO WES
(4:30 PM)

Hello, my Darling,   #52

The snow is piling up and I guess we are in for a siege—it has that look of slow determination that produces results. Guess I'll have to dig up the skis and the sled if it keeps up this pace. Gee Honey, would you like to take a trek up the Gold Lake road? That was a lot of fun, wasn't it?

Just came home from Ken's and Helen's; they are all well for a change, and Johnny had a wonderful time playing with John G. *[John Gordon Metzker].* The Metzkers are going out with the Bailey's to dinner. We are invited over to the Morrises'. Elda was over at the Metzkers and she said George was expecting to get drafted and that he wanted to get his hours in and his Instructor's rating. Don Alexander is to take his last physical tomorrow. Fergason's number is up and so is Ole Olson. I guess about 40 notices went out to prewar fathers on Jan. 1, 1944.

Sunday 7:30 PM. Had to stop to go over to Morrises' for dinner—Margaret splurged and we had a leg of lamb. Very good too. Turkey is getting very monotonous—everyone has it 'cause it doesn't cost any points.

We have about two inches of snow since noon and it isn't wasting any time right now. I guess Irene and Bud Moore didn't get in from Phoenix today 'cause we have been closed up tight. They started out about last Wednesday in CA's Luscombe and I'll just bet he will be madder than a hatter. He was pretty mad at Bud when he took his little airplane to Sweetwater, but when he takes his gal too, I'll bet CA won't be too pleased about it. They are liable to be snowed out now.

Margarite is back on the job again, but doesn't look too well. Mrs. Carter quit the 1st of the year and Margarite is taking her shift, 4 PM 'till midnight. We cleaned house over the 1st and only have a couple in. The flu seems to be subsiding and nothing else is starting up, so far.

Honey, I have no new pictures of the house, but I'll take one out of the book and send you. The house looks just about the same now. I'll try to get some more pictures off to you soon.

By the way, at the Fireman's Ball, New Year Eve, Mabel Malleague was dancing to "Why Don't We Do This More Often," and she said that it always reminds her of you. She wanted me to be sure to tell you.

There were no fights to start the New Year out. At least none that I heard about, but there certainly were a lot of swollen heads New Years day. Red Larison said he just wanted to lie down and die. I felt swell 'cause I behaved myself!!! Didn't have anyone to take me home, Honey.

John said that he was going to New Guinea, and when I asked him how he was going to get there, he said that Daddy was coming to get him. He's decided that he must take his new machine gun and go "down under" to help you. He does the old a-a-a-a- just like the rest of the little boys and gets a Jap with each burst.

I forgot to write you that you got a card from Major Simons "somewhere in Alaska." Ruthie is doing Public Health nursing in Pendleton. Ave Sturm is over in Wendover for 6 weeks or so—Pat stayed in Boise, Idaho.

Be careful, my Darling. Johnny and I say a prayer for you every night.

All our love,

                    Gail and Johnny

JANUARY 4, 1944 WES TO GAIL

Darling—   #60

As you can see, I received some more packages. Thank you, Darling, for the paper, pipe, pictures, pajamas, and especially, this pen. You've no idea how grand it is to have a decent pen again. This writes just perfectly, better than the other, I believe. I was awfully glad to get the pajamas, and the pipe I have started breaking in already. Going back to the PJ's— they're just right for fit, and perfect for the weather—I can go without a blanket on the warm nights and comfortable with just one when it's cold!

I am sort of sweating out your return from Phoenix. I haven't heard from you since the note you and the kids sent from there, but expect I'll do all right tomorrow. I love you so, Darling. I couldn't stand to have anything happen to you.

5th Jan. — Seems we were deprived of light last night so had to finish this today! I received swell fruitcake and some pictures from the Dellingers, also candy and gum. Dad and Esther's money belt was in your package.

Honey, I'm dying to know whether John is doing all this writing. Please enlighten me. Johnny, boy, thank you for the nice Christmas card. Daddy will be awfully glad to see his big boy again. Thought I would try writing on both sides of the paper to see what happens. Maybe I can save you an occasional six cents.

I've been fishing three times in the last week—all we could catch was some tiny fish about five or six inches long, which looked like tiny striped bass. There was one real outstanding kind we caught a few of—looked like a tiny sword fish *[drawing of a fish]* with a black, gristle-like snout. Its body was black and silver-also about six inches long. There was a lily pond where we caught 30 fish in an hour and a half. We knocked the barbs off the hooks so we could take the fish off and throw them back. I found a place to dig worms, and got some of the biggest you ever saw—better than Charlie's Hog Patch! There were some eight inches long and as big around as a lead pencil! Some fun!

I caught another fighter ride the other day—this time in a Thunderbolt. Boy, was it good. Can't tell you any more about it, but that is some airplane!

Well, Dearest, here's hoping today brings a letter from you—

All my love, always— Wes

P. S. Thanks also for the cigars. How about some more? (This is a request for the P. O.)

JANUARY 4, 1944 GAIL TO WES

Hi Sweet—   #53

It's snowing again. We got about 6 inches with the first storm—now it is sort of dribbling along. The six inches didn't stop our put-putt's and some of the gang were out flying, but I wasn't able to make it. Bud and Irene got back but haven't heard any details. Between the two of them they spent over $200.00. Must have had some fun somewhere along the line. Janet Cotter Peterson is confined but no baby yet. I'll probably miss it, darn it all!

Sent you a package of funnies yesterday Honey, hope you enjoy them—I'm afraid they are all mixed up though. Cut some of the excess edges off but I'm afraid I slipped and got some vital material. Have another batch to get off in a day or two. I put Johnny's nail clipper in the first batch but I won't vouch for how sharp it is.

Got letter #56 today—Did you have a hangover Christmas? Shame on you!! Glad to hear that you are getting good things to eat and that your appetite is holding out. Please don't lose too much weight—I was so proud of those few extra pounds of yours.

Take good care of yourself, Darling—you belong to me and I love you.

Yours forever,

Gail

JANUARY 6, 1944 GAIL TO WES
(7:30 PM at the office—maternaties all over the place. Written on the stationary of Bernard S. Holm, M. D.)

Hi Pop!

Does this stationary look familiar? It certainly should, and do I wish that you were back here using it again. All your old patients come in and ask about you and wish that you were here. Mrs. Mrosla is in here at the moment giving Dr. B. a workout—when I get her card back from Dr. B. I'll tell you when she is due. (May). I guess that I told you about our two babies and last night we got another baby boy, Byrums—whoever they are. I don't know half of the people who come in here.

We are having quite a time with the abovementioned Dr. B. He doesn't turn in half of the patients he sees outside of what comes right through the front door. Now he has gotten us into a jackpot—he was covering for Dr. Lasswell at night and happened to be called out to Oscar Sorenson's. Well, in the course of Oscar's sickness, he called upon Oscar three times and charged him $9.00. Oscar put up quite a howl about it, I guess, because Uncle Tiny came up from the Quincy Lumber Company office today to see about it. Now Dr. L. has to put Dr. B. in a corner and ask him "What the hell?" As Dr. L. would put it! Gee, we do have fun up here.

I went to see Lee Larison today for the first time since we went vacationing up in Canada with the Dellingers. I expected to be spending most of my time up there getting my poor teeth worked over and was I surprised and pleased to find that all he had to do was replace some cement that was falling out of one of my pegless eye teeth. Boy, oh boy, was I ever relieved! He shined them all up swell for me. Now I have a Dentine smile, Honey, just like yours; if I only had some longer eyeteeth to fill the gaps.

Janet Finnegan came into the office today with Baby Ann. She had fallen from a box that Janet had put on top of the chair, something like we did for Johnny—so Ann could eat at the table, and the little dickens fell off of it. The X-ray showed that her clavicle was humped up in a sort of an arc [hand-drawn illustration]. Not too bad. Dr. L. called it a "green stick" fracture, or something like that. Janet is due about the 21st of this month and she really is a sight—sort of like Helen was—all out in front.

I'm sending along some of the propaganda on Political Medicine—thought that you might be interested in seeing what is going on back here in Medicine.

Honey, I received $200.00 today and guess what I am going to do with it. Think I'll just put another $300.00 with it and plunk it down on the house again. This month was pretty good at the hospital and I will get about $300.00 out of it, so—where would be a better spot. Please don't worry about my finances. I think that I am doing swell—if they don't come out of the dark and soak me from behind with some income tax. Wow, would that be a blow!

Guess I'll scoot for home now, it seems to be getting late. All my love, my Darling, and a happy anniversary, I'll be thinking of you as always.

Yours,   Gail

JANUARY 7, 1944 WES TO MARIAN

Dear Marian and Gang—

Received your swell letter of Dec. 23 today—about 14 days. Honey, it is grand to hear from you when you are so busy. The box of Pralines came yesterday. I've never heard of them before. Really, they are delicious, and I'm certainly hoarding them. They certainly have a real sherry flavour. The pipe hasn't arrived as yet. One came in a package from Gail, but guess yours is on the way. I'll be glad to have an extra, as they need changing now and then.

Some pilots just dropped in for a drink, so will have to stop for awhile.

8th Jan. The session didn't break up 'till 2 AM—about 20 of the boys decided to do a little relaxing, so we did, with four quarts of Old Shenley. Don't feel so hot today!

About me being more-or-less at the front, as you say, you must realize that in the Air Corp, the duties are not as arduous as say, infantry and engineers, who have to do the real tough pioneer work and actual ground fighting, living like dogs. We have semi-permanent camps with screened mess halls, showers, and so on, and good food with plenty to drink. The only real hardship is being away from Gail and John. So you see, it doesn't take any courage to be cheerful about it all!

I'm sorry if you took my wisecracks seriously, about gardening and growing up, and cooking—I was only kidding, Honey—I think you are tops among sisters.

Had another grand ride the other day—this time in a Thunderbolt—and it really is what the name implies. I sure got a kick out of it. Wish I could tell you more—went about a hundred miles an hour faster than the other one I told you about!

We had a swell Christmas dinner, with a pound of turkey per man, and plenty of fixin's. Uncle Sam is sure looking out for his boys.

This is Saturday and I have a stack of long-winded reports to get off, so this will be all for now.

Lots of love,

Wes

JANUARY 8, 1944 MARY CARR MOORE TO WES

Dearest Wesley—

Such good letters from you—you are a darling. I am rather worried—I did not send my last letter to you by the APO which arrived the following day; I do hope you received it. Also, have you ever received the Xmas package I sent you before November 15th? There was not anything of much value in it—but I could not seem to know what to send you; however, I wanted the things I did send you to reach you. Chiefly, a book that I liked very much, by one of our ministers here, about the 23rd Psalm. As you have not mentioned having it, I am wondering where it has gone. Of course, at that date, I had your old APO number. Also, I sent you a cable, which I hope has reached you. Yours was such a comfort to me, as it was such direct news.

I am sure you are very much interested in your work — I have known all along that you are — but I hope that you will also realize, that if you take some care of your own health, it will be better for all the rest. Now – that is, after all "Motherish," isn't it? As if you did not know as well as I, and much better in fact, how necessary that is; and also, how utterly impossible, even to consider, in some crises. Then, one has to do the things that must be done, and somehow—the Dear Lord, generally takes care of us, and we come through more difficult emergencies than one would think possible—unharmed—even strengthened, by the effort.

You know, I love you very much—that is, of course, natural, and not to be marveled at, since we are mother and son. But I have always felt even a different bond of understanding between us, and it is very comforting to feel that you somehow know many of the things that I would like to say to you; and I know the reverse message, from you, is always on the way, even before mails can put our thoughts through in writing. And even writing—or words, are somewhat futile, or—rather, inadequate. One might say "too finite."

But, after all—the Universe revolves—some of us—arrive here; go on our mortal course, and mysteriously leave, taking with us the spirit, that is ALL WE ARE; those who came before us, and whom we loved, have made the same cycle. But because my beloved Father and Mother—and others, have gone before me—are they lost to me? NO. They are near me, and in my heart and mind; and I have never been—and I am always striving to accomplish that which, usually, remains unfulfilled. Yet, my waking memories are sweet and familiar, as to those who have been with me, should leave first, that I will not be far; but my heart, and my undying affection will still encircle those parts of my being, my children. And also—I feel, should they have to go first (which I pray may not be so) that the reunion will be in TIME (as it truly is, eternal and never-ending), nothing more than a breath, in eternal memories. So, perhaps you can see, Dearest, why I <u>will not</u> load your spirit with fear for your mortal safety. But <u>know</u> that your spiritual wings grow stronger, every day of your unselfish devotion to your human charges, who need your ministrations.

This is Sunday—and I seem to be delivering a sermon; but—"now endeth the first lesson."

A sweet letter from Edith gives me much news of John—he seems to be developing very fast. Won't it be fun to get acquainted with him again?

Gail is very busy, and, I am sure, writes you much more of her activities than I can. She is a darling daughter to me – and I am very devoted to her. However, I "sort of" fell down on Christmas, all 'round. I couldn't think what to get, and ended up in not getting what I wanted to send. I got for John a very nice and attractive illustrated book after just a glance at it in the store; a family of rabbits—and then discovered afterward that it was about the "MAMMA RABBIT," who was really, the "whole show" – which could not have been so stimulating to a young man like John – as if the exploits were of a masculine nature. Then, I sent Gail a necklace, which had been given to me long ago, and which I thought would be becoming to her (sort of aquamarine shades), but intended to send her something else along with it – but never did get out to buy the "something else." The weather, plus a case of Flu just before Christmas (and which I took seriously, after last year's long siege) prevented me from doing any reconnoitering in shops.

I believe I sent you the copy of the letter from General Giraud in my last letter. I have a Photostat copy made for all the grandsons; and John has already received his.

Well, Dear, I must close this long letter and get ready for a concert. The Graham sisters are here, making me a visit for a couple of weeks – and send their love to you. They remember you and Byron and Marian with great affection. We are going to the concert (as enclosed) soon. Next week, I shall have the unique experience of conducting an orchestra, made up of some of the finest players in town, for the Hollywood Canteen in my first performance of "Brief Furlough" which I have improved and scored for full orchestra; and instead of ending as I did before on some long chords, I have added the main theme of "Home-Longing" —all "pepped up" into a brisk march-time, and the bugle "Call to Arms" with the assumption in music that they are going in, double-quick, to win! I am anxious to hear it in this form. It was so inadequately done when you heard it, as the clarinetist, who was unable to come at the last moment, was replaced by an unrehearsed player, who really did well to keep his place at all, let alone to supply the "pep" and color I had allotted to that part. I was grateful to the clarinetist for even coming at all; and I am sure he would have been all right with an adequate rehearsal.

Goodbye, Honey—I love you with all sorts of mental hugs and kisses, and lots of good wishes— and "hurry back home" (as soon as you can) and my big hopes for PEACE, early in 1944.

Devotedly your mother,
M. C. M.

JANUARY 8, 1944 WES TO GAIL

Darling—   #62

I sure was glad to find out what happened to you. Am mighty glad you sat tight until it was safe. Old man weather is a rough killer. I'd like to see that Furnace Creek Inn some day— hope we can hop over there sometime after this is all over.

I've been hitting the ball hot and heavy since I last writ. My clerk is sick and I'm breaking in a new one. Saturday is report day, showing the new man the reports and finally giving and doing same myself.

I'm sorry to hear about poor old Tom, but I suppose it will be sort of a relief to the kids, after they get over the shock.

Tell Del and Ruth I'll write soon and thank them for the swell fruitcake.

We got some fresh cabbage, peaches, plums, green salads. Cold slaw is wonderful, when you can't have it for a while!

Darling, I'm pooped—so that's all for now.

I love you, always,

Wes

JANUARY 8, 1944 GAIL TO WES
(Saturday night—office)

Honey—   #55

Received your letter of Dec. 26th today; sorry my letters aren't coming through OK. I've kept to the every-other-day schedule. We had a slide down the canyon that tossed an engine into the river. That has been holding up your mail.

Darling you had a much more exciting Christmas than I did, and I certainly hope it wasn't anything near as lonesome as mine. I've tried not to write to you when I feel lonely, but I guess sometimes I slip up and you hear all about how I wish you could come home. Just keep yourself well, Sweetheart!

Doris doesn't know what to make of Chris' condition—he tells her he feels like he's got malaria and he has his legs all bandaged up 'cause some sores are running. Swell stuff you get over there!

Virgil Abbott is missing in action—you remember Alga's old flame. Nan Hazeltine is on her way to Sweetwater. Bet she is thrilled!

By the way, I dug out your log books and you have 441:02 hours total time—423:58 solo time. I thought instead of sending your logbooks (which might get lost) I'd make a notarized statement of your hours in different horsepower. Hope that will serve the purpose. If you don't want it that way, be sure to let me know.

All my love, Sweetheart,

Gail

JANUARY 9, 1944 WES TO GAIL

Darling—   #63

Hope the shock won't be too great, getting letters two days in a row. I've been at the reports again all day today. Oh for a guy with some brains who could type!

It's been hotter than the very devil the last few days. It gets just about unbearable in the middle of the day. I've been going down and taking a jump in the creek about one o'clock, then resting until about 3:30 or 4:00—just about have to sit still when the old mercury betters 120.

No letters today—but I'm satisfied, knowing you are safe back home. Going to bed now, Sweet.

All my love, always yours,
                          Wes
                    Tell John I love him.

JANUARY 10, 1944 GAIL TO WES

Dearest Wes,   #56

Received your letter of Dec. 29th (#58), and now you really have me confused as to your whereabouts. Guess my maps that I might get hold of wouldn't show any such place as Gusap, Gussap, or whichever it is that I'm trying to make out. You aren't casting any reflections on my navigation now, are you Sweet? I took it that you were down low—I mean, sort of on the coast. Oh shucks, I'm all mixed up. If you went 75 miles north of where I had you before, you'd be in the water east of Astrolabe Bay—which I certainly hope that you aren't.

I'm typing this at the office between shots, broken ribs and pelvic. If you can't make any sense to it, you will know why. The furnace has gone haywire and Margarite is keeping our two babies warm with an electric heater. I have on two coats. It's been off all day (something wrong with the pump). Luzzader was up for awhile this afternoon, but he had to go out with the engine (he works on the railroad) and said that he would come in and work on it tonight—sometime after 9. We have old Louie and two maternity's in, and they are all cold blooded, so I guess that they won't freeze to death.

Yesterday I went out with Floyd to take a spin around the Valley—it was a perfectly innocent looking day, but boy, oh boy, what a ride we had. It was a bit muddy on the takeoff. That slowed us down, besides splattering us well with mud. When we finally got off the ground, something up above gave us a slap on the back and we came down again—not too hard. About the third try, we got off and bounced around like popcorn on a hot frying pan. We got over the fence at about 20 feet and just couldn't get any altitude. That little old hill had a mess of downdrafts around it, so we kept going and went through the cut—we didn't get above the hill level until we got around by the Oakland Camp road. After we got up to about 800 feet, it treated us just about the way it did when we went out of Kern County Airport over the Tehachapi Pass. Well, we didn't stay up there very long—what a beating we took! We'd drop 200 feet and then gain it back like a bouncing ball. We came in under power, and fortunately, but quite by mistake, I made a wheel landing and came barreling into home plate. When I got out of that little T Craft and took a look at the clouds that had gathered overhead, and what they were doing, I wasn't at all surprised at the ride we had.

Last night it snowed—it was really gorgeous, we got about six inches and then the moon came out. What a picture! Today it has melted—I mean most of it, and it is pretty sloppy. Tonight it is cold enough to freeze it pretty thoroughly. I got a batch of funnies in the mail to you today. They will probably take longer, though; because I sent them straight mail.

Today I asked John when he was going to be big enough that he wouldn't have to use his duck any longer, and his answer was "When I grow a bigger bottom, Mommie, then I can sit there." He really pulls some fast ones now and then. You should hear some of them first hand. The other day he pounded his chest, "shest" as he calls it, and said, "See Grandma, I'm growing big like you!" Grandma had an awful time keeping a straight face. John's most absorbing occupation right at present is building Forest Services, hangars, airplanes, jeeps, etc. out of some blocks he got for Christmas. He and Grandpa sit on the floor and they really put out some weird concoctions. He still has some of that darned old rash and we can't seem to do anything about it. We haven't been starving him because of it, though, and he really is a husky—weighs 39 pounds—and maybe you don't think that he is a couple of armloads when we get him up at night. He certainly is doing well, though; we've only had a couple of accidents at night since he has been at Grandma's, and boy, that is a relief.

Dad has him hypnotized about going to bed. When the minute hand gets to 7:30, the Sandman starts sticking his head out of the clock. Dad has pasted a red line on the clock so that if John isn't upstairs by the time that minute hand gets to the red mark, the Sandman will jump right out of the clock and close Johnny's eyes so that he won't be able to open them. Johnny really scoots when he sees that hand approaching the red mark.

Don't worry about my would-be instructing—I'm mighty careful with this old hide of mine, and I'm not taking any chances with any lamebrains. In fact, I don't let anyone get very far into trouble 'cause I figure that I haven't gotten it down to the fine line of knowing just when to take over. If they want to go up and fly, swell; if they don't want to fly my way, that's swell too, they can let me out.

So Julian is up there on the North coast, huh! Have you heard from him lately? What about that damsel he had at Moresby? Is that current still running strong? Have you seen anything of any of the 63rd? Doris tells me that Chris lost his right hand man through a transfer. She also thinks that Chris has almost given up ever hearing about his flight training application. Guess Chris isn't too well satisfied with what he is doing.

Gosh, Honey, my fingers are just about to freeze off, so I think that I sign off and go on home. This place is like a tomb.

I love you, my Darling—

Gail

JANUARY 12, 1944—SOUTHWEST PACIFIC AREA (SWPA, Fifth Air Force): HQ V Fighter Command transfers from Port Moresby to Nadzab, New Guinea and Major General Paul B. Wurtsmith becomes Commanding General, V Fighter Command. In New Guinea, 130+ B-24's, B-25's and P-40's attack Alexishafen. B-24's bomb Gasmata Island off New Britain Island. B-24's and B-25's strike Kaukenau and Timoeka, New Guinea and score hit on a freighter off Tanimbar Island, Moluccas Islands.

JANUARY 12, 1944 WES TO GAIL

Sweetheart—   #64

That was a swell "Round Robin" you and the Gang sent me on Christmas. I got a lot of fun out of it. Old Ken is still a master of the dry wit.

I made friends with one of the liaison boys and got my first ride in an L-5, the 190 Stinson. It sure is a swell ship. I talked him into a trip for tomorrow. We are going to visit Julian, stopping by to see Van on the way. Boy, that ought to be a swell trip. Will let you know how it comes out.

Things have been burning right along, keeping me plenty busy. But am enjoying it as usual. Golly it would be nice to get home for just a day or two, though.

I think I told you I wrote to the Foley's—you asked me, but I had already done so.

I have a bunch of Christmas thank-yous to get off and can't quite find the energy. Will try to make the grade tonight. So you are going to get shorted, Dear, 'cause I want to hit the hay early.

All my love, Honey—

Your Wes

JANUARY 12, 1944 GAIL TO WES
(3:00 PM)

Hi Sweetheart,

This is the office typewriter—or do you recognize it. Have a few minutes so I thought that I would write to you airmail and send along some pictures and airmail stamps to use on all the stationary that you got for Christmas. Hope that you like the pictures—they are the best that I could do. I think that they are cute of Johnny, but those of me in the white dress are really sopin', now aren't they? At least those who have seen them say they don't flatter me at all; that is some consolation.

Blank just called up and she wants to do an operation on Mrs. Lakey. Fine thing—she (Blank) just got over the flu and she has been out in the County Hospital with a heart attack. Margarite is howling because she will have to scrub, and Blank usually takes at least 3 hours to do anything in the line of an operation.

Last night Doris and I went down to "Fort Sprague" to see Princess O'Rouke, and in the process, got in on a Newsreel of New Guinea. They seem to have some pretty speedy rivers down in that section. We watched them clearing out some tropical growth to make an airport. It said that it was somewhere near Madang and showed pictures of the "Aussies" tramping forward. The savages pictured were really dillies. I'd think that you'd run just at the sight on one of those babies with the knife through his nose—or was it bone? He looked pretty vicious. No wonder you decided to smoke your cigarettes.

Mother got your letter, written the 30th of December, this morning. It made very good time. Took just as long as your airmail to me that was written Dec. 29th. I think that they go in the same time excepting if they have a big load and can't get them all in, they give preference to the airmail.

We got a Christmas card from Soapy from Texas, did I tell you? Etz told me the other day that he is down in San Diego now towing torpedoes. I haven't quite figured out yet what in the devil he would be doing that for and neither has she. I'd think that it would be much safer to be pushing torpedoes!

Honey, I was tickled to death to hear that you are holding your weight and that you have an appetite. I was so afraid that you would lose all of that weight that you had gained—and you have lost some of it. By the way, thanks, my dear, for sticking up for my cooking; you are very gallant. Mother was quite impressed. However, I think that she has just about given me up for useless.

I bought myself some flying boots—all fleece lined. They are honeys, but I don't think that they will hold the water out. They do keep my feet warm, though, and that is what I want. After riding back from Phoenix in that Culver without any heater, I decided that they were a mighty handy thing to have. I have been wearing them in the office all day today because the darned old furnace went haywire again. Seems to be going all right now.

I'm going to type out the contents of Ruth Simons Christmas note, so here it is: "Greetings—wherever you are, have wondered about you so many times and what has happened. Ralph and Edna, Bill and Miki left Thursday for Tinker Field, Oklahoma, the fellows are in the 330th. Hope they like it there. I'm the last one left! Fax's are in Tucson, Arizona. Stanley and I saw Stan in Seattle last month for five wonderful days! Gee he looked good to me! Am working as Public Health nurse. It's good for me. Do write a note so I'll know how you are. As ever, Ruthie."

Esther and Dad Moore were right tickled to get a cable from you at Christmas and they seemed to be thrilled because I thought that I would be able to take Johnny up there some time this Spring. The way things are going, I don't know whether I'll be able to get away or not. Margarite is taking the 4-12 shift, and I seem to be able to save Dr. L. quite a bit of grief by being out here in the front office and covering while Dr. B. is here and Dr. goes home. I don't know what in the world to tell Esther now because she seemed to be planning on our coming so much. Guess that I'll have to write her this afternoon and break it to her easy, not to plan on us too much.

Guess I'd better sign off now and do a little work. All my love, my Darling—

Gail

JANUARY 14, 1944 GAIL TO WES

Hello Sweetheart,

Received your #59 of Jan. today and was glad to hear that you had gotten through New Years Eve without suffering too much New Years Day. The chocolates requested are practically on their way. Bill is wrapping them and, incidentally, he said that he would send them, but I think that maybe I'd better pay for them. Did you ever receive the camera that Bill sent you? Be sure to take good care of it Honey, 'cause it belongs to Virginia Bailey.

The boys and girls seem to be roaming the skies today—it's a beautiful day—wish that I was out there. George C. is having quite a time. Since they are cutting the Instructor list down so much, he's afraid that he won't be able to get in. The draft is closing in on him. Elda certainly isn't too happy about it. Just had a run in with Dr. B. over a money matter. Come on home, Honey, and get me out of this mess! My hair is starting to curl I get so hot sometimes.

I love you so much XXX

                    Gail

JANUARY 14, 1944 WES TO GAIL

Hello, Honey—   #65

Boy, was that ever a lovely trip. I flew the 2nd half of the way—and was Julian surprised to see me. That boy is really staying in the front line—and to top it all, he's going out to one of the latest taken areas in about a week—I envy him. I talked pretty fast, and the pilot let me take Julian up for about half an hour—we really looked the country over, with Julian flying from the back, and me making the takeoffs and landings. He hasn't had much chance to fly, and I was glad I could give him a ride. That's my first solo flight since leaving the good old U. S. Now I can say I flew a military aircraft in New Guinea during the War! If things work out, I should get in quite a little L-5 time. This officer is a pretty good guy.

No letters from you for several days, Darling—hope something comes today.

When we left yesterday, we had to sweat out a fog and drizzle for an hour and a half—finally took off with about a fifty-foot ceiling, and in ten minutes were in the bright sunshine. Reminded me of our time at Lordsberg, N. M. I was quite surprised that I made a fairly decent landing the first time. Then, when I took Julian up, I made a perfect three point "grease job"—sure tickled me—even Julian thought it was good! It's a kick to land on the metal strips—they sure make a hell of a noise when you're rolling along on them.

The heat has relaxed a bit, with a rather cloudy, windy, and drizzly spell. It's rather a relief, although it still gets pretty muggy after lunch.

Darling, please don't forget—more pictures—especially of you and John, and I do want some good ones of the house. In case I forgot—I could go for some milk chocolates.

All my love, Darling. Forever yours,

Wes

JANUARY 16, 1944 GAIL TO WES

Dearest Wes,   #58

We've had quite a weekend in this household, Sat. Mom and Dad went off to Reno so John and I kept house. We cleaned most of the morning, had lunch at the Drug Store and then went up to Bishop's so John could play in the snow with Jan. They had a wonderful time sledding—I thought that Johnny would be afraid of it, but no, he just ate it up. He'd pull the sled up the hill and come backwards just about as fast as he would go up. He'd grin and shout when he got to the bottom.

Roby went out of town, so Ann asked us to stay over night, which we did. After a couple of sessions of trying to get the kids to sleep and having them crawl in with each other, we managed to quiet them down, so we had a bridge game—Irene Lund and Barbara Baldwin, Jr., came and played with us. We really had a session. John was really a peach—he got up and took himself to the bathroom in a strange house—stayed in bed half an hour after he woke up and didn't cry—you would have been so proud of him! Maybe he would be all right if I took him to Seattle, but I sometimes wonder.

My love forever, Sweetheart,   Gail

JANUARY 17, 1944 WES TO GAIL

Dearest Sweetheart   #66

Sure wish I could have some of that snow you are talking about. It's really been hot lately—mingled with those torrential rains. I'm getting pretty brown now—hope I can bring some of it home with me.

I'm going to get an anniversary telegram off in the morning, Dear—hope it reaches you in time. I can't say much in it, but I can here. Darling you have given me the happiest five years of my life. You are dearer to me than anything in the world, and you are the best, sweetest, smartest, most beautiful little wife any man could have. And oh, how I do love you. You bore a wonderful son for us, and I love him just as much as I do you, Darling. I'll be so happy to come home to you when this is all over.

You shouldn't have sent me John's nail clipper, Dear. I don't need one that badly. Want me to send it back? Poor John will miss it.

Let me know if you still haven't received the $200.00 by the time you get this and I will have it traced. That worries me. I'd hate to have all that dough lost!

Sorry to hear old Dr. B. is still making a sap of himself. Guess he was behind the door when the brains were passed out. What will Bert do if he goes into *[unreadable]*? Did old Louis die?

My tent mate and I worked like the devil today. We put in a concrete floor in our tent. There was a small gasoline mixer which made a wheelbarrow load at a batch, so it took us about four hours of good, steady and hard work, including hauling sand and gravel from the river in a trailer. But, it's pretty nice. Over in the corner, where I piped the water in, we have a square sump hole with 2-inch pipe leading out to a hole filled with rock for a drain. It works swell. Tomorrow, I'm going to build a good big table, and I know where I can swipe a packing box. Lumber is truly a scarce item in these parts.

Well, Dearest, I'm going to put these aching bones to bed now, and don't worry about my health. I'm just bursting with it!

All my love to you and John.   Always your

                                                      Wes

JANUARY 17, 1944 GAIL TO WES

My Darling—

No mail form you for several days—hope that everything is running smoothly. I sent you a V-Mail today that I wrote last night so you can see which goes the faster. Thought maybe you'd like me to send you this airmail so I could include a few choice tidbits. Yesterday, I did a little flying. Floyd and I went XC to Susanville. He did all the flying except the landing at Susanville (which was in the snow). I didn't know how I'd make it from the right side. We landed, but I'm not saying how. Part of the field was snowy, part was icy, and the rest was made up of mud puddles and chuckholes. There was talk over there that their school might close up as the flying program has been cut so drastically. Floyd is doing pretty well although I still have to poke a little rudder on the take off and level him off on his landings.

Gee Honey, you should have been around this place today. Margarite was fit to be tied and Dr. L. was cussing every other word. Blank did her operation! Dr. Tobias (a German refugee M. D., she just looks like a little old woman to me) assisted her and Dr. B. gave the anesthetic. They started at 8:30 AM and got out at 11:30—the patient was still breathing, but I don't know why. Blank whittled away and finally made the patient neuter gender, and then she whacked off the appendix—she cut a hole somewhere and stuck a rubber tube out through the vagina for a drain. About that time she told Dr. B. to get Dr. L. to finish the anesthetic and for him to get scrubbed to take over. She almost keeled over, but Margarite poured some aromatic spirits of ammonia before she completely went out. Then, after, Dr. B. got scrubbed, she wouldn't let him in. Finally he got her to let him sew up a couple of layers. After that, Margarite and I followed her into the bathroom while she dissected the uterus and the amniotic sac almost hit her in the eye. There was a beautifully formed six-month fetus. Blank just couldn't understand it. She (the patient) had not had any morning sickness, no normal symptoms of pregnancy except possibly no period for six months or so!!! I tell you Blank will never touch a knife in this place again as long as the Lasswells are here! I'm 'fraid I'll go home and dream of awful things tonight. I was assistant "run-around girl" and did everything from pouring ether to catching the appendix (which wasn't even inflamed, to speak of).

Doris is going to take a jaunt down to Long Beach to see Chris' mother and brother Bob, who is coming home from Tarawa. It will be swell for her to get away, but I surely hope she doesn't stay! She's been a peach about sticking it out under pretty adverse conditions and she really is a swell little nurse, if her resistance can hold up under the strain.

David has just been commended for his handling of the annual review and has to take over the parade and review for a couple of Generals next week. Is Pop proud of him!

Well, my Sweet, guess I'll fold up for the night and go home. All my love forever and ever, and please take good care of yourself.

Gail

P. S. Forgot to tell you that Blank dropped a needle in the belly and they had to go fishin' for it.

JANUARY 19, 1944—SOUTHWEST PACIFIC AREA (SWPA, Fifth Air Force): 57 B-24's bomb Boram, New Guinea; 17 more bomb Ammonia Island, Moluccas Islands, and Halloing, Celebes Islands; and 2 others score hits on freighter near Aitape, New Guinea. 65 B-25's, along with RAAF airplanes, pound positions in the Shaggy Ridge, New Guinea area. 2 P-39's bomb barges in the Cape Roast, New Britain Island area. 25th Photographic Reconnaissance Squadron, 6th Photographic Reconnaissance Group begins transfer from Brisbane, Australia to Lae, New Guinea with F-5's.

JANUARY 19, 1944 GAIL TO WES

My Darling,

Got a letter from you today (#66), and was I glad to see it!! Several days since I'd heard from you. You lucky bum, to get a ride in a Thunderbolt. I envy you. Shall we buy one after the war? The fishin' sounds swell, but surely you couldn't use those whale-sized hooks on those poor little fish! I should think that the fish would be scared to death of an 8-inch worm.

Bill B. and I got busy today and sent you a box of Corina Sports and a box of chocolates. Hope that they get to you intact. Bill wrapped them well, but I don't know whether the chocolates will be a liquid mass or not.

Honey, we've had perfect weather, the snow is practically melted off and the sun has been spreading itself. It has been chilly—but not cold enough to chill my desire to get out to the airport and do a little flitting. Guess I can't make it until Sunday, however. Now that I'm getting so I can do a little something, they keep me pretty busy.

All my love Sweetheart, and take care of yourself.

Yours Gail

JANUARY 20, 1944 WES TO GAIL

Darling—   #68

Time moves along pretty fast when I'm busy—and really drags when not. The former has been true the last few days, with lots of activity about, and exciting too. Then, too, I've been having fun working about my tent. I told you of the table and chair I built, and concrete on the floor. Since, I've built a clothes cabinet for hanging up the uniform, which I never use—and shelves for khakis, shorts, sox, etc. and toilet articles. We are busy doing a little wiring at present. My tent mate and I each want a bed lamp, and we have a new member—an Aussie Captain who works in liaison with our forces and theirs. A swell fellow, and I hope he stays. So, anyway, we each are going to have a reading light, complete with switches and a central light. It'll be nice and cozy and homelike—but no wife. The Aussie is going to have a "botman" to serve him, do laundry, bring tea in the morning, etc., so we figure on kicking in a little money to get the same kind of room service! Should be just like the Hotel Statler, or something! I suppose by the time we get all nice and comfortable, we'll move on up the line—oh, well, "c'est la guerre!"

Your newsy letter from the hospital ("maternity's all over the place") of Jan. 6 came and I enjoyed it all so much. I am so hoping you will get some pictures to me soon, of you, and John, and of the house. You should find some old snaps of the hospital in my bunch of pictures if you ever run across them. Thanks for the California Physicians Serv. Statement. Looks like they might be getting the unit up to a figure that would make it worthwhile attending patients on that basis—$1.75. Of course, where we should get $2.50, we get $.75 less, but at least it's money in the hand!

Glad you got the money OK. I'm holding out on you this month as I may get to go to Australia to a special Malaria school for two or three weeks, and want to try out a few big juicy steaks, some champagne, and for a change, an iced drink of whiskey with (actually) Coca Cola in it! Hope you won't mind.

Darling, I love you, and hope you get the Anniversary telegram in time.   Always, Wes

JANUARY 23, 1944 GAIL TO WES
(Sunday)

Darling—

Doris and I got the "Round Robin" back from the girls and Marce sent along these pictures. Marce and Burke are still in Great Falls. They are expecting an addition in May. Mavis and Margaret both have baby girls. Speaking of babies, Honey—Janet came through yesterday with a miniature John Finnegan. She didn't have a bad time at all. Came into the hospital at 8 AM, started some good pains about 12:30 and by 1:19 PM the little cherub was shouting before his legs got out. She (Janet) looks better than she has in years and is most cherub. She is going to try to nurse the baby. He's a swell looking little fellow. They are so tickled to have a boy.

You asked if Johnny were doing all the writing—no Sweetheart, he hasn't grown up that much! But he is growing fast. As a matter of fact, he can't even make the letters, but he does know them by sight.

Received your letter written on Jan. 8th today. There is still one missing, #61, but expect it will be along in a day or so. #63 arrived yesterday. Sorry to hear you are having so much trouble with your secretaries. I know there might be something I could do over there. Why don't you send a request to the P. O. Dept. and I'll get Bill to wrap me up and ship me over.

"Hello Daddy—I'm being a good boy. Please come home soon so you can go sliding with me. Love Johnny" He's heckling me to go up and play with John Gordon so I guess I'd better get going.

Don't quite know what to do with the joke you sent me—don't dare show the men and I don't think the gals know enough to appreciate it.

All my love, Darling

Gail

JANUARY 23, 1944—SOUTHWEST PACIFIC AREA (SWPA, Fifth Air Force): In New Guinea, 35 B-24's, with fighter escort, bomb Wewak; 50 Japanese fighters intercept; in the ensuing air battle US aircraft claim 12 of the fighters shot down; 5 US fighters are lost; P-39's strafe barges and AA positions at Align Harbor and on the Rae Coast. In New Britain, A-20's hit forces and AA positions near Cape Roast and Gasmata Island. B-24's hit Flores Island, Lesser Sunda Islands. 25th Liaison Squadron, V Bomber Command attached to 5212th Photographic Wing (Provisional), begins moving from Brisbane, Australia to Lae, New Guinea with L-5's.

JANUARY 23, 1944 WES TO MARIAN

Dear Marian and Gang—

Thanks, Honey, for your nice letter of December 23. Guess I told you I received the pipe and *[unreadable]*. Both very welcome gifts. The pipe is a dandy, and I'm smoking it this minute.

Things have been rather exciting, and <u>good</u> lately. We are seeing big things being done, and my own boys are taking no small part. I look forward to some fairly rapid changes in the near future.

Had a nice plane ride the other day. Went over to see Julian Atkins, and took him up myself-in a trainer L-5. He got quite a kick out of it as did I. We looked over some rather forward areas together and returned to his base, then I came on back with the regular pilot. He's a couple of hundred miles from me, the way I have to go.

I wrote Mother today and told her about the heater and the rain, both of which are terrific—also, that I have a nice concrete floor, table, running water—even a bedside lamp and table. There is an Aussie Capt. Sharing quarters with a pilot and me. He's drawing some good looking nudes for me to put on my lamp shade.

Give my love to the boys. Lots of love, Wes

P. S. Send me some pictures if you ever have any. I enjoy them a lot.

JANUARY 25, 1944 GAIL TO WES

Hello Honey,

One of these days I'm going to start out on a new number series. When they get above 50 I can't seem to remember them anymore. I have a sheet of paper at home, but most of the time I write to you up here at the office and I can't remember which number goes on my next letter.

I had a busy day today—started out ironing something to wear to the office and when I got up here, decided that I'd better start knocking a few spider webs off the ceiling so people would think that we had a little business. (Really though, it isn't that bad, we are really faring pretty well.) After I got the spider webs pretty well cleaned up, the place was so darned dirty, that I started at one end and went to the other end with the broom. What it really needed was a mopping and a good one at that. Couldn't quite make that, though. Esther, Margarite's prize from The Quarters, was supposed to be in this morning, but didn't ever show up. Darn her hide anyway. She has been relieving Pearl Penman one day a week with the cooking, and the independent cuss doesn't show up until about 8 o'clock, and Doris has to cook breakfast for the patients. You can't fire her, because if you do, there just isn't any one else to hire. Oh well, when the war's over, I guess there will be people howling for jobs. Mrs. Thomas is having a time with her feet and Margarite is afraid that if she doesn't let her off for awhile, she will lose her entirely—that would almost be a tragedy.

I guess that I've told you that Margarite is working the 4-12 shift. Mrs. Thayer is working pretty regularly, now, and also Doris. That is the extent of our working force. Guess I'll have to take a practical course, Sweetheart. Will you hire me when you get back here?

Blank blew in this morning and said that she wanted to do a complete Hysterectomy on this Dr. Tobias that is staying here with her. I think that the pair of them are ready for the nut house. If Tobias could stand to have Blank dig around in her after the exhibition of a week ago, I know that she is balmy. Anyway, that announcement practically evoked an eruption of no small dimensions. However, Margarite controlled herself much better than I thought she would ever be able to, and announced that there would be no more such surgery here as long as she was around, and that in the future, Blank had better hire any surgery out to the county. Now Dr. B. is dodging her. However, he has cooked up a story that, as her physician, he feels that she is not physically—(here Dr. L. adds "and mentally")—capable of practicing medicine, and especially surgery, and that he does not want the responsibility of having to take over when she pulls one of her faints. Dr. L. voiced a suspicion of her ability to come back and be in the most buoyant of spirits, even after looking like death itself. Everyone admits that she has wild looks in her eyes pretty often. Some of the things that she does even a "shot" couldn't perpetuate.

Had dinner with the Dellingers last Sunday, and after dinner we all went to the show. Johnny stayed awake for about twenty minutes of the show. He was so proud of the fact that he had been to the show. He talked about it all the next day. Del and Ken went down to Sacto to consult with Fred, so the gals played bridge up at the Metzkers last night. Helen M. was so full of chatter that we didn't get much bridge playing done, though. I'm having the gang to dinner at the hotel tomorrow night. Charlie Bedell is sick in bed with the flu and so is Ray Smith. Guess Ray hasn't the flu, however. Dottie Parker is presiding as the host for me. Gee Darling, it certainly is the devil to be without you—not only is it lonesome as can be, but I have to do things all by myself. Have heard rumors of a bill that will send you all home after a year overseas—I hope that it goes through and you can come home to us soon.

All my love forever and ever

Gail

JANUARY 25, 1944 WES TO GAIL

Darling—   #69

Received your letter of Dec. 31. You do have such a hard time with the numbers, Dear, just let them go. I can tell from the dates just as well. I have them all neatly filed with an Acco binder and it's getting to be a decent stack. You are a good girl to write so faithfully.

In regard to the liaison rating, the purpose would be rescue work, to go out in a two-place L-5, pick up a wounded pilot and give him emergency treatment and bring him back. Unfortunately, the brass hats feel as you do, and don't seem inclined to grant it.

Sounds natural, old Bert taking his New Year's nip! He used to have a nip every evening when we were together those first few days in '36. Just one—but he would tell me I shouldn't! Ask him if it will be OK for me when I get to be his age! Sounds like you widows did pretty well New Years Eve. Sure wish I could have been there, Darling.

I like the paper and pen so much. The pen writes so easily, and the nib is perfect. Thanks again, Darling.

The gang is at the movies, so have comparative peace and quiet. It's quite comfortable and homey, now with the soft, shaded lamp, table and comfortable chair. I am sipping a whiskey and water with a dash of vermouth—warm. Oh, for some ice! I think I'll go over in a jeep and visit a native village tomorrow. The Aussie is going with me, and knows the ropes, so we should be able to do some good trading for objects d' art.

Oh-oh—here comes the gang—no more peace!

Goodnight, Dearest—all my love, always, your—

Wes

JANUARY 27, 1944 GAIL TO WES

Darling—   #1

We had a blitz up at the house today—Laura called and said that the furnace was off, the water heater wouldn't work and the toilet blew up. We rented Luzzader but he couldn't get up the hill 'cause the new snow was slippery. Finally, he got the water heater torn apart and the furnace going, but couldn't do much about the john. Honey, I knew we built that bathroom upstairs for a purpose. What happened was that the steam from the water heater backed up and hit the water in the back of the john and split it wide open.

The party last night turned out swell—but gee, Honey, we sure did miss you! I told the gang I wasn't entertaining them after dinner and they could go as they pleased. The girls ended up playing bridge at Dellingers, and I don't know what happened to the men.

I guess I won't fly Doris to Reno tomorrow—the weather is too uncertain. Mother wants to go over and see that her glasses are OK. So another reason to drive. Doris was lucky to get a plane all the way to L. A.

Got your 12th letter today, Sweet, and found out what you were flying. Sure must have been fun.

All my love
                              Gail

JANUARY 28, 1944 WES TO GAIL

Dearest,   #70

I have a fine collection of letters from you. You certainly stick by your every other day schedule like a faithful little wife.

Honey, I don't mind your telling me when you feel low. It ought to help some to get it off your chest to your old man. We can't help missing each other, and I surely wouldn't want it otherwise. And as expressing yourself, your letters are wonderfully sweet and expressive, and I love them—and you, tremendously big.

I haven't seen Chris in some time. Transportation is difficult when I get down there and I can't seem to make connections. I'm sorry to hear about his tropical sores, and will certainly look him up my next trip.

So old Virgil is missing—that's pretty rough—how's Olga take it?

Thanks for the information on my hours. I'm glad you didn't send them. The statement would be swell.

I got more amusement out of your guesses. I certainly haven't been stationed out in the middle of any bay. Make it about 300 degrees instead of 360 degrees from Chris—your navigation procedures are very good, and I'd ride cross-country blindfolded with you any day, Dearest.

So that damned old furnace is kicking up its usual winter fuss. Better have Ken take a check on the blower motor. The bearing case was a little loose, and he never did get around to getting it fixed before I left last winter.

That sounded like a really rough ride you and Floyd had. I remember an occasional day like that, and it can give you a bad time. How's old Floyd doing as a pilot?

I haven't had any further luck getting rides in the L-5 since I visited Julian. They seem to be pretty tight with them. Sure be glad when I can get home and fly whenever I damn please— and see some snow!

They say that some of the mountains in New Guinea have snow on them all year 'round. I haven't seen them so far.

The boys really got a kick out of John's remark about the size of his bottom. Golly, I'd love to see him, Dear. He must be awfully cute. Thanks for the nice pictures of him leaning on the Silvaire prop—quite nonchalant. I must agree that the pictures of yourself don't do you justice as far as your face is concerned, but you do look sweet in the white uniform. Quite business-like.

About Julian's damsel, he is apparently still deeply interested, although, of course, she is now far away—but he mentioned some very fine Christmas gifts she sent, and many letters. By the way, he was expecting a Captaincy within the week. I must write him and see if he received it, and if he made the move to the new landing place.

I was glad you sent me the airmail stamps, as they are not always available here. This is lovely paper and envelopes.

The pictures you saw of the airport being cleared in the newsreel were undoubtedly where I visited Julian, from the description, and being near the place you mentioned. There is a beautiful strip there now.

I got a swell letter from Walt Cameran—remember Major Cameran? He is at the 484th Bomb Group, AAB, Harvard, Nebraska. He is Group Surgeon. Thinks he will be going overseas about March 1st. He says Marge wants your address. I'm going to write him, so will give it to him.

Speaking of weight, I weighed 147 ½ pounds today, in pants and shoes—and I am getting to be the bronzed Adonis (?) I'm really in the pink, Dear.

Hope you get some weight, Dear. Take some vitamins and try to gain.

All my love, Dearest,

Wes

JANUARY 29, 1944 TELEGRAM WES TO GAIL

DEAREST, MY THOUGHTS ARE WITH YOU ON OUR ANNIVERSARY==OF HAP-
PINESS TOGETHER. I HOPE I WILL BE WITH YOU FOR THE NEXT.

MY FONDEST LOVE FOR YOU AND JOHN==WES MOORE

JANUARY 29, 1944 GAIL TO WES

Sweetheart,

Received your night letter this morning and was so thrilled! Gee, I wish you were here,
never to leave me again. I certainly hope that the time will come around soon Honey, I get
so lonesome sometimes. There always seems to be plenty to do, but even doing things
can't erase that loneliness.

Mother and I took Doris over and put her on the plane at 1 o'clock. They had quite a time
getting the starboard motor going—it sputtered and backfired and acted up, but when it
started, it purred right along. Last evening Mother and I took in the Riverside Bar and saw
Sophie Tucker, then we thought we'd look in at the track. While there, we ran into Ruth and
Dottie-they were taking Ed Eckstein over to catch the bus for L. A. so—the Eckstein brothers took us all to Columbos to dinner. We danced the "boys" to pieces. We got home about
midnight.

I sank another $500.00 down on the house, Honey, and we have it whittled down to $3259.40
and the interest was $18.45. Doesn't sound so horrible as it did, does it? I think that they
are bamboozling me on the interest but what can I do about it? Being as I don't understand
it, I can't complain. Pretty soon, my Darling, we are going to have a house.

I'm sending along some pictures of John that Bill Bailey took down at the store. I think
they are pretty good. He's a chip off the old block, Honey, and full of the devil.

Draper had a little misfortune out at the airport this morning. The office burned down and
with it all his records, his typewriter and calculator, couple of props—some instruments—
our precious sugar pine board, and I guess the maps. It made a clean sweep 'cause Draper
was flying and the only other two people around were down in the shop. I guess the wood
stove they put in got too hot. I haven't been out to view the wreckage, but it must be a mess.

Elda is having Supper Club tonight—I have to bring garlic bread, so you see my cooking
hasn't improved in your absence—they still don't trust me to cook anything, or else they
are being nice to me 'cause I'm at the office all day. It is nearing quitting time so will sign
off and go home and work on my garlic bread. Darling, I sure enough wish that you were
going along too!

All my love forever and ever—

Gail

"Because we haven't written does not mean that we do not think of you often. Some day
soon we will write, tho."

Margarite.

"Hello Wes: Here I am back in the swing of things again—it's a boy this time and are we glad! Everything went along fine—but I did miss the two of you. Here's hoping it won't be long before everybody is back home again and we can all be with our families and friends again. Gail keeps us all well posted as to your progress, and we do enjoy hearing about your work. Our best wishes to you always."

Sincerely,

Janet Finnegan

JANUARY 30, 1944 WES TO GAIL

Sweetheart,

Had a wonderful trip yesterday—this time by jeep. We drove about fifteen miles down the valley to visit some native villages. The Aussie Captain, the Group Surgeon, Group Dentist and myself went. We took along salt tablets, candy lifesavers, and cigarettes for trade and got a bunch of coconuts and pawpaws. There was an Aussie officer down there in control of them who is going to pick up some grass skirts, arrows, and other junk for us. We had a big time examining the children and feeling for enlarged spleens, and there were some real beauties. I've never really felt a spleen before now.

I borrowed a camera, and the other boys had some, so we got a bunch of pictures. Hope some of them come out, as I have a couple of us standing between a couple buxom belles who would make good jersey cows. It was the most fun I've ever had—talk about all sizes and shapes—they've sure got 'em! I'll send the pictures along when I get them, although it will take a month or so to get them developed.

I didn't realize that you came back from Phoenix in the Culver. Did you fly it much? How is it to land and take off?

Thanks for the letter from Ruthie Simmons. Wonder where Stan is?

Dad and Esther both wrote me. They don't seem to have been getting my letters. I wrote them in December and January. I'll send along another letter to them.

Mother sent me a photographic copy of her letter from General Giraud, and I think I'll send it to you, as I might lose it bouncing around the country, so am enclosing it.

I ran into one of my old friends from California Medical School, Ed Healy. He's a flight surgeon over here too. We met at a medical meeting last night where I heard a little talk on dengue, so I brought him back to the tent and we had some drinks and a small poker game with some of the boys. He hadn't been able to get any liquor, so I gave him a quart and he was quite delighted. I don't believe you ever knew him.

Darling, do as you please about going to Seattle—don't worry about it, as it will be OK whether you go or not.

I'm right tickled to hear that a camera is on the way, though it doesn't seem right to deprive Virginia. I'll be looking for it, and take another trip to the natives.

I'm glad you are paying Bill for the candy. That's too much for him to do. You are sweet to take care of my many requests, Dearest.

I can't imagine why George Cotter should be drafted. It's our understanding that they were slowing up on that, as we have so many men under arms at home now who could be sent for replacements. I didn't know he was trying to be an instructor in aviation—sure hope he makes it.

Darling, I'm sorry you have to put up with that Dr. B. He ought to be ashamed of himself—holding out. Want me to write to him and tell him what a heel I think he is? I'll sure do it if you say so!

Keep the old chin up, Sweetheart. I love you, and I'll come back to you just as soon as Uncle Sam will let me.

All my love, always Darling—

Your Wes

JANUARY 31, 1944 GAIL TO WES

Dearest Wes,   #2

Our fifth anniversary has come and gone. I certainly hope the next one we'll be together and every one after that!

I spent yesterday out at the airport. We raked through the ashes trying to find at least one page of Draper's logbook, but we didn't find much of anything. Among other things, Draper lost 6 props and a whole new set of instruments for Ted Swift's ship. It snowed almost all day yesterday. I took the T Craft 55 up in it, and it was quite a sensation. There was about 9 inches on the ground and everything was white. I couldn't tell when I'd taken off or when I was on the ground. That must be the way you feel when you come in on water. At any rate, you seem to have a good cushion when you land. Before I got down, the snow was really coming down. You would have loved it, Darling. Guess you can't visualize snow down there where it is so hot.

John has had a cold, so he didn't get a chance to get out in it, to his great disappointment. Now it has been raining and most of it is rained off again. Haven't been skiing yet—can't seem to find time enough.

Take good care of yourself, Darling.

All my love,   Gail

FEBRUARY 1, 1944 WES TO GAIL

My Darling,   #72

Three nice V-Mails from you today. It's so nice to hear from you, Sweetheart. You sounded so sad when you said my letters seemed to get farther and farther apart. Darling, I'll try to do better by you. There is so little to tell you about over here. One day is just the same as another when I can't wangle flying trips or be building a house, or something.

The boys have been using my tent as a clubroom, pending the building of a clubhouse (which we just started on yesterday). There are anywhere from ten to thirty in here every night to have a few drinks, sing, play poker, and what not—so that if I don't find time in the day to write, I'm generally out of luck at night.

The interesting things that do happen, I can't mention, unfortunately—so-o-o...

It's a tough war, isn't it, Honey? It's going to be wonderful when I get back to my baby. I haven't heard any more about my leave lately. Don't know when it will be. Sure wish they'd give me a leave to Quincy for about a week.

I have a new nickname. As my hair is short, and I'm not using any grease on it, it sticks straight up all over, so the boys call me "Curly Moore," and my tent is known as "Curly Moore's Bar."

The club building will be pretty good, about 60 x 30 feet. It is one of these portable building affairs that can be folded up and transported by air. Of course, it is just a framework, so we will put on a tarpaulin for a roof, screen wire sides with about four feet of paper from the ground up, concrete floor, and a false ceiling of burlap cloth for coolness. Then we will build a bar and furniture. One end will be closed off for a reading and writing room.

I just finished a book of Daman Runyon's best stories. I enjoyed them more than somewhat—and if there is anything you wish to send me, make it another batch of those little books.

Thanks, Darling, in advance, for the cigars and candy. I hope they make as good time as this fountain pen did.

About the liaison deal, no further news. Looks as though they don't care to have me fly for them in the combat zone. Ah, well, such is life.

That was pretty rough on Ken and Del, having Fred Christy knocked out at such a crucial moment. How's he getting along?

I still can't see why guys like Del and George should be getting caught up with by the draft. Poor old Del—he sure won't enjoy being a yard bird, I can promise you that. He'd better apply for Officer's Candidate School—wonder if he could make the grade? Poor Bunky didn't.

Guess I'd better try to get some shut-eye. The boys stayed late last night and I had live duty today.

Goodnight, Sweetheart—I love you always.

Wes

FEBRUARY 3, 1944 GAIL TO WES

My Darling—   #3

Haven't heard from you since Jan. 24th. It seems ages between letters and things just sort of pull at my heart. I love you, Darling, and please don't let anything happen to you. I guess I'm pretty spoiled getting at least two letters a week. Couldn't tell when you sent the wire for our anniversary, Honey, but it certainly was swell. Let's have our next anniversary together, whatsay?

Johnny and I just came in from the airport—wish I had moved from the airport over to the Stone House for the purpose of giving exams. Barbara Baldwin, Ivy and Otto Grover were taking their Private's. Ivy and Otto were really sweating. Judge Morgan blew in from Chico, hoping to reorganize the Quincy CAP Flight, and screwy Jack Murphy rolled in from Lovelock. There was really quite a hangar session at the Stone House.

Gee, Honey, hope I get a letter from you tomorrow. With no letters and it raining cats and dogs, my spirits seem to be at low tide! Wish I had you here to snuggle up to. Guess I miss getting babied.

All my love

Gail

FEBRUARY 4, 1944 WES TO GAIL

Darling,   #73

I didn't write yesterday as I was feeling a bit low. I had a bad headache and a temperature of 99. Thought perhaps I was coming down with dengue, but am OK today, so I guess not.

The General was up a few days ago and passed out a bunch of decorations to the boys in our Group—Air Medal, Distinguished Flying Cross, Purple Heart, Soldier's Medal, and two Bulova wrist watches to two of the Line Chiefs for all the hard work they have done under adverse conditions. (Line Chief is an enlisted man in charge of all the medicines out at the line.)

I received your airmail of January 2nd today, with the picture of the house. It's a beautiful sight to my eyes, Darling, and I hope that it won't be too long before we are in it together again. The snow looks so inviting. I do wish we could ski up the Gold Lake road together again this year, Sweetheart.

I am surprised at all these married men having to go (to war). I don't imagine that they will send them out of the States—probably use them to replace men who are to go over as replacements here and elsewhere.

I wish turkey would start to get monotonous over here—or lamb too! We have roast beef (well done) and bully beef pretty regularly (the latter, plenty often) and steak occasionally. Eggs seem to be fewer also. Guess it goes in spells.

How come old Bud Moore goes off with Irene? How does his wife like it? Anyway, I thought he left Quincy.

Oh, I received the cute little leather card you sent from Phoenix. The stops you outlined didn't exactly pan out, did they, Darling—such as the one in Death Valley!

The old help situation is plenty rough, isn't it Dear. It must be just terrible now the war is on. Poor Dr. and Margarite, it's pretty darn swell of them to take this thing over for us, and I'll always appreciate it. Please give them my regards and tell them how fine I think they are.

Goodnight, now, Dearest. All My love to you and John. Tell John Daddy will come and see him as soon as he can. 'Fraid I won't be able to bring him back to New Guinea this trip, though!

Your own,

                                        Wes

FEBRUARY 4, 1944 GAIL TO WES

Hello, My Darling,   #4

I got your Jan. 17th letter today and was it ever a welcome sight! It took 18 days for it to come through where it only took 9 days for your letter of the 14th—that made quite a gap with no letters and I couldn't figure out what the heck! Golly but that letter sure made my day brighter. Honey, you say things the nicest way. I wish that I had been blessed with a gift for expression so that I could tell you all the swell things I want to—to show how much you mean to me and how very much I miss you, and how I pray every day for God to keep you safe, and for Him to bring you back to me soon. But that is the only way I can say it, and although it doesn't sound dressed up at all, you know that all of me is in it!

Now to answer some of your questions—no, for heaven's sakes don't send the nail clipper back—if it ever reaches you. John and I get along beautifully with the scissors. I did receive the $200.00 and wrote you about it—perhaps you have received the word by now. And by the way, I certainly appreciated it. The house is now down to $3,285.00 and I'm still plugging away. If we aren't careful, we're liable to have the Hospital paid off by next winter too! How does that sound to you?

The situation with Dr. B. doesn't seem too bad to me now, because it is allowing Dr. L. to go home every night (although Margarite can't go with him). That means a lot to him. I don't care how much Dr. B. pockets as long as we can keep our heads above water. Right now the Plumas Industrial and the County are on the same side of the fence against Blank. Dr. B. has told her that she can't operate at the County either and I don't think that either of the Dr's will ever give anesthetic for her. However, she said that Frank (her husband) gives a beautiful anesthetic, so I guess that she won't need their assistance. I heard today that she was looking over the Evans property, thinking that she might build a hospital out there. Some fun—she's had that bug for so long now that it is getting to be a joke. If she tried it, she would die of a heart attack.

No, Louie didn't die, but I think that he is going to be a permanent border at the Plumas Industrial Hospital. They let him out once and the next morning he was right back here in the same condition as the first time he came in. He looks pretty well, but he has an awful pain in his leg that they had to give him shots for. I don't know just what the diagnosis for that was, but it seems to be over now.

How's about telling me about your tent mate. I want to see if you are in the right kind of company. Sounds as though you boys might have been busy with the laying of the floor. Must have kept you busy for awhile and out of mischief. Or do you have a chance to get into any mischief over there?

Last night the airport crowd got together out at the Stone House and celebrated examinations being over. Peter Mingrone cooked up a big pot of spaghetti and meatballs, a green salad and French bread, and we spread a feast. I got in on the dishwashing end of it. We had broom dances and all sorts of queer performances, but it was fun. I certainly wish you had been there, Honey. Josephine is still on the Jukebox. We were very fortunate in not being bothered by the trade—only a couple of people came in during the whole evening.

Guess that I'd better call a halt to this. Believe it or not, I'm going to a lecture put on by the Rotary Club. Something about Latin-American contributions to the war.

All my love   Gail

FEBRUARY 5, 1944 WES TO GAIL

Darling Gail,   #75

Your V-Mail of January 25th arrived today. Honey, don't worry about the numbers on your letters. I can tell by the dates when I've missed any.

You really are having misery with the help. Those damned coloreds are certainly independent. I wish CA had never brought them to Quincy. Yet, he creates the best part of our business, so I can't [unreadable].

You don't say much about Doris—does she like it? And do you think she will stay on? I certainly do hope so, as I imagine she is one pretty swell gal. Give her my best regards, Dear. I get a kick out of the way Dr. and Dr. B. shove poor old Blank around about surgery—that seems to be about the only point Dr. and Dr. B. agree on!

We hauled three big truckloads of sand and gravel from the river today, requiring plenty of shoveling into and out of the truck. It's for our club. I'm weary and sore tonight, and I think I'll cut this short.

Always your loving hubby—

                          Wes

FEBRUARY 6, 1944 GAIL TO WES

Sweetheart—   #5

It's 11:30 PM and time I was tucked away, but thought you'd like to know what went on in the little town today. 'Course you can guess where I spend the day—at the airport! Went out about noon, but the fog hung in at about 500 feet so that all we could do were takeoffs and landings. I sandbagged for Barbara Baldwin in Draper's Luscombe 65 (He has 5 of them now), and we came in with a dead stick twice—no harm done. The darn thing goes down to 400 rpm and promptly dies after you cut the throttle. I'd never been in it before, but it seems that sometimes it does it and sometimes it doesn't. *[Yikes!]* Then I sandbagged for Otto in the T Craft 55 and the darn wing on the left drops out too fast. *[Double yikes!]* Then I rode with Floyd, and since he hadn't soloed, I'd help him and we'd come in a little hotter.

Big Barbara and I went to the show tonight—saw "Watch On The Rhine," excellent picture. In the newsreel I saw some of your metal strips. It looked like they have holes in them. Must be quite a sensation to rattle over them.

Guess I'll call it a day, Honey. Goodnight, and all my love forever and ever—

Your Gail

FEBRUARY 7, 1944 WES TO GAIL

Dearest Gail,

Another letter from you, Honey—Jan. 27th. The V-Mail makes pretty good time.

That "Blitz" at the house sounded pretty rough. Did the water come down through the ceiling from the cracked growler? Boy, I wish I had put a decent furnace and electric water heater in the house back in pre-war days. It would only have cost around $200.00, and the savings in grief and fuel would more than paid for it by now!

I'm glad your party was a success. It will be nice to participate again someday. That Congressional Bill you mentioned is having some effects. Many of the pilots are being allowed to go home, with replacements coming in. The enlisted men have to go about eighteen months, and the other ground officers too. As for the doctors, we are a sort of bastard lot. No one seems to know what sort of a deal we get, as there aren't enough of us around—partly by reason of guys like friend Dr. B. However, it looks like I may eventually get to be Group Surgeon here, if they send the present one home and the other Squad Surgeon, who is my senior, goes through the job. Maybe six or eight months. I'd really like to come home Major Moore! I'll at least feel like I've caught up to Barney—unless he gets promoted—which is likely!

There have been many beautiful sights going by here these days—oh, just wonderful to see—we're really pouring it on those little bastards these days.

I have a new souvenir—a P-38 model made of 30 caliber shells for the booms and a 50 caliber for the fuselage. It's mounted on a 50 caliber set into a bowl which is a part of an Aussie 25 pounder. There are Australian coins around the edges to hold cigarettes. The wings are also part of the 25 pounder flattened out. I'm going to try to send it along with the Jap rifle. I have the box made, but just can't seem to get around to getting it all packed and sent on the way.

Well, Honey, nothing new, except we really are in the rainy season now. It sure does flood the place in about five minutes when it starts. I always have one outfit drying while the other is getting wet.

All my love, Dearest. Always your—

Wes

FEBRUARY 8, 1944 GAIL TO WES
JOHN W. MOORE, M. D.
BERNARD S. HOLM, M. D.
Quincy, California *[Old business stationery]*

Honey,

I'm up at the office and it is about 7:35. Dr. B. has a shot to give. Otherwise, everything is quiet. Louis had a cerebral hemorrhage today about one o'clock and his left side is paralyzed. For awhile he couldn't talk very well. This evening he seems to be doing better. He looks so entirely different than he did before the stroke that it sort of startles me when I have to go in there. He has been conscious all of the time. I don't know just how long he will last, but I guess that he will be with us until that time. I feel sorry for Louie; he can't even read that Bee that I've been bringing him every morning.

Mother and Dad are planning to leave for Phoenix on the 14th. I guess that Johnny and I will batch for a couple of weeks. I have to see Mrs. Redstreake to see if she will take John for a little while each day and I can still cover on the hours that I am supposed to. John said that he would like to go to Phoenix too. He'd like to see Uncle David and Maribelle. The other night Mrs. Baldwin asked him where you were and he answered, "New Guinea" and then she asked where that was, he said "Oh, somewhere down by Australia," then after thinking it over he added, "and Great Falls." Johnny and Dad made a snowman today, and was Johnny thrilled with it. He says that he can't make one by himself. His are just little balls and they don't make big snowmen.

The other day I wrote a letter to David and Maribelle and was going to send them some pictures—like the ones that I sent to you. I had an envelope with some pictures to send to your mother too, and what did I do but put David's letter in your mother's envelope and sent it off to her. She's going to be quite surprised to be addressed as "Kookie." I hope that she doesn't fall over in a faint. I wrote her today explaining my error; however, she will have a few days to contemplate the condition of her daughter-in-law's mind. Hope that she doesn't decide that I've gone clear off the beam.

We lost all of the snow of the first storm, and then this morning it started out with fresh gusto, only to end up in a rain that washed all the snow away again. John was most disgusted when his snowman started to run away. We'll probably get a good one before the winter is over, if this isn't the year for the floods.

Oh, I forgot to tell you that I got $150.00 from the hospital this month. We still are holding our heads above the water. I expect that this month will be a little on the lean side, however. We aren't having so very much business. Blank is mad at both Margarite and Dr. B. because neither one of them would let her use the operating rooms again unless it is an emergency, and then either Dr. L. or Dr. B. will check the patient. Blank was so mad that she went before the Board of Supervisors asking why she couldn't use the County Hospital. I don't believe that she got anywhere by doing it. Probably the next thing that we will hear is where she is doing major surgery down in her own little set up.

Guess that I'd better go home now, Darling, and iron a few uniforms so I'll be clean tomorrow.

I love you, my Sweet—more than I think you realize. All my love

Gail

[Attached is a card signed by Dottie, Bill Bailey, Ruth Dellinger, George Cotter, Helen Metzker, Del Dellinger, Helen Baldwin, Elda Cotter, Link Peckinpah, Leda Bell—Chas. has the flu—Betty Peckinpah, & Doris Hansen.]

FEBRUARY 9, 1944 WES TO GAIL

Darling,   #76

No mail since day before yesterday. They've been kind of slowing up on *[unreadable]* too, haven't they. I'm sweating out the nail clipper, cigars, candy, and what have you! Darling, you must spend half your time wrapping up stuff to send me. I sure do appreciate it.

Honey, I do so enjoy that picture of the house, too. I'll take as good care of it as I can and bring it safely home to you. I can see what they meant when they told us in Brisbane that things get damp in New Guinea. The damn envelopes stick shut and the stamps lose their goo, so have to be stuck on with glue! I hope I can keep the damn wool uniforms from going to pieces with mildew, etc.! Oh, it's a rough life, ain't it, sweet?

Darling, I worked the line today and I'm tired. I'll have to quit and get some shut-eye.

I'm reading Nero Wolfe, *The League of Frightened Men.* Just finished Ellery Queen's *Anthology of Mystery Stories.* Twenty-five short ones!

All My love, Sweet, and tell John Daddy loves him.

Wes

FEBRUARY 10, 1944 GAIL TO WES

Darling,   #7

Another day, but no letters—dern it all! Guess you feel the same way when mine don't get through to you. Don't worry, Sweetheart, I will write to you every other day unless I break my arm. 'Course I might miss a day now and then, but not very often.

John and I went to Kindergarten today and did John ever have a good time—it was his first visit. I told him yesterday that I would take him, and he awakened at 5 am to ask me if it was time to go to Kindergarten. Did he ever show off when they started on the alphabet.

What did you have in mind to rejuvenate the inside of the office with, Honey? I think that Margarite is going to have it calcimined (?). I imagine that you could get an answer back before anything is done—that is—if you put it in the letter that answers this one. That Margarite gets things done!

Louis is still with us. In fact he's the only one in right now. He looks pretty bad; expect he'll go out just any time.

Bill Bailey is pretty sore at Dr. B. He's found out that he is giving his private patients medicine from the County stock instead of writing prescriptions. Bill doesn't know if he charges for all of them, but he knows of some that he hasn't. It's probably the way that he gets his patients—his profession certainly isn't free—that bird knows how to soak them.

I got Mrs. Redstreake to take John from 3 to 5 and 7 to 8 while Mother is gone—there will be three other kids there, so he will have a marvelous time. My how he likes other children.

We had a beautiful sunny day today, and again the snow is practically all gone—except on the north side of our house. Incidentally, Ray had to get a whole new toilet—they couldn't find a tank that would go on the rest of the thing.

Lena is staying with John while I'm at the office, so I'd better get on my horse.

All my love, Honey—

Gail

Hello Wes. How are you getting along? I just came up after some cough medicine. Sure wish I had some of yours. Kill a Jap or two and come home. From yours,

C. Bedell

FEBRUARY 11, 1944 WES TO GAIL

Dearest Sweetheart,   #77

Haven't had a letter since last time, so no questions to answer! However, I did get a letter from an old sweetheart, hope you are properly jealous. Clara! Seems she made a resolution, so wrote me a V-Mail and a very nice letter too. She's been in a Gilbert and Sullivan job and done a spot of opera plus the usual teaching. It's a good thing I didn't marry her. I'm sure I'd have been jealous of her career—anyhow—I sat down and wrote her a lengthy letter telling all the dope I've given you over the past three months. Hope you won't mind, Darling. You're still my very best girl, you know, and you are the only one your poppy loves—and how.

We are having a big Group inspection tomorrow, so we have all been busy today cutting and burning grass, filling in old slit trenches, picking up cigarette butts and trash. It has been threatened that anyone whose tent area isn't neat will go to the bottom leave list!

I'm slated to go to [unreadable] School on the 22nd, at the town where I first arrived in Australia. It will be a week or ten days. Whether I get my Sydney leave directly following, or a month later, I don't know yet.

Honey, I've found out I still can't play poker. I'll have to confess, I lost about seventy-five pounds in the past month finding out, so I've reverted to my old policy of not playing. I'm sorry Dear—that's going to make two months I don't send you my extra money. Please forgive your erring husband.

It's been so hot in the day, I take a dip in the creek about 12:00, doze until 1:00 or 1:30, 'till I can't stand the puddle of sweat under my nude body, then take another dip, and maybe a third before four o'clock, when its' regular shower time. Thank goodness, the nights are cool, and usually very, very damp. I'm not complaining, Dear, still getting a kick out of it all.

Something very funny, yet at the time, a little terrifying, happened a couple of nights ago—which I can't tell about now—but you must not let me pass it up when I see you next. It was really a kick.

The battle goes on as ever, hot and heavy—and very favorable. It does seem to take a long time for each forward movement, though, in spite of continued victory. But I suppose that is to be expected.

Darling, did you get my anniversary telegram and letter in time? I thought so much how wonderful it would have been to be with you then—as always, Darling, but our time is coming, Sweet.

I love you, Dearest, always and faithfully and do miss you so.

All my love—forever and ever.

                         Wes

FEBRUARY 12, 1944 GAIL TO WES

Sweetheart,   #8

Received letters #70 (Jan 30ᵗʰ didn't have a #) yesterday, and #67 and 68 today. Guess a boat must have come in. #66 and 69 are still missing. Guess they will be along one of these days. You certainly have been building a cozy little nest for yourselves. Should be pretty comfy when you get through. Hope you get to Australia, Darling—should be quite a treat for you.

I was certainly glad to hear that you are keeping your weight. As for mine, did Dr. L. ever howl when I read him that you thought I should take Vitamins—he says that I look better than he's seen me in some time. Really, Honey, I'm packing all the weight that 5'2" can stand—besides, I'm getting a stenographer's seat, which is no addition in the line of beauty.

Dr. L's comment on your trip to the natives was good: "So he took his cigarettes down to trade with the natives!" He didn't think that was so smart! I told him that I didn't think that he needed to worry about what was traded in return.

CA came back a couple of days ago. Katherine is coming out here and live with him 'cause *[unreadable]* is transferred out West.

All my love, Sweet

                              Gail

FEBRUARY 12, 1944 WES TO GAIL

Gail, Darling,   #78

Got your letter of the 31ˢᵗ today, but haven't received the one for the 29ᵗʰ, so don't know what this is all about—this raking through the ashes trying to find Draper's log book. Somebody's plane must have burned up.

Honey, aren't you a bit brave about flying about in a snowstorm? You know, it can come down awfully hard up there sometimes. Please take extra good care of my little girl.

I agree with you, Dearest—let's have all the next seventy-five anniversaries together. I can't seem to remember your mentioning my telegram. Did you receive it all right, Darling?

You spoke about how nice it would be to have one of those planes after the war—the second one I said I rode in. Just to show you how much it would cost even to fly one, you could fly the Aeronca 22 ½ hours on the gas it would take to fly it <u>one</u> hour! So let's not plan on having one, unless you know of some rich uncle who is liable to die off and leave you three or four million!

The normal course of events passes by (period)! I've quit playing poker, though I am sorely tempted, looking at the games. However, if I don't, I won't have enough to get to Malaria School and on leave, let alone gypping you out of your cut! I have been such a bad boy, Dearest—I'm truly sorry.

We had an inspection today. Everybody was all shined up, and the camp policed (that means picking up papers, etc.) to a fare-thee-well. Apparently we did OK. Am having some very satisfying results in the anti-mosquito campaign which we all are working. Of course, I'm not allowed to give you figures, but I've been working up some pretty colored graphs which show some very fine improvement in mosquito-borne diseases. I kind of enjoy fiddling with statistics once in awhile, although I do prefer the more active side of medical practice—as you know—no babies to hold in the oven, or work over, around here!

Darling, you were such a big help then, and I had no idea you were going to be mine. I'm terribly happy I love you, Sweetheart.

I love you, always. Your own—

Wes

DATED FEBRUARY 14, 1944

A tattered and burned piece of a parachute was shipped home to Gail with the following India ink inscription: "Nip chute deliberately picked up on wing of P-40 by pilot, Bill Ferris, after Nip was shot down by another pilot over Wewak."

FEBRUARY 14, 1944 WES TO GAIL

Darling,   #79

No mail for a couple of days, though I did get a nice note from CA. He's pretty swell to write as often as he does. Can't understand why he isn't wintering back East.

I haven't had a chance to see Julian again, and am wondering if he has moved to the new spot. I've been busy with paperwork, getting the pilot's individual records up to date and trying to run them over to the dentist for their identification charts. They are like a bunch of kids—have to practically lead each one over there by the ear.

I got hold of *For Whom the Bell Tolls* (Hemingway) and am going to start it as soon as I finish with the present mystery story. Have you read it?

The food has been a little below normal lately—all nourishing, but just too damned much canned bully beef—four nights and lunches in a row. We are looking forward to some lamb tomorrow night.

Action continues about the same. No excitement lately. The old slit trench is getting full of weeds from disuse!

How's my Johnnie boy? I'll bet he's getting to be a real big boy now, and taking good care of his Mama while Daddy is away.

'Night, Darling. I love you so much.

Your Wes

FEBRUARY 15, 1944 GAIL TO WES

Hello Darling, #9

Seems like an awful lot has happened in the last few days. Mother and Dad left Sunday for Sacramento and parts east. Sunday afternoon, I went out to the airport and got a ride in the Silvaire. I took Nina up to Portola to see a P-39 that had cracked up somewhere up there, but never did find it. Seems like something happened to the oil line and the cockpit filled up with smoke—the kid thought that it was a fire, so he jumped. From what they say, the 39 was all over the landscape.

Sunday night, I went up to Beckwith with the Metzkers, Cotters, Bedells, and Baileys. We had dinner up there, and a nice one too. John had a marvelous time running back and forth with John Gordon; however, I think that he wore himself down slightly.

When the Baileys and the Cotters arrived, they told us that CA had taken big Barbara up for her first plane ride and that he had run out of gas and made a forced landing out in Bresciani's field. They apparently made a beautiful landing, but before they came to a stop, they hit a ditch and nosed over. Barbara is in the hospital—nothing serious, but plenty sore in spots. CA broke his glasses and got a cut over his eye. He certainly is mortified. I didn't see the plane, but from what CA said, one side of the landing gear is washed out and the underside of the cowling was mashed. I think that he is going to sell the remains to Walker, and he has his eye on another Silvaire. He says that it would take too long to patch it up. Last night he said that they had an organization—he and Julian. Julian is the president and CA the vice president. I guess the association is for the washing out of Silvaires.

Yesterday morning, John woke up with a temperature, so I phoned Dr. and told him that John had a temperature and what do I do now? He told me to bring him up, so John is reposing in the Xray examination room and getting along quite nicely. His temp is practically gone and he is sleeping peacefully—being a good boy, believe it or not. I guess he had an intestinal upset, and after chewing up two doses of Dr's. pink pills (and asking for more) everything is rosy. He doesn't seem to mind staying here and he likes all of the nurses. Yesterday, when he came tramping out here in his bathrobe and slippers looking for me, Dr., in his gruff voice said, "Here, young man, you get yourself back into bed!" Johnny went a kiting and has been earnestly working at getting back into Doris' good graces. That really impressed him.

Morgan Haun is up here putting a board around the examination table in the treatment room. The table had gouged out some of the plaster. Then he is going to repaint the room. Later on, we are going to have him do the rest of the inside. He has just finished doing Willis King's office (the same kind of plaster) with Kem-tone and it looks very nice. It really needs it and should look much better.

I went down to the bank today and closed out that beautiful bank account that I told you Dr. had given us. I put down on the hospital loan, which at this moment is in the amount of $845.00. In nine months the hospital should belong to us again, Honey. Now won't that be something? (You should hear Morg out there talking away to himself—wonder if he knows what he's talking about?)

Helen Metzker has invited me over to dinner tonight. Bill and Margaret Hays are up and looking for a house—the last check on Margaret's blood pressure was 240, so they decided that they might just as well come back up here to live. I think that Bill is buying an interest in Ken's Associated *[Oil Jobber]* business. Haven't gotten all of the details on it yet.

Your letter #69 came through today, Honey—sorry I got so mixed up in my numbers. Honest, I'm trying to do better. I'm one day late with this one, but you know, it's liable to happen every so often!

Bye now, Sweetheart. Johnny and I love you with all our hearts.

Always your   Gail

FEBRUARY 16, 1944—SOUTHWEST PACIFIC AREA (SWPA, Fifth Air Force): 40+ B-25s attack a convoy off New Hanover Island. 30+ B-24s bomb Panapai Airfield and Kavieng on New Ireland Island, and some hit Cape Balangori and Talasea, New Britain Island. 19 B-24s and B-25s bomb Halong in the Celebes Islands. P-40s hit shipping and barges in the Wewak, New Guinea area. Transfers in New Guinea: HQ 345th Bombardment Group (Medium) from Dobodura to Nadzab; 25th Liaison Squadron, 5212th Photographic Wing (Provisional), from Lae to Nadzab with L-5s.

FEBRUARY 16, 1944 WES TO GAIL

Hello, Sweetheart,   #80

How's my baby tonight? Happy? I want you to be, Dearest. We'll have such fun when Daddy gets back. War is a hell of a note, ain't it?

Darling, I had a marvelous ride today. The squadron has the use of a two-seater P-40 for a couple of days, and the boys were giving all the crew chiefs and line men rides. Did they get a thrill—first time for a lot of them. My chance came late in the afternoon. I had scheduled typhoid shots for 6 PM and forgot all about it. When I came in at 6:45, the medical enlisted man was practically through with them, so I didn't have a thing to do except to get my own.

We had <u>ice cream</u> tonight—first I've tasted in six months, and was it good.

Well, anyway, the C. O. took me up. There is a fuselage tank behind the pilot in the regular job, which is removed to make room for a spare seat—no dual controls, unfortunately. But it's a world more comfortable than having the pilot on your lap! We went over and took a look at some of the spots the boys have dive-bombed, but no Nips showed up. Then he put on a real act. I had to lean forward and push my breath with all my might to keep from blacking out, especially in a peel off. They get right upside down then rack the old stick back. Once or twice I couldn't even lift my hands off my lap, and I really got a bit grayed out. He did some perfectly beautiful slow rolls, and then held us inverted for about a minute. All the mud in the cockpit fell up into our faces! On the way home, he got right down on the river and tore along wide open xxx miles an hour. Then he'd bank up one way and the other, all but putting the wingtip in the water. Boy, what a thrill. We buzzed camp and practically took the roof off the mess hall.

Well, well, I sort of ran away with myself about that ride, didn't I?

Guess I told you I'm going to Malaria school on the 22nd. I may get my regular leave to follow, in which case, I'll be away almost a month. Darling, wouldn't it be swell if we could see Sydney together? Someday, Sweetheart.

All my love, Darling, your own husband who loves you—

Wes

P. S. No letters for about four days! Tsk tsk!

FEBRUARY 17, 1944 GAIL TO WES

Dearest—   #10

John and I are back home again. I kept John in the hospital two days. His fever was down yesterday morning and then went to 99 at 4:00 yesterday afternoon. He goes in and lies down after he eats as though his tummy might be complaining. Does he get that form his Dad? Maybe he should try a little front line "grub" to cure him of that!

It's trying awfully hard to cook up a good storm. Last night the wind howled around and finally it squeezed out about an inch of snow, which didn't last long when the sun hit it this morning.

Del got a six months deferment—after Ruth insisted that he straighten out his business before he got mixed up in the draft. Whoever told you they are slowing up on the inductions is crazy!

Ran out of ink! They seem to be taking them faster, if anything. Someone is really getting ready for a big push somewhere. The news is sounding mighty good from your side of the globe. They seem to have bottled up quite a number of Japs on Bouganville, and from what I can gather, Rabaul is pretty well sewed up. With the Navy cleaning up the Islands in Mid-Pacific and your outfits mopping up in the southwest Pacific, Truk looks like a pretty vulnerable spot.

Johnny has gone to sleep—he really must be sick. Never heard of such a thing as that little man even dozing in the middle of the day. My, but it is quiet.

The Bishops are trying to sell their house for $7500.00. I've heard that they have bought that little number just this side of Long Bridge. They are going into ranching, giving up the store. I guess ranching will be a side issue. Blank attempted to buy the Home Hotel for a hospital, but she couldn't put the cash on the line, so it didn't go through—have heard that she is dickering over the Clinch Ranch again. She wants to sell her outfit down here for $7000.00, and she can't seem to get any buyers!

I'm going to try to scoot up to the P. O. with this now, so bye my sweet,

Love Gail

Dearest Darling Gail,   #81

Your airmail of the 17th of Jan. came today. You wanted to know how much faster the V-Mail was. The one on the 16th got here about 12 or 13 days ago. Sometimes the airmail gets here faster.

Thank you for the pictures, Dearest. They are cute of John and the grandparents. Dave has his usual twinkle, but Mom looks a little severe. Is John getting her down?!

Also, got your V letter of Feb. 3rd today and the funnies Edith sent. Thanks, Mom. I enjoy your talk about flying, even tho' it does make me a little jealous. You sure must have the hours piled up by now. How many, Dear?

Tonight, we had wine with roast beef. There was Chablis, Port, Claret, and Burgundy. I stuck to the Chablis, and it was delicious, chilled. We must have wine with our meals occasionally. It sure improves my appetite.

Today, I worked on the officers club, tacking down the canvas on the roof. I was up there about an hour and a half without my shirt on, and I believe it's the hottest day we had yet. I'll swear it was 140 degrees up there. I couldn't touch the canvas it was so hot. I nearly passed out from the heat, so I got down and went for the showers—the water was practically hot, although the pipe is buried, so finally I went down to the creek and lay in it for about 30 minutes. That was really a life-saver. Then I snoozed for a couple of hours.

I'm getting so tan that I can go around for three or four hours without a shirt during the hottest part of the day, and I don't burn a bit. Hope I can bring the tan home with me.

I weigh 147 ½ pounds. I thought I had lost weight during that canned bully-beef session, but apparently not.

I've been writing pretty regularly, Dear. The letters must bunch up a bit. Maybe you'll get several at once. Are you getting them according to sequence? I won't get any mail from you for about a month when I go away. That's going to be bad. But it will be fun having a whole bunch waiting for me. You might write me once or twice right away, c/o American Red Cross, APO 923. If I don't get it, they can shoot it back up here. I should be there between March 6 and March 20.

Say, that was horrible, about Dr. Blank doing a hysterectomy on a pregnant woman. Certainly, she must not do any more surgery there. I want to know how the woman came out of it. Let me know, Dear.

Hurrah for David! Guess he's getting to be a big shot. They ought to be giving him railroad tracks soon. Give the newly wed my regards when you write.

Don't know why I used this side of the paper. I thought I was all through!

Goodnight, Darling. I love you, always,   Wes

FEBRUARY 19, 1944 GAIL TO WES

Darling—   #11

I'm at Redstreake's playing Cops and Robbers with the little guys while Mrs. Redstreake does her shopping, and then I go back to the office for the afternoon. John says he's going to eat his before they eat him. There are Germans and Japs climbing on the windows—Boy! What fun we're having.

At the office— #72—Feb. 1st arrived today. Sounds as though "Curly Moore's Bar" must be the hot spot of New Guinea. Can't understand how they missed calling you Gus. The hair sounds like Gus to me. Never mind Sweetie Pie, I still love you more'n anything!

It's been winding itself up to snow but all it can do is spit a couple of times and then it gets tired—we're having a "flying good winter."

John and I both got a cold when he left the hospital—you should have seen me last night giving us both steam inhalations—one hour on, two hours off. I had to set the alarm clock so we wouldn't suffocate. I'm 'fraid the back room is too big and drafty for it to be very successful.

Must write Mother—Bye now and all my love—

                                    Gail

FEBRUARY 21, 1944 GAIL TO WES

My Darling—   #12

Got out of the office tonight—Margarite is watching it for me 'cause Louise is the only one in. Dr. cleaned house when he came back after his weekend. John and I both have colds, so it will do us good to go to bed early.

Last night we had dinner out at CA's with Irene and Barbara and Ardis. The first three drove to Reno to pick up Katherine and Bunky and the kids. Bun goes to S. F. and the rest of the family is going to live with CA for the duration, I guess. We put on a bang-up snowstorm for Katherine—it started last night and it's still going strong. Shall I put a little on dry ice and ship it down to you Honey?

Peck tells me that Julian is in a hospital somewhere with malaria—know anything about it?

Saturday night, the airport gang celebrated Irene Lund's solo. Had a steak fry down in the old Legion Hall—which is now Grover Bros. Storehouse. We danced, ate and had a pretty good time. I wake up shivering every morning. I need you to keep me warm, Honey.

We had about a 6 foot ceiling by the time the steaks came off the coals, but it didn't seem to bother anyone. The consensus of opinion was that there wasn't as much smoke as in the Sump, and it was a lot better smoke at that.

Bud Young is in for limited service. Smitty might work for us. George is looking into active CAP service.

All my love, Darling

Gail

FEBRUARY 23, 1944 WES TO GAIL

Darling,   #83

I forgot to put a number on yesterday's letter.

Well, school is going on fine. We are receiving the curious peregrinations of the eukylostania and the domestic secrets of the lady mosquito, not to mention various bugs, worms, insects and what have you. We had a good talk on typhus this morning.

You know, there seems even less I can tell you here than I could up there. All we do is go to class 'til 2 or 3 PM, rest 'til 5:00, go down town and eat, then blot up the beer at the Officer's Club until about 10:30, come back and hit the hay. My one variation is the Masonic Club. I met the Aussie-Scotch steam ship engineer again last night—typical of the Saturday evening past stories about the ship, "Glencastle." He tells me they have an eleven-story Masonic Club in Sydney, and we have it all fixed up to meet there for lunch. It's the only one of that kind in the world, he tells me.

This place is lots better than last July and August. In fact, it was really cold then.

I hope these letters get there. I haven't been able to get to town early enough to get stamps at the APO, so have to send them "Free" for the [unreadable].

Darling, I'm going to get out of this hot tent and go back to class. By the way, I am really enjoying the fresh meat, eggs, milk and fruit we are getting here. I ought to look like a tub when I return.

All my love Darling, your   Wes

FEBRUARY 23, 1944 GAIL TO WES

Sweetheart,   #13

Letter #75 arrived yesterday—it was very short, but there was one more day that I knew you were all right. A letter from you, Darling, changes the complexion of my day.

Helen told me yesterday that Del is trying to get in the Navy. I don't know whether anyone knows definitely, or not. Someone saw him in the city and he was taking a physical for something. He isn't due home until next Monday—will let you know when I hear.

We are having a CAP meeting tonight trying to reorganize. Morgan from Chico will be here. We've all had to make new applications. I think they are trying to weed out those who really aren't interested and get the rest of us going on something. I don't know what it will be, but just anything would help.

Haven't heard from Mom since they left S. F. Hope they got to Phoenix OK. Airmail service has been pretty rotten the last couple of weeks. One thing after another has happened down the canyon.

Johnny and I had dinner with Ken and Helen last night—Helen went to Wed. Club, but John and I hid ourselves home with our colds—we are both better today. I'll learn to keep this furnace going yet!!

Be careful, Honey. All my love forever and ever—

Gail

FEBRUARY 24, 1944 WES TO GAIL

Dearest Gail,

Hello, Darling. Am writing this one in the classroom waiting for school to start. As I don't have my pad, am again without a number, but I think it is 84.

On my way down, I met Van (that's several days ago at APO 929) on his way back. He had been to school and on leave, also. We chatted just a short time as he was waiting for a plane north and I for one south. He said Vern is in the hospital down here with his old chest complaint. I expect he'll probably get to go home on it this time. I'm going to try to get out to see him this afternoon. Van was in the hospital himself, down south of here, with an ear infection, of all things for an old man to get! He looks somewhat aged. I don't believe that the tropics are agreeing with him! Oh, oh, class starting.

Well, just learned a little about eukrylastania deiodenale, necator amricious and ascaris lumbricides, not to mention enteroluius and trichuris.

I got caught in the rain trying to find a cab home last night. Sneezing today, but guess that I won't get pneumonia. This is quite a climatic change for us. I presume it will be considerably cooler when I get further south on my leave next week.

I keep asking all the many people I see if any of them have seen Barney, or know where the *[unreadable]* is—no luck. I'd sure like to run into him. I was supposed to meet Julian again last night, but he didn't show up, so I had a couple of beers, watched a pretty rough poker game awhile, then came on back to the pyramidal tent for a night's rest.

They are about to start the next class—dengue fever—so I'll seal this up and get it off in the early mail.

I miss your letters, Dearest. I'm going to be glad to get back to camp.

All my love, always. Your own

Wes

FEBRUARY 25, 1944 GAIL TO WES

My Darling,   #14

Your letter of Feb 3 (when you had the fever) came. After the letter of Feb 5 in which everything seemed to be all right. Golly, Honey, I pray for you every night—God has to keep you safe—I hope He listens to me. *[Both letters missing.]*

Had a letter from Mom today—from Phoenix—and they think Kookie is grand. I knew they would. They have had quite a time getting there. Guess the train trip was no lark. Mom has one of those runny colds and I guess it's been raining everywhere they went. They were expecting to get a ride in David's AT6. (the lucky bums) if it wasn't raining! Dad has an appointment with Dr. Barkan on the 2nd of March and then I guess they'll be home. We've kind of missed them around here—I've finally learned how to keep the furnace going, but it was quite a struggle.

There's nothing exciting at the office. Louie is still the only one in, but I guess he's going kind of batty—why in the devil didn't you limit the care on dollar a month patients when you made that contract? Oh well, it's all in the day's work. Guess next week I'll have to start struggling with the Hospital Income Tax.

All my love, Sweetheart, and take care of yourself.   Your Gail

FEBRUARY 25, 1944 WES TO GAIL
[Red Cross stationary]

Darling,

I thought I would write you from the Club. I've blotted up the allotted number of beers (about ten, depending on how fast one is on the trigger). I think I got around nine tonight, as I'm slowing up a bit in my old age. Any—how, I'm waiting for my train which leaves in about thirty minutes, and it takes me about fifteen to get there from the Club.

I miss you so, Honey. Golly, sitting around drinking beer and listening to the music, and I don't know a soul. Julian and all the brass hats are gone off on their trip, and I'm alone amongst a multitude. I did strike up a short acquaintance with an infantry officer, but he went away awhile ago to catch an earlier train—to a different place—so I wondered in here to look around, and seeing paper, could think of nothing that would make me happier than talking to you, Sweetheart. (I love you, my Dearest.)

Tomorrow we will have our last classes and finals. Then I'll have to "sweat out" my orders for leave which haven't shown up yet, so will be going south in the next two days.

All my love as always, Dearest. Your adoring and longing husband,

Wes

FEBRUARY 26, 1944 WES TO GAIL

Darling,

This is the last day of school. We are supposed to have a few lectures from 8 to 10, then a final examination. I've got to do a little bustling around after that, as there has been some hitch in my orders for leave. They were to be forwarded to me here, but have not arrived, so I'll have to do a little telegraphing. I may be up here 'til Monday or Tuesday.

I went to the movies last night and saw *Change of Heart*. I really enjoyed it, as it was the first time I had viewed a movie from anything but a wooden box or jeep seat in quite some time. The picture was good, and I bought some ice cream from the vendor at intermission.

Took a rest from the club last night and didn't go in for any beer. I wish I could take about a hundred cases of it back with me. There is where it would really be appreciated.

Only three more days to the end of this month. Time is rolling along pretty fast. Things seem to be going ahead with more force, with the latest attacks on Truck and Carolines, and the two *[unreadable]* in Europe. I hope it means that things will be speeded up. I don't dare speculate on how long this will last. I'm just going to keep going along, "fat, dumb and happy." No help worrying about it.

Darling, it will be swell to see you again on that big homecoming day!

I love you truly, Sweetheart—always,

Your Wes

FEBRUARY 27, 1944 WES TO GAIL
[Queensland Masonic Club stationery]

Hello, Darling,

I've been taking the worst kicking around the last few days. After finishing up at the school, I had to arrange another billet in town while awaiting orders. They put me up in an awful little dump of a hotel, in a room about 8 x 12 feet, with another officer. Just room to turn around. My bed is full of ants, cockroaches running around. The bathroom is filthy and no hot water. I'd rather be back at camp. My leave orders haven't come through and I just have to keep running to the Surgeon's office. Meals are horrible in town—the only saving grace is the beer. Of course, there is the fresh *[unreadable]*, ice creams, etc., but the meat is usually all gone, and the crowds are terrific. You have to make reservations one or two days in advance to get into the movies, even! I'm sure upset and damn mad—I don't get burned up like this very often, Honey, so excuse me for taking it out on you. It's sure a help to tell you about it.

Dearest, I miss getting your letters and am afraid that my leave is going to be not so much fun. Seems so much easier up there with the squadron where I have my work and friends. I don't know a soul here, nor down south in the leave area. Hope some of my pilots turn up down there.

I love you, Sweetheart, and miss you lots, and I would so love to see John. He'll soon be four years old, and no daddy to celebrate with him.

All my love, always, Darling. Your   Wes

FEBRUARY 28, 1944 GAIL TO WES

Darling—   #15

Winter has set in. It started snowing last night and hasn't quit yet. We only have a foot or so, but it looks like it means business.

Received three letters yesterday, Honey, #'s 75, 76, and 77. Guess I won't get any more for a week or so. I was certainly glad to get these. To answer some of your questions, it was the downstairs growler and the water didn't get any further than the bedroom.

The Group Surgeon sounds good—however, my Sweet. I'll welcome you back with open arms-Major or no Major. I'm looking forward to seeing the souvenir P-38; sounds like quite a concoction!

I'm properly jealous of Clara, Darling, but I'd certainly be a fine chump if I thought it necessary for you to give up your old pals—after all Honey—the old friends are the best friends, aren't they?

I'd like to have seen the activity that the inspection brought on—bet it was good! How did it turn out? Anyone lose a leave? I imagine that you will be kind of glad to see Brisbane again one of these days. I imagine a little civilized territory would be quite unique at this point. Honey, for Pete's sake, if you can have any fun with money over there, don't worry about how I feel about it 'cause I feel you have a little fun coming to you!!

Please take care of yourself, and here's all my love Sweetheart—

                    Yours, Gail

FEBRUARY 28, 1944 WES TO GAIL
[Red Cross stationery]

Darling,

I seem to write letters from most any old place around this town. I'm still sweating out my orders. The delay is maddening. Especially, as there is so little to do around here. Just eat and sleep, and go to the movies when you can get in. I took in a vaudeville last night. Very second rate, with a bunch of corny jokes and acts. The girls were all covered up too—no thrill!

I don't think I remembered to tell you I saw Vern. He is in a hospital near here with a chest condition—chronic bronchitis—which he has had for years and which got worse up north. Now he is expecting to be re-classified and probably will be kept in Australia. He may be sent to Darwin. Anyway, he got a pass, so we went to dinner at a hotel here and then spent the evening at the club quaffing beer. On our way to dinner, the hotel elevator got stuck between floors. After much prying and pounding, we managed to crawl through the upper part of the door below us! What a place!

It's hotter than hell around here and so boring. Golly, I hope I get my orders today.

Honey, I love you to pieces—always your devoted

Wes

FEBRUARY 29, 1944 WES TO GAIL

Dearest Darling,

I am packing up tonight to leave this little hole in the wall. I fly south in the morning. A car will pick me up at 3 AM for the airport. I'm certainly anxious to get away from here. This one week school and two weeks leave will amount to six weeks by the time I get back.

I ran into the Aussie Liaison Officer from the group today. I took him to where our beer ration is cached and we had a few with the gang. Then he took me to the Australian Officers Club where I met some of his friends and we had a few beers and dinner. It was a very nice club, and the roast chicken was good.

Last night one of the beer gang, Captain Hewpar out of the old 63rd, and I took in a steak dinner and saw *Flight for Freedom*. A swell picture, about Amelia Earhart.

I wonder—did I tell you about running into Hewpar yesterday? I guess I didn't. I went down to get my ration of one brandy and one wine. We also can get 24 quarts of beer per month, but I wasn't going to bother with mine, having no place to keep it. He had a room with some pilots and the hotel would ice the beer, so I got mine, and we had some crabs and beer—wonderful afternoon!

MARCH 2, 1944 —SOUTHWEST PACIFIC AREA (SWPA, Fifth Air Force): In New Guinea, 80+ B-24's and P-40's hit the Hansa Bay area, the airstrip at Nubia, and the Madang Alexishafen area. 60+ B-25's and A-20's pound enemy forces on Los Negros Island as Allied ground forces occupy Momote Airfield; P-47's providing cover for the B-25's claim 7 enemy fighters shot down.

MARCH 3, 1944 GAIL TO WES

Sweetheart,   #17

I am sitting here at home in quite a quandary. I'm suppose to be at the office at 4 and Mom and Dad wired that they would be home this afternoon. Being that John has quite a cold and the weather is a mess, I'm hoping that they make it home in time to stay with John so I won't have to take him to Redstreake's while I go to the office. That is all quite involved, but you can probably get what I mean. Gee, what mucky weather to tramp around in. Guess you remember what it's like to have about three feet of snow and then have it just pour!

Last night I went out to the airport with the Mingroves—(don't know whether you remember Barbara and Peter Mingrove). Barbara cooked up some beans, which she poured on rice and then each one flavors his own beans to taste with Oil Vinegar and Fresh Onions. They were mighty good and I seem to have suffered no ill effects from the concoction.

Gee, Honey, (as John would say) I luff you and certainly wish that you were here and we were home—wouldn't that be fun? Get jealous of the Smith's up there having each other and our house too!

All my love, my Precious

                    Gail

MARCH 4, 1944 WES TO GAIL
[Stationery address: 40 Fairfax Road, Bellvue Hill, Australia]

Dearest Sweetheart,

I've had a wild time since I last wrote. I spent three terrible days trying to get out of _____. I had to go back and forth to the airport with my bag, which was terrifically heavy, and so disappointed each time. It's an all day job to sweat one out, because you don't know from 5 AM to 5 PM whether you will get on or not.

I just got to Sydney today, and one of my pals told me of a place to go. I'm here, and Darling, it's so lonely I just can't believe it.

This wonderful woman, Mrs. Hay, has devoted her home for the past two years to pilots. She keeps scads of veal, eggs, <u>rare</u> roast beef, ham and chicken around all the time. I'm to have breakfast in bed whenever I want it, and she has a maid to do all the laundry. Darling, it's just like heaven compared to what I've had <u>way up</u> north. It's been terribly expensive, with nearly three weeks up at the other town, and costing me two pounds a day here which is better than the two and one half I had to pay there, plus beer, food, etc. I'm going to be so broke, it's pitiful.

Dearest, I wish you could be with me — we'd have so much fun here — it's quite like old S. F.

More tomorrow, Darling. I'm going to get a tremendous night's sleep tonight.

All my love, Darling

Wes

MARCH 4, 1944 —SOUTHWEST PACIFIC AREA (SWPA, Fifth Air Force): In New Guinea, 30+ B-24's hit the Hansa Bay and Alexishafen areas while 20 P-39's attack Madang and Bogadjim and 22 A-20's pound Erima. 14 A-20's and B-25's hit enemy positions on Los Negros Island.

<u>MARCH 5, 1944 WES TO GAIL</u>

Dearest Baby,

I'm having a hard time managing to write to you, Sweetheart—you know why? I'm getting so lazy and spoiled I can hardly think of doing anything energetic! Mrs. Hay is a most marvelous looker-out-after. She takes care of our laundry and cleaning, sends breakfast to us in bed, arranges tickets for shows and reservations for dinner. Golly, she's been doing this for two years now, and I don't see why these crazy kids don't drive her mad. The house is a lovely two-story affair with seven big bedrooms upstairs and two baths—all nice twin beds, etc. The walls are covered with the pilot's names, drawings, their photos tacked up all over and squadron insignia. There is a swell tennis court, and Dear, I'd forgotten how much fun it was to play. I have had three sets today, and if I'm able to move tomorrow I'll be lucky.

We get six bottles of beer a day and one bottle of liquor, but only two packs of cigarettes a week. That's rough, but fortunately, I brought a few extra cartons with me.

Honey, Darling, this would be so much fun if I had you with me. It's funny, but I'm more lonely for you here than I am up north where there aren't a bunch of strange white women running around. Darling, I love you more than anything in the world, and remember that, won't you, Sweet—I'm <u>all yours</u>, now and always. You know that, don't you.

Wes

MARCH 8, 1944· GAIL TO WES

Sweetheart—

Back at the office again after a very hectic afternoon. Johnny fell off a chair at Margaret Morris' and broke the emphasis on the right humerus—it seems it's just a chip—Dr. B.'s pictures weren't so hot, but good enough to show that the rest of the bones were intact—I think. Dr. L. hadn't gotten out of town yet, and I knew where he was, so I got him to come back just to ease my mind. It apparently isn't anything serious and Johnny is comfortable tonight. He thinks it is quite a lark now that it has quit hurting and Grandma has to feed him.

I'm going up to Ruth's to Wednesday Club this evening—haven't played bridge for so long, probably will mess everybody up. Oh well!

I got all of the material together for Mrs. Butcher to fix the Hospital Tax return and delivered it to her this morning. I'm certainly glad that is off my chest.

Darling, either the boats or the Japs are holding up my mail again. I haven't gotten a letter for a week, and boy do I miss them. Seems like ages between letters.

All my love my Sweet.   Gail

MARCH 10, 1944 GAIL TO WES

My Darling-

Had a regular Blitz on letters the last few days—5 in two days, and how very wonderful—#'s 78, 79, 80 and 81, and then one written on the 26th while you were at school. The letter of the 17th gave me an address to write to you at school, but Honey, I knew it couldn't possibly get to you by the 20th, so I'll just keep on writing to 713. Guess you must have missed my letter telling you that the telegram arrived in plenty of time; land, I was so thrilled to get it. Will try to get more on this letter with the typewriter.

Good work on controlling the mosquitoes! (They tell me that Wendell Hogan is home with Elephantiasis; don't know how true it is.)

I saw the picture "For Whom the Bells Toll" when I went to the city with Ruth. It won something in the Academy Award line.

I'm certainly glad to hear that the slit trench is getting full of weeds. Hope that thing grows over and you don't need it again.

Boy! Am I green over that ride that you had. I'd probably have been sick as a goose, but I'd certainly love to get the chance to do that! Best I could do was go up with Al Classen today after he got his commercial and sit there while he tried everything he'd ever heard of a light plane doing. By the way, Quincy scored 100% on tests with the CAA. Irene got her Private, Floyd passed his check for his hand, Al got his Commercial and so did Peter Mingrove.

Quincy is turning out pilots at a great rate! Aren't you proud? Our runway is dry as a bone and Beckwith is under about three feet of snow. They have tried skis up there, but I don't think that they did very well because there were holes in the snow. Can you imagine that!

Golly, Sweetheart, I'm so glad that you haven't lost any weight. Keep up the good work. The tan sounds marvelous, but good godfry, the heat sounds terrific. I certainly couldn't stand anything like that.

Sequence means nothing to the boys that put out the mail. By stacking your letters in rotation, however, I can get a pretty good picture of what you are writing about.

Dr. B. got a letter from Fletcher telling him that he has been made available, so he is on his way down to the city to apply to the Navy again. I don't think that the so and so will ever get into the service. The Board is asking for another deferment for him. It is up to the County to get someone to replace him, and I don't know how in the devil they can find anyone.

If this gets a little jumbled to you, it is because I've been trying to answer your questions without using up space for paragraphs. I should have started this on the typewriter, I guess.

Last night there was an airport party out at CA's given by the happy pilots. It was really a bang-up party as usual. I came home about 12:30, but they tell me that the inspectors didn't leave until 5 AM. Horrible, isn't it. When we do things, we do them in a big way. The inspectors had a big time. So did everyone else. Peter cooked the spaghetti, and he really did a job on it.

I love you, my Sweet, and sure do miss you!

Gail

MARCH 10, 1944—SOUTHWEST PACIFIC AREA (SWPA, Fifth Air Force): B-25's pound Lorengau and other targets on Manus Island. Numerous other Fifth Air Force aircraft carry out armed reconnaissance over wide reaches of the SWPA, attacking a variety of targets.

MARCH 12, 1944 GAIL TO WES

Sweetheart,

Another Sunday nearly gone and my Darling is so far away. Gee, Honey, we did have a lot of fun on our Sundays and all days, didn't we? Seems so long ago—hope it won't be as long before we can take up where we left off. I love you, Pop, and sure do wish you were here.

Johnny is getting along swell with his arm all tied up. Dr. L. says that he doesn't think that there is anything broken. The break that B. diagnosed, Dr. L. says is an outline of the bone.

Saturday I had a blow up with Dr. Blank's husband and told him if he had things like that to say that he'd better come up to the office and quit blabbing over the phone. He didn't come up—just hung up. I'll let you know what it is all about when I find out myself.

Blank and Guyer went to CA to see if he wouldn't back them in buying the Home Hotel (hoping to get the Industrial trade, I guess). CA was laughing about it. Didn't you say once—C'est le guerre? Or something of the sort?

All my love Darling,

Gail

MARCH 13, 1944—SOUTHWEST PACIFIC AREA (SWPA, Fifth Air Force): In New Guinea, 200+ B-24's, B-25's, A-20's, P-38's, P-47's and P-40's pound Wewak township, blasting docks, warehouses, gun positions, and numerous other targets; fighters claim 11 enemy aircraft shot down. 36 B-25's bomb Tingo village and Lugos Mission area on Manus Island, where elements of the 1st Cavalry Division make an amphibious landing, take the mission and head E toward Lorengau.

MARCH 14, 1944 GAIL TO WES

Hello my Darling—

Spring has sprung in Quincy today. Gave me the itch to go up to Gold Lake—with you, my Sweet. I 'spose I won't get up there this year—they've cut way down to two gallons now, and I can't get to the airport and Gold Lake too.

I got up early this morning and flew to Susanville with Barbara Baldwin in Draper's Luscombe. It was her first cross country. She did OK. She'll make a good pilot. We took some instruments over for Harry Alley to put in CA's ship—if and when it gets put together again.

Johnny is getting to be quite a fellow. He went shopping the other day—over to Kilpactrick's and came home with a can of cold tongue. He did this all on his own, you understand. No points, no money, no nothin' but brass.

Oh yes, he did mooch a penny out of Ruby. I had to go trotting back with his groceries and explained to the clerks that they weren't to give him anything unless he has a note. Was my face red when they didn't even know he had taken it.

Gee Sweetheart, I miss you so and I do want you home so much! Sure do wish you could hop a bomber home for your leave. Hope you enjoy your leave, Sweet.

All my love forever and ever,

Gail

MARCH 14, 1944—SOUTHWEST PACIFIC AREA (SWPA, Fifth Air Force): In New Guinea, 80+ B-24's, B-25's, and A-20's, supported by Allied fighters, pound the Wewak area; 17 other B-24's bomb the airfield at Tadji; and 8 A-20's carry out a sweep over the Madang area while 12 bomb the airstrip at Alexishafen. HQ 8th Fighter Group and 35th and 36th Fighter Squadrons move from Cape Gloucester, New Britain Island to Nadzab, New Guinea with P-40's and P-47's respectively.

MARCH 14, 1944 GAIL TO WES

Sweetheart,

I'm writing on borrowed time again—at the office. There is absolutely nothing going on— not even anyone (but Louie) at the Hospital.

Ruth took Johnny and me down to the mill and we watched the wheels go around. They seem to be doing OK. They need Fred Christy rather badly. He should be back in another three weeks. Today the wind was blowing a small cyclone, and the boys were afraid the mill might burn up. They wired for another $25,000 insurance and begged some hose from the USFS because the wind was blowing the flames and smoke from the burner right back at the mill.

I'm going to try to draw you a picture of Johnny's arm—hope you get the idea. *[Drawing of bones.]* This is the way I see it from the latest X ray. His arm is still swollen and green, but doesn't seem to bother him very much. He's even gotten so he can eat with his left hand. Grandpa has taught him his alphabet and numerals and is he the wise guy. Believe it or not, Pop, he'll be four years old the 3rd of April! Gee, Darling, wish you could hop a bomber home for that month of leave.

All my love, always   Gail

MARCH 15, 1944—SOUTHWEST PACIFIC AREA (SWPA, Fifth Air Force): In New Guinea, 200+ B-24's, B-25's, A-20's, P-38's, P-47's and P-40's pound Wewak township, blasting docks, warehouses, gun positions, and numerous other targets; fighters claim 11 enemy aircraft shot down. 36 B-25's bomb Tingo village and Lugos Mission area on Manus Island, where elements of the 1st Cavalry Division make an amphibious landing, take the mission and head E toward Lorengau.

MARCH 16, 1944—SOUTHWEST PACIFIC AREA (SWPA, Fifth Air Force): On New Guinea, 70+ B-24's, B-25's and A-20's hit AA positions, buildings and salvage dumps at Wewak and nearby Brandi Plantation; 19 B-25's bomb personnel and storage areas at Nubia; and B-24's and Catalinas attack a Japanese convoy near Hollandia. Other B-24's bomb docks and factory area at Soerabaja, Java. 8th Photographic Reconnaissance Squadron, 6th Photographic Reconnaissance Group, moves from Port Moresby to Nadzab, New Guinea with F-5's.

MARCH 17, 1944—SOUTHWEST PACIFIC AREA (SWPA, Fifth Air Force): In New Guinea, almost 100 B-24's, B-25's and A-20's attack the Wewak area; P-38's hit the Hansa Bay area while other B-25's bomb the Madang-Alexishafen area. Soerabaja, Java naval base is bombed by B-24's.

MARCH 18, 1944—SOUTHWEST PACIFIC AREA (SWPA, Fifth Air Force): In New Guinea, 100+ B-24's, B-25's, and A-20's continue to pound the Wewak area, hitting AA positions and nearby Brandi Plantation; a Japanese supply convoy reaches Wewak but escapes bombardment.

MARCH 19, 1944—SOUTHWEST PACIFIC AREA (SWPA, Fifth Air Force): In New Guinea, 100+ B-24's, B-25's, A-20's and P-47's pound the Wewak area, hitting especially hard the Cape Moem and Cape Boram areas; other B-25's and P-39's, along with RAAF aircraft, bomb the Hansa Bay, Nubia, Madang, and Alexishafen areas and hit targets along Bogadjim Road; and 130 B-24's, B-25's, A-20's, and P-38's virtually destroy a supply convoy proceeding from Wewak toward Hollandia, sinking at least 5 vessels. P-40's attack a bivouac area and AA on Garove Island, Bismarck Archipelago.

MARCH 20, 1944 WESTERN UNION TO JOHNNY 8:47 AM

MASTER JOHN DAVID MOORE

HAPPY BIRTHDAY JOHNNIE WHAT A BIG FELLOW YOU ARE GETTING TO BE. DADDY WILL COME HOME TO SEE YOU AS SOON AS HE CAN.

LOVE FROM DADDY   JOHN MOORE

MARCH 20, 1944 WESTERN UNION WES TO GAIL 8:48 AM

MRS. JOHN W. MOORE:

DEAREST, I HAVE BEEN ILL. IRITIS IMPROVING. NOT WRITTEN SEVERAL DAYS AND DON'T WANT TO WORRY FONDEST LOVE.

WES MOORE

MARCH 20, 1944—SOUTHWEST PACIFIC AREA (SWPA, Fifth Air Force): In New Guinea, 30+ B-24's bomb the airfield at Aitape; 20+ P-39's and A-20's hit Japanese HQ and other targets along the Bogadjim Road while B-25's and P-39's on armed reconnaissance hit targets at Milhanak, along the Gogol River, at Yeschan, Burui Airfield and at Erima; and at night B-24's bomb remnants of a supply convoy off Cape Terabu. On New Britain Island, P-40's on armed reconnaissance hit villages and barges along the Bangula Bay coast. [John Wesley Moore, M. D., killed.—JM]

MARCH 20, 1944 GAIL TO WES

My Darling,

We got the two telegrams this morning and hope you are all better. Gee, Pop, what caused the Iritis? I got the medical dictionary to see what it was all about and frankly, I'm not too much enlightened. I found out that it hurt like the devil, contracted the pupils, discolored the iris, and as for the cause—well, it gave a few and then said "etc." So, just what happened to you? Why can't you come home to recuperate? We'd gladly send Dr. B. over to take over. I think that I told you that he applied to the Navy again—a stall for another three months. Mrs. B. is "on the way" so it looks as though he intended to stay awhile.

I tried to send you a wire today, Darling, to let you know that we had gotten yours, but I couldn't figure out where to send it. There is no way of knowing where you are or when the cable was sent. I rather suspect that you are still in Brisbane, because your last letter had the earmarks of having been written by a sick person. However, you could be anywhere from Sydney to New Guinea, so I'll write to 713; you'll be back there eventually. I'll try not to get too worried when I wait for two weeks for a letter, Honey, or will it be longer? Have you been in a hospital and just where in the dickens are you? It's too bad that we can't put more in the wires, isn't it?

Saturday I had quite a day. I washed windows and woodwork up here at the office and spent the whole afternoon "unbuttoning" the cans that Pearl had just dumped the contents out of and then piled on the back porch—jeepers, what a dirty job. On the strength of my starting it, however, the girls finished it up yesterday. Now I'll try to get them hauled down to the store for the tin drive.

I think that Doris went skiing yesterday—I got out my ski boots for her.

Saturday night, a bunch of us were invited up to Bill Bailey's—we had quite a time. What a bull session! Bill provided us with ample liquids, and the party just went on and on. I spent most of the evening trying to get a job running shuttle service for Draper between here and Reno. Of course that would necessitate my getting a C ticket, but I guess that it could be done. CA was very much opposed to my doing it, saying that I didn't have to do such things, that I could get in all of the flying that I wanted to. But fooey, Honey, I'd like to do something on my own just once.

Yesterday, Sunday, Barbara B. and I went out and took a cross country to Beckwith. We got out real early and was it beautiful! She did all of the flying and I did all of the looking. I flew for awhile with Floyd (he still hasn't gotten his written OK from Washington for his solo). Then Draper asked me if I would check a fellow out for him. The fellow had been instructing at basic somewhere down the line. Did I feel silly! Anyhow, I checked him out—did he ever tromp on those rudders. He certainly seemed jittery as the dickens. When he landed, it was on one wheel. I jumped the right rudder and hauled the stick clear back and he didn't even know that I had touched it. Fine pilot. He did all right the second time around—I turned him loose, 'cause he could fly the thing, so he took a passenger and cruised around the valley at about 3,000 feet. Those valley cats don't like our mountains.

[My earliest memories were of flying with Mom before I was four. I remember the sound and smell of the airplane and the image of the sunlight reflecting off the instruments. I also remember how she uttered a squeal of delight when she let me have the yoke of the Taylorcraft. I pushed forward as hard as I could and loved the floating sensation. —JM]

Guess I'd better get to work, Sweetheart, I haven't done a thing up here today, did clean house at home though, so the day isn't a total loss.

Please take care of yourself, Darling—don't forget that I love you more than anything in the world.

Always your   Gail

MARCH 22, 1944 GAIL TO WES

My Darling—

Got two letters from Sydney yesterday, written March 4 and 5, and one today written Feb. 28th. The ones from Sydney sounded very cheerful and as though you were enjoying yourself, and it is hard to realize, Sweet, that you are sick. However, you must have gotten sick about the 10th if my super-sleuth deductions are correct. Hope you've got everything under control, Pop, and are enjoying your leave. Do you want me to send you some cash? I'd hate to think that you didn't have enough to see you through a good vacation. I'd certainly give a million—if I had it—to be there with you. Honey, we'd really have fun. We had a beautiful day today, and I spent most of the afternoon out getting speckled in the face. I must look like a goose egg. I haven't been in the sunshine for so long that I guess my skin is tender.

Mrs. Hay sounds like a super person. I am grateful to her for taking in my Honey and making life pleasant for him for awhile.

I love you, Darling, and want you to be happy and have fun.

Forever your Gail

MARCH 26, 1944 GAIL TO WES

Darling—

Johnny and Dad have built a steamboat out of chairs in the living room and they just left me off at New Guinea. Sure do wish that they had. Golly, Honey, I'd even like to get just a glimpse of you. Hope you're well and safe and happy!

I spent most of the afternoon out at the airport and got a ride with Bill Bailey. He doesn't get out very often, but when he does, he certainly does wring that poor little Aeronca out. It got pretty gusty by the time we got down and it felt as though we were getting spanked in the pants. Bill made a lousy landing, but his air work was swell—a BT came in just as we got out of the ship—it was from Chico. It didn't use any more of the field than the Cubs do. I've been trying to wangle a ride in it, but I'm not making much progress. Guess even up here in the sticks they are afraid to break the rules. Oh well, maybe after the war I'll get a ride in something more than a 65.

I got your letter of Feb. 29 today, Sweet—practically a month after you wrote it—telling all about leaving school and heading South. Gee, the letters certainly are mixed up! But I've gotten the story—I think. I don't believe I knew Vern or the fellow form the 63rd you gave your beer to.

All my love, Darling. Forever your   Gail

MARCH 28, 1944 GAIL TO WES

Hello Honey—

It's five to 7 and I am sitting at your desk like the Chief Executive himself. It is still daylight, but the radio works swell—some class, eh? I sure do wish that I'd hear from you. I know you said that you hadn't written but I'd certainly like to know how you are getting along.

Chris wrote Doris that they were taking him to a rest home. Guess he must have had some kind of a mental crackup—however, he didn't elucidate.

CA had a letter from Julian, and I guess he is back on the job again.

Today Dr. took the cast off of Johnny and he is in the sling only. Yesterday, he got hit on the right ear with a baseball bat when he got too interested in the boy's ball game. It didn't hurt him badly, and not long after he stopped howling, he was back there asking for more. He's certainly all boy, Darling, and you need have no fears about that! Everyone in town knows him—people that I have never seen before say, "Hello, Johnny."

Gosh Honey, they are playing Hawaiian music, and it brings up some of the grandest memories. We sure did have fun together, didn't we Pop. Hurry back so we can take up where we left off.

I love you XXX   Gail

MARCH 30, 1944 DOUGLAS McARTHUR TO GAIL
GENERAL HEADQUARTERS
SOUTHWEST PACIFIC AREA

Dear Mrs. Moore:

My deepest sympathy goes to you in the death of your husband, Captain John W. Moore. Your consolation for his loss may be that he died in the service of our country in a just cause which, with Victory, will give freedom from oppression to all peoples.

Very faithfully,   Douglas McArthur

UNDATED, SUNDAY ESTHER TO GAIL

Gail Dear—

Nothing I can say—had Wes been my own son I couldn't have loved him more. Dad is crushed—only once before have I seen him cry. He isn't any too well as it is. We do so want you to come up as soon as possible—please try and of course if there is anything we can do let us know.

Our love to you and the folks—
                                    Esther

APRIL 6, 1944 FEATHER RIVER BULLETIN

CAPTAIN MOORE DIES AT NEW GUINEA FRONT

The war came very close to Quincy this week. Dr. John Wesley Moore, officer in the United States Army Air Forces, was killed in New Guinea March 20. The fateful War Department telegram was delivered to Mrs. Moore on Saturday.

Community stunned: The news spread rapidly. It stunned the community. Captain Moore was the friend of hundreds, a civic leader, active in the Rotary Club, a past master of the Masonic Lodge, founder of Quincy Sky Harbor. His wife is the former Gail Rogers, daughter of Forest Supervisor and Mrs. D. N. Rogers. She is left with four-year old John David Moore, the "tin-type" of his father. Everybody stops and talks to Johnny when he comes downtown.

Captain Moore went on active duty Oct. 22, 1942, reporting at Pendleton Field. He trained in the Army's schools of medicine at Randolph Field and Santa Ana and in March last year was sent to the 63rd Service Group at Spokane. Six weeks more of training followed at Great Falls, Montana, and in midsummer of last year, Captain Moore sailed for Australia. He was sent to New Guinea and was kept very busy there in the line of duty as a flight surgeon until a few weeks ago when he became ill himself. He was returned to Australia for hospitalization. According to the meager details in the War Department telegram, he was killed in the crash of the bombing plane which was returning him to New Guinea.

He was born at Seattle Aug. 2, 1907, son of Dr. John C. Moore and Dr. Mary Carr Moore. After he graduated in 1934 from the University of California with the degree of Doctor of Medicine, he practiced at Seattle for a year as his father's associate. He held licenses in both Washington and California. In 1935 he became a camp physician for the Civilian Conservation Corps, being stationed at DeSabla, Butte County.

Owned Hospital Here: He bought the Plumas Industrial Hospital in Quincy April 1, 1936, from Dr. B. Lasswell, and later Dr. Bernard Holm, now a Lieutenant Commander in the U. S. Navy, and he became partners in the operation of the institution. Dr. Lasswell came out of retirement when the young doctors joined the colors, and is in charge of the hospital now. Mrs. Moore assists in the office.

Captain Moore is also survived by his brother, Captain Byron O. Carr, and a sister, Mrs. Marian Moore Quinn of Los Angeles. Captain Carr is a ferry pilot for American Airlines.

Little John David Moore's birthday is April 3, and a party has been planned for him at the Quincy Forest Service campgrounds Sunday. It was held, because his daddy would have preferred it that way. At the height of the fine birthday party, an Army training plane zoomed into Quincy Sky Harbor. Aboard it was Mrs. Moore's brother, Lt. David H. Rogers of Luke Field, Phoenix. His mother had telephoned the news to him Sunday morning and he obtained permission to fly here at once. He returned to his station Monday.

Father of Airport: Dr. Moore put Quincy on the air map. There was no airport here when he started flying back in 1936. He and Fred Russell, who had an airplane here, rented some ground from Harry Lee, and spent their own money to grade it. Quincy rapidly became one of the most air-minded communities in the country, until today half the businessmen in town are aviators. The project became so important that responsibility for managing the airport was assumed by the county supervisors.

Captain Moore was a member of the VFW post here—Kenneth M. Hayes Post No. 3825. He had recently written to Chester Hard, commander, to say, "I feel my membership will prove a most pleasant association. Give my regards to the boys."

APRIL 10, 1944 ROTARY ROOTER
(Link Peckinpah, Editor)

"Wes"

Notified last week of the death of our own Rotarian, Captain Wes Moore, victim of a bomber crash in New Guinea on March 20, was a severe shock to every member of this club and to the entire community where he was loved and greatly admired. Expressions of grief will help little in assuaging the feeling of loved ones at home, but certainly Gail and little Johnny have our deepest sympathy and we all feel with them their irreplaceable loss.

Wes became a member of this club during 1936 shortly after establishing himself as physician and surgeon and head of Quincy's Industrial Hospital. He was elected a Director of the Club in 1940 and served as the Club's Vice President in 1941. Playing an active part in Rotary work and in the general welfare of this community Wes will live long in the memory of Quincy people for his unselfish service. Outstanding in Wes' accomplishments was the establishment of an airport for this community. We are all rather proud of the Quincy Sky Harbor and we have it because of Wes Moore's leadership and untiring efforts. Wes' dream of a standard size fully equipped airport in American Valley will become a reality in the not too distant future if we carry on. When that airfield is established it should be dedicated to the memory of this fellow who with courage, foresight and enthusiasm, sold the importance of aviation to this community.

We honor and deeply revere the memory of our fellow Rotarian Captain John Wesley Moore, whose life was distinguished in "Service above Self" to his home and community and to his Country.

APRIL 13, 1944 MARY CARR MOORE

Strange, this dream: all these days and nights I've been trying to "contact" Wesley, or dream about him…As I sat at my desk, thinking, I had a momentary glimpse of Wesley, thin and disheveled, face looking bruised and he was standing in tall growth of something; just for a moment!

APRIL 30, 1944 JULIAN ATKINS TO GAIL
[In New Guinea]

Dear Gail—

It has been awfully hard for me to delay this so long, as I know how you must feel with so little information about Wes. The authorities have now given me permission to write, and I hasten to send you the meager information I have, and whatever consolation I can afford you.

I saw Wes briefly in Australia as I was returning from my leave. He said it was almost time for him to return also. I came through here on March 12th on the way up where I was stationed at that time; and he must have come along within a few days…The first I learned of his death was when I was transferred down here. I arrived Sunday, April 2nd, and in the afternoon I met Chaplain Roman, who was a total stranger to me. In our conversation I mentioned that Mrs. Moore told CA King in Quincy, that her husband Dr. Moore and I had a short visit in Australia. Small world! He said, "Do you mean Capt. John Moore?" When I said yes, he told me he had conducted services for him that afternoon, and had just returned from the cemetery. It seemed an incredible coincidence, and I questioned him exhaustively, but he didn't know any particulars, except that there had been no survivors, and that services had been conducted for all ten, jointly, by him and a Catholic Chaplain, and that it had been a very beautiful and impressive service. I have been to the cemetery several times. It is in a beautiful valley with mountains in the background in three directions. The place has been landscaped and is carefully and thoroughly tended. There is a regulation against making pictures of the cemetery, or I would enclose some here.

He was in a B-24 airplane out of the 43rd Bomb Group, which took off from here about 2:30 in the afternoon. At about three o'clock it was seen by some Australian troops in a steep spiral, obviously out of control, and disappearing behind a mountain. They notified the authorities, and it took some time to reach the scene. The plane was completely destroyed, but did not burn. They were brought out by soldiers and natives to the road near the falls, and thence to town. This was on March 20th, and since I didn't learn of it until April 2nd, it has been impossible for me to trace any other information. They wouldn't let me go to his station to see about his property, but everyone assures me that those things are always taken care of most carefully. I know that he had collected a number of mementos for you and John David, and I have asked a number of people from up there about them, but haven't found anyone with specific information. I am told that official details will come to you from the Adjutant General, War Dept, Washington D. C., and that you can get information from the Quartermaster General, War Department, Washington.

Gail, I know that I can't help you much with this belated relation of the slight, sketchy information I have been able to collect—and it is my earnest wish that it hasn't been told in a way that will give you anything but comfort. Please appreciate that it is very difficult for me to know what to say, or how to say it, but be assured that I would do anything I can for you, and would appreciate any request, if I have neglected anything.

Wes was a good friend, and the few visits I had with him over here were thoroughly enjoyed, and are even more appreciated now. Everyone in the 63rd Service Group had a high regard for him, as did all the other officers and men who know him. Unfortunately, we were farther apart after he transferred to his last organization, and I didn't know very many of his new friends.

Captain Roman is a fine Chaplain, and assures me he will do anything for you that he can, and will be glad of any opportunity that you could give him.

With very best regards to you and your fine family, I am sincerely yours,

Julian.

DECEMBER 15, 1944 FEATHER RIVER BULLETIN

QUINCY WOMAN TAKEN IN PLANE CRASH AT AIRPORT
Motor Failure Brings Death to Two in First Fatality At Sky Harbor

Gail Rogers Moore, prominent Quincy woman, was instantly killed late Tuesday afternoon when the ship in which she was flying with Edward R. Hansen of Quincy crashed following a takeoff from Quincy Sky Harbor. Hanson, fatally injured, lived but a few hours following the crash and did not regain consciousness before death. Only meager information is available since no witness to the actual crash has been found. However, experienced flyers who arrived at the scene of the accident shortly after were certain that the plane's motor went dead, allowing it to fall in a nose dive without having sufficient elevation for pulling it out.

R. J. Cotter, local logger and experienced flyer, saw the plane, a 2-place Taylorcraft, take off from the airport from Mt. Hough mill pond where he was unloading logs. Seeing nothing out of the ordinary Cotter turned to his work and, looking up an instant later, saw the plane on the ground with the nose buried and tail in the air.

The fallen plane was also seen about the same time by attendants at the airport, who called for the Quincy Ambulance immediately and rushed out to the scene. Dr. Emailing Blank of Quincy, who examined Mrs. Moore, stated she had met instant death from the impact.

Gail Rogers Moore, born August 19, 1916, was the daughter of Mr. and Mrs. D. N. Rogers of this city and sister of Captain David Rogers of the United State Air Forces, now stationed in Florida. Her husband, the former Captain John Wesley Moore, lost his life in a crash of an Army plane in New Guinea in March of this year. He had been serving as a Flight Surgeon with his unit in the South Pacific.

Dr. and Mrs. Moore were married here on January 30, 1939. Mrs. Moore is survived by her little son, John David Moore, born April 3, 1940.

Residing all of her life in Quincy, Mrs. Moore attended Quincy schools, graduating from the local high school with the class of 1934. She attended the University of California, graduating in 1938.

Following Dr. Moore's enlistment in the Air Corps in 1942, Mrs. Moore became active in carrying on the business of the Plumas Industrial Hospital, which was owned by Dr. Moore and Dr. Bernard S. Holm. Dr. Lasswell replaced Dr. Moore as resident physician and carried on until the Hospital was sold by Mrs. Moore early this summer to Dr. B.

Mrs. Moore has been one of Quincy's most enthusiastic boosters for aviation and learned to fly expertly under the training of her husband, who ranked high among local flyers. Quincy Sky Harbor owes its start to the hard work and farsightedness of the former Dr. Moore and it is ironical that the first fatal accident to occur in the operation of the local airfield should take the life of the wife of its founder.

It was 54 years ago, but I still remember the tall graceful oak trees at the Quincy Cemetery gravesite. There were throngs of people. The casket was being lowered slowly down into the deep, dark perfectly squared-off pit. One woman embraced me crying, "Oh you poor child!" I didn't really know what she was talking about.

I would keep getting presents from Mommie and Daddie because Grandma and Grandpa couldn't find a way to tell me about death. One day Grandma found me crying with my head in my hands. I said, "I guess she just went away." And Grandma said, "Yes, she went away on a long trip." — JM

May 1943

Mary Elizabeth Barker-Rogers

Luther Bailey Rogers

CHAPTER 9

AFTER

[Mary Elizabeth Barker-Rogers of Maine continues her narrative]... then came the World War. Only two in our family were eligible for service. David, with other foresters in California, being already in government employ, was organized for coast defense in case of need. The railroads went into government hands as soon as the United States went into the war, so Luther, though examined and listed as fit, was never mobilized. There seemed to be need at home for all railroad men with special training.

The last year of the war the Grand Army appointed their national reunion at Portland, Oregon. Secretary McAdoo permitted them to take the only railroad excursion of the year. We decided to go.

As many of the family as could get a vacation in those busy times gathered at the farm and helped us pack and get on our way. We left home in August and traveled leisurely, stopping a day each in Boston, Niagara Falls and Chicago. Then there were three days and three nights without stopping. The majority of our car companions were going to the reunion too, and were pleasant people to meet. Our accommodations were comfortable; we were perfectly well and thoroughly enjoying ourselves. What more was needed? At Portland all the Grand Army people received every courtesy possible from the city. Mr. Rogers and I were domiciled at Headquarters, the best hotel in the city. Ladies placed their cars and themselves as chauffeurs at the service of the old veterans and their wives. There were excursions on the Columbia Highway and to the heights around the city; and as a final courtesy carriage-loads of roses were brought in to be distributed among the men wearing the bronze button.

After a three-days' rest we took the wonderful Shasta route to San Francisco and spent one beautiful day on the Pacific shore where the clear green water came rolling in to break on the sands at our feet.

Back over the sun-baked land, through miles of grape orchards, we rode to Sacramento, and there we turned off up the Feather River Canyon to the town of Quincy. As we climbed, just above us could be seen here and there marks of the trail of the forty-niners who mined this canyon. There was just room between the mountains for the river. The railroad and the automobile road were cut from the side of the mountain and tunnels frequent.

We remained with David a month at Quincy, taking hair-raising rides over the mountain grades, turning hairpin curves with the horrifying

impression that we were shooting off into space. There were picnics and rides into lovely little shut-in valleys with tiny villages. There was frequently the phone signal of fire started by lightning or by some careless camper back in the hills. Then would follow the rapid gathering of the extra fire fighters, loading the cars with provisions and fire-fighting utensils, and they with David in charge, would be off to the spot for one or half a dozen days—according to the start it got before they arrived.

It was all very new and exciting to us, but we could not stay forever. Our return brought us through the Royal Gorge across the salt fields to Salt Lake. We stopped a day there seeing the city and attending a sermon in the Tabernacle. The ride from there by way of Pueblo to Denver and Colorado Springs was very fine.

As a child, when they were putting the first transcontinental railroad across I heard a great deal about Pike's Peak. I must say I was disappointed when I first saw it. Owing to the fact that the surrounding country is at so great an elevation the mountain itself seemed dwarfed compared with those we had seen on the Pacific Coast. The Mississippi, which we crossed at St. Louis, was another disappointment. The Father of Waters looked shallow and muddy as if it had just been overflowing the meadows along the shores. I would probably have to be a pilot on a boat to have a proper respect for it. The Hudson or the St. Lawrence is to me much more impressive.

Not long after we reached home, Peace was declared. We settled down now for a quiet year at home. Our farm activities were attended to by the son of the man who had formerly done the work. We were very comfortable and contented. The following summer, the girls came home to their vacation with a project about which they were very enthusiastic. They wanted to give us a golden wedding anniversary celebration. I demurred. I disliked assuming so much importance for myself. I did not desire to be so much in the community limelight, and lastly, I didn't want them to take upon themselves in their short playtime the work involved in such an undertaking. The matter was argued until I gave a reluctant consent.

They would have a church wedding with all the accessories. Ushers, bridesmaids, maid of honor and best man were selected from friends of our own age, and Lore consented to give the bride away. The youngest grandson, a lad of six years with a mop of yellow curls, was flower bearer or as he put it, flower barrel. The village pastors were away, so one from a neighboring town, an old friend of our family, came to our aid. It was the task of our family, helped by volunteer friends, to trim the church and vestry. Buttercups, yellow daisies and ferns were selected, and the old church became a bower of beauty. I had to wear a white dress and veil, mind you, fastened with water lilies. Everything went off without a hitch. There was some music, two or three appropriate songs; then the bridal party walked up the aisle to the wedding march. The "Flower Barrel" smiled so broadly, was so pleased with himself, carrying his basket of yellow daisies, everybody smiled with him. There were refreshments, and a reception in the vestry. The church was full of our friends of this and other towns.

After the "wedding," we bought a small car and made preparations to take a camping trip each summer. We wanted to go for a month across country, returning before the August vacation. Mr. Rogers was eighty years old. I was some years younger, but our age did not deter us for a minute. We got our camping outfit, tent, cot beds, sleeping bags, a portable stove and such dishes as were absolutely necessary. We made arrangements with our man to drive for us on our first and second trips. Our itinerary was first Peaks Island for the regimental reunion, then the White Mountains. It was very successful, and the next year found us again on the trail.

Mr. Rogers had an attack of erysipelas the following summer from which he did not fully recover for a year. Consequently, we took no journey that summer. He also began to have serious trouble with his eyes. The oculist was not very sanguine about benefiting him but said there was a chance that they could be cured, so we went each month to Bangor for treatment. We got a young friend to drive us down to Connecticut, where Annie, now Mrs. Howard Smith *[pen name, Lou Rogers]*, had a summer home. Ruth was there, and Angus, her husband, came out for the weekends. It was a beautiful countryside, and we very much enjoyed our stay.

On the way back, we camped on top of one of the Blue Ridge Mountains where we had an enchanting outlook over the beautiful valleys with their picturesque farm buildings and the many small streams flashing in the blue atmosphere. The whole country had a quaint, primitive air as if man's occupation were only a trivial incident. I was struck by the vivid red color of the soil wherever uncovered. We took a crossroad to get back into the main highway and had an atrocious time with the mud, but we came out of the woods near the Natural Bridge, where we camped on a grassy flat beside a rivulet across which we laid a board for a bridge.

I thought it a good time to wash the towels and my smock. A sudden shower came up, and I dropped the articles and ran into the tent. When the downpour ceased and I poked my head out of the tent, to my amazement I found the brook had overflowed and the flat was covered with its muddiest water nearly to the tent. Towels, smock, basin and soap were somewhere on their way to the Natural Bridge. In an hour the brook was down to normal size and I recovered the wash hung up on the shrubs along the bank and the basin caught in a tiny dam made by the debris.

We drove straight north up the Susquehanna Valley through the mining district to Scranton and visited one of the many caves. We turned before we came to Binghamton and went across at West Point, crossed the Hudson at Bear Mountain Bridge and settled down at Brookfield, Connecticut for a three days' rest *[Lou's home]*. From there we went back to Maine by way of the White Mountains. We were just in time for the arrival of the family at Shin Pond.

Mr. Rogers was in excellent spirits and seemed to have benefited by the journey. His eyesight, however, was certainly failing. Only the Elliott's from Montreal and Lore's family from Washington were able to leave their business, so we had a very quiet time. The Montreal party left us the last of August and the remainder of us were preparing to go when Mr. Rogers had a bad fall. He was bruised and had a broken rib and was badly shaken. A physician was summoned who did for him what was needful, and in a few days he was able to be taken home.

Lore had to be back in his laboratories, and Annie came to stay with us. Mr. Rogers recovered rapidly from his hurts and was able to take his daily rides in the car. The doctor advised keeping him out in the air as long as he was comfortable. The roads were fine, the weather warm and sunny and the forests glorious with the colors of autumn. So we devoted our time to him, occasionally taking our lunch and eating it beside some stream or on some hill from which we could see Katahdin and its foothills. The doctor and we were soon conscious that, though Mr. Rogers had recovered from his hurts, the shock had been too great to overcome, and all the symptoms of the dissolution of old age were setting in. He suffered very little other than increasing weakness and within a month passed away with only a week of confinement to his bed.

As he lay waiting for interment, the casket draped with the flag for which in his later years he had spent much time cultivating a respect and loyalty, the tributes of flowers from warm hearted friends came pouring in until the place was a bower of beauty. Some of the sons and daughters could not come to us. David was too far away; Luther had been sent by his company to Chile for a year, and Ruth could not travel with her small baby. The others were there. The American Legion were his escort, bearing in addition to their own flags, the flag of the Post of which he was the last member. One man came from a distance to fulfill a promise made several years before, to play taps at his grave.

MARCH 29, 1946 SACRAMENTO BEE

QUINCY WOMAN PLANS TO DONATE AIRPORT SITE

QUINCY (Plumas Co.), March 28. Final arrangements are being completed whereby Quincy will be provided with an adequate airfield. Mrs. Nellie C. Gansner is having a deed drawn which will be presented to the board of supervisors Monday. She will donate 103 acres of land on Spanish Creek…this will provide for an airstrip which completed will measure 3,500 by 500 feet without obstructions. Also available for recreation development for the community will be sufficient space for a swimming pool and picnic grounds, as the area embraced in the deed includes property bordering both sides of Spanish Creek. The airport will be located one quarter mile from Quincy and will meet all requirements of the Civil Aeronautics Authority…will take care of any commercial planes. The preliminary survey for the site was completed this week.

The proposed airport has been a project of Plumas County Planning Board. The executive committee is composed of D. N. Rogers, S. L. Bailey and CA King. *[Incidentally, after the war, CA married Zona Brown (Orville Brown's sister). Zona flew in two women's transcontinental air races, winning one of them.*

I remember being out at the new airport. I was just past the "age of reason" and watching Grandpa striding next to the grader. He was going to make sure that this project was done right! Grandma and Grandpa were horrified when I announced at that very early age that "I Must Fly!"

Mary Lee Metzker was wondering how the family should address her younger brother John and me so that we didn't both answer at once. She decided to call me "Johnny," and the name stuck.

One day, John and I decided we would try to fly together. I just knew I could! We jumped off the garage roof holding hands. He, being a year older, survived unscathed, but I broke my arm and found out something about flying!

When I was older, my grandparents would take me over to Ken and Helen Metzker's vacation home on Lake Tahoe. They had a boathouse that stood about twenty feet above the sparkling waters; I loved to run as fast as I could on the roof of the boathouse and sail out over the water. I would spread my arms and pretend that I could fly!

During the summer of 1959, I was nineteen and was not to be denied the thrill of flight any longer. Over the next 40 years, I made aviation my life, earning all the necessary ratings and spending more than twenty-three thousand hours in the air to date.

In 1998, I published an autobiography I called I MUST FLY! It outlines my career as a pilot for an Alaskan bush airline, landing a twelve thousand pound C-46 on a frozen lake. I thundered down deep canyons in giant fire bombers during death-defying slurry drops. I learned to fly floats and sprayed crops at night in a powerful open-cockpit biplane crashing three different times. Once I took off into blinding fog at night at a dangerous mountain airport only to discover that my cockpit lights were inadequate to illuminate vital instruments. I felt the thrill of simulating a spectacular crash into a pristine High Sierra lake for a Hollywood movie. I performed air show loops and rolls and survived a near-disaster in a glider. I experienced engine failure and a forced landing out of a spin in an antique Aeronca like Mom used to fly. I have appreciated the world from a beautiful balloon.

My fortunes have ranged from being a flat-broke guitar pickin' college student and flight instructor to a successful flying business proprietor.

I'll bet Mom and Dad would have loved doing the flying that I have been privileged to do. I'm deeply sorry I couldn't know them better. — JM]

EPILOGUE

Researching *Family Centennial* was fun! While following the trail of my ancestors, I gathered a sense of pride and belonging to a group of dynamic and interesting people.

It is truly ironic that the people that Mom and Dad were in conflict with would win. Dr. Blank, who was banned from operating at the hospital, would be the one to pronounce Mom dead; Dr. B., a constant thorn, would end up owning the Plumas Industrial Hospital.

A word about Dr. B., now deceased. From the time I first learned to fly until he sold the Plumas Industrial Hospital years later, Dr. B. was kind to me, administering to my FAA Airman Physical examinations at no charge—in memory of my Father, he said. He raised a fine family, practiced medicine honorably, became a member of the Bill Bailey backroom "poker group" and was a friend to many. I sincerely believe my Mom and Dad would applaud his accomplishments if they could.

<u>SEPTEMBER 1, 1997 SANDRA LEE SHERRINGTON TO JOHNNY MOORE</u>

Dear Johnny,

My cousin Harriett recently sent me a copy of your book *[I MUST FLY!]*. In my thank you letter, I told her the following: "I am just thrilled to have this copy of Johnny Moore's book. There are so many things to share about Johnny Moore before even reading the book, which I just can't wait to do. First of all Johnny and I are the same age and we went all through school together. The first home movie Daddy ever took was during the winter of 1946 and I was sledding down the hill in front of Ray Smith's house. Of course you know that the home across the street belonged to Johnny parents ….anyway, Johnny was there in his snowsuit and he jumped off a hill, did a somersault and landed on his head in the snow. He was a dare devil from day one.

Johnny always had a really wonderful tree house in this grandparent's back yard. I was allowed to climb up and sit in it once. Johnny would swing down from the tree house on a rope.

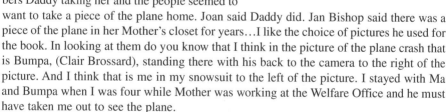

Johnny's father delivered me. I'm sending a copy of my birth announcement listing Drs. Moore and Holmes as the "directors." Do either of you remember Dr. Holmes? Wes Moore must have gone into the service around 1942 or 1943—maybe the book will say.

I don't know how Edith and Dave Rogers ever made it through 1944 losing their son-in-law and then their beloved daughter, both to tragic accidents. It seems that everyone in Quincy had to go out and look at Gail's plane when it crashed. Joan remembers Daddy taking her and the people seemed to want to take a piece of the plane home. Joan said Daddy did. Jan Bishop said there was a piece of the plane in her Mother's closet for years…I like the choice of pictures he used for the book. In looking at them do you know that I think in the picture of the plane crash that is Bumpa, (Clair Brossard), standing there with his back to the camera to the right of the picture. And I think that is me in my snowsuit to the left of the picture. I stayed with Ma and Bumpa when I was four while Mother was working at the Welfare Office and he must have taken me out to see the plane.

Well, that's my Johnny Moore stories. Joan and I think the book should be made into a movie and I want Brad Pitt (my heartthrob) to play the lead. Joan had a few tears when she saw the book and read the covers.

Love, Sandra

REFERENCES CITED

Air Force Combat Units of World War II, Office of Air Force History,
     Headquarters USAF, 1961, ISBN 0-912799-02-1.

Combat Squadrons of the Air Force, World War II, Office of Air Force
     History, Headquarters USAF, 1982.

Hersey, Elliott, Genealogist. Harrison, ME.

Holms, Norman W. My Pacific Railroad: An Engineers Journey.
     Steel Rails West Publishing,1966.

The Army Air Forces in World War II: combat chronology-1945. Office of Air Force
History, Headquarters USAF, 1973.

The Caduceus of Kappa Sigma International Fraternity, Page 21, Chapter Celestial.

Dunn, Temtyan. Abilene. Unpublished manuscript.

Moore, Byron. The First Five Million Miles. New York, Harper & Brothers, 1955, Library
     of Congress catalog card number: 55-8028.

Moore, Johnny. I Must Fly! Quincy, California, Sugarpine Aviators, 1998,
     ISBN 0-9658720-5-X.

Moore, Mary Louise Carr. My Little Story. Moore Archives.

Rogers, David Nathan. Forest Service Record. Unpublished manuscript.

Rogers, Luther Bailey. Civil War Record. Unpublished manuscript.

Rogers, Mary Elizabeth Barker. Down East. Unpublished manuscript.

Sheppard, Alice. Cartooning for Suffrage. Albuquerque, University of New Mexico Press,
     1994. ISBN 0-8263-1458-9

APPENDIX

Family Centennial Genealogy
Family Part I

Barker, Addison Perley (I) — Son of Cyrus Barker and Mary Jane Berry.

Barker, Addison Perley (II) — Son of Addison Perley Barker and Susan A. Brown.

Barker, Cyrus (I) — Father of Addison Perley Barker.

Barker, Mary Elizabeth — Daughter of Addison Perley Barker (I) and Susan A. Brown.

Barker, Mary Ellen — Daughter of Cyrus Barker (I) and Mary Jane Berry.

Barker, Rodney Clinton — Son of Cyrus Barker (I) and Mary Jane Berry. Captain, Union Army.

Barker, Steven Cutler — Son of Cyrus Barker (I) and Mary Jane Berry. Captain, Union Army.

Berry, Mary Jane — Wife of Cyrus Barker (I).

Brown, Susan A. — Wife of Addison Perley Barker (I).

Buck, Mary — First wife of Byron Oscar Carr.

Carr, Byron Oscar — Son of Merwin Carr and Delia Ann Torry. Colonel, U.S. Army.

Carr, Byron Thorpe — Son of Byron Oscar Can and Mary Buck.

Carr, Clark "CIarkie" — Son of Clark E. Can.

Carr, Clark E. — Son of Clark Merwin Carr & Delia Ann Torry. Capt. Washington State Militia. Author

Carr, Clark Merwin Can — Emigrated from England to America. Reverend.

Carr, Eugene A. — Son of Clark Merwin Carr and Delia Ann Tony. General, U.S. Army.

Carr, Eugene Merwin — Son of Byron Oscar Carr and Mary Buck. Captain, Washington State Militia.

Carr, George Pratt "Georgie" — Son of Byron Oscar Can and Sarah Amelia Pratt

Carr, Horace M. — Son of Clark Merwin Can and Delia Ann Torry. Ambassador to Denmark.

Carr, Mary Louise — Daughter of Byron Oscar Carr and Sarah Amelia Pratt.

Carr, Torry Wray — Son of Byron Oscar Carr and Sarah Amelia Pratt.

Fish, Squire — Husband of Mary L. Rogers. Founder of Patten, Maine.

Hall, Amanda Jordan — Wife of John Wesley Moore (I).

Hersey, Mary Matilda — First wife of Luther Bailey Rogers.

Kanaday, Mary — Wife of William Watson. Teacher.

Maguire, Mary — Wife of Eugene A. Carr.

Merrill, Louisa — Wife of Robert Henry Pratt.

Moore, Byron Carr — Son of John Claude Moore and Mary Louise Carr.

Moore, Fred T. — Son of John Wesley Moore (I) and Amanda Jordan Hall.

Moore, John Claude, M.D. — Son of John Wesley Moore (I) and Amanda Jordan Hall.

Moore, John Wesley — Son of John Claude Moore and Mary Louise Carr.

Moore, Marian Hall — Daughter of John Claude Moore and Mary Louise Carr.

Pratt, Alice Edwards, Ph.D. — Daughter of Simian Pratt and Joanna Dennison. Teacher, Author.

Pratt, Carlin Louise — Daughter of Robert Henry Pratt and Louisa Merrill. Playwright, Author.

Pratt, John Haraden — Son of Simian Pratt and Joanna Dennison. Music Scholar.

Pratt, Lucy — Daughter of Simian Pratt and Joanna Dennison

Pratt, Robert Henry — Son of Simian Pratt and Philendia Lincoln. Seaman, Miner, Railroader.

Pratt, Sarah Amelia "Nanna" — Daughter of Robert Henry Pratt and Louisa Merrill. Feminist, Musician, Author.

Pratt, Simian - Singer and teacher. Colonel, Maine State Militia.

Rogers, Annie Lucasta "Lou" - Daughter of Luther Bailey Rogers and Mary Elizabeth Barker. Feminist, Cartoonist, Author.

Rogers, David Nathan - Son of Luther Bailey Rogers and Mary Elizabeth Barker. Forester.

Rogers, Edwin Searles (I) - Son of Luther Rogers and Hanna Bailey. First Lieutenant, Union Army.

Rogers, Edwin Searles (II) - Son of Luther Bailey Rogers and Mary Elizabeth Barker.

Forester.Rogers, Lore A. Ph.D. — Son of Luther Bailey Rogers and Mary Elizabeth Barker. Scientist.

Rogers, Luther Bailey "The Boss" — Son of Luther Rogers, M. D. Captain, Union Army. Forester.

Rogers, Luther Barker — Son of Luther Bailey Rogers and Mary Elizabeth Barker. Electrical Engineer, Pilot.

Rogers, Luther, M. D. — Pioneer doctor in "Down East Maine."

Rogers, Mary Hersey — Daughter of Luther Bailey Rogers and Mary Matilda Hersey.

Hersey, Mary Matilda — First wife of Luther Bailey Rogers.

Rogers, Ruth - Daughter of Luther Bailey Rogers and Mary Elizabeth Barker.

Rogers, Sarah L. — Daughter of Luther Bailey Rogers and Mary Elizabeth Barker.

Watson, Edith Lenore — Daughter of William Watson and Mary Kanaday.

Woodard, Winchell —Husband of Mary Ellen Barker.

Family Part II

Carr, Mary Louise "Nonnie" Ph.D. — First wife of John Claude Moore, M. D. Composer.

Hudson, Clyde Benton Jr. "Mick" — Son of Clyde Benton Hudson and Marian Hall Moore. Future Pilot.

Hudson, Robert Wray "Bob" — Son of Clyde Benton Hudson and Marian Hall Moore. Future Pilot.

Lepley, Anne Blench — Second wife of Herbert Sydney Watson. Probation Officer for the County of Plumas.

Moore, Byron Carr "Dinty" — Son of John Claude Moore and Mary Louise Carr. Pilot, Author.

Moore, John Claude, M.D. — First husband of Mary Louise Carr.

Moore, John David "Johnny"— Son of John Wesley Moore and Frances Gail Rogers. Future Pilot and Author.

Moore, John Wesley "Wes" M. D.— Son of John Claude Moore and Mary Louise Carr. Captain U. S. Army Air Corps. Flight Surgeon, Pilot.

Moore, Marian Hall — Daughter of John Claude Moore and Mary Louise Carr.

Moore, Richard Carr— Son of Byron Carr Moore

Pratt, Sarah Amelia "Nanna"— Wife of Byron Oscar Carr. Musician, Theologian, Author.

Quinn, Cyril "Cy"— Second husband of Marian Hall Moore.

Ricker, Man belle E. "Kookie"— Wife of David Harold Rogers.

Rogers, David Harold — Son of David Nathan Rogers and Edith Lenore Watson. Pilot.

Rogers, David Nathan — Son of Luther Bailey Rogers and Mary Elizabeth Barker. U.S. Forest Service Supervisor.

Rogers, Frances Gail — Daughter of David Nathan Rogers and Edith Lenore Watson. Pilot.

Sax, Esther — Second wife of John Claude Moore, M. D.

Watson Herbert Sydney "Tiny"— Son of William Watson and Mary Kanaday. Quincy Lumber Company Employee.

Watson, Arthur Joseph "Dot" — Son of William Watson and Mary Kanaday. Engineer for the County of Plumas.

Watson, Arthur R. — Son of Arthur Joseph Watson and Katherine R. Woods. Lieutenant U.S. Army. Pilot.

Watson, Edith Lenore — Daughter of William Watson and Mary Kanaday.

Watson, Ernest — Son of William Watson and Mary Kanaday. Jesuit Priest.

Watson, Virginia — Daughter of Arthur Joseph Watson and Katherine R. Woods.

Watson, William — Emigrated from England. Surveyor for the County of Plumas.

Woods, Katherine R. — Wife of Arthur Joseph Watson. Librarian for the County of Plumas.

Friends and Characters Part II

Atkins, Julian R. — Captain, U. S. Fifth Air Force. Pilot

Austin, Emile — Owner of Quincy Hotel.

B., Dr. "Dr. B." — Physician in Quincy.

Bailey, "Bill"— Owner of the Quincy Drug Store. Pilot.

Baldwin, Barbara "Jr." — Daughter of E. "Dan" Baldwin and Helen.

Baldwin, Dan — Son of E. Dan Baldwin and Barbara Sr. Pilot.

Baldwin, E. "Dan" — Quincy Lumber Company Employee.

Barbara "Sr." — Wife of E. "Dan" Baldwin.

Bedell, "Buddie" — Son of C. T. Bedell and Lila. Future Pilot.

Bedell, C. T. "Charlie" — Cattle Rancher.

Bell, Leda — Friend of Gail Rogers Moore.

Bishop, Roby — Grocery Store Proprietor.

Blank, Emailing, M.D. — Physician in Quincy.

Brossard, Clair "Bumpa" — Father of Edna Brossard

Brossard, Edna — Wife of John Corydon Lee.

Brown, Arizona "Zona" — Sister of Orville Brown. Pilot.

Brown, Orville — U.S. Forest Service, Quincy Lumber Company Employee, Sea Bee.

Brown, Roy — U.S. Forest Service Employee. Sea Bee.

Cotter, George — Auto Dealership Proprietor. Pilot.

Cotter, Robert J. "Bob" — Logger, Pilot.

Gaulden, Ruth — Wife of A. C. Dillenger

Grover, Freeman E. "Bud" — Proprietor, Grover's Drug Store. Pilot.

Grover, Otto — Proprietor, Grover's Drug Store. Pilot.

Hallstead, Ivy — Wife of Freeman E. Grover. Pilot.

Hard, Chester — U.S. Forest Service Employee.

Helen Armstrong — Wife of Bill Bailey

Helen Bolte — Wife of J. K. Metzker.

King, "CA" — Owner, Quincy Lumber Company. Pilot.

Larison, Lee — Dentist.

Lasswell, "Dr." M. D. — Resident Physician, Plumas Industrial Hospital.

Lee, Corydon John "Stub" — Proprietor of the Town Hall Theater.

Lee, Sandra — Daughter of John Corydon Lee and Edna Brossard. Married name
       Sherrington.

Leila — Wife of C. T. Bedell.

Lund, Irene — Pilot

Maggie — Wife of Owen Morris.

Margery — Wife of Chester Hard.

Margarite — Wife of Dr. Lasswell. Head nurse at Plumas Industrial Hospital.

McCurley, "Mac" — Military Pilot.

Metzker, J. K. "Ken" — Lumberman.

Metzker, John Gordon — Son of J. K. Metzker and Helen. Future entrepreneur, Pilot.

Metzker, Mary Lee — Daughter of J. K. Metzker and Helen.

Moncur, J. 0. — Judge of the Superior Court.

Moore, Bud — Pilot.

Morris, Owen — Quincy Lumber Company employee.

Nina — Wife of Roy Brown. Nurse at Plumas Industrial Hospital.

Ole — Wife of Clarence Schott.

Peckinpah, C. Lincoln "Peck" — U.S. Forest Service employee.

Redstreake, Angelinea "Lena" — Babysitter for John David Moore

Redstreake, Douglas "Itchy" — Son of Angelinea Redstreake. Quincy
       Track Star, Grocer.

Redstreake, John "Johnny" — Son of Angelinea Redstreake. Quincy
       Skier, Postmaster.

Russell, Fred L. — Pilot.

Ruth Gaulden — Wife of A. C. Dellinger

Schott, Clarence R. — Builder of Wes and Gail Moore's house. Musician, Pilot.

Smith, Raymond "Ray" — Owner of Meadow Valley Lumber Company.

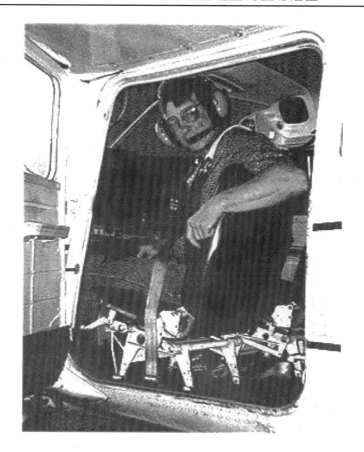

About the Author

Johnny Moore was born on April 3, 1940 of parents who were products of very different backgrounds—those from the East being practical and earthy pioneers, while the Westerners were aristocratic wielders of power. All were smart and courageous.

Johnny holds a Master's Degree in Anthropology and lifetime adult teach credentials in the fields of Anthropology and Aviation. Owner/Operator of Sugarpine Aviators, he is a professional pilot with more than twenty-three thousand hours. He enjoys hiking, skiing and studies Kodenkan jujitsu.

Johnny is also the author of *I Must Fly!* — the sequel to *Family Centennial*—which covers his true aviation adventures including Alaskan bush flying, firebombing, crop dusting and movie stunts. He is also an Inspection Authorized Aircraft and Powerplant Mechanic, FAA Designated Pilot Examiner. Johnny's children represent the fifth generation in Quincy.